ENCOUNTERS

Chinese Language and Culture

Use the Registration Code below to register for the *Encounters: Chinese Language and Culture* Website.

1. Go to: www.EncountersChinese.com
2. Click "Create an Account" and register as a student
3. Enter this code in the "Registration Code" field

ENCOUNTERS
ENCOUNTERS
hjzdfyrdwd
ENCOUNTERS
ENCOUNTERS

This code may be used only once. To purchase a new code, visit http://goo.gl/6MZLrh.

D1075611

Yale UNIVERSITY PI
New Haven and London

yalebooks.com/languages

ENCOUNTERS

Chinese Language and Culture

Student Book 4

ENCOUNTERS

Chinese Language and Culture

Student Book 4

汉语和中国文化

Cynthia Y. Ning
University of Hawai‘i at Mānoa

Stephen L. Tschudi
University of Hawai‘i at Mānoa

John S. Montanaro
Yale University

Instructor's Annotations by **Amy Shen**
Berkshire School

Audio Program by **Cynthia Y. Ning** and the **Confucius Institute**
University of Hawai‘i at Mānoa

Yale UNIVERSITY PRESS
New Haven and London

华语教学出版社
SINOLINGUA

Published with assistance from the Office of the President, Yale University.

Yale University Press books may be purchased in quantity for educational, business, or promotional use. For information, please e-mail sales.press@yale.edu (U.S. office) or sales@yaleup.co.uk (U.K. office).

Project Developers: Mary Jane Peluso and Timothy J. Shea
Project Director: Sarah Miller
Editorial Assistant: Ashley E. Lago
Developmental Editor: Martin Yu
Project Manager: Karen Hohner
Copy Editor: Jamie Greene
Managing Editor: Jenya Weinreb
Designer and Compositor: Wanda España/Wee Design Group
Illustrator: Nora Guo
Cover Designers: Sonia Shannon and Wanda España/Wee Design Group
Art Managers: Melissa Flamson and Poyee Oster
Production Controller: Maureen Noonan
Digital Product Manager: Sara Sapire
Digital Product Assistant: Thomas Breen
Marketing Manager: Dawn Gerrity

Printed in the United States of America.

ISBN: 978-0-300-16165-6 (student edition)
ISBN: 978-0-300-16169-4 (annotated instructor's edition)
Library of Congress Control Number: 2015952146

A catalogue record for this book is available from the British Library.

This paper meets the requirements of ANSI/NISO Z39.48-1992 (Permanence of Paper).

10 9 8 7 6 5 4 3 2 1

We dedicate ***Encounters*** to the memory of John DeFrancis, who began his seven-decade career as the first Ph.D. student in Chinese Studies at Yale University and who then published numerous books and articles on the subject of China and the Chinese language. He was a gentle man who lived a full, good life and gave so much to so many.

Contents

Preface

Congratulations, you've reached Book 4 of ***Encounters: Chinese Language and Culture!*** We hope that by now, you have a grounding in useful language skills that allow you to meet many basic needs with facility. We also hope that you have been able to get to know more about people and allow them to get to know you better by using Chinese. Book 4 explores more facets of modern life: we visit a bookstore, dip into TV and film media, surf the Chinese Internet, and discuss sporting events. We comment on the ideal career, life partner, place to live, and lifestyle. We explore spirituality. Finally, as in Level 1, we conclude with reflections on learning Chinese and how to continue beyond this level.

Book 4 maintains the four-skill approach with which you have become familiar. You will work on listening, speaking, reading, and writing—all in a cultural context—but as in Books 1, 2, and 3, the curriculum emphasizes listening and speaking. We believe that these skills will help you build the strongest foundation to develop competency in Chinese.

Book 4 integrates content from the dramatic series, filmed in present-day Beijing. The episodes, available at ***www.EncountersChinese.com***, provide the basic content of each unit. You will find that you are able to understand much more of the language used in these episodes than you did in Books 1, 2, and 3. The language in the episodes is useful both for training in comprehension and as the basis for picking up new vocabulary and grammar and for developing functional competence. As in the past, though, don't try to learn *everything* in each unit; there is simply too much.

The illustrated, self-contained stories for reading, linked to the theme of each unit, were introduced in Book 3 and continue in Book 4. It is our hope that these stories will inspire you to write your own and that these student-written texts can become additional reading material for your class. Selected student texts may, with permission, be uploaded to the ***Encounters*** website in the future, so that students can choose freely and extensively among texts of high interest, to further develop reading ability. Reading becomes an increasingly important focus as language skills improve, and reading widely is the most effective way to familiarize students with the more formal language and contexts of the advanced level.

At this level, we are not providing a workbook to teach stroke order for character writing, since the basic principles relating to stroke order will have been internalized by now. If you need stroke order support, please use the ***Encounters*** Character Trainer App that is accessible via ***www.EncountersChinese.com***.

We wish you continuing success on your journey of learning Chinese!

—Cynthia Y. Ning
—Stephen L. Tschudi
University of Hawai'i at Mānoa

Academic Committee

YALE UNIVERSITY PRESS

Richard C. Levin
理查德雷文
Former President, Yale University
前耶鲁大学校长

Peter Salovey
彼德 萨罗维
President, Yale University
耶鲁大学 校长

Linda K. Lorimer
罗琳达
Vice President for Global and Strategic Initiatives, Yale University
耶鲁大学副校长兼环球策略负责人

Dorothy Robinson
多乐茜 罗宾逊
Senior Counselor to the President, Yale University
耶鲁大学校长资深顾问

John Donatich
约翰 多纳蒂奇
Director, Yale University Press
耶鲁大学出版社 社长

Mary Jane Peluso
玛丽珍 珀卢索
Project Developer
项目发展人
Former Publisher of World Languages, Yale University Press
前耶鲁大学出版社世界语言部 发行人

Timothy Shea
提姆 西薛
Project Developer
项目发展人
Former Editor of World Languages, Yale University Press
前耶鲁大学出版社世界语言部编辑

Sarah Miller
莎拉 米勒
Project Director
项目主任
Editor of Course Books and World Languages, Yale University Press
耶鲁大学出版社世界语言部 教科书编辑

Cynthia Y. Ning
任友梅
Author
语言教学部分撰稿人
Associate Director, University of Hawai'i Center for Chinese Studies
夏威夷大学中国研究中心 副主任
U.S. Director, Confucius Institute at the University of Hawai'i
孔子学院 院长
Executive Director, Chinese Language Teachers Association, 2000–2009
中文教师学会 执行主任

Stephen L. Tschudi
唐润
Author
语言教学部分撰稿人
Specialist in Technology for Foreign Language Education, University of Hawai'i at Mānoa
夏威夷大学外语教育技术专家

John S. Montanaro
孟德儒
Author
语言教学部分撰稿人
Senior Lector in Chinese, Yale University
耶鲁大学 资深中文讲师

Hugo Krispyn
胡果 克理思平
Executive Producer and Creative Director
总制片、总导演

Xiao Yu
于晓
Producer and Screenwriter
制片人、编剧

CHINA INTERNATIONAL PUBLISHING GROUP

Cai Mingzhao
蔡名照
President Emeritus, China International Publishing Group
中国国际出版集团 前任总裁

Zhou Mingwei
周明伟
President, China International Publishing Group
中国国际出版集团 总裁

Huang Youyi
黄友义
Former Vice President, China International Publishing Group
中国国际出版集团 前任副总裁

Wang Gangyi
王刚毅
Vice President, China International Publishing Group
中国国际出版集团 副总裁

Wang Junxiao
王君校
Senior Project Officer
学术顾问
President, Sinolingua
华语教学出版社 社长

Han Hui
韩晖
Project Director
项目主任
Editor-in-Chief, Sinolingua
华语教学出版社 总编辑

Guo Hui
郭辉
Former Associate-Editor-in-Chief, Sinolingua
华语教学出版社 前任副总编辑

Zhou Kuijie
周奎杰
Culture Consultant
文化顾问
Former Editor-in-Chief, New World Press
原新世界出版社总编辑

Zhao Rongguo
赵荣国
Producer
制片

Liu Jiefeng
刘杰峰
Producer
制片

Lu Jianming
陆俭明
Professor, Peking University
北京大学中文系 教授

Cui Xiliang
崔希亮
President, Beijing Language and Culture University
北京语言大学 校长

Li Xiaoqi
李晓琪
Professor, School of Chinese as a Second Language, Peking University
北京大学汉语教育学院 教授

Wu Zhongwei
吴中伟
President, School of International Cultural Exchanges, Fudan University
复旦大学国际文化交流学院院长

Liu Songhao
刘颂浩
Professor, International College for Chinese Language Studies, Peking University
北京大学对外汉语教育学院 教授

Ma Jianfei
马箭飞
Deputy Chief Executive, Confucius Institute Headquarters/Hanban
孔子学院总部 副总干事

Wu Yongyi
吴勇毅
Vice President, Professor, East China Normal University
华东师范大学对外汉语学院副院长、教授

Zhou Xiaobing
周小兵
President, Professor, School of Chinese as a Second Language, Sun Yat-sen University
广州中山大学国际交流学院 副院长、教授

Sun Dejin
孙德金
Professor, Beijing Language and Culture University
北京语言大学 教授

Acknowledgments

Cynthia Y. Ning dedicates her work to the memory of her parents, Grace and Chung Fong Ning, who made her conversant in Chinese in a decidedly non-Chinese environment; to the memory of her husband, Allan Ngai Lim Yee, who died too young; to her talented and loving daughter, Robyn Yee; to her brother and frequent dining companion, Sam Ning; to her yoga, dining, movie, and adventure buddies, Myrtle Wong, Janeen Kuhn, Robert Kohn, and Robert Brumblay; and to her mentor in filmmaking, Eric Gustafson.

Stephen L. Tschudi dedicates his work to his amazing parents, Martha and Morton Wood, who by their example taught him to love life, music, dance, and nature; to his husband, Daniel Tschudi, who delicately imposes a modicum of order on Stephen's chaos; and to the friends in China who were his earliest and best teachers.

The authors and publishers thank their professional friends and colleagues, including the staff of the Center for Chinese Studies at the University of Hawai'i and in particular its Confucius Institute; the University's Department of East Asian Languages and Literatures, Center for Language and Technology, and National Foreign Language Resource Center; and the following individuals: Li Qikeng, Zha Yunyun, Dong Xu, Qu Yaojia, Liu Meiyi, Zhai Mengying, Yang Jia, Yang Piao, Wang Yajun, Chuang Huiya, Gao Chenghua, Xing Yi, Tiger Wu, Tien Chenshan, Zhang Zihe, Frederick Lau, Sun Jialin, Samuel Ning, Amy Shen, Chunman Gissing, Kristine Wogstad, Joanne Shang, Terry Waltz, Reed Riggs, and Martin Yu.

Introduction

Overview

The comprehensive ***Encounters*** program:

- Includes two complete levels of two books each (Level 1: Books 1 and 2; Level 2: Books 3 and 4).
- Employs a functional, task-based approach.
- Presents authentic language and culture through engaging dramatic video episodes.
- Focuses on communication in the spoken language.
- Includes reading material in both traditional and simplified characters.
- Links cultural video interviews to language functions.
- Presents clearly focused grammar instruction and practice.
- Adheres to ACTFL Proficiency Guidelines.
- Assists teachers with a fully annotated instructor's edition, materials to excite students' interest, and a wide selection of useful tools in various media.

Program Components

The ***Encounters*** program comprises:

- A beautifully produced ***video series***, filmed entirely on location in China and featuring a dramatic story line and segments devoted to Chinese culture and history.
- A full-color ***student textbook***, completely integrated with the video series and other ***Encounters*** components.
- An ***annotated instructor's edition*** of the textbook, packed with teaching tips, extra classroom activities, and suggestions for using the program in the classroom.
- ***Screenplays*** containing the transcripts of the dramatic episodes.
- An ***audio program*** to assist students with listening comprehension, pronunciation, vocabulary, and model conversations.
- A ***website, www.EncountersChinese.com,*** that offers students and teachers streaming video and audio content, and other resources for speaking, reading, and writing Chinese.

Recap of Books 1, 2, and 3

The 20 units in Level 1 (Books 1 and 2) touched on making introductions and sharing personal information; dealing with time and money; talking about travel, foreign languages, and currency; discussing school, study, and daily routines; arranging for food and eating; discussing leisure activities; comparing living arrangements; moving around town and going on excursions; and chatting about the experience of learning Chinese.

Level 1 followed the experiences of expatriates living and learning in China, a pair of visitors to China, and the Chinese professionals and students they came to know. Some of these people you meet again, several years later, in Level 2. There were also 20 mini-documentaries in Level 1, which presented the points of view of a diverse range of people on the topics covered in each unit. The mini-documentaries were expanded in Level 2.

The 10 units in Book 3 touched on catching up with old friends, dealing with illnesses, setting up a bank account, getting a haircut in a beauty salon, buying and using a cell phone, going shopping in malls and neighborhood stores, grocery shopping and cooking, describing personal appearance and personality, discussing relationships with parents, and chatting about the experience of settling into a new place.

The Cast of Characters

MAO ZHIPENG (Máo Zhìpéng, 毛志鵬／毛志鹏) In Level 2, Mao Zhipeng returns as a core character. He is no longer working with Chen Feng but has instead become a professor at the Communications University of China (the true profession of the actor who plays him).

LUO XUETING (Luó Xuětíng, 羅雪婷／罗雪婷) Professor Mao is now engaged to a Chinese American physician, Luo Xueting, played by a woman previously interviewed in the mini-documentary section of Level 1. Dr. Luo is interning at the clinic of the Communications University of China.

MICK (Mǐkè, 米克) Also returning is Mick, the Australian tea connoisseur. The actor who plays him is really a tea connoisseur and the owner of a real-life establishment called *The Hutong*, which also figures in Level 2.

FANG LAN (Fāng Lán, 方蘭／方兰) Fang Lan, a puckish student of Professor Mao's, returns as a core character in Book 4. She is outspoken and strong-minded, and she has an opinion about everything. She lives at home with her parents, who also appear in the series.

EMMA (Àimǎ, 艾瑪／艾玛) Emma also returns as a core character in Book 4. She is an American exchange student at the Communications University of China and is living at the home of Fang Lan and her parents. Emma has a positive outlook and is not afraid of making mistakes.

TANG YUAN (Táng Yuǎn, 唐遠／唐远) Tang Yuan comes to the capital as well, with A-Juan, now his wife. He is a successful artist seeking to establish himself in the art community in Beijing.

A-JUAN (Ā-Juān, 阿娟) A-Juan is now married to Tang Yuan and expecting their first child. The character is played by a different actress than in Level 1 (the original actress left the cast to start a family).

CHEN FENG (Chén Fēng, 陳峰／陈峰) Chen Feng is still in advertising, and although he and Xiao Mao are no longer partners, he still calls on his old friend for help with an occasional project.

XIAO FEI (Xiǎo Fēi, 小飛／小飞) Chen Feng's cousin, Xiao Fei, still works for Chen Feng's company but is now almost presentable as a member of the team.

LAO FANG (Lǎo Fāng, 老方) Fang Lan's father is a teacher who sings Jingju (Chinese opera) and does all the cooking at home.

ZHANG SUYUN (張蘇雲/张苏云) Fang Lan's mother is a highly successful real estate agent. She is the family's major breadwinner.

A number of other memorable characters round out the cast: a famous actress, Fang Lan and Emma's school friends, Professor Mao's colleagues, and an agile martial arts instructor and his students. All work together to portray life in the rich and diverse communities of metropolitan Beijing.

The Dramatic Story Line

The lives of all the major characters intersect in the course of an academic year. Fang Lan and Emma meet a famous actress, and Fang Lan produces a news segment about this meeting; Emma becomes disenchanted with her friends' obsessions with their cell phones; Fang Lan interviews a martial arts instructor and begins an internship at Chen Feng's company, where Xiao Fei is instantly smitten with her; they work together to develop a dating website; Tang Yuan and A-Juan come to town and find a comfortable place to live; Fang Lan and Emma reminisce about the time they have spent together; and Emma experiences a Dragon Boat Festival before finally saying good-bye to Fang Lan. The characters experience many of the normal ups and downs of life at home, in school, and at work.

The Mini-documentaries

The content of the documentary series could constitute a parallel and completely independent textbook. Here, the documentaries serve to enrich the video offerings of Level 2 significantly. Via a plethora of interviews intercut with footage of sites, products, and activities, the depth of Chinese culture pertaining to each topic in the textbook is explored. We hope you will take the time to savor the wealth of knowledge on offer in this documentary series and come away with a much fuller sense of the breadth and depth of contemporary Chinese culture.

A Unit Tour

The ***Encounters*** textbook presents a carefully structured and cumulative approach to learning Mandarin Chinese. Students progress from listening and speaking activities to the more challenging skills of reading and writing Chinese characters. The emphasis is on communicative skills, as the primary goal of the ***Encounters*** program is to foster proficiency in everyday Chinese.

Each unit offers an inviting combination of in-class, individual, pair, and group activities. Humor and a lighthearted attitude encourage learners to approach the study of Chinese with enthusiasm and confidence. "FYI" boxes provide in-depth glimpses into Chinese language and culture, and appealing illustrations keep interest levels high. By weaving cultural information throughout the text—rather than relegating it only to end-of-unit notes—***Encounters*** reinforces the notion that language is inseparable from culture.

Unit titles are presented in English, in Chinese characters, and in pinyin. Traditional characters are used here to evoke decorative calligraphy, which is often presented only in the traditional form, even in China.

The introductory page for each unit features a photograph from the corresponding video episode. Skills taught and practiced in the unit are related to the events that students observe in the episode.

A list of skills to be covered in the unit clarifies learning goals and helps students stay organized.

UNIT 38

"No attachments, no worries—happy and free"

無牽無掛樂逍遙

Wúqiānwúguà lè xiāoyáo

The ideal lifestyle

In this unit, you will learn how to:

- talk about your thoughts on an ideal lifestyle.
- describe what you wish for your own future lifestyle.
- talk about what you most appreciate about your current life.
- describe what you hope for in an overseas study program.
- decipher the main ideas of an online discussion about studying abroad.
- read a brief autobiography.
- write a brief autobiography.

一百七十五 175

Encounter 1 Discussing an ideal future lifestyle

Each unit contains several interesting and enlightening "Encounters," presenting material that covers common real-life situations.

38.1 *Emma and Fang Lan are home with Fang Lan's parents, chatting about lifestyles.* 請把中文跟英文對上。／请把中文跟英文对上。

____ a. lìhai 厲害／厉害	1. *peanuts*
____ b. xiàohua 笑話／笑话	2. *lifestyle*
____ c. huāshēngmǐ 花生米	3. *satisfied, contented*
____ d. xìngfú 幸福	4. *powerful, formidable*
____ e. mǎnzú 滿足／满足	5. *make a toast to life*
____ f. lǐxiǎng de 理想的	6. *joke*
____ g. shēnghuó fāngshì 生活方式	7. *ideal*
____ h. wèi shēnghuó gānbēi 為生活乾杯／为生活干杯	8. *happy*

Various listening and learning activities are enriched by their connections to the ongoing video and by their insights into Chinese culture.

38.2 *View Episode 38, Vignette 1. Emma and Fang Lan's family are chatting around the dinner table. Indicate who says each of the following sentences (presented in the order in which they appear).* 請注明這話是誰說的。／请注明这话是谁说的。

	方蘭／方兰	父親／父亲	母親／母亲	艾瑪／艾玛
a. Lái, wǒmen gōngxǐ māma.	☐	☐	☐	☐
b. Yòu zhuàn le hǎo duō qián!	☐	☐	☐	☐
c. Nǐ mā lìhai ba!	☐	☐	☐	☐
d. Wǒ tīngdào le yí ge fēicháng hǎoxiào de xiàohua.	☐	☐	☐	☐
e. Wǒmen yǒu xuǎnzé de quánlì ma?	☐	☐	☐	☐
f. Wǒ shì kāi ge wánxiào.	☐	☐	☐	☐
g. Zhēn xiànmù nǐ.	☐	☐	☐	☐
h. Nǐmen zhēn xìngfú!	☐	☐	☐	☐
i. Wèi háizimen de wèilái, gānbēi!	☐	☐	☐	☐

FYI 供你参考

FYI boxes provide relevant cultural information that will both fascinate students and deepen their understanding of the Chinese language and the culture and people of China.

Speak of the devil

Cao Cao (*Cáo Cāo* 曹操; 155–220 CE) was the warlord of the region that became the State of Wei during China's Three Kingdoms period (220–280 CE). He's famous for fighting, albeit unsuccessfully, against the generals Liu Bei and Sun Quan at the Battle of the Red Cliffs. The history of the period inspired the classic novel *Sānguó Yǎnyì* 三國演義／三国演义 *Romance of the Three Kingdoms*—one of the four great classical novels discussed in Unit 31—which has been dramatized in many folk operas, movies, and TV dramas. But his popularity among China's youth derives primarily from the video game series called *Romance of the Three Kingdoms*, published by the Japanese Koei Company.

How did Cao Cao become the subject of this widely used saying? According to a popular theory, he was very suspicious and untrusting by nature, and given the tensions that surrounded him, he resorted to employing a small army of spies to gather information and spy on people. These spies were ubiquitous and mobile; they could suddenly appear out of nowhere. This phrase was coined to remind people to watch what they said and did because danger lurked everywhere—one small misstep could land you in trouble with Cao Cao!

38.7 *Fang Lan's father comes across as a wonderful person in this vignette.* 請把中文跟英文對上。／请把中文跟英文对上。

____ a. zhème bàng de lǎogōng 這麼棒的老公／这么棒的老公	1. *has a good character*
____ b. yòu huì chàngxì yòu huì zuòfàn 又會唱戲又會做飯／又会唱戏又会做饭	2. *can both sing and cook*
____ c. xǐhuan gěi nǚ'ér hé lǎopo mánghuo 喜歡給女兒和老婆忙活／喜欢给女儿和老婆忙活	3. *is talented*
____ d. rénpǐn hǎo 人品好	4. *is such a great husband*
____ e. yǒu cáihuá 有才華／有才华	5. *likes to busy himself for his wife and daughter*

Both traditional and simplified characters are used throughout the materials. Only 20 percent of characters have two forms, and students will encounter both forms in areas where Chinese is spoken. Students can easily learn to recognize both but need to write only in the form that is meaningful or useful to them.

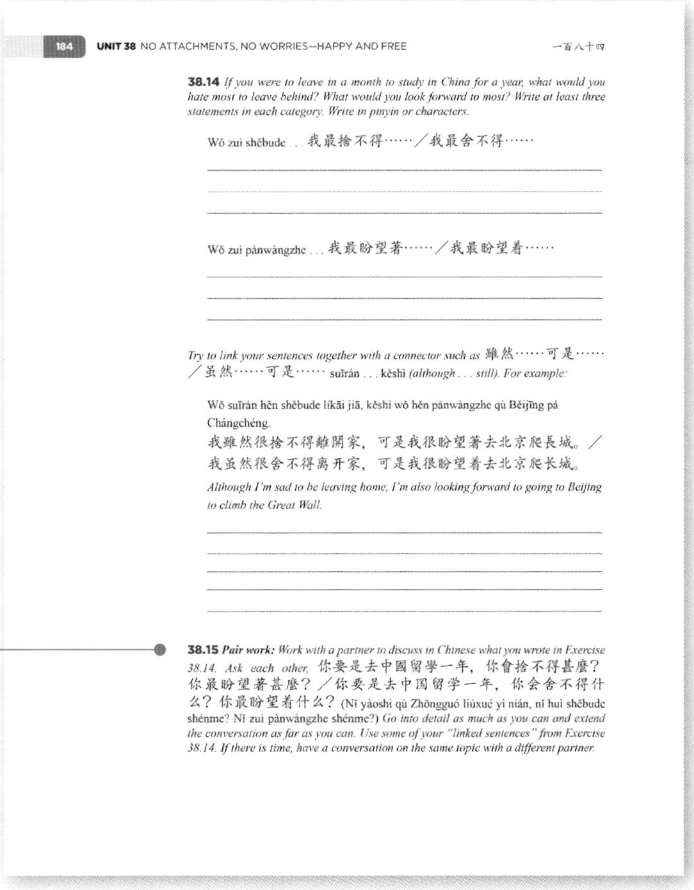

184 **UNIT 38** NO ATTACHMENTS, NO WORRIES—HAPPY AND FREE 一百八十四

38.14 *If you were to leave in a month to study in China for a year, what would you hate most to leave behind? What would you look forward to most? Write at least three statements in each category. Write in pinyin or characters.*

Wǒ zuì shěbude . . . 我最捨不得……／我最舍不得……

Wǒ zuì pànwàngzhe . . . 我最盼望著……／我最盼望着……

Try to link your sentences together with a connector such as 雖然……可是……／虽然……可是…… suīrán . . . kěshì *(although . . . still). For example:*

Wǒ suīrán hěn shěbude líkāi jiā, kěshì wǒ hěn pànwàngzhe qù Běijīng pá Chángchéng.

我雖然很捨不得離開家，可是我很盼望著去北京爬長城。／我虽然很舍不得离开家，可是我很盼望着去北京爬长城。

Although I'm sad to be leaving home, I'm also looking forward to going to Beijing to climb the Great Wall.

38.15 ***Pair work:*** *Work with a partner to discuss in Chinese what you wrote in Exercise 38.14. Ask each other,* 你要是去中國留學一年，你會捨不得甚麼？你最盼望著甚麼？／你要是去中国留学一年，你会舍不得什么？你最盼望着什么？(Nǐ yàoshi qù Zhōngguó liúxué yì nián, nǐ huì shěbude shénme? Nǐ zuì pànwàngzhe shénme?) *Go into detail as much as you can and extend the conversation as far as you can. Use some of your "linked sentences" from Exercise 38.14. If there is time, have a conversation on the same topic with a different partner.*

Suggestions for conversation practice appear throughout each unit. Students build confidence and practical conversational skills through these entertaining oral exercises.

一百八十七 **ENCOUNTER 3** 187

38.17 *The search described in Exercise 38.16 will also lead to information for Chinese students seeking to study overseas. For example, you might find the advertisement provided below at this website:* http://www.wiseway.com.cn/zhuanti/cglx/?baidu-jiaoyu.

首页 | 英国 | 美国 | 澳洲 | 加拿大 | 德国 | 荷兰 | 瑞士 | 日本 | 韩国 | 中国香港 | 新加坡 | 爱尔兰 | 马来西亚 | 意大利 | 俄罗斯 | 法国 | 西班牙

a *Across the top of the ad, there is a banner listing countries where information about their programs can be found on the site:* 英国、美国、澳洲、加拿大、德国、荷兰、瑞士、日本、韩国 、中国香港、新加坡、爱尔兰、马来西亚、意大利、俄罗斯、法国、西班牙. *Using the banner as a guide, write the Chinese terms for the following countries.* 請寫漢字。／请写汉字。

Germany		*Canada*		*Spain*	
Ireland		*Malaysia*		*Japan*	
Australia		*United States*		*South Korea*	
France		*Switzerland*		*Italy*	
Holland		*Russia*		*Singapore*	
England		*Hong Kong (in China)*			

b *The ad is simple and direct. Please write characters for the English below.*

1. *Whether you have money or not, just follow your impulses!*

2. *Studying abroad will give you*

3. *Study abroad: if you want to go, go!*

By incorporating materials found in real life—an online ad, for example—lessons provide practical information enabling students to perform everyday tasks in Chinese.

Interesting stories written in characters facilitate intensive reading and develop reading comprehension skills. Extensive character-recognition exercises cultivate students' ability to gather meaning from context. The engrossing storyline also deepens their understanding of the unit topic.

一百八十九 ENCOUNTER 3 189
Reading a story
38.19 故事 Find the following terms in either the traditional or simplified text and circle them. Write in the accompanying number.
Shanghai after a Japanese air attack
At home in Lahore, Pakistan. Author is the 5-year-old girl in the middle.

Mini-documentaries extend students' control of the language and enrich their understanding of the unit topics. Authentic interviews offer a closer look into Chinese society and its people, encouraging students to investigate how Chinese culture is different from or similar to their own.

A complete Recap section appears at the conclusion of every unit. These pages include a summary of grammar topics, a vocabulary list, and a checklist of tasks that students are expected to have mastered in the unit. The Recap encourages students to review their progress, identify gaps in their learning, and congratulate themselves on their accomplishments.

UNIT

31

“Reading is always beneficial”

開卷有益

Kāijuànyǒuyì

Books and media

In this unit, you will learn how to:

- talk about books and magazines.
- identify different genres of books.
- talk about “following” media celebrities.
- decipher some book and magazine titles and signs in a bookstore.
- identify the author, translator, and publisher of a book you haven’t seen before.
- comprehend summaries of popular stories.
- write a summary of a favorite story.

Encounter 1 Browsing a bookstore

31.1 *Fang Lan is accompanying Emma on a visit to a neighborhood bookstore to buy her books for school.* 請圈選正確的意思。／请圈选正确的意思。

a. guàng shūdiàn 逛書店／逛书店 *(browse a bookstore / shop for books)*

b. zài túshūguǎn dāizhe 在圖書館呆著／在图书馆呆着 *(hang out in a library / look for a library)*

c. diànyǐng zázhì 電影雜誌／电影杂志 *(movie theater / movie magazine)*

d. shūjià 書架／书架 *(bookcase / bookmobile)*

e. xiǎoshuō 小説／小说 *(gossip / novel)*

31.2 *View Episode 31, Vignette 1 and indicate the speaker.*

	Fang Lan	Emma
a. I like browsing in bookstores too.	☐	☐
b. When I was little, I liked to hang out in the library.	☐	☐
c. I've seen the Harry Potter movies.	☐	☐
d. Let's buy a magazine and read it together at home.	☐	☐
e. This bookstore is a bit small; it may not have all the books you're looking for.	☐	☐
f. The teacher recommended I buy a bilingual edition of a novel.	☐	☐
g. You should choose an English novel you're familiar with.	☐	☐
h. I've read the original version; I liked it very much.	☐	☐

31.3 請再一次聽錄像片斷，然後圈選正確的答案。／请再一次听录像片断，然后圈选正确的答案。

Part 1

Àimă: A, zhè xiăo shūdiàn bú dà, dànshì hĕn . . .

Fāng Lán: Wŏ juéde zhèr hĕn ___ (yăzhì *elegant* / yòuzhì *immature*).

Àimă: Hĕn yăzhì? Shénme yìsi?

Fāng Lán: Jiùshì hĕn yŏu pĭnwèi, hmm, *tasteful*.

Àimă: O, wŏ dŏng le. Zhēn de shì zhèyàng. Xièxie nĭ ___ (bēi *carry on the back* / péi *accompany*) wŏ lái zhè jiā shūdiàn.

Fāng Lán: Méiguānxi! Qíshí wŏ yĕ hĕn ài ___ (guāng *light* / guàng *browse*) shūdiàn.

Àimă: Wŏ yĕshì! Wŏ juéde wŏ suànshì ge . . . shūchóng?

Fāng Lán: *Bookworm!* Shū___ (dāizi *idiot* / dàizi *tape*).

Àimă: Méicuò, shūdāizi. Wŏ xiăoshíhou, tèbié xĭhuan zài wŏ zhù de nèi ge chéngli de túshūguăn ___ (dàizhe *bringing along* / dāizhe *hanging out*).

Fāng Lán: Shì ma? Nà nĭ dōu xĭhuan yìxiē shénme ___ (lèixíng *type of* / nèixīn *inner feelings*) de shū?

Àimă: Chángpiān xiăoshuō, tèbié shì ___ (lìshĭ *history* / lìzhì *motivational)* xiăoshuō. Dànshì dāngrán hái xĭhuan Hālĭ Bōtè zhī lèi.

Fāng Lán: Wŏ yĕ tèbié xĭhuan Hālĭ Bōtè zhèyàng de ___ (huánxiāng *returning to one's hometown* / huànxiăng *fantasy*) xiăoshuō! Wŏ hái kànguo Hālĭ Bōtè de diànyĭng. Tā de nǚ___ (zhŭjué *lead role* / zhùjiào *teaching assistant*) jiào Emma Watson, tèbié piàoliang. Gēn nĭ hái yíyàng de míngzi ne!

Part 2

Àimă: Duì ya! Wŏ yĕ hĕn xĭhuan tā. A! Zhèr yŏu ___ (bāgē *mynah bird* / bāguà *gossip*) zázhì.

Fāng Lán: A, hái yŏu diànyĭng zázhì. Kànkan zhè qī de ___ (mĕiróng *beauty* / nèiróng *content*) huìbuhuì yŏu tā de ___ (qīnwĕn *kiss* / xīnwén *news*). Wa, zhè qī hái tĭng ____ (fēngfù *plentiful* / fănfù *repeatedly*) a.

Àimă: N, duì a, kàn ___ (pèngmiàn *meet* / fēngmiàn *cover*) jiù zhīdào nèiróng hĕn fēngfù.

Fāng Lán: Āi! Zhè bú jiùshì tā ma! Nà wŏmen măi yì bĕn, huíqu yìqĭ dú. Wŏ hái kĕyĭ zuò nĭ de _____ (huŏ *fire* / huó *living*) zìdiăn.

Àimă: Hăo de!

Fāng Lán: Duìle, nĭ de lăoshī ràng nĭ măi xiē shénmeyàngr de shū?

Àimă: N, xiān dĕi măi "Huánqiú hànyŭ" de _____ (gēbĕn *songbook* / kèbĕn *textbook*). Hái yŏu wénxué, lìshĭ, kējì, gōngjù shū, jīnróng jīngjì hé jìsuànjī . . .

Fāng Lán: Nà hái tĭng duō a. Zhăozhăo ba, zhèr kĕnéng bùyídìng huì yŏu.

Àimă: Yīnggāi huì yŏu . . .

Fāng Lán: Dànshì zhè ge shūdiàn yŏudiăn xiăo, kĕnéng zhăobudào nĭ xiăng yào de nà xiē shū. Guò liăng tiān wŏ dài nĭ qù yí ge dà yìdiăn de shūdiàn, yīnggāi jiù néng măi dào.

Àimǎ: Hǎo de, hǎo de! Ó, duìle, lǎoshī hái jiànyì wǒ mǎi yì běn Zhōng-Yīng duìzhàoběn de_____ (xiǎoshuō *novel* / shuōxiào *tell a joke*), kànkan zhèr yǒu méiyǒu.

Fāng Lán: Zhōng-Yīng duìzhào xiǎoshuō . . . nà yīnggāi yǒu. Qù nàr kànkan. Yīnggāi hái tǐng duō de.

Àimǎ: Nǐ yǒu méiyǒu shénme kěyǐ ___ (tuījiàn *recommend* / tuìqián *get a refund*) de?

Fāng Lán: Yīnggāi xuǎn yì běn nǐ bǐjiào ___ (chúxī *New Year's Eve* / shúxī *familiar*) de Yīngwén xiǎoshuō. Āi, zhèr yǒu hǎo duō Zhōng-Yīng duìzhàobǎn. Àomàn yǔ Piānjiàn? Shì Jiǎn Àosīdīng xiě de?

Àimǎ: Ō, hǎo zhǔyi! Wǒ dúguo ___ (yuánzǐ *atom* / yuánzhù *original work*), tǐng xǐhuan zhè běn shū de! Hǎo _____ (làngmàn *romantic* / lángbèi *awkward*)!

31.4 *Foreign names and titles can be translated into Chinese based on their sound, meaning, or a combination of both. Check the appropriate column and write the number for the English equivalent in the word bank that follows.*

	Sound	Meaning	Combination	#
a. Hālǐ Bōtè 哈里波特	☐	☐	☐	
b. Àomàn yǔ Piānjiàn 傲慢與偏見／傲慢与偏见	☐	☐	☐	
c. Jiǎn Àosīdīng 簡・奧斯丁／简・奥斯丁	☐	☐	☐	
d. Shāsǐ yì zhī zhīgēngniǎo 殺死一隻知更鳥／杀死一只知更鸟	☐	☐	☐	
e. Piāo 飄／飘	☐	☐	☐	
f. Táng lǎo yā 唐老鴨／唐老鸭	☐	☐	☐	
g. Jī'è yóuxì 飢餓遊戲／饥饿游戏	☐	☐	☐	
h. Mǐ lǎoshǔ 米老鼠	☐	☐	☐	

1. Jane Austen
2. Harry Potter
3. *To Kill a Mockingbird*
4. Donald Duck
5. *Pride and Prejudice*
6. *The Hunger Games*
7. Mickey Mouse
8. *Gone with the Wind*

31.5 *Write the traditional characters, simplified characters, and English in the appropriate places in the chart to match the pinyin.*

漢英字典	長篇小説	短篇小説	電影雜誌	八卦雜誌
工具書	對照版	漢語課本	科幻小説	歷史小説

长篇小说	短篇小说	汉语课本	科幻小说	历史小说
工具书	电影杂志	八卦杂志	对照版	汉英字典

Chinese textbook	*short story*	*gossip magazine*	*Chinese-English dictionary*	*reference book*
bilingual edition	*novel*	*movie magazine*	*science fiction*	*historical novel*

拼音	繁體字	简体字	英文
chángpiān xiǎoshuō			
duǎnpiān xiǎoshuō			
diànyǐng zázhì			
bāguà zázhì			
Hàn-Yīng zìdiǎn			
duìzhào bǎn			
Hànyǔ kèběn			
kēhuàn xiǎoshuō			
lìshǐ xiǎoshuō			
gōngjùshū			

31.6 ***Pair work:*** *Work with a partner to read the following conversation.*

艾玛：啊，这小书店不大，但是很……

方兰：我觉得这儿很雅致。

艾玛：很雅致？什么意思？

方兰：就是很有品位 (pǐnwèi *taste*)。Hmm, tasteful.

艾玛：噢，我懂了。真的是这样。谢谢你陪我来这家书店。

方兰：没关系！其实我也爱逛书店。

艾玛：我也是！我觉得我算是个……书虫 (shūchóng *bookworm*)?

方兰：Bookworm! 书呆子 (shūdāizi *bookworm*)!

艾玛：没错，书呆子，我小时候，特别喜欢在我住的那个城里的图书馆呆着。

方兰：是吗？那你都喜欢一些什么类型 (lèixíng *type*) 的书？

艾玛: 长篇小说，特别是历史小说。但是当然还喜欢哈里波特之类。

方兰: 我也特别喜欢哈里波特这样的幻想小说 (huànxiǎng xiǎoshuō *fantasy novel*)！我还看过哈里波特的电影。它的女主角叫 Emma Watson，特别漂亮。跟你还一样的名字呢！

艾玛: 对呀！我也很喜欢她。啊！这儿有八卦杂志。

方兰: 啊，还有电影杂志。看看这期的内容 (nèiróng *contents*) 会不会有她的新闻。哇，这期还挺丰富 (fēngfù *abundant*) 啊。

艾玛: 嗯，对啊，看封面 (fēngmiàn *cover*) 就知道内容很丰富。

方兰: 哎！这不就是她嘛！那我们买一本，回去一起读。我还可以做你的活字典。

艾玛: 好的！

方兰: 对了，你的老师让你买些什么样儿的书？

艾玛: 嗯，先得买《环球汉语》(Huánqiú Hànyǔ *Encounters*) 的课本。还有文学、历史、科技、工具书、金融经济和计算机……

方兰: 那还挺多啊。找找吧，这儿可能不一定会有。

艾玛: 应该会有……

方兰: 但是这个书店有点小，可能找不到你想要的那些书。过两天我带你去一个大一点的书店，应该就能买到。

艾玛: 好的，好的！哦，对了，老师还建议我买一本中英对照本的小说，看看这儿有没有。

方兰: 中英对照小说……那应该有。去那儿看看。应该还挺多的。

艾玛: 你有没有什么可以推荐 (tuījiàn *recommend*) 的？

方兰: 应该选一本你比较熟悉的英文小说。哎，这儿有好多中英对照版。傲慢与偏见 (Àomàn yǔ Piānjiàn *Pride and Prejudice*)？是简•奥斯丁写的？

艾玛: 噢，好主意！我读过原著 (yuánzhù *original*)，挺喜欢这本书的！好浪漫 (làngmàn *romantic*)！

Switch roles and try it again with traditional characters.

艾瑪: 啊，這小書店不大，但是很……

方蘭: 我覺得這兒很雅緻。

艾瑪: 很雅緻？甚麼意思？

方蘭: 就是很有品位。Hmm, tasteful.

艾瑪：噢，我懂了。真的是這樣。謝謝你陪我來這家書店。

方蘭：没關係！其實我也愛逛書店。

艾瑪：我也是！我覺得我算是個……書蟲？

方蘭：Bookworm! 書呆子！

艾瑪：没錯，書呆子，我小時候，特別喜歡在我住的那個城裡的圖書館呆著。

方蘭：是嗎？那你都喜歡一些甚麼類型的書？

艾瑪：長篇小説，特別是歷史小説。但是當然還喜歡哈里波特之類。

方蘭：我也特別喜歡哈里波特這樣的幻想小説！我還看過哈里波特的電影。它的女主角叫 Emma Watson，特別漂亮。跟你還一樣的名字呢！

艾瑪：對呀！我也很喜歡她。啊！這兒有八卦雜誌。

方蘭：啊，還有電影雜誌。看看這期的內容會不會有她的新聞。哇，這期還挺豐富啊。

艾瑪：嗯，對啊，看封面就知道內容很豐富。

方蘭：哎！這不就是她嘛！那我們買一本，回去一起讀。我還可以做你的活字典。

艾瑪：好的！

方蘭：對了，你的老師讓你買些甚麼樣兒的書？

艾瑪：嗯，先得買《環球漢語》的課本。還有文學、歷史、科技、工具書、金融經濟和計算機……

方蘭：那還挺多啊。找找吧，這兒可能不一定會有。

艾瑪：應該會有……

方蘭：但是這個書店有點小，可能找不到你想要的那些書。過兩天我帶你去一個大一點的書店，應該就能買到。

艾瑪：好的，好的！哦，對了，老師還建議我買一本中英對照本的小説，看看這兒有没有。

方蘭：中英對照小説……那應該有。去那兒看看。應該還挺多的。

艾瑪：你有没有甚麼可以推薦的？

方蘭：應該選一本你比較熟悉的英文小説。哎，這兒有好多中英對照版。傲慢與偏見？是簡•奥斯丁寫的？

艾瑪：噢，好主意！我讀過原著，挺喜歡這本書的！好浪漫！

31.7 *If you were going to chat with a friend about books, magazines, bookstores, or films, what would you say? What are your favorite books and magazines? Do you like to hang out in bookstores? Do you often go to the movies? What are your favorite movies? Take some notes in Chinese.*

31.8 ***Mingling:*** *Now chat with at least three people in your class for 2–3 minutes each. Talk about books, magazines, bookstores, or films.*

Encounter 2 Meeting an idol

31.9 *Fang Lan recognizes Huang Yalan, a well-known actress, in the bookstore. To prepare for viewing this episode, match the vocabulary below.* 請把中文跟英文對上。／请把中文跟英文对上。

____ a. diànyǐng yǎnyuán 電影演員／电影演员	1. *fan(s)*
____ b. ǒuxiàng 偶像	2. Dream of the Red Chamber
____ c. zhuàngjiàn 撞見／撞见	3. *idol*
____ d. fěnsī 粉絲／粉丝	4. *Phoenix Wang (a character)*
____ e. Hóng Lóu Mèng 紅樓夢／红楼梦	5. *film actor*
____ f. Qīngcháo 清朝	6. *take a photo together*
____ g. ràokǒulìng 繞口令／绕口令	7. *run into*
____ h. hé zhāng zhào 合張照／合张照	8. *tongue twister*
____ i. Wáng Xīfèng 王熙鳳／王熙凤	9. *Qing Dynasty*

31.10 *View Episode 31, Vignette 2. Identify who makes each of the following statements (presented in the order in which they are made).*

i. Emma ii. Fang Lan iii. Actress

______ a. Oh, sorry, am I blocking your way?
______ b. Are you the film actress Huang Yalan?
______ c. My mom is a fan of yours.
______ d. I came to buy the new edition of *Dream of the Red Chamber*.
______ e. It takes place in the Qing Dynasty.
______ f. I'm happy too. Very happy.
______ g. May I have my picture taken with you?
______ h. Let me help you. Cheese! Beautiful!
______ i. Our teacher asked us to work on tongue twisters and standard pronunciation.

31.11 請把下面的拼音跟上面的英文對上。／请把下面的拼音跟上面的英文对上。

______ 1. Wǒ māma shì nín de fěnsī.
______ 2. Wǒ lái mǎi xīnbǎn Hóng Lóu Mèng.
______ 3. Tā fāshēng zài Qīngcháo.
______ 4. O, duìbuqǐ, wǒ shìbushì dǎngzhe nǐmen la?
______ 5. Wǒ néng gēn nín hé zhāng zhào ma?
______ 6. Nín shìbushì diànyǐng yǎnyuán Huáng Yǎlán?
______ 7. Lǎoshī ràng wǒmen xué ràokǒulìng hé biāozhǔn de fāyīn.
______ 8. Wǒ bāng nǐ. Qiézi. Tài piàoliang le!
______ 9. Wǒ yě kāixīn, hěn kāixīn.

31.12 *Fang Lan mentions the following proof that her mother is a fan of Huang Yalan.*
請把拼音、漢字和英文對上。／请把拼音、汉字和英文对上。

a. tèbié xǐhuan kàn nín yǎn de diànyǐng	1. 给我取名叫方蘭，因為您的名字裡有個“蘭”字。／给我取名叫方兰，因为您的名字里有个“兰”字。	A. *often reads news about you online*
b. gěi wǒ qǔ míng jiào Fāng Lán, yīnwèi nín de míngzi li yǒu ge “lán” zì	2. 看過您在報紙上的觀眾問答專欄／看过您在报纸上的观众问答专栏	B. *named me Fang Lan because there's a “lan” (orchid) in your name*
c. kànguo nín zài bàozhǐ shàng de guānzhòng wèndá zhuānlán	3. 下了好多您的照片	C. *especially likes to watch your movies*
d. jīngcháng zài wǎngshàng kàn nín de xīnwén	4. 特別喜歡看您演的電影／特别喜欢看您演的电影	D. *has downloaded many of your photographs*
e. xià le hǎo duō nín de zhàopiàn	5. 經常在網上看您的新聞／经常在网上看您的新闻	E. *has read columns in the newspaper on your answers to readers' questions*

Would you say you exhibit any of the behaviors listed above in relation to someone you admire?

誰是你的偶像呢？請寫名字。／谁是你的偶像呢？请写名字。

31.13 ***Think-pair-share:*** *First, come up with several statements describing a celebrity or someone you adore and what you do as a fan. Take notes in the space below.*

Tell your partner about this person and try to improve your statements. Take notes about your partner's "idol."

Finally, share your statements with the class and make a list of people held in high regard by your classmates.

FYI 供你参考

The four great classical novels of Chinese literature (*sì dà míngzhù* 四大名著)

With increasing literacy rates and publication for wider audiences, these long (100+ chapters) novels of the Ming and Qing Dynasties are celebrated as the best of premodern Chinese fiction. They were written in a mixture of vernacular and classical language, leaning more toward the colloquial—which is very different from the literary language that had predominated previously. English translations of all four novels are available in more abridged and fuller versions—read them if you have the time and interest!

a. 請把中文跟英文對上。／请把中文跟英文对上。

____ 1. *Dream of the Red Chamber* A. Shuǐhǔ Zhuàn 水滸傳／水浒传
____ 2. *Water Margin* B. Hóng Lóu Mèng 紅樓夢／红楼梦
____ 3. *Journey to the West* C. Sānguó Yǎnyì 三國演義／三国演义
____ 4. *Romance of the Three Kingdoms* D. Xī Yóu Jì 西遊記／西游记

b. *Here is some further information about each of the four great classical novels. Write the Chinese title of each in the spaces provided.* 請寫拼音或者漢字。／请写拼音或者汉字。

1. ______________________________

Written in the 14th century, this novel tells tales about the exploits of 108 outlaws who flee the rule of a corrupt government and make their home around the marshes of distant Mt. Liang (*Liángshān* 梁山). It is loosely based on historical figures such as *Sòng Jiāng* 宋江, *Wǔ Sōng* 武松, *Lǔ Zhìshēn* 魯智深／鲁智深, *Lín Chōng* 林冲, and their brethren—heroes who can uproot a tree or kill a tiger with their bare hands and who beat off successive attempts by government forces and other opponents to capture or suppress them. The novel also tells popular stories about their martial adventures, which have been widely circulated through oral storytelling before being collected here. Most of the outlaws are eventually granted amnesty by the Song Dynasty government and recruited into the army to fight against foreign invaders and suppress rebel uprisings. Authorship is attributed variously to *Shī Nài'ān* 施耐庵 and *Luó Guànzhōng* 羅貫中／罗贯中.

2. ______________________________

Two branches of a wealthy family surnamed *Jiǎ* 賈／贾 live in adjacent compounds in Beijing during the Qing Dynasty. One is the *Róngguó* 榮國／荣国 (Glorify the Country) House, and the other is the *Níngguó* 寧國／宁国 (Pacify the Country) House. The scion of the Rongguo House is a sensitive young man named *Bǎoyù* 寶玉／宝玉 (Precious Jade), since he was born with a piece of jade in his mouth. He is in love with a tragic young cousin named *Dàiyù* 黛玉 (Blue-Black Jade), who has been sent to live at the Rongguo House following the death of her mother. But Baoyu is expected to marry his other cousin, the beautiful *Bǎochāi* 寶釵／宝钗 (Precious Hairpin). The novel focuses on these three primary characters along with several dozen other major characters and several hundred minor ones. The tremendous wealth of detail provided in this sprawling epic novel has given rise to a subfield in the study of Chinese literature called Redology (*Hóngxué* 紅學／红学). Written by *Cáo Xuěqín* 曹雪芹.

3. ______________________________

A historical novel set during the century of disunion that began with the end of the *Hàn* 漢／汉 Dynasty (2nd century CE), the plot follows the legendary battles and intrigues among the leaders of the three states of Cao Wei, Shu Han, and Eastern Wu. The protagonists include the warlord *Dǒng Zhuó* 董卓; the generals *Cáo Cāo* 曹操, *Sūn Quán* 孫權／孙权, *Liú Bèi* 劉備／刘备, and *Guān Yǔ* 關羽／关羽; and the brilliant strategist *Zhūgě Liàng* 諸葛亮／诸葛亮. Written in the 14th century, this novel depicts idealized rulers and ministers pitted against villains and the rise and fall of each of them. The central tragic theme of the novel is that union must ineluctably move toward disunion (and eventually back again) in the historical flow of the empire. Stories from this novel are the basis of several wildly popular computer games. Authorship is attributed to *Luó Guànzhōng* 羅貫中／罗贯中.

4. ______________________________

Written in the 16th century, this novel is based on the travels of the historical priest *Xuánzàng* 玄奘 (602–664) of the Tang Dynasty, who went to India to obtain Buddhist scriptures, brought them back to China, and translated them into Chinese. In this novel, though, he gains the company of four fantastical companions: the magical Monkey King named *Sūn Wùkōng* 孫悟空／孙悟空; the perpetually ravenous Pigsy (*Zhū Bājiè* 豬八戒／猪八戒); the serious, devoted Sandy Monk (*Shā Héshàng* 沙和尚); and a dragon in the shape of a horse. Since Xuanzang has not shed a drop of semen in multiple lifetimes, eating his flesh is reputed to impart immortality, so along the way, Xuanzang's disciples have to fight off a myriad of demons and monsters who try to get to the priest through direct and deceptive means. Although the novel has layers of spiritual meaning, it has been a perpetual favorite with children in remade formats. Written by *Wú Chéng'ēn* 吳承恩／吴承恩.

c. *A principal character in* Dream of the Red Chamber *is called Phoenix in the English translation. She is married to Baoyu's elder cousin and runs the world of the Rongguo Mansion. She is an extremely interesting character: smart, capable, beautiful, assertive, strong-willed, outspoken, funny, and sometimes cruel. What is she called in the original Chinese?* 請寫拼音或者漢字。／请写拼音或者汉字。

____

31.14 *Fang Lan says the following about* Dream of the Red Chamber*:*

Tā fāshēng zài Qīngcháo, shì yí ge fēicháng fùyǒu de rén de jiātíng li, yǒu xǔduō xìnggé gè yì de rénwù.

它發生在清朝，是一個非常富有的人的家庭裡，有許多性格各異的人物。／它发生在清朝，是一个非常富有的人的家庭里，有许多性格各异的人物。

It takes place during the Qing Dynasty, in the household of a very rich family. There are many very strong personalities.

Think-pair-share: *Fill in the blanks below to come up with a statement in Chinese about a book or movie that you like.*

Tā fāshēng zài ___________________________, zài yí ge ___________________________ lǐtou.
(Where does the story take place?) *(In what kind of a setting?)*

Zhǔyào rénwù shì ____.
(Who are the main characters?)

____.
(Say anything else you'd like about the story.)

Zhè běn xiǎoshuō / Zhè bù diànyǐng de míngzi jiào ___________________________.
(Write the name in Chinese if you can; otherwise write English.)

Share your statement with your partner and see if you can improve it. Then take notes in pinyin and/or characters on your partner's statement.

Finally, share your statement with the class. As a group, make a simple, annotated list (in pinyin and/or characters) of the books or movies your class likes.

31.15 *View Episode 31, Vignette 2 again and follow along in the dialogue below. Then work with two classmates to act out the scene. Switch roles and repeat twice.*

艾瑪: 誰啊?
方蘭: 跟我來。
演員: 哦, 對不起, 我是不是擋著 (dǎngzhe *block one's way*) 你們啦?
方蘭: 不不不...... 您特別像一個人。
演員: 哦?
方蘭: 不好意思啊, 冒昧地問一下 (màomèi de wènyíxià *may I be so bold as to ask*), 您是不是電影演員黃雅蘭?
演員: 你看我像嗎?
方蘭: 哎呀, 太像了! 您一定就是, 對不對?

[Fang Lan laughs in delight.]
方蘭: 艾瑪, 太棒了! 我親眼見到我的偶像啦! 哎呀, 真沒想到能在這兒撞見您! *[turns to the actress]* 我媽媽是您的粉絲, 她從年輕的時候就特別喜歡看您演的電影!
您看, 她給我取名叫方蘭, 也是因為您的名字裡有一個"蘭"字。
我還看過您在報紙上的觀眾 (guānzhòng *audience*) 問答 (wèndá *Q&A*) 專欄 (zhuānlán *column*)。
我媽還經常在網上看您的新聞, 對了, 她還下了好多您的照片呢!
演員: 噢, 真謝謝你了, 小姑娘! 哎, 也替我 (tì wǒ *on my behalf*) 謝謝你媽媽!
方蘭: 哎, 您是在看《紅樓夢》嗎?
演員: 嗯, 是啊。我來這邊買一本新版 (xīnbǎn *new edition*)《紅樓夢》。
艾瑪:《紅樓夢》是甚麼?
方蘭:《紅樓夢》就是一本經典 (jīngdiǎn *classic*) 的中國小說, 是四大名著之一。它發生在清朝, 是一個非常富有的人的家庭裡, 有許多性格各異的人物......

艾玛: 谁啊?
方兰: 跟我来。
演员: 哦, 对不起, 我是不是挡着 (dǎngzhe *block one's way*) 你们啦?
方兰: 不不不...... 您特别像一个人。
演员: 哦?
方兰: 不好意思啊, 冒昧地问一下 (màomèi de wènyíxià *may I be so bold as to ask*), 您是不是电影演员黄雅兰?
演员: 你看我像吗?
方兰: 哎呀, 太像了! 您一定就是, 对不对?

[Fang Lan laughs in delight.]
方兰: 艾玛, 太棒了! 我亲眼见到我的偶像啦! 哎呀, 真没想到能在这儿撞见您! *[turns to the actress]* 我妈妈是您的粉丝, 她从年轻的时候就特别喜欢看您演的电影!
您看, 她给我取名叫方兰, 也是因为您的名字里有一个"兰"字。
我还看过您在报纸上的观众 (guānzhòng *audience*) 问答 (wèndá *Q&A*) 专栏 (zhuānlán *column*)。
我妈还经常在网上看您的新闻, 对了, 她还下了好多您的照片呢!
演员: 噢, 真谢谢你了, 小姑娘! 哎, 也替我 (tì wǒ *on my behalf*) 谢谢你妈妈!
方兰: 哎, 您是在看《红楼梦》吗?
演员: 嗯, 是啊。我来这边买一本新版 (xīnbǎn *new edition*)《红楼梦》。
艾玛:《红楼梦》是什么?
方兰:《红楼梦》就是一本经典 (jīngdiǎn *classic*) 的中国小说, 是四大名著之一。它发生在清朝, 是一个非常富有的人的家庭里, 有许多性格各异的人物......

艾瑪: 有意思……
方蘭: 聽説《紅樓夢》要被翻拍成 (fānpāi chéng *turned into*) 電影版了，您是不是要在裡面演甚麼角色啊？

[Actress smiles but says nothing.]
方蘭: 一定是！對不對？那您是要演誰呢？讓我想想，是王熙鳳 (Wáng Xīfèng *Phoenix Wang*) 吧！

[Actress laughs.]
方蘭: 哎，艾瑪，我太開心啦！*[to Emma]* 你開心嗎？
艾瑪: 嗯，我也開心，很開心。
方蘭: *[to actress]* 我能跟您合張照嗎？
演員: 啊，當然可以！來來來，來來來。
方蘭: 謝謝！
艾瑪: 我幫你。茄子。太漂亮了！

[Actress and Fang Lan pose.]
方蘭: 真好！謝謝您！
演員: 不客氣。
方蘭: 那……不打擾了。再見！
演員: 再見，再見。

艾玛: 有意思……
方兰: 听说《红楼梦》要被翻拍成 (fānpāi chéng *turned into*) 电影版了，您是不是要在里面演什么角色啊？

[Actress smiles but says nothing.]
方兰: 一定是！对不对？那您是要演谁呢？让我想想，是王熙凤 (Wáng Xīfèng *Phoenix Wang*) 吧！

[Actress laughs.]
方兰: 哎，艾玛，我太开心啦！*[to Emma]* 你开心吗？
艾玛: 嗯，我也开心，很开心。
方兰: *[to actress]* 我能跟您合张照吗？
演员: 啊，当然可以！来来来，来来来。
方兰: 谢谢！
艾玛: 我帮你。茄子。太漂亮了！

[Actress and Fang Lan pose.]
方兰: 真好！谢谢您！
演员: 不客气。
方兰: 那……不打扰了。再见！
演员: 再见，再见。

31.16 ***Group work:*** *Work in groups of three (double up if necessary). Following the example of the conversation in 31.15, write a script (on a separate sheet of paper) and act out a skit in which a famous person interacts with two fans. Perform for another group or for the class.*

Encounter 3 Reading and writing

Reading real-life texts

31.17 *Here are some signs and books Fang Lan and Emma saw at the bookstore.*

a *This book has been placed in a prominent position in the bookstore.*
請把漢字填上。／请把汉字填上。

Discovering Laozi (Fāxiàn Lǎozǐ)

____

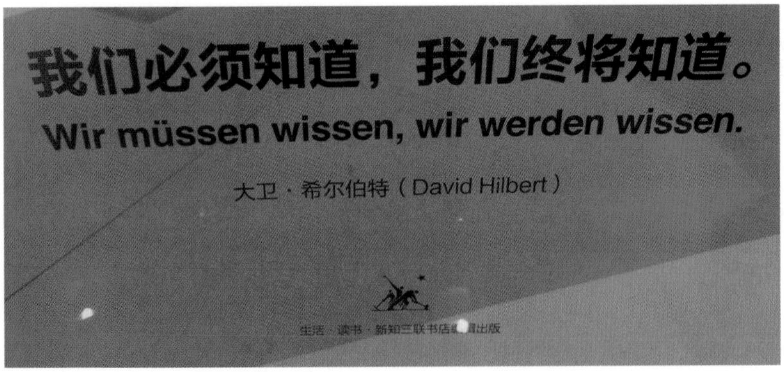

b *Urban Chinese bookstores often have translated editions of books written in different foreign languages. This one was written by* 大卫・希尔伯特 *(*Dàwèi Xī'ěrbótè *David Hilbert).*

1. *Note the transliteration of the Western name. Can you remember the transliteration of "Harry Potter"? Write the pinyin here:* ______________________.
2. *Complete the title of the book in English: We must* __________*, we will eventually* __________.
3. *Write the* 漢字／汉字 *for the following terms:*

   must ____________ (bìxū)

   will eventually ____________ (zhōng jiāng)

   know ____________ (zhīdào).

[*The traditional characters for these terms, in scrambled order, are* 知道、必須、終將.]

c *You may be familiar with this book by the American author* Jiékè Kǎilǔyǎkè. *What do you think the circled phrase* 王永年译 Wáng Yǒngnián yì *means? Fill in the blank in English:*

________________________ Wang Yongnian

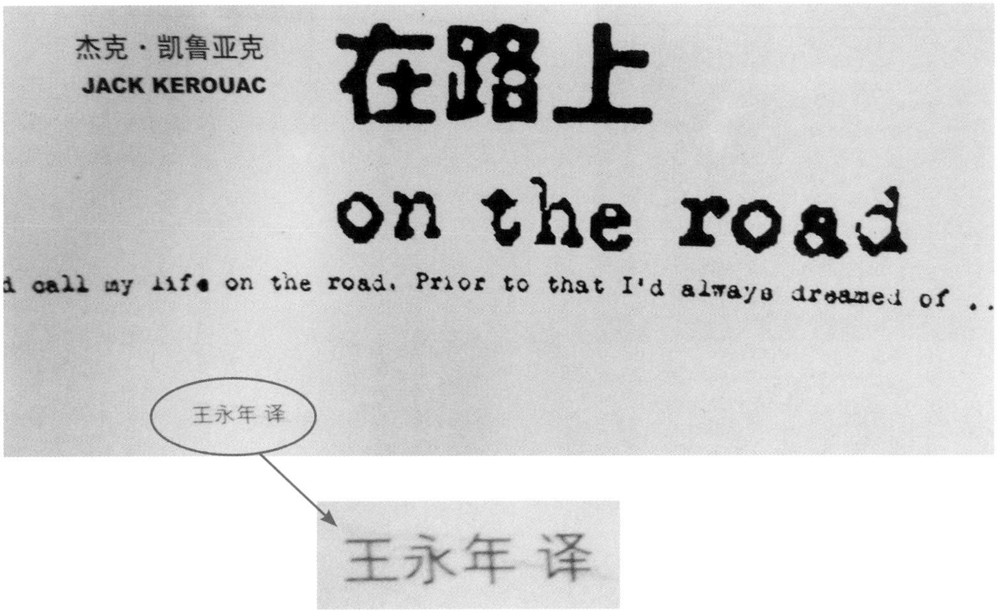

d *This American novel is* Raven Stole the Moon *by Garth Stein.* 請填空。／请填空。

1. *Chinese title (in pinyin):*

   ____

2. *Meaning of the Chinese title:*

   ____

3. *Author's name in Chinese (pinyin):*

   ____________ • Sītǎn

4. Wǔ Jiànbó *is the*

   ________________________.

e *This section is called "Youth literature—Qīngchūn wénxué."*
請用拼音填空。／请用拼音填空。

剩者为王。 *The survivor is king.* Shèngzhě wéi ______.

我在你遥远的身旁。 *You are far away, but I am by your side.* Wǒ zài nǐ yáoyuǎn de ____________.

2 条命 *Two lives* Liǎng ______ mìng

南方旅店 *The inn in the south* ____________ lǚdiàn

你可以爱我。 *Go ahead and love me.* Nǐ ______ ài wǒ.

如愿 *As you wish* ______ yuàn

f *Books in this section fall under three categories. Write the English categories in the appropriate blanks to match the order of the characters (from left to right).*

philosophy
religion
psychology

____________ • ____________ • ____________

Now match the Chinese with the English.

___1. 中国哲学史 A. *Jesus Also Lectured on Zen*

___2. 耶稣也说禅 B. *Did You Think That What You Thought Was What You Thought?*

___3. 你以为你以为的就是你以为的吗？ C. *History of Chinese Philosophy*

g

1. *What is the Chinese for* Art: The Whole Story? 請寫拼音。／请写拼音。

   ____

2. *Circle and label the following books:*

   A. History of World Civilization

   B. History of Contemporary Western Art

h *This is one of the magazines Fang Lan and Emma picked up.*

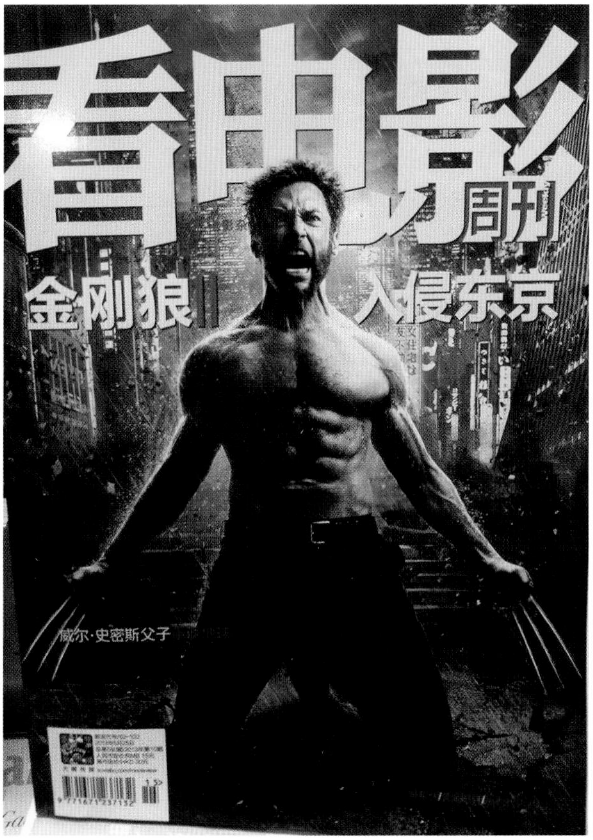

1. *What is the name of the magazine?* 請寫拼音。／请写拼音。 ______________________

2. *How often does it come out?* 圈選正確答案。／圈选正确答案。

   daily weekly monthly annually

3. 刊 kān = *periodical.* 圈選正確答案。／圈选正确答案。

   日刊 = *daily weekly monthly annually*

   週刊／周刊 = *daily weekly monthly annually*

   月刊 = *daily weekly monthly annually*

   年刊 = *daily weekly monthly annually*

4. *The cover article states, "*Wolverine II *invades* ______________." （請用英文填空。／请用英文填空。）

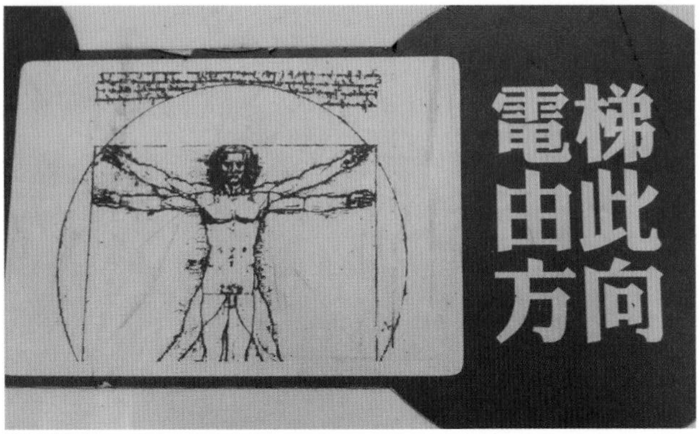

i *This sign is posted on the wall.*

1. *Circle the set of numbers below that indicates the correct order the six characters on the sign should be read.*

4, 1	2, 1	1, 2	1, 4
5, 2	4, 3	3, 4	2, 5
6, 3	6, 5	5, 6	3, 6

2. *What does this sign say?* 請寫英文。／请写英文。 ________________

j *The advertisement on the window makes use of a pun. Literally, it states:*

Your coffee library—
the "comfortable" room for your spirit

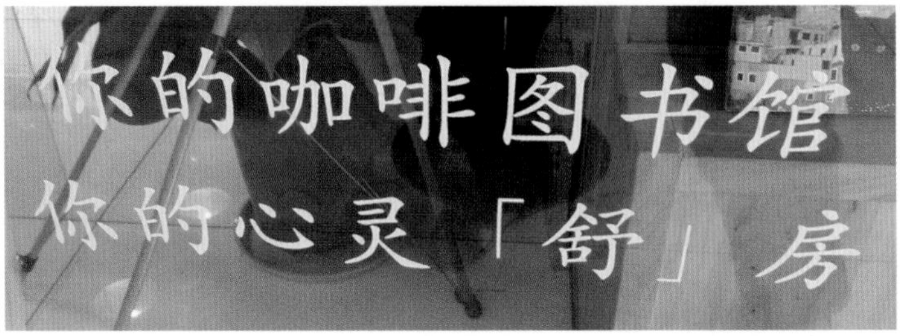

1. 舒 = shū = *comfortable. What other character on the sign is also pronounced* shū? 請寫漢字。／请写汉字。 ________

2. *What would the second line mean, if this other character were used for* 舒? 請寫英文。／请写英文。

____.

Reading a story

31.18 故事 *Following are the plot outlines of three well-known stories. Write their English titles.*

a. ________________________

b. ________________________

c. ________________________

a 故事發生於南北戰爭時代的美國南部。在喬治亞州，亞特蘭大市附近有一個名叫【塔拉】的大農場。那兒住著一個年輕美貌名叫郝思嘉的少女。她愛上了一個男的，可是這個男的跟別人結婚了。同時，有另外一個叫白瑞德的俊男喜歡她。過了一段時間，北方軍隊占领了亞特蘭大。白瑞德帮助郝思嘉逃難。這本很長的小說被拍成一部很有名的電影。

b 很久以后的将来，北美变成了一个很黑暗、殘酷的地方。全国被划分成十三个区。每过几年，政府就要举办一个被叫做【饥饿游戏】的比赛。每区必須派一个少男、一个少女参加比赛，决斗到死。只有一名選手可以活著回家。故事的主人公是一位十六歲的女孩子，她和一位也是十六歲的男鄰居代表第十二區。兩個人一起想辦法生存。

c 有一個小男孩過著很艱苦的生活。他父母去世得很早，他在親戚的家庭裡長大。他親戚對他很不好，一直虐待他。在他十一歲的生日那一天，他收到了一封很神秘的信，說他其實是一個神通兒童，而他的父母是被一個很邪惡的，叫伏地魔 Fúdìmó 的人害死的。信裡還勸他要儘快地來到一所叫【霍格華兹 Huògéhuázī】的学校开始受训。

Match the titles you discerned with their Chinese versions below.

____ 哈里波特 Hālǐ Bōtè

____ 飄／飘 piāo *float, flutter*

____ 飢餓遊戲／饥饿游戏 jī'è yóuxì

31.19 *Write a summary of a favorite story or film using* 漢字／汉字. *Have your draft checked by your teacher or someone else who is fluent in Chinese. Share your summary with the class.*

Encounter 4 Extension: Cultural mini-documentary

View the cultural mini-documentary for this unit and complete the exercises below.

31.20 *This video is a spoken description of the* China Youth Daily (CYD) *by* 張坤／张坤 Zhāng Kūn, *the paper's Deputy Chief Editor. CYD is the official organ of the Chinese Communist Youth League (*共青團／共青团 Gòngqīngtuán*). The paper is well regarded in China; it was the first national paper to push the envelope in terms of reporting on official corruption in the early days of opening and reform in the late 1970s (following the Cultural Revolution). Before watching, brush up on some key words about newspapers. Copy the following vocabulary items in pinyin into the places where they belong.*

bǎn	bàoshè	bàozhǐ	biānjí	biānjíbù	dúzhě	fùzǒngbiān
jìzhě	jìzhězhàn	rìbào	yìnshuāchǎng	Zhōngguó qīngnián bào		

People:

a. 編輯／编辑 *editor* ______________

b. 副總編／副总编 *Deputy Chief Editor* ______________

c. 讀者／读者 *reader* ______________
d. 記者／记者 *reporter* ______________

Places, objects, and organizations:
e. 編輯部／编辑部 *editorial office* ______________
f. 報社／报社 *newspaper (as an organization)* ______________
g.《中國青年報》／《中国青年报》China Youth Daily ______________
h. 記者站／记者站 *local news bureau* ______________
i. 日報／日报 *news daily, daily paper* ______________
j. 報紙／报纸 *newspaper (as a thing)* ______________
k. 印刷廠／印刷厂 *print shop (printing factory)* ______________
l. 版 *a page of a newspaper (refers to the printing plate)* ______________

31.21 *Watch the video. Number the following topics in the order in which the speaker mentions them.*

_____ *The role of the media in civil society*
_____ *CYD's production and distribution*
_____ *CYD, its reporters and its bureaus*
_____ *Categories of readers*
_____ *Categories of reader expectations*
_____ *Categories of pages (sections of the paper)*

Now match each topic with one of the statements below that describes the topic. Translations for the statements appear below, in no particular order.

____ a. 第二類的期待是希望看到《中國青年報》對於一些社會不公正的現象、不公正的行為進行一些批評性的，揭露性的報導。／第二类的期待是希望看到《中国青年报》对于一些社会不公正的现象、不公正的行为进行一些批评性的，揭露性的报导。Dì èr lèi de qīdài shì xīwàng kàn dào Zhōngguó qīngnián bào duìyú yìxiē shèhuì bù gōngzhèng de xiànxiàng, bù gōngzhèng de xíngwéi jìnxíng yìxiē pīpíng xìng de, jiēlù xìng de bàodǎo.

____ b. 每個國家的媒體都應該是除了自身對於新聞的基本的判斷之外，應該還有國家利益、公眾的利益在裡面。／每个国家的媒体都应该是除了自身对于新闻的基本的判断之外，应该还有国家利益、公众的利益在里面。Měi ge guójiā de méitǐ dōu yīnggāi shì chúle zìshēn duìyú xīnwén de jīběn de pànduàn zhī wài, yīnggāi hái yǒu guójiā lìyì, gōngzhòng de lìyì zài lǐmian.

____ c. 我們讀者有四大類型：中國大陸的黨政機關；以大學生為主的青年群體；我們的部隊，就是中國人民解放軍；共青團。／我们读者有四大类型：中国大陆的党政机关；以大学生为主的青年群体；我们的部队，就是中国人民解放军；共青团。Wǒmen dúzhě yǒu sì dà lèixíng: Zhōngguó dàlù de dǎngzhèng jīguān; yǐ dàxuéshēng wéi zhǔ de qīngnián qúntǐ; wǒmen de bùduì, jiùshì Zhōngguó Rénmín Jiěfàngjūn; Gòngqīngtuán.

____ d. 我們的記者都是專業記者和編輯。／我们的记者都是专业记者和编辑。Wǒmen de jìzhě dōu shì zhuānyè jìzhě hé biānjí.

____ e. 我們日常的報紙是十二個版，大致分為綜合類、專業類、副刊類、評論類，大概分為這樣四大類。／我们日常的报纸是十二个版，大致分为综合类、专业类、副刊类、评论类，大概分为这样四大类。Wǒmen rìcháng de bàozhǐ shì shí'èr ge bǎn, dàzhì fēn wéi zōnghé lèi, zhuānyè lèi, fùkān lèi, pínglùn lèi, dàgài fēn wéi zhèyàng sì dà lèi.

____ f. 可以進行同步的衛星傳輸、排版。所以一篇稿件在晚上進行總編輯最后簽完以后，發到報社的夜班車間印刷，但是同時通過傳版，到全國二十多個分印點，第二天能保証盡快速度地到達讀者的手中。／可以进行同步的卫星传输、排版。所以一篇稿件在晚上进行总编辑最后签完以后，发到报社的夜班车间印刷，但是同时通过传版，到全国二十多个分印点，第二天能保证尽快速度地到达读者的手中。Kěyǐ jìnxíng tóngbù de wèixīng chuánshū, páibǎn. Suǒyǐ yì piān gǎojiàn zài wǎnshang jìnxíng zǒng biānjí zuìhòu qiān wán yǐhòu, fā dào bàoshè de yèbān chējiān yìnshuā, dànshì tóngshí tōngguò chuánbǎn, dào quánguó èrshí duō ge fēn yìn diǎn, dì'èr tiān néng bǎozhèng jìnkuài sùdù de dàodá dúzhě de shǒuzhōng.

- *We can do synchronized satellite transmission and typesetting. So after the editor-in-chief gives the final sign-off on a manuscript in the evening, it's sent to the newspaper's print shop night shift, but it is simultaneously transmitted to more than twenty printing places so as to ensure the next day it will reach the hands of readers with the greatest possible speed.*
- *The media in each country should, in addition to relying on their own judgment in reporting basic news, include the national and public interest [as factors in their decisions].*
- *Our typical issue is twelve pages, roughly divided into general content, specialized content, supplements, and commentary. Those are roughly the four categories.*
- *Our reporters are all professional reporters and editors.*
- *The second type of expectation is that they will see reporting in the* China Youth Daily *that criticizes and exposes social injustices and unjust conduct.*
- *We have four types of readers: those in China's party and government organizations; youths (mostly college students); our troops, that is to say the PLA; and [members of] the Communist Youth League.*

31.22 *Watch the video one more time and jot down five to ten expressions you would like as part of your "takeaway" from this video.*

Recap

Grammar

What if you run into "Khrushchev" in Chinese?

How does the Chinese language handle foreign names such as Khrushchev? Well, the answer is straightforward: the same way we do. When Khrushchev first burst onto the world scene, someone had to figure out how to represent "Хрущев" for English readers. The answer then and now was to use transliteration—the phonetic rendering of the original name in a different script. Sound out the name and use similar-sounding English letters to represent it. Simple solution. Therefore, Хрущев became Khrushchev for readers of English and 赫魯曉夫／赫鲁晓夫 (*Hèlǔxiǎofū*) for Chinese readers. Names of people are handled this way along with the names of places and a host of other things foreign.

Washington (the place and the president) becomes 華盛頓／华盛顿 (*Huáshèngdùn*), aspirin becomes 阿司匹林 (*āsīpǐlín*), and Coca-Cola becomes 可口可樂／可口可乐 (*kěkǒukělè*). This last example shows yet another feature: "translating" the sound but also incorporating some meaning. 可口 means "tasty, delicious" in Chinese, and 可樂／可乐 means something like "delightful"—a pleasant representation of "cola." 可口可樂／可口可乐 therefore means "tasty and delightful." Some are fuller translations of meaning: Cinderella becomes 灰姑娘 (*Huī gūniang*)—"the girl of the ashes." Remember when you learned the names of foreign countries. Recall:

德國／德国 *from* **Deutsch**land
英國／英国 *from* **Eng**land
美國／美国 *from* A-**me**-(ri-ca)
意大利 *from* **Itali**a. *And so on.*

The characters chosen for use are not randomly selected but usually come from an "approved" list. The characters on the list are not commonly used, so they pose considerable difficulties for many Western readers. But there are some bright spots that can make things a bit easier for us to spot names. Here are four:

1. Context, context, context. Context, as always in language comprehension, is key. When reading an article about Russia, expect Putin (普京 *Pǔjīng*) to show up. When reading about U.S politics, expect 奥巴馬／奥巴马 *Àobāmǎ.*
2. Official titles are often name markers. When Putin or Obama show up, you can expect the title 總統／总统 (*zǒngtǒng* president) to be there as well. See a title, expect a name.

3. If you find a string of five or six unfamiliar characters, you might suspect a name, especially if these characters defy your best efforts at understanding. Keep in mind: if all else fails, it's probably a name.

4. Of course, use whatever the text provides, such as photos, illustrations, or orthographical markers (e.g., brackets) that often signal the names of people and books.

Vocabulary

Please refer to page R-2 for a list of grammatical abbreviations used throughout this book.

Àomàn yǔ piānjiàn 傲慢與偏見／傲慢与偏见 *Pride and Prejudice* N

bāguà 八卦 gossip (originally eight trigrams of the *Book of Changes* used in divination) N

chūbǎnshè 出版社 publishing house; publisher; press N

dāi 呆 stay; hang out V

dǎng 擋／挡 get in the way of; block V

dǎrǎo 打擾／打扰 disturb; trouble V

duìzhào 對照／对照 contrast; compare; place side by side for comparison (as parallel texts) V; **duìzhàobǎn** 對照版／对照版 bilingual edition

fānpāi 翻拍 adapt (as a movie) V

fāshēng 發生／发生 happen; occur; take place V

fēngfù 豐富／丰富 rich; plentiful; abundant SV; enrich V

fēngmiàn 封面 cover (of a publication) N

fěnsī 粉絲／粉丝 fan (loan word) N

fùyǒu 富有 rich; wealthy SV

gè yì 各異／各异 each different VP

gōngjùshū 工具書／工具书 reference book N

guàng 逛 stroll; ramble; roam; browse V

guānzhòng 觀眾／观众 spectator; audience N

hé zhāng zhào 合張照／合张照 take a photo together VP

Hóng Lóu Mèng 紅樓夢／红楼梦 *Dream of the Red Chamber* N

huánqiú 環球／环球 the earth; the whole world N; worldwide PREF

huànxiǎng 幻想 fantasy; illusion N/V

Jiǎn Àosīdīng 簡・奧斯丁／简・奥斯丁 Jane Austen N

jīngcháng 經常／经常 often; constantly; frequently; regularly A

jīngdiǎn 經典／经典 classics; scriptures; text N

jīngjì 經濟／经济 economy; financial condition N; **jīngjìxué** 經濟學／经济学 economics (as a field of study)

jīnróng 金融 finance; banking N

juésè 角色 role; part N

kāixīn 開心／开心 feel happy; rejoice V

kējì 科技 science and technology N

lèixíng 類型／类型 type; category; genre N

màomèi 冒昧 make bold; venture to V

nèiróng 内容 content; substance N

ǒuxiàng 偶像 idol; image; model N

pāi 拍 shoot a movie; take pictures V

péi 陪 accompany; keep someone company V

pǐnwèi 品味 taste N; taste; savor VO

qiézi 茄子 eggplant N (*transliteration of "cheese" when photographing*)

Qīngcháo 清朝 Qing Dynasty (1644–1911) N

qīnyǎn 親眼／亲眼 with one's own eyes; personally A

qǔ míng 取名 name; christen VO

ràokǒulìng 繞口令／绕口令 tongue twister N

rénwù 人物 character; personage N

Sānguó Yǎnyì 三國演義／三国演义 *Romance of the Three Kingdoms* N

shūchóng 書蟲／书虫 bookworm N

Shuǐhǔ Zhuàn 水滸傳／水浒传 *Water Margin* N

shúxī (*also pronounced* **shóuxi**) 熟悉 know something/somebody well SV/V

sì dà míngzhù 四大名著 four great classical novels (of Chinese literature) N

tuījiàn 推薦／推荐 recommend

Wáng Xīfèng 王熙鳳／王熙凤 Phoenix Wang (a character in *Dream of the Red Chamber*) N

wèndá 問答／问答 questions and answers; interrogation N/V

xià 下 download V

xiàng 像 resemble; take after; be like V

xiǎo gūniang 小姑娘 young girl/lady N

xīnbǎn 新版 new edition; new version N

xìnggé 性格 (person's) nature; disposition; temperament N

Xī Yóu Jì 西遊記／西游记 *Journey to the West* N

yǎn 演 perform; play; act ; show (a film) V

yǎnyuán 演員／演员 performer; actor; actress N

yǎzhì 雅緻／雅致 refined; tasteful SV; refinement N

yǔ 與／与 and; together with (*used only in written Chinese*) C

yuánzhù 原著 original work N

zázhì 雜誌／杂志 magazine; journal; periodical N

zhī lèi 之類／之类 and such/like S

zhù 著 write books, etc. V

zhuàngjiàn 撞見／撞见 meet/discover by chance V

zhuānlán 專欄／专栏 special column (in a newspaper, etc.) N

Checklist of "can do" statements

After completing this unit, you should be able to perform each of the following tasks:

Listening and speaking

- ☐ Name different types of books and magazines in a bookstore.
- ☐ Talk about your own reading habits, such as what you like to read.
- ☐ Briefly describe a favorite book.
- ☐ Talk about what movies you like and how often you go to the movies.
- ☐ Name a media celebrity you admire and describe the extent to which you are a "fan."

Reading and writing

- ☐ Decipher some titles of books and magazines.
- ☐ Identify the author, translator, and publisher of a book you haven't seen before.
- ☐ Identify how often a magazine is published.
- ☐ Comprehend some brief descriptions of famous novels.
- ☐ Write a description of your own.

Understanding culture

- ☐ Make several accurate statements about the four great classical novels of Chinese literature.
- ☐ Make several accurate statements about *China Youth Daily*.

UNIT 32

"To each his own"

各有所好

Gè yǒu suǒ hào

TV shows and films

In this unit, you will learn how to:

- talk about TV shows.
- identify different types of TV shows.
- understand an entertainment news report.
- describe an encounter with a media celebrity.
- decipher some signs posted around a media studio.
- comprehend a description of a famous movie director.
- write a description of a favorite movie director.

Encounter 1 Identifying types of TV shows

32.1 *Xiao Mao has given his media class an assignment—to make a TV show.* 請圈選正確的意思。／请圈选正确的意思。

a. diànshì jiémù 電視節目／电视节目 *(TV channel / TV program)*

b. diànshì tái 電視台／电视台 *(TV station / TV program)*

c. pāi 拍 *(shoot / hit)*

d. xìliè 系列 *(department / series)*

e. xīnwén 新聞／新闻 *(news / show)*

32.2 *View Episode 32, Vignette 1. The students have a week to make a half-hour program. They are trying to decide what kind of TV show to make. Match each type of show with what the students decide about making that type of show.*

____ a. TV drama	1. No; nothing happens on campus.
____ b. reality cop show	2. No; too hard to organize.
____ c. talent show	3. No; too much writing.
____ d. travel show	4. Yes!
____ e. entertainment news program	5. No; too exhausting, too time-consuming.

32.3 請把英文跟中文對上。／请把英文跟中文对上。

____ a. jiémù de tícái 節目的題材／节目的题材	1. *theme of the program*
____ b. jiémù de nèiróng 節目的內容／节目的内容	2. *reality show*
____ c. diànshì liánxùjù 電視連續劇／电视连续剧	3. *documentary*
____ d. tuōkǒu xiù 脱口秀	4. *content of the program*
____ e. zhēnrén xiù 真人秀	5. *sitcom*
____ f. qíngjǐng duǎnjù 情景短劇／情景短剧	6. *TV series*
____ g. jìlùpiān 紀錄片／纪录片	7. *evening news*
____ h. wǎnjiān xīnwén 晚間新聞／晚间新闻	8. *talk show*
____ i. xíngzhēnjù 刑偵劇／刑侦剧	9. *entertainment news*
____ j. xuǎnxiù jiémù 選秀節目／选秀节目	10. *travel show*
____ k. lǚyóu jiémù 旅遊節目／旅游节目	11. *crime investigation show*
____ l. yúlè xīnwén 娛樂新聞／娱乐新闻	12. *talent show*

32.4 *Every Chinese count noun is "measured" by a measure word or counter. In this unit, programs (*節目／节目 jiémù*) are measured by either* 個／个 *or* 檔／档 dàng *(often pronounced* dǎng*), whereas single episodes of a program are measured by* 集 jí. *Fill in the blanks below with either* dǎng 檔／档 *or* jí 集.

Máo Jiàoshòu ràng xuéshengmen pāi yì _____ bú xiàn tícái hé nèiróng de diànshì jiémù. Yǒu xiē xuésheng jiànyì pāi yì _____ diànshì liánxùjù, kěshì Máo Jiàoshòu shuō, nèi yàng yě děi bǎ zhěngge xìliè de gùshì dàgāng xiěchūlai.

毛教授讓學生們拍一 ______ 不限題材和內容的電視節目。有些學生建議拍一 ______ 電視連續劇，可是毛教授説，那樣也得把整個系列的故事大綱寫出來。／

毛教授让学生们拍一 ______ 不限题材和内容的电视节目。有些学生建议拍一 ______ 电视连续剧，可是毛教授说，那样也得把整个系列的故事大纲写出来。

Prof. Mao asked the students to make a program with no limit on topic or content. Some students suggested filming one episode of a dramatic series, but Prof. Mao said that for that, they'd have to develop a plot outline for the entire series.

32.5 *Match each type of TV program with its description.* 請把英文跟中文對上。／请把英文跟中文对上。

____ a. diànshì liánxùjù 電視連續劇／电视连续剧

____ b. tuōkǒu xiù 脱口秀

____ c. zhēnrén xiù 真人秀

____ d. qíngjǐng duǎnjù 情景短劇／情景短剧

____ e. jìlùpiān 紀錄片／纪录片

____ f. wǎnjiān xīnwén 晚間新聞／晚间新闻

____ g. lǚyóu jiémù 旅遊節目／旅游节目

____ h. xíngzhēnjù 刑偵劇／刑侦剧

____ i. xuǎnxiù jiémù 選秀節目／选秀节目

1. 可以聽一系列的名人在聊天／可以听一系列的名人在聊天
2. 讓我們即使不出門也可以看看很多地方／让我们即使不出门也可以看看很多地方
3. 讓我們一集接著一集，想知道故事的結局／让我们一集接着一集，想知道故事的结局
4. 選拔在某方面（例如跳舞、唱歌）表現優秀的人／选拔在某方面（例如跳舞、唱歌）表现优秀的人
5. 可以讓我們知道世界上最近發生了一些甚麼事／可以让我们知道世界上最近发生了一些什么事
6. 讓我們對真實的人、事、物有更多的認識／让我们对真实的人、事、物有更多的认识
7. 可以看看一般人（非演員）在不同的情況下會做甚麼／可以看看一般人（非演员）在不同的情况下会做什么
8. 有趣、搞笑，可以讓我們哈哈笑／有趣、搞笑，可以让我们哈哈笑
9. 警察抓壞人的故事／警察抓坏人的故事

32.6 *For each type of TV program, list one or two of your favorite shows (*可以用英文*), and jot down several descriptive phrases about each show (*請寫中文／请写中文*).*

32.7 ***Mingling:*** *Talk to several of your classmates. Find out what TV shows they like to watch, and note how they describe (*形容 xíngróng*) those shows.*

同學的名字／同学的名字	他們最喜歡的電視節目／他们最喜欢的电视节目	他們怎麼形容這些節目／他们怎么形容这些节目

Encounter 2 A news report

32.8 *Fang Lan reports on her encounter with Huang Yalan. To prepare for viewing this episode, match the vocabulary below.* 請把中文跟英文對上。／请把中文跟英文对上。

____ a. dújiā xīnwén 獨家新聞／独家新闻 — 1. *exclusive news*

____ b. zhǔchírén 主持人 — 2. *box office*

____ c. jìzhě 記者／记者 — 3. *classical literature*

____ d. gǔdiǎn wénxué 古典文學／古典文学 — 4. *host of the show*

____ e. piàofáng 票房 — 5. *portray*

____ f. chūyǎn 出演 — 6. *reporter*

32.9 *View Episode 32, Vignette 2. Does Fang Lan make each of the following statements? Mark* Yes *or* No.

	Yes	No
a. My friend and I ate dumplings.	☐	☐
b. We had not intended to go to a bookstore.	☐	☐
c. I wanted to introduce my friend to classical Chinese literature.	☐	☐
d. I almost didn't recognize Huang Yalan.	☐	☐
e. I rushed over and greeted her.	☐	☐
f. She agreed to have her picture taken with me.	☐	☐
g. She denied that she would play Wang Xifeng.	☐	☐
h. I never really was one of her fans.	☐	☐

32.10 請把下面的中文跟上面的英文對上。／请把下面的中文跟上面的英文对上。

_____ 1. Wǒmen méi xiǎng qù shūdiàn. 我們沒想去書店。／我们没想去书店。

_____ 2. Wǒ chōng shàngqu hé tā dǎ zhāohu. 我衝上去和她打招呼。／我冲上去和她打招呼。

_____ 3. Tā fǒurèn le jiāng yào yǎn Wáng Xīfèng. 她否認了將要演王熙鳳。／她否认了将要演王熙凤。

_____ 4. Wǒ hé wǒ de péngyou chī le shuǐjiǎo. 我和我的朋友吃了水餃。／我和我的朋友吃了水饺。

_____ 5. Tā tóngyì hé wǒ hé zhāng zhào. 她同意和我合張照。／她同意和我合张照。

_____ 6. Wǒ xiǎng gěi wǒ péngyou jièshào yí xià Zhōngguó de gǔdiǎn wénxué. 我想給我朋友介紹一下中國的古典文學。／我想给我朋友介绍一下中国的古典文学。

_____ 7. Wǒ qíshí cónglái dōu bù shǔyú tā de fěnsī. 我其實從來都不屬於她的粉絲。／我其实从来都不属于她的粉丝。

_____ 8. Wǒ chāyidiǎn méi rènchū Huáng Yǎlán. 我差一點沒認出黄雅蘭。／我差一点没认出黄雅兰。

32.11 *Fang Lan briefly describes her encounter with Huang Yalan in this segment. Take a flight of fancy: Pretend that you ran into one of your favorite celebrities (or use one of the people pictured below). Where did the meeting take place? What happened? Take a few notes below on how you might describe your encounter. Use known vocabulary or ask your teacher for some help, but don't be too ambitious!* 請寫漢字或者拼音。／请写汉字或者拼音。

成龍／成龙

Chéng Lóng

Jackie Chan

Hong Kong actor

王菲

Wáng Fēi

Faye Wong

Chinese singer/actress

珍妮佛・勞倫斯／珍妮佛・劳伦斯

Zhēnnífó Láolúnsī

Jennifer Lawrence

American actress

法瑞爾・威廉姆斯／法瑞尔・威廉姆斯

Fǎruì'ěr Wēiliánmǔsī

Pharrell Williams

American singer/songwriter

周杰倫／周杰伦

Zhōu Jiélún

Jay Chou

Taiwanese singer/songwriter/actor

32.12 *Tell a small group about your "meeting" with the celebrity you chose. Take notes below on what they say about their experiences.*

32.13 *To introduce Fang Lan's report, the host of the show makes the following remarks. Watch the beginning of Vignette 2 again and select the correct pinyin to fill in the blanks.*

dújiā xīnwén	jiémù	jìzhě	mài ge guānzi
péngyoumen	shōukàn	yǒu qǐng	zhǔchírén

(1) Guānzhòng ____________, dàjiā hǎo! (2) Huānyíng nín ____________ jīntiān de "Yúlè xīnwén bǎi fēn bǎi." (3) Wǒ shì ____________ Cuī Xiāo, (4) nàme jīntiān de ___________ne, wǒ jiāng gěi dàjiā shuō yìtiáo ____________, (5) jùtǐ zhè tiáo xīnwén shì shénme? (6) Gěi nín_____________, (7) yóu wǒmen de ____________Fāng Lán wèi nín jiǎngshù, (8) ______________.

Now number the English sentences below to match the order of the Chinese.

____ *Over to you.*

____ *What is this news item exactly?*

____ *Our own reporter Fang Lan will tell you all about it.*

____ *Welcome to today's "100% Entertainment News."*

____ *Now for today's show, I'm going to give you a news scoop.*

____ *You'll never guess.*

____ *Hello, audience members and friends!*

____ *I am your host, Cui Xiao.*

32.14 *Pretend you are the host of the show. Read your "script" out loud.*

觀眾朋友們，大家好！歡迎您收看今天的《娛樂新聞百分百》。我是主持人崔蕭，那麼今天的節目呢，我將給大家説一條獨家新聞，具體這條新聞是甚麼？給您賣個關子，由我們的記者方蘭為您講述，有請。

Read it again!

观众朋友们，大家好！欢迎您收看今天的《娱乐新闻百分百》。我是主持人崔萧，那么今天的节目呢，我将给大家说一条独家新闻，具体这条新闻是什么？给您卖个关子，由我们的记者方兰为您讲述，有请。

32.15 *To close out the show, the host makes the following concluding remarks. Watch the ending of the vignette again and select the correct pinyin to fill in the blanks.*

dàlù xīn diànyǐng jiǎngshù jiē xiàlái jìlù shàngyìng zhídǎo

(1) Hǎo de, gǎnxiè Fāng Lán. (2) _________ne, wǒmen lái guānzhù yǒuguān __________fāngmiàn de xiāoxi. (3) Yóu Chén Kěxīn dǎoyǎn _________de zuìxīn diànyǐng "Zhōngguó Héhuǒ Rén" cóng 5 yuè 17 hào zài Zhōngguó dàlù __________ zhīhòu ne, (4) chuàngxià le yǒu wǔ yì duō piàofáng de __________, (5) zhè yěshì Chén Kěxīn zhídǎo de diànyǐng zài ___________de zuìxīn jìlù. (6) Nàme zhè bù diànyǐng ___________de shì sān ge niánqīng rén . . .

Now number the English sentences below to match the order of the Chinese.

____ *This is a new record for director Chen Kexin in Mainland China.*

____ *Since the new movie* American Dreams in China *[The Chinese Partner] by director Chen Kexin opened on May 17,*

____ *Next, let's turn our attention to news about new movies.*

____ *And this movie is about three young men . . .*

____ *OK, thank you, Fang Lan.*

____ *it has earned a record 500 million yuan at the box office.*

32.16 *Pretend you are the host of the show. Read your "script" out loud.*

好的，感謝方蘭。接下來呢，我們來關注有關新電影方面的消息。由陳可辛導演執導的最新電影《中國合夥人》從5月17號在中國大陸上映之後呢，創下了有五億多票房的記錄，這也是陳可辛執導的電影在大陸的最新紀錄。那麼這部電影講述的是三個年輕人……

Read it again!

好的，感谢方兰。接下来呢，我们来关注有关新电影方面的消息。由陈可辛导演执导的最新电影《中国合伙人》从5月17号在中国大陆上映之后呢，创下了有五亿多票房的记录，这也是陈可辛执导的电影在大陆的最新纪录。那么这部电影讲述的是三个年轻人……

32.17 American Dreams in China *set a Chinese box office record. Do some research on this film, and write a short plot summary below.* 請寫中文。／请写中文。

32.18 *Work in a small group. One of you will be the host, and the others can be reporters. You can talk about the movie* American Dreams in China *or about your meetings with one of the celebrities you "ran into." Put together a brief entertainment news show.*

Encounter 3 Reading and writing

Reading real-life texts

32.19 *These are signs posted around a media studio at the Communication University of China, where Fang Lan is recording her show.*

a

請填上拼音。／请填上拼音。______ ______ ______

b *This is the sign on the makeup room. Number the pinyin to match the characters.*

___ zhuāng ___ shì ___ huà

c *This is a sign on another door. Write the pinyin for the term:*

____

What is this room? Choose one:

☐ bathroom ☐ dressing room ☐ rest area ☐ props room

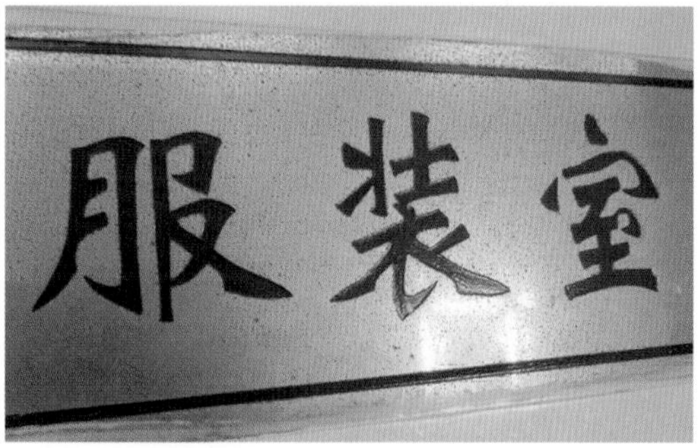

d *Do you remember this sign from Unit 28 in Book 3?*
請寫英文和拼音。／请写英文和拼音。

英文: ______________________________

拼音: ______________________________

e *This area is exclusively for use by:*

☐ reporters ☐ engineers

f *Since the video for this textbook was filmed in this space, the crew was directed to go to the right. Write out the pinyin for the Chinese name of this textbook:*

____

Reading a story

32.20 故事 *Find the following terms in either the traditional or simplified text and circle them. Write in the accompanying number.*

Chinese film director Zhang Yimou, born 1950

Scene from the movie *Hero*

1. diànyǐng dǎoyǎn *film director*
2. zuì yǒumíng *most famous*
3. kěnéng *perhaps*
4. Zhāng Yìmóu *Zhang Yimou*
5. dǎoyǎn *direct*
6. bāokuò *include*
7. Hóng Gāoliang *"Red Sorghum"*
8. Dà Hóng Dēnglong Gāogāo Guà *"Hang High the Big Red Lanterns" = "Raise the Red Lanterns"*
9. Húozhe *"To Live"*
10. Yí ge Dōu Bù Néng Shǎo *"Not One Can Be Missing" = "Not One Less"*
11. Wǒ de Fùqīn-Mǔqīn *"My Parents" = "The Road Home"*
12. Yīngxióng *"Hero"*
13. chūguó *go abroad*
14. Xiàwēiyí *Hawaii*
15. cānjiā *take part in*
16. guójì diànyǐngjié *international film festival*
17. chūmíng *become famous*
18. gōutōng *communicate*
19. qítā *other*
20. dǎoyǎn *director*
21. yǔyán bùtōng *doesn't know the language*
22. zìmù *subtitles*
23. hěn wéinán *had a very hard time*
24. biànchéng *become*
25. suīrán *although*
26. jìxù *continue to*
27. fāxiàn *discover*
28. duìhuà *dialogue*
29. qíshí *actually*
30. huàmiàn *image*
31. yàojǐn *important*
32. jiùshì shuō *which is to say*
33. nénggòu *be able to*
34. dàgài *broadly, generally*
35. lǐjiě *understand*
36. gùshi *story*
37. xīnshǎng *appreciate*
38. yìshù *artistry*
39. pāi *shoot, film*
40. bǐjiào *relatively*
41. zhùzhòng *pay attention to*
42. yīnwèi huàmiàn ér chéngmíng *become famous because of the imagery*

中國電影導演中最有名的可能就是張藝謀了。他導演的電影包括1987 年的《紅高粱》，1991 年的《大紅燈籠高高掛》，1994年的《活著》，1999 年的《一個都不能少》、《我的父親母親》，還有2002年的《英雄》。張導演第一次出國是1985年去夏威夷參

中国电影导演中最有名的可能就是张艺谋了。他导演的电影包括1987 年的《红高粱》，1991 年的《大红灯笼高高挂》，1994年的《活着》，1999 年的《一个都不能少》、《我的父亲母亲》，还有2002年的《英雄》。张导演第一次出国是1985年去夏威夷参

加國際電影節。他那時候還沒有出名，到了夏威夷他因為不會説英文，很難跟別人溝通。他在電影節上看了很多其他導演的電影，可是因為他語言不通，看不懂英文的字幕，很為難。他想，怎麼辦？看不懂其他導演的電影，自己怎麼能夠變成好導演呢？雖然看不懂，可是他還是繼續去看電影。後來，他發現，電影裡頭的對話其實沒有畫面要緊。就是説，看電影比聽電影要緊。他發現，語言聽不懂，還是能夠大概理解電影的故事，還是能夠欣賞電影的藝術。他自己拍的電影，都比較注重畫面，不那麼注重對話。張藝謀的電影畫面特別的美。他的電影是因為畫面而成名的。

加国际电影节。他那时候还没有出名，到了夏威夷他因为不会说英文，很难跟别人沟通。他在电影节上看了很多其他导演的电影，可是因为他语言不通，看不懂英文的字幕，很为难。他想，怎么办？看不懂其他导演的电影，自己怎么能够变成好导演呢？虽然看不懂，可是他还是继续去看电影。后来，他发现，电影里头的对话其实没有画面要紧。就是说，看电影比听电影要紧。他发现，语言听不懂，还是能够大概理解电影的故事，还是能够欣赏电影的艺术。他自己拍的电影，都比较注重画面，不那么注重对话。张艺谋的电影画面特别的美。他的电影是因为画面而成名的。

32.21 *Do you agree that the imagery is the most important feature of a movie? Check one of the statements below.*

_____ 我同意。電影的畫面最重要。／
我同意。电影的画面最重要。

_____ 我不同意。電影的對話最重要。／
我不同意。电影的对话最重要。

If you like, take a survey of your friends. Ask and answer the following question:
你覺得電影的畫面最重要嗎？／你觉得电影的画面最重要吗？

32.22 *Research and write a short paragraph about your favorite movie director. Write in Chinese characters on a separate sheet of paper. Have it corrected by your teacher or other tutor, and produce a new draft that you can share with your classmates, in print or online (e.g., on a class website).*

Encounter 4 Extension: Cultural mini-documentary

View the cultural mini-documentary for this unit and complete the exercises that follow.

32.23 *This video is an introduction to the media production education facilities at the Communication University of China (CUC) by* 劉杰鋒／刘杰锋 Liú Jiéfēng, *a dean at the school. Before watching, brush up on some key words about broadcast media.* 請把中文跟英文對上。／请把中文跟英文对上。

____ a. diànshìtái 電視台／电视台	1. *programming department*
____ b. chuánméi 傳媒／传媒	2. *news department*
____ c. zǒngbiānshì 總編室／总编室	3. *research and development department*
____ d. xīnwénbù 新聞部／新闻部	4. *technology department*
____ e. jiémùbù 節目部／节目部	5. *communications media*
____ f. yánfābù 研發部／研发部	6. *main editorial office*
____ g. jìshùbù 技術部／技术部	7. *television station*

32.24 *Prof. Liu goes into a lot of detail about operations at the student-run television station at CUC. Watch and listen for overall topics without worrying too much about language details. Orient yourself to his introduction by numbering the following summary paragraphs to reflect the actual spoken order. Begin by sorting out paragraphs* a–d *and then* e–i.

Paragraphs a through d:

____ a. *There's another reason behind the whole thing—just about every postsecondary school in China now has a degree program in communications. I personally know of almost a thousand schools that have them. If each one of those schools produces only one person [majoring in communications], that puts tremendous competitive pressure on us at CUC. It was when faced with this competition that the school established the station.*

____ b. *As far as basic equipment is concerned, we follow the standards of a professional station. For example, hardware such as you might find at China Central TV—shooting, editing, broadcasting, transmitting, and storage—we've got it all. Our organizational design is also based on the organizational structure of a highly professional TV station. Education in communications has to strongly emphasize practice; it's a field that really stresses operational skills. So if in the classroom we were to only lecture about theory, most of the time we wouldn't be giving students that chance for real practice.*

____ c. *So the station is organized just like a professional one. The main units are the main editorial office, the news department, the programming department, the research and development department, and one more department that is probably different from any postsecondary school station: the technology department. These departments are actually organized according to the academic majors we offer.*

____ d. *CUC's television station was established in May of 2008 with the aim of providing a platform for experiential learning so that all students at CUC could benefit through actual practice. The idea was to build the station to paraprofessional standards, so the school gave us our own separate building and established almost 30 production units.*

Paragraphs e through i:

____ e. *So then our news host takes these dozen or so news stories and strings them together, including our subtitling—everything gets put in. Once it's all in, if . . . actually, in principle, it could be broadcast directly at this point, but we'll probably bring it back, at the end, so that after it's out we have the teachers in the news department and the leaders of the station, the head of station, examine and approve. When this happens, if they feel there's no problem with the form or the content, then we'll send it to the transmission room for transmission at the scheduled time. So that's the whole process for the news.*

____ f. *Our school, CUC, is an integrated university in the communications field, touching on all the professional specializations and positions in the field. In our school's television station, each department has its own independent workflow. Take the news department for example. Our news [department] broadcasts two episodes each week as well as the show "Campus Life" and the news in English, titled "CUC News." No matter which of these types of news we're talking about, they are all operated according to a very integrated workflow.*

____ g. *So as of now, having been through five years of building it up, our TV station now has 35 teachers and close to 900 student reporters. That is, every year we will have 900 reporters who come to our station for real practice and internship.*

____ h. *So with this process, as far as a professional television station is concerned, that news [program] may be over. But for our school, for CUCTV, the news production process is not ended yet. Once an episode of the news has been broadcast, the teachers will want to organize all the students for a viewing party and wrap up by telling the students which news items were great, which ones had problems, and which items could be improved or be perfected from another angle. So, if we do this, then this news [episode] is in fact over.*

____ i. *First of all, there is a work team, and if for example they are to be responsible for next week's news, then under a teacher's direction they must choose topics and plan things out. One episode of news will feature 12–15 news stories. After the content has been planned out, then we start shaping a script. Then, with the script in hand, we form teams and start shooting. The news has to be shot story by story. After the entire episode has been shot, then we take the material, the unorganized bits of material that have been shot, and bring them back to the supporting editing room and edit them. Finally, we take them to the broadcasting studio, where we finish organizing them into a news sequence.*

32.25 *Match each Chinese statement with an English summary from Exercise 32.24. (Note: Each Chinese statement corresponds to a key point in the English summary; it's not a word-for-word translation.)*

____ 1. 學校給我們專門的一個獨立的大樓，又給了我們將近三十個編制的機構。／学校给我们专门的一个独立的大楼，又给了我们将近三十个编制的机构。Xuéxiào gěi wǒmen zhuānmén de yí ge dúlì de dàlóu, yòu gěile wǒmen jiāngjìn sānshí ge biānzhì de jīgòu.

____ 2. 我們的部門設置也是按照一個非常專業的電視台的機構來進行設置的。／我们的部门设置也是按照一个非常专业的电视台的机构来进行设置的。Wǒmen de bùmén shèzhì yě shì ànzhào yí ge fēicháng zhuānyè de diànshìtái de jīgòu lái jìnxíng shèzhì de.

____ 3. 現在中國幾乎所有的高校都在辦傳媒專業......他們每一個學校，他只要出一個人，我們傳媒大學的競爭壓力就會非常非常的大。／现在中国几乎所有的高校都在办传媒专业......他们每一个学校，他只要出一个人，我们传媒大学的竞争压力就会非常非常的大。Xiànzài Zhōngguó jīhū suǒyǒu de gāoxiào dōu zài bàn chuánméi zhuānyè. . . . Tāmen měi yí ge xuéxiào, tā zhǐyào chū yí ge rén, wǒmen Chuánméi Dàxué de jìngzhēng yālì jiù huì fēicháng fēicháng de dà.

____ 4. 我們學校電視台......主要有總編室、新聞部、節目部、研發部，還有......技術部。／我们学校电视台......主要有总编室、新闻部、节目部、研发部，还有......技术部。Wǒmen xuéxiào diànshìtái . . . zhǔyào yǒu zǒngbiānshì, xīnwénbù, jiémùbù, yánfābù, hái yǒu . . . jìshùbù.

____ 5. 我們的新聞是每週要有兩期必須要播出的，另外還有一段《校園生活》，還有一段叫英文新聞，叫 "CUC News"。／我们的新闻是每周要有两期必须要播出的，另外还有一段《校园生活》，还有一段叫英文新闻，叫 "CUC News"。Wǒmen de xīnwén shì měi zhōu yào yǒu liǎng qī bìxū yào bōchū de, lìngwài hái yǒu yí duàn "Xiàoyuán shēnghuó", hái yǒu yí duàn jiào Yīngwén xīnwén, jiào "CUC News."

____ 6. 我們一期新聞可能有十二條到十五條新聞......新聞要逐條逐條地去拍。／我们一期新闻可能有十二条到十五条新闻......新闻要逐条逐条地去拍。Wǒmen yì qī xīnwén kěnéng yǒu shí'èr tiáo dào shíwǔ tiáo xīnwén . . . xīnwén yào zhútiáo zhútiáo de qù pāi.

____ 7. 這個就是一個新聞的整個的流程。／这个就是一个新闻的整个的流程。Zhè ge jiù shì yí ge xīnwén de zhěnggè de liúchéng.

____ 8. 老師......最後來告訴同學哪條新聞不錯，哪條新聞有問題，哪條新聞還是可以改善的。／老师......最后来告诉同学哪条新闻不错，哪条新闻有问题，哪条新闻还是可以改善的。Lǎoshī . . . zuìhòu lái gàosu tóngxué nǎ tiáo xīnwén búcuò, nǎ tiáo xīnwén yǒu wèntí, nǎ tiáo xīnwén háishi kěyǐ gǎishàn de.

____ 9. 現在我們電視台擁有了三十五位老師，然後我們有將近九百名學生記者。／现在我们电视台拥有了三十五位老师，然后我们有将近九百名学生记者。Xiànzài wǒmen diànshìtái yōngyǒu le sānshíwǔ wèi lǎoshī, ránhòu wǒmen yǒu jiāngjìn jiǔbǎi míng xuésheng jìzhě.

Recap

Grammar

The many uses of 的

Let's take another look at 的. There are at least four uses for this grammatical particle.

- **Possession, belonging**

我們的電視台有將近三十個機構。／我们的电视台有将近三十个机构。

Wǒmen de diànshìtái yǒu jiāngjìn sānshí ge jīgòu.

Our *station has almost thirty organizational units.*

- **Attaching a modifier to a noun**

每一期新聞我們都按照專業的標準去拍。／每一期新闻我们都按照专业的标准去拍。

Měi yì qī xīnwén wǒmen dōu ànzhào **zhuānyè de** biāozhǔn qù pāi.

We shoot every episode of the news according to ***professional*** *standards.*

- **Providing additional detail about a known past event (usually preceded by 是)**

中國傳媒大學電視台是2008年成立的。／中国传媒大学电视台是2008年成立的。

Zhōngguó Chuánméi Dàxué diànshìtái shì **èrlínglíngbā nián chénglì de.**

CUCTV was ***established in 2008.***

- **Characterizing something as a categorical truth or as a member of a category or type (usually preceded by 是)**

我們的新聞是每周有兩期必須要播出的。／我们的新闻是每周有两期必须要播出的。

Wǒmen de xīnwén shì měizhōu yǒu liǎng qī **bìxū yào bōchū de.**

Our news ***[is the type that] must broadcast*** *two episodes per week. / As for our news, we* ***must broadcast*** *two shows weekly.*

Exercise 1: Look at each use of 的 that you see in the following quotes from the cultural mini-documentary. Can you match each use of 的 to one of the types described above? Write the appropriate code in the blank.

P: possessive
M: modifier
D: details about a known past event
C: categorical

______ 1. Tā shèjí dào chuánméi lǐngyù de gègè zhuānyè. 它涉及到傳媒領域的各個專業。／它涉及到传媒领域的各个专业。 *It involves every specialization in the media field.*

______ 2. Chuánméi lèi de zhè zhǒng jiàoxué qíshí shì fēicháng zhòngshì shíjiàn gōngzuò de. 傳媒類的這種教學其實是非常重視實踐工作的。／传媒类的这种教学其实是非常重视实践工作的。 *Media-type education of this sort actually regards experiential work as extremely important.*

______ 3. Wǒmen yào ná dào wǒmen de yǎnbō shì. 我們要拿到我們的演播室。／我们要拿到我们的演播室。 *We have to take it to our broadcast room.*

______ 4. Xuéxiào gěi wǒmen zhuānmén de yí ge dúlì de dàlóu. 學校給我們專門的一個獨立的大樓。／学校给我们专门的一个独立的大楼。 *The school gave us our very own freestanding building.*

______ 5. Lǎoshīmen lái gàosu tóngxué nǎ tiáo xīnwén búcuò, nǎ tiáo xīnwén yǒu wèntí, nǎ tiáo xīnwén háishi kěyǐ gǎishàn de. 老師們來告訴同學哪條新聞不錯，哪條新聞有問題，哪條新聞還是可以改善的。／老师们来告诉同学哪条新闻不错，哪条新闻有问题，哪条新闻还是可以改善的。 *The teachers tell the students which news items are great, which news items have problems, and which news items could stand some improvement.*

______ 6. Zhōngguó Chuánméi Dàxué diànshìtái shíjì shang shì 2008 nián 5 yuèfèn zhèngshì chénglì de. 中國傳媒大學電視台實際上是2008年5月份正式成立的。／中国传媒大学电视台实际上是2008年5月份正式成立的。 *CUCTV was actually formally established in May of 2008.*

Exercise 2: Jot down a few notes of your "takeaways" from this interview. 試試用中文寫吧！／试试用中文写吧！

Vocabulary

Please refer to page R-2 for a list of grammatical abbreviations used throughout this book.

bǎo'ān 保安 security personnel N

bàodǎo 報導／报导 report V; information N

bōchū 播出 broadcast; disseminate RV

cǎifǎng 採訪／采访 cover; interview; gather news V

chāyidiǎn 差一點／差一点 almost A

chōngshàngqu 衝上去／冲上去 charge; rush; dash (over to) RV

chūyǎn 出演 play the part of; act; portray VO

dàgāng 大綱／大纲 outline; synopsis; summary N

dǎng 檔／档 *(for programs and TV series)* M

dǎoyǎn 導演／导演 director *(of plays, films)* N

dárén 達人／达人 talent *(loan word from English word* talent*)* N/PL

dǎ zhāohu 打招呼 say hello to; greet *(somebody)* VO

dújiā 獨家／独家 exclusive; sole ATTR

fēngōng 分工 division of labor N

fǒurèn 否認／否认 deny; repudiate V

gǔdiǎn 古典 classical ATTR

guòhuǒ 過火／过火 extreme; going too far SV

huǒ 火 hot; popular SV

jí 集 *(for episodes in a TV series)* M

jiǎngshù 講述／讲述 tell about; narrate; relate V

jiāngyào 將要／将要 be going to; will; shall AV

jiémù 節目／节目 program; item *(on a program)* N

jìlùpiān 紀錄片／纪录片 documentary N

jìzhě 記者／记者 reporter N

jù 劇／剧 theatrical work; drama; play N

káng 扛 carry V

liánxù 連續／连续 continuous; successive; running ATTR; continuously; successively; in a row A

liánxùjù 連續劇／连续剧 TV series N

lǚyóu 旅遊／旅游 tour V; tourism N

mài(ge) guānzi 賣（個）關子／卖（个）关子 hold in suspense *(in storytelling)* VO

piàofáng 票房 box office N

pò'àn 破案 solve a criminal case VO

pōlà 潑辣／泼辣 bad-tempered; aggressive; fierce and tough SV

qī 期 *(for magazines and periodicals)* M

qíngjǐng duǎnjù 情景短劇／情景短剧 sitcom N

qīnqiè 親切／亲切 cordial; genial SV

rènwu 任務／任务 task N

shàngyìng 上映 show a film V

shèxiàngjī 攝像機／摄像机 video camera; camcorder N

shōukàn 收看 tune into; watch (TV) V

shuǐjiǎo 水餃／水饺 dumpling N

shǔyú 屬於／属于 belong to; be a part of V

tái 台 channel; station N

tiǎozhàn 挑戰／挑战 challenge N

tícái 題材／题材 subject matter; theme N

tuánduì 團隊／团队 team N

tuōkǒu xiù 脱口秀 talk show N/PL

wǎnjiān 晚間／晚间 evening; at night N

wǎnyuē 婉約／婉约 graceful and restrained ATTR

wēnróu 温柔 gentle and soft SV

xiàn 限 set a limit; restrict V

xiànshí 現實／现实 practical; pragmatic SV

xiāoshí 消食 help to digest VO

xìliè 系列 series; set N

xíngzhēnjù 刑偵劇／刑侦剧 crime investigation show N

xīnwén 新聞／新闻 news N

xiù 秀 show *(loan word from the English word* show*)* N/PL

xuǎnxiù jiémù 選秀節目／选秀节目 talent show N

yúlè 娛樂／娱乐 amusement; entertainment; recreation N

zhēnrén xiù 真人秀 reality show N

zhídǎo 執導／执导 direct *(a film)* V

zhìzuò 製作／制作 produce V

zhǔchírén 主持人 host; anchor N

zuìfàn 罪犯 criminal N

zǔzhī 組織／组织 organize V

Checklist of "can do" statements

After completing this unit, you should be able to perform each of the following tasks:

Listening and speaking

- ☐ Talk about different kinds of TV shows.
- ☐ Understand an entertainment news report.
- ☐ Describe a "pretend" meeting with a media celebrity.
- ☐ Contribute to a mock news show.

Reading and writing

- ☐ Decipher some signs posted around a media studio.
- ☐ Comprehend a short essay about a famous Chinese director.
- ☐ Write a short essay about your favorite movie director.

Understanding culture

- ☐ Make several accurate statements about the media production facilities of the Communication University of China.

UNIT

33

"Searching the globe for curiosities"

寰宇搜奇

Huányǔsōuqí

Searching the Internet

In this unit, you will learn how to:

- talk about finding news items online.
- identify key PRC websites and their functions.
- talk about communicating online.
- decipher some items on pages of a key Chinese website.
- read a story about a website.
- write a story about a favorite website.

Encounter 1 Identifying Chinese sites

33.1 *Fang Lan discovers that her news report has spread across the Internet.* 請把中文跟英文對上。／请把中文跟英文对上。

____ a. shàng le Sōuhú 上了搜狐	1. *got many hits or views*
____ b. diǎnjīliàng gāo 點擊量高／点击量高	2. *reposted*
____ c. fā yì tiáo zhuàngtài 發一條狀態／发一条状态	3. *went viral*
____ d. zhuǎnfā 轉發／转发	4. *try doing a search*
____ e. xiàng bìngdú yíyàng chuánbō kāi 像病毒一樣傳播開／像病毒一样传播开	5. *got on Sohu*
____ f. sōusōukan 搜搜看	6. *sent out a post*

33.2 *View Episode 33, Vignette 1. The students are excited about all the places the video is showing up. Number the sites below in the order they are named.*

___ Kāixīn (wǎng) 開心網／开心网 *Kaixin001 (Network) [literally, "Happy Net"]*
___ Téngxùn yúlè (wǎng) 騰訊娛樂(網)／腾讯娱乐(网) *Tencent Entertainment (Network)*
___ Tǔdòu (wǎng) 土豆(網)／土豆(网) *Tudou (Network)*
___ Yōukù (wǎng) 優酷(網)／优酷(网) *Youku (Network)*
___ Sōuhú (wǎng) 搜狐(網)／ 搜狐(网) *Sohu (Network)*
___ xiàonèi (wǎng) 校内(網)／校内(网) *campus intranet (network)*

Visit the following six commercial sites at ent.qq.com, www.tudou.com, www.youku.com, *and* www.sohu.com, *and browse them;* www.baidu.com *and* www.weibo.com *are not mentioned in the episode but are important to know about. Then, in the spaces that follow, write the names of equivalent sites, such as YouTube and Google, with which you are familiar. (The site www.*开心*.com, also mentioned in the episode, is a social networking site like* www.weibo.com.*)*

a. 优酷 = ______________________
b. 土豆 = ______________________
c. 搜狐 = ______________________
d. 腾讯娱乐 = ______________________
e. 百度 = ______________________
f. 微博 = Twitter; Facebook

33.3 *The students make many statements about what has happened to Fang Lan's report online. View the vignette again and match the statements below with the students who made them.*

i.

ii.

iii.

iv.

v.

____ a. Shàng le Sōuhú. *It's on Sohu.*

____ b. Diǎnjīliàng hái tǐng gāo de. *The click rate is pretty high, too. [There are lots of views.]*

____ c. Téngxùn Yúlè shang yě yǒu. *It's on Tencent Entertainment Network too.*

____ d. Yǒu rén gěi wǒ fā le duǎnxìn. *Someone sent me a text [about it].*

____ e. Zài xiàonèi shang fā le yìtiáo zhuàngtài. *Someone put up a post on the school's intranet.*

____ f. Kāixīnwǎng shang yě yǒu rén zhuǎnfā le. *Kaixin001 is forwarding it too.*

____ g. Xiànzài yǐjing xiàng bìngdú yíyàng chuánbō kāi le. *It's gone viral.*

____ h. Xiànzài yǐjing shì jìnrénjiēzhī le. *It's already become something everyone knows about.*

____ i. Tǔdòu yě zhuǎn le. *Tudou passed it on too.*

____ j. Xiànzài wǎngshang dàochù dōu shì. *It's everywhere on the Net now.*

____ k. Tèbié huǒbào. *It's explosive.*

33.4 請把上面的拼音和英文與下面的漢字對上。／请把上面的拼音和英文与下面的汉字对上。

____ 1. 騰訊娛樂上也有。／腾讯娱乐上也有。
____ 2. 在校內上發了一條狀態。／在校内上发了一条状态。
____ 3. 土豆也轉了。／土豆也转了。
____ 4. 上了搜狐。
____ 5. 有人給我發了短信。／有人给我发了短信。
____ 6. 現在網上到處都是。／现在网上到处都是。
____ 7. 點擊量還挺高的。／点击量还挺高的。
____ 8. 現在已經是盡人皆知了。／现在已经是尽人皆知了。
____ 9. 現在已經像病毒一樣傳播開了。／现在已经像病毒一样传播开了。
____ 10. 特別火爆。／特别火爆。
____ 11. 開心網上也有人轉發了。／开心网上也有人转发了。

33.5 *After viewing the video of Huang Yalan dealing with the paparazzi, the students discuss whether she affirmed or denied the news that Fang Lan had put out.* 請選英語填空。／请选英语填空。

confirm	*affirmative (sure)*	*deny*

Student A: She didn't really completely ____________ (the news report); she just couldn't ____________ it.

Emma: But when she told you, wasn't she very ____________?

Write the four terms below into the "Confirm" or "Deny" columns.

確定／确定 quèdìng	否定 fǒudìng	否認／否认 fǒurèn	肯定 kěndìng

Confirm, affirm, "say yes"	Deny, "say no"

33.6 ***Mingling:*** *Walk around the room talking to your classmates. Make up a guess about each (*Nǐ de zhuānyè shì Zhōngwén; Nǐ yǒu yí ge mèimei; Nǐ dǎ lánqiú dǎ de hěn hǎo; Nǐ xǐhuan kàn diànyǐng; *etc.). To your classmates' guesses, say,* "Zhèi ge wǒ néng kěndìng" *if it's true or* "Zhèi ge wǒ fǒudìng" *if it's false.*

33.7 *What are three websites you visit frequently? List them below.*

____________________ ____________________ ____________________

Why do you go to these websites? Check the reasons below, or make up some of your own.

☐ Wǒ shàngwǎng chá xìnxī.
我上網查信息。／我上网查信息。*(look up information)*

☐ Wǒ shàngwǎng wán yóuxì.
我上網玩遊戲。／我上网玩游戏。*(play games)*

☐ Wǒ shàngwǎng gòumǎi dōngxi.
我上網購買東西。／我上网购买东西。*(shop for things)*

☐ Wǒ shàngwǎng liánxì péngyou.
我上網聯繫朋友。／我上网联系朋友。*(contact friends)*

☐ Wǒ shàngwǎng kàn xīnwén.
我上網看新聞。／我上网看新闻。*(watch or read news)*

☐ Wǒ shàngwǎng kàn shìpín.
我上網看視頻。／我上网看视频。 *(watch videos)*

☐ ____

☐ ____

Mingling: *Chat with some classmates. Ask,* 你最喜歡上甚麼網站？為甚麼？／你最喜欢上什么网站？为什么？ *Answer their questions according to your answers above.*

Encounter 2 Smartphone communications

33.8 *After class, Fang Lan, Emma, and some other students are relaxing at a café. All except Emma are absorbed with their phones.* 請把中文和英文對上。／请把中文和英文对上。

____ a. qúnfā xiāoxi 群發消息／群发消息	1. *receive a response*
____ b. shōu dào huífù 收到回覆／收到回复	2. *play with your cell phone*
____ c. shōu dào duǎnxìn 收到短信	3. *stare at the screen*
____ d. wánr shǒujī 玩兒手機／玩儿手机	4. *send a group message*
____ e. pāi yì zhāng (zhàopiàn) 拍一張(照片)／拍一张(照片)	5. *means of communication*
____ f. dīngzhe píngmù 盯著屏幕／盯着屏幕	6. *take a picture*
____ g. jiāoliú fāngshì 交流方式	7. *receive text messages*

33.9 *View Episode 33, Vignette 2, and match the statements below with the students who made them. (Statements are listed in the order they were made).*

i. ii. iii. iv. v.

____ a. Can you believe that Fang Lan's report is this popular?

____ b. I'm sending a group message with this news to my elementary school classmates.

____ c. I just got a response from my friend in Africa.

____ d. Don't play with your cell phones anymore.

____ e. I want to take a photo and send it to my friend in Seattle.

____ f. None of us are looking at each other; we're all staring at our cell phone screens.

____ g. This is how we communicate.

____ h. Just let me finish sending this text.

____ i. The first one to touch a phone pays for our food!

33.10 請把上面的英文與下面的拼音和漢字對上。／请把上面的英文与下面的拼音和汉字对上。

____ 1. Wǒ yào pāi yì zhāng zhào, fā gěi wǒ zài Xīyǎtú de péngyou.
我要拍一張照，發給我在西雅圖的朋友。／我要拍一张照，发给我在西雅图的朋友。

____ 2. Shéi dì-yī ge ná shǒujī, shéi jiù qǐngkè.
誰第一個拿手機，誰就請客。／谁第一个拿手机，谁就请客。

____ 3. Bié wánr shǒujī le.
別玩兒手機了。／别玩儿手机了。

____ 4. Wǒ gāng shōu dào wǒ zài Fēizhōu de péngyou de huífù.
我剛收到我在非洲的朋友的回覆。／我刚收到我在非洲的朋友的回复。

____ 5. Nǐmen gǎn xiāngxìn Fāng Lán de bàodǎo zhème huǒ ma?
你們敢相信方蘭的報導這麼火嗎？／你们敢相信方兰的报导这么火吗？

____ 6. Děng wǒ fā wán zhè tiáo duǎnxìn.
等我發完這條短信。／等我发完这条短信。

____ 7. Zhè shì wǒmen de jiāoliú fāngshì.
這是我們的交流方式。／这是我们的交流方式。

____ 8. Měi ge rén dōu názhe shǒujī zhǐ dīngzhe píngmù, gēnběn jiù bú kàn bǐcǐ.
每個人都拿著手機只盯著屏幕，根本就不看彼此。／每个人都拿着手机只盯着屏幕，根本就不看彼此。

____ 9. Wǒ zhèngzài gěi wǒ de xiǎoxué xiàoyǒuzǔ qúnfā zhè tiáo xiāoxi.
我正在給我的小學校友組群發這條消息。／我正在给我的小学校友组群发这条消息。

33.11 *How do you feel about friends spending time on the phone when you're all out together? Write several sentences about what you think.* 請寫漢字或者拼音。／请写汉字或者拼音。

33.12 *Ask several of your classmates the following question:* 你對朋友們在一起的時候老玩兒手機有甚麼看法？／你对朋友们在一起的时候老玩儿手机有什么看法？ *Respond using the notes you wrote in Exercise 33.11. Take notes below on what your friends say.*

Encounter 3 Reading and writing

Reading real-life texts

33.13 *This is the banner for a Chinese search engine.*

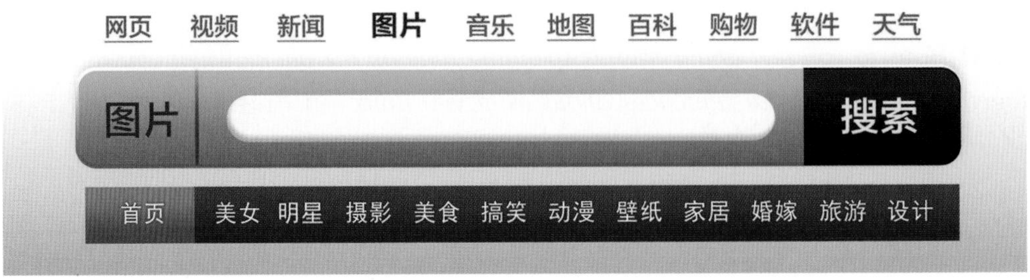

The following categories are given in the top line (in green):

网页 视频 新闻 图片 音乐 地图 百科 购物 软件 天气

Write the characters next to the glosses below.

________ xīnwén *news* ________ gòuwù *shopping* ______ dìtú *maps*

________ ruǎnjiàn *software* ________ tiānqì *weather* ______ wǎngyè *splash page*

________ yīnyuè *music* ________ bǎikē *encyclopedia* ______ shìpín *video*

________ túpiàn *images*

33.14 *The banner shown in Exercise 33.13 is from the home page of the Images category.*

a. *Write the characters for* shǒuyè *(home page; literally, "head page"):* ______________

b. *The text box allows you to type in key words for the image(s) you are searching for. The button to the right of this box includes a term that is the equivalent of "search." Write the characters for* sōusuǒ*:* ______________

33.15 *Refer again to the image from Exercise 33.13. The brown bar at the bottom of the banner lists the following searchable image categories:*

美女 明星 摄影 美食 搞笑 动漫 壁纸 家居 婚嫁 旅游 设计

Write the characters next to the glosses below.

______ bìzhǐ *wallpaper* ______ měishí *gourmet food* ______ míngxīng *celebrities*

______ dòngmàn *graphic novels* ______ hūnjià *wedding* ______ shèyǐng *photography*

______ měinǚ *beauties* ______ gǎoxiào *comedy* ______ shèjì *design*

______ jiājū *homes* ______ lǚyóu *travel*

33.16 *Circle the appropriate category from the choices given for each sample image. The caption for each image is given below.*

a **Caption:** 这不会是亲哥俩吧!

These couldn't be a pair of blood ________! (用英文填空)

Category:

明星 美女 搞笑 家居 动漫

b **Caption:** 最热男明星

The ____________ male stars (用英文填空)

Category:

旅游 设计 美食 明星 美女

c **Caption:** 自信的完美新娘

The confident perfect bride

Category:

搞笑 美食 动漫 旅游 婚嫁

d **Caption:** 足球之都——巴西

The capital of soccer—__________ (用英文填空)

Category:

美女　搞笑　婚嫁　动漫　旅游

e **Caption:** 下次我在沙滩也这么玩

Next time I'm at the __________, I'll play this joke too. (用英文填空)

Category:

搞笑　动漫　旅游　家居　设计

f **Caption:** 味浓情更浓—巧克力让你心动

The flavor is intense but the feelings are even more intense—__________ moves your heart. (用英文填空)

Category:

搞笑　动漫　婚嫁　设计　美食

Reading a story

33.17 故事 *Find the following terms in either the traditional or simplified text and circle them. Write in the accompanying number.*

1. Gǔgē *Google*
2. zhùmíng *famous*
3. gōngsī *companies*
4. yóu *by*
5. tiāncái *genius*
6. jiǎnlòu *crude*
7. huánjìng *environment*
8. chuànglì *created*
9. lìwài *be an exception*
10. sīrén *private*
11. chēkù *garage*
12. kāichuàng *begin, establish*
13. dàdǎn *bold*
14. zhǔyi *idea*
15. quán shìjiè *the whole world*
16. suǒyǒude *all that there is*
17. xìnxī *informatio*
18. zhěnghé *organize, integrate*
19. wǎngluò *the Web*

20. jìsuànjī *computer*
21. Mìxiēgēn Dàxué *University of Michigan*
22. jìshù *technology*
23. juédìng *decide*
24. Sītǎnfú Dàxué *Stanford University*
25. rènshi *become acquainted with*
26. Éluósī *Russia*
27. Mǎlǐlán Dàxué *University of Maryland*
28. qǔdé *obtain*
29. xuéshì xuéwèi *bachelor's degree*
30. bóshì *Ph.D.*
31. kāifā *develop*
32. zuìchū *at the beginning*
33. bān dào *moved to*
34. sōusuǒ yǐnqíng *search engine*
35. mìngmíng *to name*

36. yìwèizhe *denote*
37. wúxiàn de *limitless*
38. méiyǒu biānjiè *boundless*
39. shùzì *number*
40. mùbiāo *goal*
41. zǔzhī zhěnghé *organize and integrate*
42. kǒuhào *slogan*
43. bú zuò'è *do no evil*

44. quēdiǎn *shortcoming*
45. biànchéng *turn into*
46. yúshì *therefore*
47. gù *hire*
48. zhuànqián *earn money*
49. fāngshì *means, method*
50. xiāngdāng *quite*
51. jiǎndān *simple*
52. Měiguó *American*
53. bìxū *need to*
54. juédìng *decide*
55. mài guǎnggaò *sell ads*
56. rènhé *any*
57. xiāngguān *related*
58. wúguān *not related*
59. diǎnjī *click on*
60. yì bǐ qián *a sum of money*

61. jùdà *enormous*
62. yǐngxiǎng *impact*
63. shènzhì *even*
64. yǔyán *language*
65. dá'àn *answer*

"谷歌一下，就知道了！"

有很多著名的公司是由一兩個天才在很簡陋的環境下創立的。谷歌也不例外。谷歌是兩個年輕人在加州 Menlo Park 的一個私人車庫裡開創的。他們想出了一個大膽的主意，要把全世界所有的信息

"谷歌一下，就知道了！"

有很多著名的公司是由一两个天才在很简陋的环境下创立的。谷歌也不例外。谷歌是两个年轻人在加州 Menlo Park 的一个私人车库里开创的。他们想出了一个大胆的主意，要把全世界所有的信息

都整合起來，放到網絡上，讓每個人都能上網去看。

都整合起来，放到网络上，让每个人都能上网去看。

這兩位天才是誰呢？他們的名字叫拉裡・佩奇 (Lālǐ Pèiqí *Larry Page*) 和謝爾蓋・布林 (Xiè'ěrgài Bùlín *Sergey Brin*)。佩奇是一個美國人。他從小就對計算機特別感興趣。在他只有六歲的時候，他父親就給他買了一台計算機。後來他上了密歇根大學讀計算機工程。畢業以後，他做了幾年計算機技術方面的工作。24歲那年，他決定去斯坦福大學學習計算機科學。在斯坦福他認識了布林，一個出生在俄羅斯，六歲來到了美國的同學。布林在馬裡蘭大學取得計算機科學學士學位後，也去了斯坦福大學讀博士。兩個人就是在斯坦福大學的時候開始開發谷歌的。最初，他們只是在自己的宿舍裡工作；後來，他們搬到了一個朋友的車庫裡去了。他們把新開發的搜索引擎命名為谷歌 (Google)。

这两位天才是谁呢？他们的名字叫拉里・佩奇 (Lālǐ Pèiqí *Larry Page*) 和谢尔盖・布林 (Xiè'ěrgài Bùlín *Sergey Brin*)。佩奇是一个美国人。他从小就对计算机特别感兴趣。在他只有六岁的时候，他父亲就给他买了一台计算机。后来他上了密歇根大学读计算机工程。毕业以后，他做了几年计算机技术方面的工作。24岁那年，他决定去斯坦福大学学习计算机科学。在斯坦福他认识了布林，一个出生在俄罗斯，六岁来到了美国的同学。布林在马里兰大学取得计算机科学学士学位后，也去了斯坦福大学读博士。两个人就是在斯坦福大学的时候开始开发谷歌的。最初，他们只是在自己的宿舍里工作；后来，他们搬到了一个朋友的车库里去了。他们把新开发的搜索引擎命名为谷歌 (Google)。

Google 是甚麼意思呢？是1加上100個零，也就是意味著無限的、沒有邊界的數字。這個名字就是他們的目標——把網絡上無數的信息組織整合起來。谷歌的口號是"不作惡"。

Google 是什么意思呢？是1加上100个零，也就是意味着无限的、没有边界的数字。这个名字就是他们的目标——把网络上无数的信息组织整合起来。谷歌的口号是"不作恶"。

佩奇和布林這兩個天才有一個缺點，那就是他們兩個都不知道怎麼把產品變成錢。於是他們雇了一位叫埃裡克・施密特 (Āilǐkè Shīmìtè *Eric Schmidt*) 的同事。他賺錢的方式相當簡單，也相當美國。如果想賺錢，就必需找東西賣。谷歌能賣甚麼呢？他們決定在搜索引擎上賣廣告。現在，你每次上網搜索任何信息的時候，都會看到跟它相關或者無關的廣告。每點擊一個廣告一次，谷歌就會賺一筆錢。

佩奇和布林这两个天才有一个缺点，那就是他们两个都不知道怎么把产品变成钱。于是他们雇了一位叫埃里克・施密特 (Āilǐkè Shīmìtè *Eric Schmidt*) 的同事。他赚钱的方式相当简单，也相当美国。如果想赚钱，就必需找东西卖。谷歌能卖什么呢？他们决定在搜索引擎上卖广告。现在，你每次上网搜索任何信息的时候，都会看到跟它相关或者无关的广告。每点击一个广告一次，谷歌就会赚一笔钱。

谷歌對我們的生活有巨大的影響。它甚至影響到了我們的語言。現在，如果你想對任何一個問題找出一個答案，人們會說，“你去谷歌一下吧！”

谷歌对我们的生活有巨大的影响。它甚至影响到了我们的语言。现在，如果你想对任何一个问题找出一个答案，人们会说，“你去谷歌一下吧！”

33.18 *Write a short description in Chinese of a favorite website on a separate sheet of paper. Have it corrected by your teacher or other tutor, and produce a new draft that you can share with your classmates, in print or online (e.g., a class website).*

Encounter 4 Extension: Cultural mini-documentary

View the cultural mini-documentary for this unit and complete the exercises that follow.

33.19 *In this video, a variety of people discuss how they use the Internet. Online megastores such as* 淘寶／淘宝 Táobǎo *and communications apps such as* 微信 Wēixìn *(the Chinese version of WeChat) have caused tremendous shifts in commerce and communication in China. You may find some interesting differences from your own Internet habits. Before watching, brush up on some key words related to the Internet.* 請把中文跟英文對上。／请把中文跟英文对上。

____ a. hùliánwǎng 互聯網／互联网	1. *shop, buy stuff*
____ b. xiàzǎi (*or* xiàzài) 下載／下载	2. *look up, search*
____ c. shìpín 視頻／视频	3. *play games*
____ d. zīliào 資料／资料	4. *the Internet*
____ e. gòuwù 購物／购物	5. *videos*
____ f. wánr yóuxì 玩兒遊戲／玩儿游戏	6. *download*
____ g. chá 查	7. *materials, information*

33.20 *In the first part of the video (0:00–1:53), people tell us in 18 short clips how they use the Internet. For each word in the list above, make a tally of the number of times it appears in this part.*

a. hùliánwǎng 互聯網／互联网	
b. xiàzǎi (*or* xiàzài) 下載／下载	
c. shìpín 視頻／视频	
d. zīliào 資料／资料	
e. gòuwù 購物／购物	
f. wánr yóuxì 玩兒遊戲／玩儿游戏	
g. chá 查	

33.21 *Here are a few more useful phrases from the first part of the video. Using them, prepare a few sentences in Chinese to describe your own use of the Internet.*

Zuòwéi xuésheng de huà, . . .
做為學生的話，……／作为学生的话，……
As a student, . . .

Wǒ yìbān shàngwǎng zuì zhǔyào jiùshì . . .
我一般上網最主要就是……／我一般上网最主要就是……
Typically I go on the Web mostly to . . .

shàng wǎngzhàn qù liúlǎn yìxiē nèiróng
上網站去瀏覽一些內容／上网站去浏览一些内容
go to websites to browse content

Zhǐyǒu . . . de shíhou wǒ cái huì yòng diànzǐ yóujiàn
只有……的時候我才會用電子郵件／只有……的时候我才会用电子邮件
I only use e-mail when . . .

yào chá yíxià dāngdì de xiángxì zīliào
要查一下當地的詳細資料／要查一下当地的详细资料
if I need to look up detailed local information

zàixiàn kàn diànyǐng
在線看電影／在线看电影
to watch movies online

Wǒ yìbān qíngkuàng yòng hùliánwǎng qù zuò wǒ de gōngzuò.
我一般情況用互聯網去做我的工作。／我一般情况用互联网去做我的工作。
Typically I use the Internet to do my work.

Write some statements about your own Internet use:

33.22 *In the second part of the video (1:54–2:38), respondents answer the question* 你用互聯網與親友溝通嗎？／你用互联网与亲友沟通吗？ Nǐ yòng hùliánwǎng yǔ qīnyǒu gōutōng ma? "*Do you use the Internet to communicate with friends and family?" Five of the seven respondents are pictured below; write the appropriate letter under each picture to match each person with his or her usage profiles.*

1. ____

2. ____

3. ____

4. ____

5. ____

Profiles:

a. uses the Internet to communicate only rarely; prefers meeting in person or calling on a cell phone
b. connects with friends a lot, using e-mail and chat tools
c. remarks how many Internet chat tools there are now; uses QQ to connect with friends in China and Skype for friends overseas
d. chats with friends on e-mail [sic] to find out how they're doing and what's new
e. likes using WeChat on the cell phone because it's convenient for getting your friends all in a group

33.23 *In the third part of the video (2:40 until the end), respondents are asked,* 互聯網對人際關係有甚麼影響？／互联网对人际关系有什么影响？ Hùliánwǎng duì rénjì guānxi yǒu shénme yǐngxiǎng? "*How has the Internet affected human relationships?"* 請把中文跟英文對上。／请把中文跟英文对上。

____ a. shíjiān yuèláiyuè cháng 時間越來越長／时间越来越长	1. *between people*
____ b. rén yǔ rén zhījiān 人與人之間／人与人之间	2. *emotional connections are somewhat weakened*
____ c. miàn duì miàn de gōutōng 面對面的溝通／面对面的沟通	3. *lame, boring*
____ d. jiǎnshǎo 減少／减少	4. *as time goes on*
____ e. gǎnqíng yǒusuǒ dànhuà 感情有所淡化	5. *most [of my] friends*
____ f. dà bùfen péngyou 大部分朋友	6. *face-to-face communication*
____ g. méijìn 沒勁／没劲	7. *be reduced, lessen*

Now make your own statement about the Internet and emotional connections, using some of these terms and phrases, no matter whether you agree or disagree.

33.24 *Here are some more words the respondents used.* 請把中文跟英文對上。／请把中文跟英文对上。

____ a. duìyú zánmen lái jiǎng
對於咱們來講／对于咱们来讲

____ b. xiàng Tiānfāng Yètán
像天方夜譚／像天方夜谭

____ c. huì jù zài yìqǐ
會聚在一起／会聚在一起

____ d. hùxiāng yúlè
互相娛樂／互相娱乐

____ e. wǎngluò hěn fādá le
網絡很發達了／网络很发达了

____ f. zhìnéng shǒujī
智能手機／智能手机

____ g. wǒ gèrén rènwéi
我個人認為／我个人认为

____ h. qíshí shì shūyuǎn le péngyou de jùlí
其實是疏遠了朋友的距離／
其实是疏远了朋友的距离

1. *entertain one another, have fun together*
2. *as far as we are concerned*
3. *actually it has created distance between friends*
4. *smartphones*
5. *my personal opinion is that . . .*
6. *the Web has become very developed*
7. *like the Arabian Nights; like a fairy tale*
8. *would get together*

Try making another statement about the Internet and emotional connections, using some of these terms and phrases.

Recap

Grammar

Question words to express the indefinite

Q: When is a question word *not* a question word?
A: When it indicates an *indefinite* quantity, quality, person, place, thing, time, etc.

Words that express the indefinite—for example, *anybody, anything, nobody, nothing, everywhere,* and *anywhere*—can be tricky to express in a foreign language. In Chinese, the key is not in learning new words but in using words you already know—question words such as 誰／谁, 哪, 哪裡／哪里, 哪個／哪个, and 甚麼／什么—in a new way. Here are some examples:

1. Combine the question word with 也 or 都, in a positive or negative statement.

Shéi xiǎng qù? *Who wants to go?*
Shéi dōu xiǎng qù. *Everyone would want to go.*
Shéi yě bù xiǎng qù. *No one wants to go.*

Nǐ rènshi tā ma? *Do you know her?*
Dāngrán. Wǒ shéi dōu rènshi. *Of course. I know everyone.*
Tā hěn yǒumíng. Shéi dōu rènshi tā. *She's famous. Anyone would know her.*
Wǒ zhèr shéi dōu bú rènshi. *I don't know anyone here.*
Tā shì shéi? Shéi yě bú rènshi tā. *Who's she? No one knows her.*

Nǐ xiǎng mǎi shénme? *What would you like to buy?*
Dōngxi dōu hěn piányi. Wǒ shénme dōu xiǎng mǎi. *The things are all inexpensive. I want to buy everything.*
Dōngxi dōu tài guì le, wǒ shénme dōu mǎibùqǐ. *The things are too expensive. I can't afford anything.*
Wǒ shénme dōu bù xiǎng mǎi. Wǒ dōngxi tài duō le. *I don't want to buy anything. I have too much stuff.*

Nǐ xiǎng dào nǎr qù? *Where do you feel like going?*
Qù nǎr dōu xíng. Nǐ shuō ba! *Anywhere is fine. You decide!*
Wǒ nǎr dōu xiǎng qù, kěshì qián bú gòu. *I want to go everywhere, but I don't have enough money.*
Wǒ nǎr yě bù néng qù. Tàitai bìng le. *I can't go anywhere. My wife is sick.*

Nǐ yào něi ge? Něi ge bǐjiào hǎo? *Which one do you want? Which one is better?*
Něi ge dōu xíng. *Either [whichever one] will do.*
Něi ge dōu bù xíng. Dōngxi dōu bù hǎo. *Neither [none of them] will do. They're not good items.*

2. Use the question word in a paired construction.

Nǐ xiǎng chī diǎnr shénme? *What would you like to eat?*
Suíbiàn, nǐ yǒu shénme, wǒ jiù chī shénme. *Anything. I'll eat whatever you have.*

Nǐ xǐhuan zhèi ge dìfang ma? *Do you like this place?*
Bù xǐhuan. Yào shénme, méi shénme. *No. It doesn't have anything we want.*

Fang Lan's statement is an example of this construction. She said:

Shéi dì-yī ge ná shǒujī, shéi jiù qǐngkè! *Whoever is the first to touch a phone will pay for all the food!*

3. Statements in which the question word indicates an indefinite can be turned into questions by adding *ma*.

Nǎr dōu xíng ma? *Would just anyplace be OK?*
Shénme dōu kěyǐ ma? *Would just anything do?*
Shéi dōu xiǎng qù ma? *Does everyone want to go?*

Exercise 1: Try it out. Insert the appropriate question word in the blanks below.

Tā rén tèbié hǎo. _______ dōu xiǎng hé tā dāng péngyou.
He is a really nice person. Everyone wants to be his friend.

Wǒ è sǐ le. Bù guǎn qù něi ge fànguǎn chīfàn, ________ dōu xíng.
I'm starving. I don't care which restaurant we go to; anyplace will do.

Wǒ děi sòng tā yí ge lǐwù. _________ dōu kěyǐ.
I have to give her a gift. Anything would work.

Exercise 2: Now read the content above in characters.

1.
誰想去？／谁想去？
誰都想去。／谁都想去。
誰也不想去。／谁也不想去。

你認識她嗎？／你认识她吗？
當然。我誰都認識。／当然。我谁都认识。
她很有名。誰都認識她。／她很有名。谁都认识她。
我這兒誰都不認識。／我这儿谁都不认识。
她是誰？誰也不認識她。／她是谁？谁也不认识她。

你想買甚麼？／你想买什么？
東西都很便宜。我甚麼都想買。／东西都很便宜。我什么都想买。
東西都太貴了。我甚麼都買不起。／东西都太贵了。我什么都买不起。
我甚麼都不想買。我東西太多了。／我什么都不想买。我东西太多了。

你想到哪兒去？／你想到哪儿去？
去哪兒都行。你説吧！／去哪儿都行。你说吧！
我哪兒都想去，可是錢不夠。／我哪儿都想去，可是钱不够。
我哪兒也不能去。太太病了。／我哪儿也不能去。太太病了。

你要哪個？哪個比較好？／你要哪个？哪个比较好？
哪個都行。／哪个都行。
哪個都不行。東西都不好。／哪个都不行。东西都不好。

2.
你想吃點兒甚麼？／你想吃点儿什么？
隨便。你有甚麼，我就吃甚麼。／随便。你有什么，我就吃什么。

你喜歡這個地方嗎？／你喜欢这个地方吗？
不喜歡。要甚麼，沒甚麼。／不喜欢。要什么，没什么。

誰第一個拿手機，誰就請客！／谁第一个拿手机，谁就请客！

3.
哪兒都行嗎？／哪儿都行吗？
甚麼都可以嗎？／什么都可以吗？
誰都想去嗎？／谁都想去吗？

Exercise 1:
他人特別好，誰都想和他當朋友。／他人特别好，谁都想和他当朋友。
我餓死了。不管去哪個飯館吃飯，哪兒都行。／我饿死了。不管去哪个饭馆吃饭，哪儿都行。
我得送她一個禮物，甚麼都可以。／我得送她一个礼物，什么都可以。

Vocabulary

Please refer to page R-2 for a list of grammatical abbreviations used throughout this book.

bǎikē 百科 encyclopedia N

bàodǎo 報導／报导 news report; story N; report (the news) V

Bāxī 巴西 Brazil PW

bǐcǐ 彼此 each other; one another A

bìngdú 病毒 virus N

bìzhǐ 壁紙／壁纸 wallpaper N

chuánbō(kāi) 傳播(開)／传播(开) disseminate; propagate; spread V

dàochù (dōu) 到處(都)／到处(都) everywhere; at all places A

diǎnjīliàng 點擊量／点击量 click rate; number of "hits" or views N

dīngzhe 盯著／盯着 fix one's eyes on; gaze/stare at V

dòngmàn 動漫／动漫 cartoons; comics; graphic novels N

dū 都 capital; metropolis BF

fā duǎnxìn 發短信／发短信 send a text message VP

fāngshì 方式 way; fashion; method; means N

fǒudìng 否定 negate; deny V

fǒurèn 否認／否认 deny; repudiate V

gǎoxiào 搞笑 funny SV

gēn pāi 跟拍 follow somebody with a camera to record an event V

gòumǎi 購買／购买 purchase; buy V

huífù 回覆／回复 reply *(to a letter/message)* V; response N

hūnjià 婚嫁 marriage N; marry V

huǒ 火 popular SV

huǒbào 火爆 explosively popular SV

jiājū 家居 home N

jiāoliú 交流 exchange; communicate V; communication N

jìnrénjiēzhī 盡人皆知／尽人皆知 be known to all IE

Kāixīnwǎng 開心網／开心网 Kaixin001 Network *(a Chinese Internet company) (literally, "Happy Net")* N

kàn shìpín 看視頻／看视频 watch videos V

kěndìng 肯定 positive; affirmative SV

liánxì 聯繫／联系 link up with; get in touch with V

lǚyóu 旅遊／旅游 travel; tour; tourism N/V

měinǚ 美女 beautiful woman; beauty N

měishí 美食 gourmet/delicious food N

míngxīng 明星 (movie/pop) star; celebrity N

nóng 濃／浓 dense; thick; concentrated; strong; intense SV

píngmù 屏幕 screen *(TV, computer, etc.)* N

qiǎokèlì 巧克力 chocolate *(loan word)* N/PL

qīn 親／亲 blood relation N

qíng 情 feelings N

quèdìng 確定／确定 be certain, confirm V

qúnfā 群發／群发 group/mass/multiple mailing V

rè 熱／热 popular SV

shàng(wǎng) 上(網)／上(网) to go on (the Internet) V

shèjì 設計／设计 design; plan N/V

shèyǐng 攝影／摄影 photography N; take a photograph; shoot a film; film V

shǒuyè 首頁／首页 home page; title page N

sōu 搜 search; collect; gather V

Sōuhú 搜狐 Sohu *(one of the largest Chinese Internet companies) (literally, "Search-fox")* N

túpiàn 圖片／图片 picture; photograph; images N

wán yóuxì 玩遊戲／玩游戏 play games VP

wǎngyè 網頁／网页 Web page N

wǎngzhàn 網站／网站 website N

wánměi 完美 perfect; consummate SV

wèi 味 flavor; taste; smell N

xiàng X yíyàng 像X一樣／像X一样 identical to/very similar to *X* PH

xiàonèi 校內／校内 inside/within the school PW/ATTR

xiàoyǒu 校友 alumni; classmates N

xìnxī 信息 information; news; message N

Xīyǎtú 西雅圖／西雅图 Seattle PW

zhuǎn 轉／转 pass on; transfer V

zhuǎnfā 轉發／转发 forward *(a message, etc)*; transmit V

zhuàngtài 狀態／状态 state (of affairs); conditions; status N

zìxìn 自信 self-confident; confident V

zǔ 組／组 section; group N

Checklist of "can do" statements

After completing this unit, you should be able to perform each of the following tasks:

Listening and speaking

- ☐ Talk about finding news on the Internet.
- ☐ Identify key PRC websites and their functions.
- ☐ Describe some websites that you visit often.
- ☐ Talk about how you communicate with friends on a smartphone.

Reading and writing

- ☐ Decipher some items on pages of a Chinese website.
- ☐ Comprehend a short essay about Google.
- ☐ Write a short essay about a favorite website.

Understanding culture

- ☐ Make several accurate statements about Taobao, Weixin, and QQ.
- ☐ Make several accurate statements about how some Chinese people use Internet sites.

UNIT

34

"Life is in movement"

生命在於運動

Shēngmìng zàiyú yùndòng

Sports and sporting events

In this unit, you will learn how to:

- talk about sports.
- make comments during sporting events.
- comment on your own engagement with sports.
- describe the rules of a favorite sport.
- comment on which countries are particularly strong in certain sports.
- comment on a key sports figure.
- comment on Chinese martial arts.
- read and comprehend some key details from a Chinese martial arts website.
- read a story about a sports celebrity.
- write a story about a sports figure.

Encounter 1 Discussing sports

34.1 *Xiao Mao and Mick are jogging.* 請把中文和英文對上。／请把中文和英文对上。

____ a. shàng yùndòngchǎng 上運動場／上运动场	1. *play tennis*
____ b. dǎ lánqiú 打籃球／打篮球	2. *play soccer*
____ c. dǎ wǎngqiú 打網球／打网球	3. *walk and talk*
____ d. dǎ pīngpāngqiú 打乒乓球	4. *kick it back*
____ e. tī zúqiú 踢足球	5. *go onto the athletic field*
____ f. mànpǎo 慢跑	6. *catch a soccer ball*
____ g. biānzǒu-biānliáo 邊走邊聊／边走边聊	7. *play basketball*
____ h. jiēzhù zúqiú 接住足球	8. *jog*
____ i. tīhuíqu 踢回去	9. *play table tennis*

34.2 *View Episode 34, Vignette 1. Xiao Mao and Mick discuss their past experiences with sports. Identify who says each of the following sentences.*

	小毛	米克
a. Your footwork isn't bad!	☐	☐
b. Do you play soccer?	☐	☐
c. I used to play soccer, but who has time now?	☐	☐
d. Can you play table tennis?	☐	☐
e. When I was little, I played table tennis, but then I stopped.	☐	☐
f. How about badminton or tennis? Can you play those?	☐	☐
g. I can play badminton but not tennis.	☐	☐
h. Can you play basketball?	☐	☐

i. When I was little, I hurt my fingers. I don't play much now.	☐	☐
j. I like watching basketball games, especially America's NBA.	☐	☐
k. Do you like watching any other sports?	☐	☐
l. I like watching martial arts competitions as well.	☐	☐
m. I've studied a bit of martial arts too.	☐	☐
n. Let's exercise some more.	☐	☐
o. You'll buy me a beer for each round we complete?	☐	☐

34.3 請把下面的拼音跟上面的英文對上。/ 请把下面的拼音跟上面的英文对上。

____ 1. Wǒ huì dǎ yǔmáoqiú, dànshì bú huì dǎ wǎngqiú.

____ 2. Nǐ huì dǎ pīngpāngqiú ma?

____ 3. Nǐ tī zúqiú ma?

____ 4. Nǐ huì dǎ lánqiú ma?

____ 5. Jiǎofǎ búcuò!

____ 6. Wǒ xiǎoshíhou dǎguo pīngpāngqiú, dànshì hòulái jiù bù dǎ le.

____ 7. Nǐ huì dǎ yǔmáoqiú huòzhě wǎngqiú ma?

____ 8. Wǒ xǐhuan kàn lánqiú bǐsài, yóuqí shì Měiguó de NBA.

____ 9. Nǐ xǐhuan kàn qítā de yùndòng ma?

____ 10. Wǒmen duō yùndòng ba.

____ 11. Wǒ hái xǐhuan kàn wǔshù bǐsài.

____ 12. Wǒ yě xuéguo yìdiǎnr wǔshù.

____ 13. Měi pǎo yì quān nǐ qǐng wǒ hē yì píng píjiǔ?

____ 14. Wǒ xiǎo de shíhou wǒ de shǒuzhǐ shòushāng le, wǒ xiànzài bù zěnme dǎ.

____ 15. Wǒ yuánlái tī zúqiú, kěshì xiànzài nǎr yǒu shíjiān a?

34.4 請把上面的拼音與下面的漢字對上。／请把上面的拼音与下面的汉字对上。

____A. 你會打乒乓球嗎？／你会打乒乓球吗？

____B. 腳法不錯！／脚法不错！

____C. 你會打羽毛球或者網球嗎？／你会打羽毛球或者网球吗？

____D. 我也學過一點兒武術。／我也学过一点儿武术。

____E. 你會打籃球嗎？／你会打篮球吗？

____F. 你踢足球嗎？／你踢足球吗？

____G. 我小時候打過乒乓球，但是後來就不打了。／我小时候打过乒乓球，但是后来就不打了。

____H. 我小的時候我的手指受傷了，我現在不怎麼打。／我小的时候我的手指受伤了，我现在不怎么打。

____I. 我會打羽毛球，但是不會打網球。／我会打羽毛球，但是不会打网球。

____J. 每跑一圈你請我喝一瓶啤酒？／每跑一圈你请我喝一瓶啤酒？

____K. 我原來踢足球，可是現在哪兒有時間啊？／我原来踢足球，可是现在哪儿有时间啊？

____L. 我們多運動吧。／我们多运动吧。

____M. 你喜歡看其他的運動嗎？／你喜欢看其他的运动吗？

____N. 我喜歡看籃球比賽，尤其是美國的NBA。／我喜欢看篮球比赛，尤其是美国的NBA。

____O. 我還喜歡看武術比賽。／我还喜欢看武术比赛。

34.5 ***Pair work:*** *Talk to a partner and find out about his or her experiences with taking part in or watching sports. Some additional sports vocabulary (with the appropriate verb) is provided for your convenience. Take notes in the space provided. Report on what your partner tells you to someone else or to the class as a whole.*

yoga	zuò yújiā	做瑜伽	*skiing*	huáxuě	滑雪
volleyball	dǎ páiqiú	打排球	*surfing*	chōnglàng	衝浪／冲浪
baseball	dǎ bàngqiú	打棒球	*skateboarding*	huábǎn	滑板
softball	dǎ lěiqiú	打壘球／打垒球	*golf*	dǎ gāo'ěrfūqiú	打高爾夫球／打高尔夫球
field hockey	dǎ qūgùnqiú	打曲棍球	*(American) football*	tī Měishì zúqiú	踢美式足球

34.6 *Following is how Mick and Xiao Mao together describe the rules of soccer.* 請用英文填空。／请用英文填空。

問: 足球是甚麼規則?

答: 很簡單。

每一隊有十一個人,

有進攻球員,

還有防守球員,

還有守門員。

手不能碰球。

目標就是把球踢進對方的球門。

然後就得分了。

问: 足球是什么规则?

答: 很简单。

每一队有十一个人,

有进攻球员,

还有防守球员,

还有守门员。

手不能碰球。

目标就是把球踢进对方的球门。

然后就得分了。

Wèn: Zúqiú shì shénme guīzé?

Dá: Hěn jiǎndān.

Měi yí duì yǒu shí yī ge rén,

yǒu jìngōng qiúyuán,

hái yǒu fángshǒu qiúyuán,

hái yǒu shǒuményuán.

Shǒu bùnéng pèng qiú.

Mùbiāo jiùshì bǎ qiú tī jìn duìfāng de qiúmén.

Ránhòu jiù défēn le.

Q: *What are the rules for soccer?*

A: ______________________.

Each team ______________________;

there are offensive players,

and ______________________,

and a goalkeeper.

______________________.

The goal is to ______________________.

______________________.

34.7 *Mick and Xiao Mao compare soccer and (American) football and note that the difference (*區別／区别 qūbié*) is that in football, players can touch the ball with their hands and tackle other players. Reconstruct what they say by filling in each blank with the correct characters or pinyin.*

碰球 pèngqiú	美式足球 Měishì zúqiú
球員／球员 qiúyuán	撞擊／撞击 zhuàngjī

問: 足球和美式足球有甚麼區別呢？／

问: 足球和美式足球有什么区别呢？

Wèn: Zúqiú hé Měishì zúqiú yǒu shénme qūbié ne?

答: 區別在 _________ 可以用手 _________，還有，_________ 可以 _________ 別人。／

答: 区别在 _________ 可以用手 _________，还有，_________ 可以 _________ 别人。

Dá: Qūbié zài _________ kěyǐ yòng shǒu _________, hái yǒu, _________ kěyǐ _________ biéren.

34.8 *How would you describe the basic rules of basketball?* 請把英文跟中文對上。／请把英文跟中文对上。

____ a. lánqiú 籃球／篮球	1. *team*
____ b. tuánduì bǐsài 團隊比賽／团队比赛	2. *goal*
____ c. duì 隊／队	3. *opponent*
____ d. qiúyuán 球員／球员	4. *win*
____ e. mùbiāo 目標／目标	5. *basketball*
____ f. tóu jìn 投進／投进	6. *as much as possible*
____ g. duìfāng 對方／对方	7. *period*
____ h. lánkuāng 籃筐／篮筐	8. *tie*
____ i. jìnliàng 盡量／尽量	9. *player*

____ j. sānfēnxiàn 三分線／三分线
____ k. jié 節／节
____ l. yíng 赢
____ m. píngjú 平局
____ n. jiāshí 加時／加时

10. *team sport*
11. *basket hoop*
12. *overtime*
13. *throw into*
14. *three-point line*

Now work with a partner or small group to pool your knowledge of basketball. 請用中文填空。／请用中文填空。

篮球是团队比赛。有_____队，每队有_____个球员。比赛目标是把_____投进对方的篮筐里，同时尽量不让对方把球投进自己的篮筐里。投进一球得____分，三分线之外投进得____分。比赛一般分有四节，每节____分钟，一共是四十八分钟。最后得分多的那队赢了。如果打成平局，那就要打____分钟加时。

Check your work by turning your book upside down and rereading this description.

籃球是團隊比賽。有兩隊，每隊有五個球員。比賽目標是把球投進對方的籃筐裡，同時盡量不讓對方把球投進自己的籃筐裡。投進一球得兩分，三分線之外投進得三分。比賽一般分有四節，每節十二分鐘，一共是四十八分鐘。最後得分多的那隊贏了。如果打成平局，那就要打五分鐘加時。

34.9 ***Group work:*** *Find someone (or several people) interested in the same sport as you [are]. Work together to write a simple description of that sport. Ask for help or look online as necessary. Have your composition corrected, prepare a new draft, and share the final description with the rest of your class.*

34.10 ***Group work:*** *Mick and Xiao Mao agree that some countries seem to be particularly strong in certain sports.* 在2012年的倫敦奧運會，以下每個運動是哪個國家得到最多獎牌的？／在2012年的伦敦奥运会，以下每个运动是哪个国家得到最多奖牌的？ *Talk with a small group IN CHINESE to decide which nation to insert in each blank. Some sample sentences are included here:*

Lánqiú shì Měiguórén de tiānxià. 籃球是美國人的天下。／篮球是美国人的天下。

Pīngpāngqiú shì Zhōngguó zuì qiáng. 乒乓球是中國最強。／乒乓球是中国最强。

Yóuyǒng shì Měiguó yíng zuì duō jīnpái de. 游泳是美國贏最多金牌的。／游泳是美国赢最多金牌的。

Yǔmáoqiú shì Zhōngguódui dǎ de zuì hǎo. 羽毛球是中國隊打得最好。／羽毛球是中国队打得最好。

Nǐ tóngyì ma? 你同意嗎？/ 你同意吗？

Wǒ bù tóngyì, wǒ juéde nǐ cuò le. 我不同意，我覺得你错了。／我不同意，我觉得你错了。

Wǒ tóngyì. Wǒ yě zhème rènwéi. 我同意。我也這麼認為。／我同意。我也这么认为。

_____ a. shèjiàn 射箭 *archery*
_____ b. yǔmáoqiú 羽毛球 *badminton*
_____ c. lánqiú 籃球／篮球 *basketball*
_____ d. quánjī 拳擊／拳击 *boxing*
_____ e. qí chē 騎車／骑车 *cycling*
_____ f. tiàoshuǐ 跳水 *diving*
_____ g. mǎshù 馬術／马术 *equestrian arts*
_____ h. jījiàn 擊劍／击剑 *fencing*
_____ i. zúqiú 足球 *soccer*
_____ j. tǐcāo 體操／体操 *gymnastics*
_____ k. róudào 柔道 *judo*
_____ l. yóuyǒng 游泳 *swimming*
_____ m. pīngpāngqiú 乒乓球 *table tennis*
_____ n. wǎngqiú 網球／网球 *tennis*
_____ o. páiqiú 排球 *volleyball*
_____ p. shuāijiāo 摔跤 *wrestling*

1. 中國／中国
2. 英國／英国
3. 德國／德国
4. 意大利
5. 古巴
6. 西班牙
7. 日本
8. 俄羅斯／俄罗斯
9. 韓國／韩国
10. 美國／美国

Take turns testing a partner's recall. Ask questions such as, Shuāijiāo shì něi ge guójiā zuì qiáng? *and check the answer. Switch roles when done.*

34.11 *Mick and Xiao Mao make some comments on specific sports and sporting actions.* 請選英語填空。／请选英语填空。

competitions	*ball*	*terrible*	*can't really*	*beauty*	*footwork*	*soccer*

a. Jiǎofǎ búcuò ma! 腳法不错嘛!／脚法不错嘛!

Your ____________ is pretty good!

b. Wèishénme yào zhuīzhe yíge qiú pǎo lái pǎo qù? 為甚麼要追著一個球跑來跑去？／为什么要追着一个球跑来跑去？

Why would you want to go running around after a _________?

c. Nǐ zúqiú hěn lìhai. 你足球很厲害。／你足球很厉害。

You are really good at ___________.

d. Wǒ bù zěnme huì dǎ pīngpāngqiú. 我不怎麼會打乒乓球。／我不怎麼会打乒乓球。

I ________________ play table tennis.

e. Wǒ de jìshù hěn làn, jiùshì yíge càiniǎo. 我的技術很爛，就是一個菜鳥。／我的技术很烂，就是一个菜鸟。

My technique is ____________; I'm only a beginner.

f. Wǒ xǐhuan kàn wǔshù bǐsài, yīnwèi wǒ juéde wǔshù shì lì yǔ měi de jiéhé. 我喜歡看武術比賽, 因為我覺得武術是力與美的結合。／我喜欢看武术比赛, 因为我觉得武术是力与美的结合。

I like to watch martial arts ________________, because I think martial arts is a combination of strength and _______________.

34.12 ***Mingling:*** *Use the comments in Exercise 34.11 as a guide, or make up some of your own. Walk around the room and ask about each of the athletes below:* Nǐ juéde X zěnmeyàng? *In response, make a comment about that person or the sport he or she plays.*

Tiger Woods
Lǎohǔ Wǔzī
老虎伍兹／老虎伍兹

Serena Williams
Xiǎo Wēi
小威

Michael Phelps
Fēi'ěrpǔsī
菲爾普斯／菲尔普斯

LeBron James
Lè Bùlǎng Zhānmǔsī
勒布朗・詹姆斯

34.13 ***Pair work:*** *Have a free conversation with a partner for about 5–10 minutes about anything related to sports.*

Encounter 2 Having fun with martial arts

34.14 *Prof. Mao's class is about to tape a martial arts demonstration.* 請把中文跟英文對上。／请把中文跟英文对上。

____ a. wǔshù biǎoyǎn 武術表演／武术表演
____ b. fēicháng jīngcǎi 非常精彩
____ c. Wáng jiàoliàn 王教練／王教练
____ d. Běijīng Tǐyù Dàxué 北京體育大學／北京体育大学
____ e. Shàolínquán 少林拳
____ f. jiǎndān dòngzuò 簡單動作／简单动作
____ g. jīběn dòngzuò 基本動作／基本动作
____ h. gāo nándù de dòngzuò 高難度的動作／高难度的动作

1. *Coach Wang*
2. *Shaolin kung fu*
3. *simple moves*
4. *martial-arts performance*
5. *Beijing Sport University*
6. *very exciting, really excellent*
7. *moves of a high degree of difficulty*
8. *basic moves*

34.15 *View Episode 34, Vignette 2. Indicate whether Prof. Mao, Coach Wang, or Fang Lan makes each of the following statements (given in the order they are made).*

i.

ii.

iii.

____ a. OK, here we go, get ready! Ready . . . begin!
____ b. Ready! Go! Go! Go!
____ c. That's really excellent.
____ d. Thanks so much to you and your students for taking the time to participate in our program.
____ e. Coach Wang has been teaching martial arts at the Beijing Sport University.
____ f. He and his students often take part in competitions and demonstrations and have won multiple awards.
____ g. Chinese martial arts are vast and deep and have a long history.
____ h. Shaolin uses minimal force to deflect maximal force.
____ i. It takes a long period of training to attain such results.
____ j. This is the end of the interview.

34.16 請把下面的拼音跟上面的英文對上。／请把下面的拼音跟上面的英文对上。

____ 1. Zhōngguó de wǔshù bódàjīngshēn, lìshǐ yōujiǔ.

____ 2. Tā hé tā de xuéshengmen jīngcháng cānjiā yì xiē bǐsài hé biǎoyǎn, bìngqiě lǚcì huòjiǎng.

____ 3. Cǎifǎng jiù dào cǐ.

____ 4. Jīngguò chángshíjiān de xùnliàn cáinéng dádào zhè ge xiàoguǒ.

____ 5. Hǎo, lái, wǒmen zhǔnbèi! Yùbèi! Kāishǐ!

____ 6. Fēicháng gǎnxiè nín hé nín de xuésheng kěyǐ chōukòng lái cānjiā wǒmen de jiémù.

____ 7. Yùbèi! Zǒu! Zǒu! Zǒu!

____ 8. Wáng jiàoliàn yìzhí zài Běijīng Tǐyù Dàxué jiāoshòu wǔshù.

____ 9. Zhēn de hěn jīngcǎi.

____ 10. Shàolínquán yǐ sìliǎng bō qiānjīn.

34.17 請把下面的漢字跟上面的拼音對上。／请把下面的汉字跟上面的拼音对上。

____ A. 王教練一直在北京體育大學教授武術。／王教练一直在北京体育大学教授武术。

____ B. 真的很精彩。

____ C. 採訪就到此。／采访就到此。

____ D. 好，來，我們準備！預備！開始！／好，来，我们准备！预备！开始！

____ E. 非常感謝您和您的學生可以抽空來參加我們的節目。／非常感谢您和您的学生可以抽空来参加我们的节目。

____ F. 少林拳以四兩撥千斤。／少林拳以四两拨千斤。

____ G. 中國的武術博大精深，歷史悠久。／中国的武术博大精深，历史悠久。

____ H. 他和他的學生們經常參加一些比賽和表演，並且屢次獲獎。／他和他的学生们经常参加一些比赛和表演，并且屡次获奖。

____ I. 經過長時間的訓練才能達到這個效果。／经过长时间的训练才能达到这个效果。

____ J. 預備！走！走！走！／预备！走！走！走！

FYI 供你参考

Chinese martial arts

There are hundreds of schools and families of traditional Chinese martial arts. Coach Wang mentions three styles linked to famous mountains—the styles of Emei Mountain (峨眉山 *Éméishān*), Wudang Mountain (武當山／武当山 *Wǔdāngshān*); Mount Song (嵩山 *Sōngshān*), which is also home to the Shaolin Temple (少林寺 *Shàolínsì*); and Yong Chun (詠春／咏春 *Yǒngchūn*, "Wing Chun" in Cantonese), which is generally believed to be named for the woman who first practiced it. The Shaolin style is practiced by the warrior monks of Shaolin Temple and has been popularized by a series of films starring Jet Li. The Yong Chun style was practiced by Bruce Lee and Ip Man. Wudang martial arts, including "internal" and "external" practice, is popular at many training centers in the United States.

34.18 *Coach Wang makes some brief introductory statements about martial arts, states that there are different styles, identifies their performance here as Shaolin martial arts, and then briefly describes this style. Put the following phrases in the correct order to yield the statement "The sequence we performed just now belongs to the Shaolin style" (literally, "Shaolin fist").*

zhè yí tào	suǒ biǎoyǎn de	shì shǔyú Shàolínquán	wǒmen gāngcái
這一套／这一套	所表演的	是屬於少林拳／是属于少林拳	我們剛才／我们刚才
______	______	______	______

34.19 *Match the Chinese with the English, and then indicate whether the phrases describe (I) martial arts in general, or (II) Shaolin martial arts.*

		I	II
a. yǐlì-huánlì 以力還力／以力还力	1. *profound (literally, broad-vast-refined-deep)*	☐	☐
b. bódàjīngshēn 博大精深	2. *have a long history*	☐	☐
c. duǎnxiǎo jīngzhàn 短小精湛	3. *return force with force*	☐	☐
d. lìshǐ yōujiǔ 歷史悠久／历史悠久	4. *divided into many styles*	☐	☐
e. fēn hěn duō ménpài 分很多門派／分很多门派	5. *deflect maximal force using minimal energy (literally, using four ounces to set aside a thousand catties [a weight])*	☐	☐
f. yǐ sìliǎng bō qiānjīn 以四兩撥千斤／以四两拨千斤	6. *short and penetrating (literally, short-small-fine-deep)*	☐	☐

34.20 ***Pair work:*** *Have a brief conversation in Chinese with a partner about Chinese martial arts. You can talk about the demonstration from the video, Coach Wang's remarks, or some previous experience or knowledge you have of martial arts. If there is time, report in Chinese on your conversation to a group or the class.*

Encounter 3 Reading and writing

Reading real-life texts

34.21 *If you do a search on "少林寺" on* images.baidu.com, *you may find the following photograph with the attached caption.* 用英文填空。

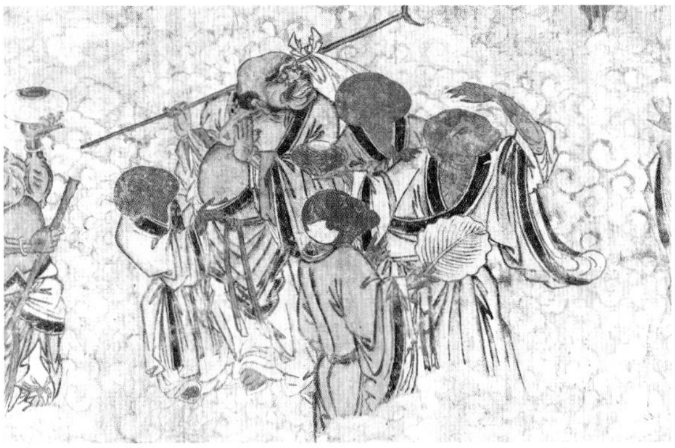

国内旅游推荐——不到少林寺就不算来到河南

Guónèi lǚyóu tuījiàn——bú dào Shàolínsì jiù bú suàn lái dào Hénán

Domestic tourism recommendation—If you don't visit the Shaolin Temple, you can't say

______________________________.

34.22 *The following are screen shots from a martial arts school website.* 請填空。／请填空。

a Chóngwǔ zhuānyè ______________

___________ zhāoshēng _____

Chongwu Professional Martial Arts School recruitment site

b 1. _________ miǎnfèi bàomíng zhuānxiàn: 4000-555-678 (jǐn shōu shì huà fèi)

National ____________ registration line: 4000-555-678 (only local call fee assessed)

全国免费报名专线：4000-555-678（仅收市话费）
24 小时咨询电话：15106555789

2. 24 _______ zīxún _______________: 15106555789 ___________ *inquiry telephone: 15106555789*

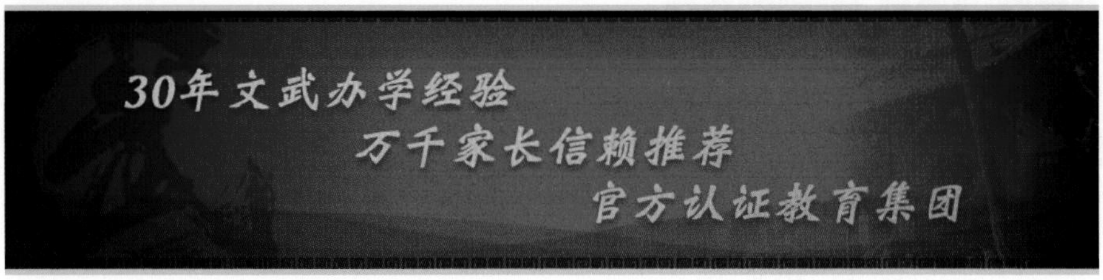

c 30 nián wénwǔ bànxué jīngyàn

wànqiān jiāzhǎng xìnlài tuījiàn

guānfāng rènzhèng jiàoyù jítuán

______________ *experience in offering education in civil and military arts*

Trusted and recommended by hundreds of thousands of parents

Officially certified ____________ *group*

d ________dǎoháng	*Service directory (literally, navigation)*
__________ __________	*Online registration*
__________ jiǎnzhāng	*Recruitment brochure*
__________ jiǎnjiè	*Overview of the* _____________
__________ biāozhǔn	*Fee schedule (literally, standards)*
_________ zīxún ________	__________ *inquiry* ___________
4000-555-678	*4000-555-678*

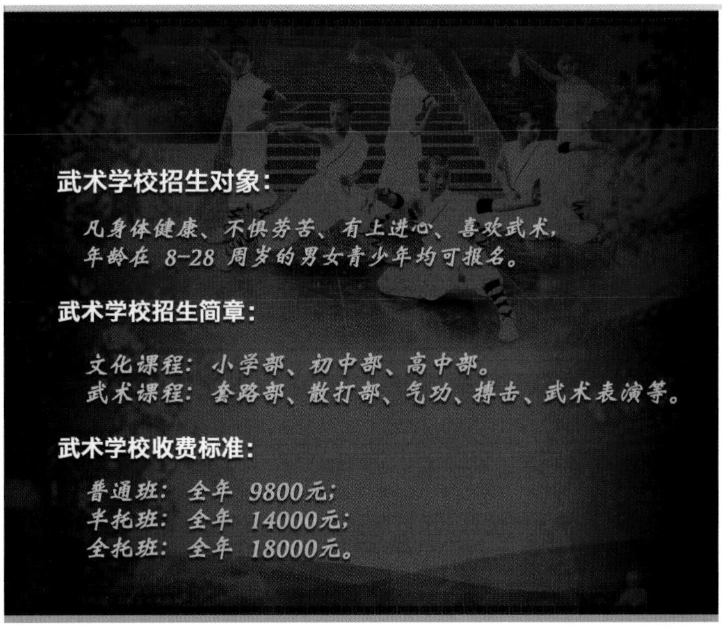
武术学校招生对象：
凡身体健康、不惧劳苦、有上进心、喜欢武术，
年龄在 8–28 周岁的男女青少年均可报名。
武术学校招生简章：
文化课程：小学部、初中部、高中部。
武术课程：套路部、散打部、气功、搏击、武术表演等。
武术学校收费标准：
普通班：全年 9800元；
半托班：全年 14000元；
全托班：全年 18000元。

e __________ __________ **zhāoshēng duìxiàng:**

Fán __________ jiànkāng, bújù láokǔ, yǒu shàngjìnxīn, __________ __________, niánlíng zài 8–28 zhōusuì de __________ qīngshàonián jūn kě __________.

__________ **xuéxiào** __________ **jiǎnzhāng:**

__________ kèchéng: xiǎoxuébù, __________, __________.

__________ __________: tàolùbù, sǎndǎ____, qìgōng, bójī, __________ __________ děng.

__________ __________ __________ **biāozhǔn:**

pǔtōngbān: __________ 9800 yuán;

bàntuōbān: quánnián 14000 yuán;

__________: quánnián 18000 yuán.

Martial arts school recruitment target:

All boys and girls aged __________ who are healthy, not afraid of hard work, self-motivated, and like __________, are eligible to __________.

Martial arts school recruitment brochure:

Cultural curriculum: elementary school section, __________ section, __________ section.

Martial arts __________: routines section, sparring section, Qigong, fighting, martial arts performance, etc.

Fee schedule of the __________:

regular class: ¥9,800 for the year;

half-residential class: ¥14,000 __________;

full-residential class: ¥18,000 for the year.

f *Finally, the website features this clickable link. Why would you want to click here?*

____

Reading a story

34.23 故事 *Find the following terms in either the traditional or simplified text and circle them. Write in the accompanying number.*

1. Lín Shūháo *Jeremy Lin*
2. zhíyè *professional*
3. zhōngqī *middle period*
4. yímín *emigrate*
5. shēng yú *be born on*
6. Luòshānjī *Los Angeles*
7. zhīhòu *later; afterward*
8. Pàluò'ā'ěrtuō Zhèn *Palo Alto*
9. kàojìn *close to*
10. Jiùjīnshān *San Francisco*
11. mǐ *meter*
12. yéye *(paternal) grandfather*
13. shēngāo *height (of a person)*
14. chāoguò *surpass; exceed*

15. duìzhǎng *captain*
16. chéngjì *grades*
17. rùxuǎn *be chosen*
18. Jiāzhōu *California*
19. mǒu ge *a certain*
20. xiàngmù *program*
21. rú *such as; for example*
22. Sītǎnfú *Stanford*
23. fēnxiào *branch campus*
24. Bókèlì *Berkeley*
25. shíxiàn *realize; achieve; bring about*
26. Hāfó *Harvard*
27. lùqǔ *admit; recruit*
28. chūsè *outstanding*
29. dàsì *college senior*
30. shuāxīn *break a record*
31. xiàng *measure word for items, clauses, etc.*
32. xiào jìlù *school record*
33. píngjūn chéngjì *grade point average*
34. huòdé *gain; achieve*
35. xuéshì *B.A. degree*
36. xuéwèi *academic degree*

37. Jīnzhōu Yǒngshì duì *Golden State Warriors*
38. qiānxià *sign*
39. héyuē *contract*
40. cóngcǐ *henceforth*
41. xuètǒng *blood relationship; lineage*
42. niánxīn *annual salary*
43. fěnsī *fan*
44. shǒu pèngdào qiú *hand touches the ball*
45. dàshēng *loudly*
46. huānhū *cheer*
47. sàijì *sports competition season*
48. jiārù *join*
49. Níkèsī *Knicks*
50. miǎo *second*
51. shènglì *win*
52. shíkè *moment; time*
53. Lín lái fēng *"Linsanity"*
54. kǒuhào *slogan*
55. dànshēng *come into being*

56. shìjiè zhīmíng *world-famous*
57. Xiūsīdùn *Houston*
58. Huǒjiàn duì *Rockets*
59. Yàzhōu bǎn *Asian edition*
60. fēngmiàn *cover*
61. jìlùpiàn *documentary film*
62. pāishè *shoot (a film)*
63. bìng *and*
64. fāxíng *distribute*
65. qiānxū *modest; unassuming*
66. qiánchéng *pious; devout*
67. Jīdūtú *Christian*
68. wèi(le) N ér V *to V on behalf of N*
69. róngyào *glory*

林書豪 (Jeremy Lin) 是個職業籃球運動員。 他父母在70年代中期從臺灣移民到美國。林書豪生於1988年8月23日，在洛杉磯附近，之後在帕洛阿爾托鎮（靠近舊金山）長大。他有一個哥哥、一個弟弟。雖然他的父母只有 5 尺 6 寸（1.68米）高，不過他母親的爺爺身高超過了6 尺（1.8米）。 林書豪本人有6 尺 3 寸（1.91米）高。

林书豪 (Jeremy Lin) 是个职业篮球运动员。 他父母在70年代中期从台湾移民到美国。林书豪生于1988年8月23日，在洛杉矶附近，之后在帕洛阿尔托镇（靠近旧金山）长大。他有一个哥哥、一个弟弟。虽然他的父母只有 5 尺 6 寸 （1.68米）高，不过他母亲的爷爷身高超过了6 尺 （1.8米）。 林书豪本人有6 尺 3 寸 （1.91米）高。

他上中學就開始打籃球，並成了他們高中隊的隊長。而且他學習成績也很好，所以他很希望能夠入選加州某個大學的籃球項目，如斯坦福大學，加州大學洛杉磯分校和加州大學伯克利分校。但他的希望沒能實現。最後，他被哈佛大學錄取了。他在哈佛籃球隊的第一年不是特別出色，但每過一年都好一些。他上大四那年，幫助哈佛隊刷新了多項校紀錄。他2010畢業的那年，平均成績是3.1，並且獲得了經濟學學士學位。

他上中学就开始打篮球，并成了他们高中队的队长。而且他学习成绩也很好，所以他很希望能够入选加州某个大学的篮球项目，如斯坦福大学，加州大学洛杉矶分校和加州大学伯克利分校。但他的希望没能实现。最后，他被哈佛大学录取了。他在哈佛篮球队的第一年不是特别出色，但每过一年都好一些。他上大四那年，帮助哈佛队刷新了多项校纪录。他2010毕业的那年，平均成绩是3.1，并且获得了经济学学士学位。

2010年金州勇士隊與他簽下合約，從此他成了NBA第一位有中國血統的球

2010年金州勇士队与他签下合约，从此他成了NBA第一位有中国血统的球

員。那年他的年薪在50萬美元左右。從那以後他的粉絲也開始迅速增加了。他在舊金山比賽時，每次手碰到球，觀眾們都會大聲歡呼。2011－12賽季，林書豪加入了紐約尼克斯隊。2012年2月14日，他在比賽的最後幾秒鐘投進了一個3分球，幫助尼克斯隊取得了比賽的勝利。在那一時刻，"林來瘋"的口號誕生了。

林書豪開始變得世界知名了。2012－14年，他加入了休斯頓的火箭隊，並在2014年被洛杉磯的湖人隊以1500萬美元的年薪簽了下來。林書豪已經兩次登上了《體育畫報》的封面，還上過一次《時代雜誌》（亞洲版）的封面。2013年，有一部叫《林來瘋》的紀錄片被拍攝並發行。但林書豪仍然很謙虛。他一直都是一個很虔誠的基督徒。他只是說："我就是想打籃球，想好好地打，為了上帝的榮耀而打。"

员。那年他的年薪在50万美元左右。从那以后他的粉丝也开始迅速增加了。他在旧金山比赛时，每次手碰到球，观众们都会大声欢呼。2011-12赛季，林书豪加入了纽约尼克斯队。2012年2月14日，他在比赛的最后几秒钟投进了一个3分球，帮助尼克斯队取得了比赛的胜利。在那一时刻，"林来疯"的口号诞生了。

林书豪开始变得世界知名了。2012－14年，他加入了休斯顿的火箭队，并在2014年被洛杉矶的湖人队以1500万美元的年薪签了下来。林书豪已经两次登上了《体育画报》的封面，还上过一次《时代杂志》（亚洲版）的封面。2013年，有一部叫《林来疯》的纪录片被拍摄并发行。但林书豪仍然很谦虚。他一直都是一个很虔诚的基督徒。他只是说："我就是想打篮球，想好好地打，为了上帝的荣耀而打。"

34.24 *Do you have a favorite sports figure? Write a brief biography of this person, using the description of Jeremy Lin as a model.*

Encounter 4 Extension: Cultural mini-documentary

View the cultural mini-documentary for this unit and complete the exercises that follow.

34.25 *This five-minute video begins with shots of several leisure activities enjoyed by elderly people at* 龍潭湖公園／龙潭湖公园 Lóngtánhú Gōngyuán, *one of Beijing's major parks, and it continues with a monologue by the president of an "amity club"* (友情俱樂部／友情俱乐部 yǒuqíng jùlèbù) *that meets in the park. Write numbers in the blanks to indicate the order in which the following leisure activities are shown in the first half-minute of the video.*

____ tī jiànzi 踢毽子 *(Hint: a shuttlecock is involved)*

____ dǎ Tàijíjiàn 打太極劍／打太极剑 *(Hint: a weapon is involved)*

____ dǎ Tàijíquán 打太極拳／打太极拳

____ dǎ pīngpāngqiú 打乒乓球

____ dǒu kōngzhú 抖空竹 *(Hint: it makes a humming noise)*

34.26 *Based on the president's monologue, can you figure out the answers to the following questions? The questions are ordered to match the content, so try pausing the video to answer each question before continuing on with the next question.*

a. (0:31–0:45) *The things he does as leader of the club include* 服務／服务 fúwù、管理 guǎnlǐ、協調／协调 xiétiáo.

☐ *competing, judging, and organizing* ☐ *chatting, entertaining, and socializing*
☐ *coaching, training, and refereeing* ☐ *serving, managing, and coordinating*

b. (0:45–2:05) *Mark the following statements* Zhēnde 真的 *(true) or* Jiǎde 假的 *(false).*

	Zhēnde 真的	**Jiǎde** 假的
1. He is 62 years old.	☐	☐
2. He has played table tennis here for more than ten years.	☐	☐
3. He has always liked playing ball sports.	☐	☐
4. He thinks it's a good fitness regimen (健身項目／健身项目 *jiànshēn xiàngmù*).	☐	☐
5. Usually in the mornings, more than 50 club members are active here.	☐	☐
6. The place is full morning, noon, and night.	☐	☐
7. The club supplied all the tables, fences, and seating.	☐	☐
8. The park administration supplies the nets, paddles, and balls.	☐	☐
9. Aside from table tennis, the club also sponsors other sports, such as shuttlecock kicking (similar to hacky sack).	☐	☐
10. The club also sponsors travel excursions, with more than ten trips this year, mostly to the nearby countryside.	☐	☐

c. (2:05–2:45) *The factors he mentions as reasons for China's international dominance in table tennis include*

- ☐ *its suitability to the Chinese temperament, its resource efficiency, and its simplicity.*
- ☐ *its popularization in society, state-sponsored training from a young age, and the strength of regional teams.*
- ☐ *its role in diplomacy, its competitive psychology, and its intensity.*
- ☐ *its audience appeal, its universality, and its emphasis on efficiency of movement.*

d. (2:45–3:00) *The club welcomes foreigners and has hosted friends from*

- ☐ *France, Senegal, and South Africa.*
- ☐ *Japan, Thailand, and India.*
- ☐ *Sweden, Russia, and England.*
- ☐ *Spain, Ecuador, and Canada.*

e. (3:00–3:30) *In elaborating on the welcome the club offers to foreigners, the president refers to China as* 禮儀之邦／礼仪之邦 lǐyí zhī bāng, *a nation of*

- ☐ *courtesy.*
- ☐ *generosity.*
- ☐ *friendliness.*
- ☐ *candor.*

f. (3:30–4:00) *He explains that the club does not hold many competitions because they would rather stress* 健身 jiànshēn *and* 娛樂／娱乐 yúlè—*that is,*

- ☐ *fitness and amusement.*
- ☐ *nutrition and harmony.*
- ☐ *bodybuilding and personal grooming.*
- ☐ *technique and strategy.*

g. (4:00–4:30) *He expresses the idea that each park has its own distinct characteristics (including the sports most people pursue there). He uses the phrase*

- ☐ Měi ge gōngyuán yǒu zìjǐ de tèsè.
- ☐ Měi ge gōngyuán yǒu tā de tèsè.
- ☐ Měi ge gōngyuán dōu hěn yǒu tèsè.
- ☐ Měi ge gōngyuán yǒu měi ge gōngyuán de tèsè.

h. (4:30–end) *A television station asked practitioners from three parks to demonstrate their leisure sports on a show. Match each park with the sport from that park.*

____ 1. *Dragon Pool Lake* (龍潭湖／龙潭湖) *Park*	A. *shuttlecock kicking*
____ 2. *Altar of Heaven* (天壇／天坛) *Park*	B. *table tennis*
____ 3. *North Lake* (北海) *Park*	C. *giant yo-yo / diabolo*

Recap

Grammar

Double-duty verbs: Resultative complements

This unit has many examples of resultative verbs (RV), a form you have seen many times before, where verb one (V1), the root, is followed by verb two (V2). V1, the base verb, expresses the primary action (for example, *chī* 吃 eat), whereas V2 shows the result or the extent of the action (for example, *bǎo* 飽／饱 be full).

我吃飽了。／我吃饱了。
I am full. (literally, I ate until I was full.)

If there is an *object*, it always follows V2 (我看完那本書了／我看完那本书了) or stands in the transposed position (那本書我看完了／那本书我看完了).

There are two types of resultative complements:

1. actual, in which the result or extent has been actually attained (我聽懂了／我听懂了)
2. potential, in which the result or extent of the action is conceived of as being possible or impossible to attain. This type is formed by inserting the infix 得 for the positive or 不 for the negative. (我聽得懂，我聽不懂，你聽得懂聽不懂？／我听得懂，我听不懂，你听得懂听不懂？)

CAUTION: Not all compound verbs are resultative. For example, see the compounds 聽説／听说, 認識／认识, 明白, and 預備／预备. The test is whether or not the compound can be converted into the potential type or not. Therefore, *聽不説／听不说 does not work.

Exercise: Provide full answers to the questions, showing your understanding of the meanings of the verbal complements.

1. Zhè ge dìfang wǒmen jìndeqù kěshì chūbùlái.
   這個地方我們進得去可是出不來。／这个地方我们进得去可是出不来。
   What's really strange about this place?

   ____

2. Nà fēng xìn wǒ shōudào le, kěshì qíguài, xìn shang yí ge zì yě méiyǒu.
   那封信我收到了，可是奇怪，信上一個字也沒有。／那封信我收到了，可是奇怪，信上一个字也没有。
   What's odd about this letter?

   ____

3. Dōngxi dōu chīwán le, kěshì wǒ hái méi chībǎo ne.
   東西都吃完了，可是我還沒吃飽呢。／东西都吃完了，可是我还没吃饱呢。
   What is this diner's problem?

   ____

4. Zuótiān wǒ shuìguòtóu le, kěshì hái méi shuìgòu.
   昨天我睡過頭了，可是還沒睡夠。／昨天我睡过头了，可是还没睡够。
   What is this person's problem?

   ____

5. Zhè ge wūzi tài hēi le, shénme dōu kànbújiàn. Lākāi chuānglián ba!
   這個屋子太黑了，甚麼都看不見。拉開窗簾吧！／这个屋子太黑了，什么都看不见。拉开窗帘吧！
   What is this person's problem? And what is the solution suggested?

   ____

6. Xué Hànzì duì wǒ lái shuō hěn nán, yǒu de xiěbùhǎo, yǒu de jìbúzhù, hái yǒu hěn duō kànbùdǒng, zhēn méi bànfǎ.
學漢字對我來說很難，有的寫不好，有的記不住，還有很多看不懂，真没辦法。／学汉字对我来说很难，有的写不好，有的记不住，还有很多看不懂，真没办法。
What are this student's problems with Chinese characters? Is he/she hopeful?

____

7. Nà běn shū mài de fēicháng hǎo, nǐ xiǎng mǎi, kǒngpà mǎibúdào.
那本書賣得非常好，你想買，恐怕買不到。／那本书卖得非常好，你想买，恐怕买不到。
What's the likelihood that the person addressed will be able to buy the book?

____

8. Wǒ jīntiān bù shūfu, hěn è, kěshì shénme dōu chībúxià.
我今天不舒服，很餓，可是甚麼都吃不下。／我今天不舒服，很饿，可是什么都吃不下。
This person is unwell. What's his/her major symptom?

____

9. Nà ge lǎoshī de wàiguó kǒuyīn tài zhòng. Tā shuō de huà, wǒ yí jù yě tīngbùdǒng. Tā xiě de zì, wǒ yě kànbùchūlái shì shénme yìsi.
那個老師的外國口音太重。他說的話，我一句也聽不懂。他寫的字，我也看不出來是甚麼意思。／那个老师的外国口音太重。他说的话，我一句也听不懂。他写的字，我也看不出来是什么意思。
This student might have some trouble passing this course. Why is that?

____

10. Tāmen míngtiān huídelái ma? Kǒngpà huíbùlái, yīnwèi tāmen yào zǒu de lù hái hěn yuǎn.
他們明天回得來嗎？恐怕回不來，因為他們要走的路還很遠。／他们明天回得来吗？恐怕回不来，因为他们要走的路还很远。
Can the people being discussed make their appointment tomorrow? If not, why not?

____

Vocabulary

Please refer to page R-2 for a list of grammatical abbreviations used throughout this book.

Àoyùnhuì 奧運會／奥运会 *abbr. for* **Àolínpǐkè Yùndònghuì** 奧林匹克運動會／奥林匹克运动会 Olympic Games N

bàngqiú 棒球 baseball N

biān V1 biān V2 邊V1邊V2／边V1边V2 do V1 and V2 simultaneously C

biǎoyǎn 表演 performance; exhibition N; perform; act; demonstrate V

bǐsài 比賽／比赛 match; competition N

bódà 博大 broad; extensive; wide-ranging VP

càiniǎo 菜鳥／菜鸟 beginner; rookie; somebody new to a subject or activity N

chōnglàng 衝浪／冲浪 surf VO; surfing N

défēn 得分 score VO

dòngzuò 動作／动作 movement; motion; action; moves N

duǎnxiǎo 短小 brief VP

duì 隊／队 team N

duìfāng 對方／对方 adversary; the other side N

fángshǒuqiúyuán 防守球員／防守球员 defensive player N

fēn 分 divide; separate; allot V

gāo'ěrfūqiú 高爾夫球／高尔夫球 golf *(loan word)* N/PL

huábǎn 滑板 skateboarding N

huáxuě 滑雪 skiing N; ski V

jiǎngpái 獎牌／奖牌 prize medal N

jiǎofǎ 腳法／脚法 footwork/kicking skill *(in soccer)* N

jiàoliàn 教練／教练 coach; instructor N

jiāshí 加時／加时 overtime *(in sports)* N

jīběn 基本 basic; fundamental; elementary SV/N

jié 節／节 segment; part; period *(in a game)* M

jiéhé 結合／结合 fusion; combination N; combine; link; unite V

jiēzhù 接住 catch *(something thrown)* RV

jījiàn 擊劍／击剑 fencing *(sport)* N

jīngcǎi 精彩 brilliant; splendid; wonderful; excellent SV

jìngōngqiúyuán 進攻球員／进攻球员 offensive player N

jīngshēn 精深 profound; penetrating VP

jīngzhàn 精湛 exquisite; fine SV

jìnliàng 盡量／尽量 to the best of one's ability; as far as possible A

jīnpái 金牌 gold medal N

jìshù 技術／技术 skill; technique N

làn 爛／烂 rotten; really bad *(usually of fruit or other foods, but here denoting lack of skill)* SV

lánkuāng 籃筐／篮筐 basket; rim of a basket N

lánqiú 籃球／篮球 basketball N

lěiqiú 壘球／垒球 softball N

lì yǔ měi 力與美／力与美 strength and beauty N

lìhai 厲害／厉害 tough; capable; sharp SV

Lúndūn 倫敦／伦敦 London PW

mànpǎo 慢跑 jog; go jogging N/V

mǎshù 馬術／马术 horsemanship; equestrian arts N

Měishì zúqiú 美式足球 American football N

ménpài 門派／门派 sect; schools N

mùbiāo 目標／目标 goal; target; objective N

nándù 難度／难度 (degree of) difficulty N

páiqiú 排球 volleyball N

pèng 碰 touch V

píngjú 平局 draw; tie *(in sports, chess, etc.)* N

pīngpāngqiú 乒乓球 table tennis N

qí chē 騎車／骑车 bicycling N; ride a bicycle VO

qiáng 強／强 strong; powerful SV

qítā 其他 other(s); the rest PR

qiúmén 球門／球门 goal N

qiúyuán 球員／球员 player; team member N

quān 圈 *(lap around a track)* M

quánjī 拳擊／拳击 boxing N

qūbié 區別／区别 difference; distinction N; differentiate V

qūgùnqiú 曲棍球 field hockey N

róudào 柔道 judo N

shàng 上 go to V

Shàolínquán 少林拳 Shaolin form of boxing N

Shàolínsì 少林寺 (Buddhist) Shaolin Temple, Henan Province, China; the cradle of Chinese martial arts PW

shèjiàn 射箭 archery N; shoot arrows VO

shǒuményuán 守門員／守门员 goalie; goalkeeper N

shuāijiāo 摔跤 wrestling N; wrestle V

shǔyú 屬於／属于 belong to; be a part of V

tào 套 *(for sets, series, etc.)* M

tī jìn 踢進／踢进 kick into RV

tī zúqiú 踢足球 play soccer/football VO

tiānxià 天下 world; dominion; territory N

tiàoshuǐ 跳水 diving N; dive into the water VO

tǐcāo 體操／体操 gymnastics; calisthenics N

tīhuíqu 踢回去 kick back *(in soccer, etc.)* RV

tǐyù 體育／体育 physical education/training; sports N

tóu jìn 投進／投进 throw into RV

tuánduì 團隊／团队 team N

wǎngqiú 網球／网球 tennis N

wǔshù 武術／武术 martial arts N

xiàn 線／线 line; boundary N

yǐ lì huán lì 以力還力／以力还力 return **(huán)** force **(lì)** with **(yǐ)** force **(lì)** IE

yǐ sì liǎng bō qiān jīn 以四兩撥千斤／以四两拨千斤 move **(bō)** 1,000 **(qiān)** catties **(jīn)** with **(yǐ)** four **(sì)** ounces **(liǎng)** = Give me a lever and I will move the earth. IE

yìbān 一般 generally; ordinarily; usually A

yíng 贏／赢 win; gain V

yōujiǔ 悠久 long in time; long-standing; age-old SV

yóuqíshì 尤其是 especially VP

yóuyǒng 游泳 swimming N; swim V

yǔmáoqiú 羽毛球 badminton; feathercock N

zhuàngjī 撞擊／撞击 dash against; strike *(here: tackle)* V

zhuī 追 chase; pursue; run after V

zuò yújiā 做瑜伽 do/perform yoga *(loan word)* VO

zúqiú 足球 football; soccer N

Checklist of "can do" statements

After completing this unit, you should be able to perform each of the following tasks:

Listening and speaking

- ☐ Talk about sports.
- ☐ Make comments during sporting events.
- ☐ Comment about your own engagement with sports.
- ☐ Describe the rules of a favorite sport.
- ☐ Comment on which countries are particularly strong in certain sports.
- ☐ Comment on a key sports figure.
- ☐ Comment on Chinese martial arts.

Reading and writing

- ☐ Decipher some key details from a Chinese martial arts website.
- ☐ Comprehend a short story about a sports figure.
- ☐ Write a short story of your own.

Understanding culture

- ☐ Make some observations about physical activities people enjoy in Beijing's public spaces.

UNIT

35

"Every walk of life produces a virtuoso"

三百六十行，行行出狀元

Sānbǎi liùshí háng, háng háng chū zhuàngyuán

The ideal career

In this unit, you will learn how to:

- talk about any work you did in the past or that you do now.
- describe what you like and dislike about your work.
- describe your ideal career, including what you hope to have as compensation.
- decipher some items on pages of a Chinese employment website.
- read a story about the professional career of a comedian and actor.
- write a story about a favorite comedian or actor.
- make some accurate comments about common Chinese careers.
- make some accurate comments about what should appear on a Chinese résumé.

Encounter 1 Discussing career aspirations

35.1 *Fang Lan and Xiao Mao talk after class.* 請把中文和英文對上。／请把中文和英文对上。

____ a. yèyú shíjiān 業餘時間／业余时间	1. *specialized internship*
____ b. zhuānyè shíxí 專業實習／专业实习	2. *a job in media*
____ c. jīhuì 機會／机会	3. *important*
____ d. zhíyè 職業／职业	4. *professional guidance*
____ e. chuánméi gōngzuò 傳媒工作／传媒工作	5. *extracurricular time*
____ f. nǎ fāngmiàn de gōngzuò 哪方面的工作	6. *profession*
____ g. méitǐ gōngsī 媒體公司／媒体公司	7. *a job in what area*
____ h. zhuānyè zhǐdǎo 專業指導／专业指导	8. *media company*
____ i. zhòngyào 重要	9. *opportunity*

35.2 *View Episode 35, Vignette 1. Xiao Mao is offering Fang Lan an opportunity at an internship. Indicate who says each of the following sentences.*

	小毛	方蘭／方兰
a. Wait up a moment.	☐	☐
b. Are you offering me a chance at an internship?	☐	☐
c. I would like a job in something like communications.	☐	☐
d. In the past, I wanted to make my own movies.	☐	☐
e. My parents hoped I could become a scientist.	☐	☐
f. I prefer to have interactions with people.	☐	☐
g. The competition is too intense in the business world.	☐	☐
h. It is nothing more than contracts, deadlines, and cash flow.	☐	☐
i. You're really someone with ambitions and ideals.	☐	☐

j. Taking part in a professional internship before getting a real job lets you know what it is you really want.	☐	☐
k. You can call him directly.	☐	☐
l. All the students are waiting for you.	☐	☐

35.3 請把下面的拼音跟上面的英文對上。／请把下面的拼音跟上面的英文对上。

____ 1. Wǒ bǐjiào xǐhuan hé rén jiāoliú.

____ 2. Yǐqián wǒ xiǎng zìjǐ pāi diànyǐng.

____ 3. Shāo děng yíxià.

____ 4. Shāngyèjiè de jìngzhēng tài jīliè le.

____ 5. Nǐ shì yí ge yǒu bàofù yǒu lǐxiǎng de rén.

____ 6. Nín gěi wǒ jièshào shíxí de jīhuì ma?

____ 7. Nǐ kěyǐ zhíjiē gěi tā dǎ diànhuà.

____ 8. Wǒ xiǎng zuò chuánméi lèi de gōngzuò.

____ 9. Zài zhèngshì gōngzuò qián cānjiā zhuānyè shíxí cáinéng zhīdào zìjǐ zhēnzhèng xiǎng yào de shìshénme.

____ 10. Jiùshì yì xiē hétong, qīxiàn, xiànjīn liú.

____ 11. Tóngxuémen dōu zài děng nǐ.

____ 12. Wǒ bàmā xīwàng wǒ néng zuò yí ge kēxuéjiā.

35.4 請把下面的漢字跟上面的拼音對上。／请把下面的汉字跟上面的拼音对上。

____ A. 以前我想自己拍電影。／以前我想自己拍电影。

____ B. 我比較喜歡和人交流。／我比较喜欢和人交流。

____ C. 就是一些合同、期限、現金流。／就是一些合同、期限、现金流。

____ D. 我想做傳媒類的工作。／我想做传媒类的工作。

____ E. 您給我介紹實習的機會嗎？／您给我介绍实习的机会吗？

____ F. 在正式工作前參加專業實習，才能知道自己真正想要的是甚麼。／在正式工作前参加专业实习，才能知道自己真正想要的是什么。

____ G. 稍等一下。

____H. 商業界的競爭太激烈了。／商业界的竞争太激烈了。

____I. 同學們都在等你。／同学们都在等你。

____J. 你是一個有抱負有理想的人。／你是一个有抱负有理想的人。

____K. 你可以直接給他打電話。／你可以直接给他打电话。

____L. 我爸媽希望我能做一個科學家。／我爸妈希望我能做一个科学家。

35.5 *What are you looking for in your career? Most people seek a type of work that . . .*

a. provides an opportunity to grow in knowledge and skill.

b. offers a high salary and good benefits.

c. offers meaning and satisfaction.

d. is stable.

How would you express these aspirations in Chinese? 請把下面的拼音與上面的英文對上。／请把下面的拼音与上面的英文对上。

____ 1. Wǒ xīwàng yǒu yí fèn gōngzī gāo, fúlì hǎo de gōngzuò.

____ 2. Wǒ xīwàng yǒu yí fèn néng zhǎng zhīshi hé jìnéng de gōngzuò.

____ 3. Wǒ xīwàng yǒu yí fèn wěndìng de gōngzuò.

____ 4. Wǒ xīwàng yǒu yí fèn yǒu yìyì, néng ràng rén mǎnyì de gōngzuò.

請再把下面的漢字與上面的拼音對上。／请再把下面的汉字与上面的拼音对上。

____A. 我希望有一份能長知識和技能的工作。／我希望有一份能长知识和技能的工作。

____B. 我希望有一份穩定的工作。／我希望有一份稳定的工作。

____C. 我希望有一份工資高、福利好的工作。／我希望有一份工资高、福利好的工作。

____D. 我希望有一份有意義、能讓人滿意的工作。／我希望有一份有意义、能让人满意的工作。

35.6 *The most popular careers after graduation from college are in the following fields.*
請把英文與拼音對上。／请把英文与拼音对上。

a. Management
b. Sales and Marketing
c. Law
d. Information Technology
e. Engineering and Architecture
f. Health Care
g. Business and Financial
h. Graphic Design
i. Research and Development
j. Education and Training
k. Communications

____ 1. Wǒ xiǎng zuò chuánméi fāngmiàn de gōngzuò.
____ 2. Wǒ xiǎng zuò gōngchéng yǔ jiànzhù fāngmiàn de gōngzuò.
____ 3. Wǒ xiǎng zuò yánjiū yǔ kāifā fāngmiàn de gōngzuò.
____ 4. Wǒ xiǎng zuò guǎnlǐ fāngmiàn de gōngzuò.
____ 5. Wǒ xiǎng zuò shāngwù yǔ jīnróng fāngmiàn de gōngzuò.
____ 6. Wǒ xiǎng zuò jiàoyù yǔ péixùn fāngmiàn de gōngzuò.
____ 7. Wǒ xiǎng zuò fǎlǜ fāngmiàn de gōngzuò.
____ 8. Wǒ xiǎng zuò měishù shèjì fāngmiàn de gōngzuò.
____ 9. Wǒ xiǎng zuò xiāoshòu hé yíngxiāo fāngmiàn de gōngzuò.
____ 10. Wǒ xiǎng zuò yīliáo bǎojiàn fāngmiàn de gōngzuò.
____ 11. Wǒ xiǎng zuò xìnxī jìshù fāngmiàn de gōngzuò.

請再把下面的漢字與上面的拼音對上。／请再把下面的汉字与上面的拼音对上。

____ A. 我想做銷售和營銷方面的工作。／我想做销售和营销方面的工作。
____ B. 我想做商務與金融方面的工作。／我想做商务与金融方面的工作。
____ C. 我想做信息技術方面的工作。／我想做信息技术方面的工作。
____ D. 我想做研究與開發方面的工作。／我想做研究与开发方面的工作。
____ E. 我想做傳媒方面的工作。／我想做传媒方面的工作。
____ F. 我想做教育與培訓方面的工作。／我想做教育与培训方面的工作。
____ G. 我想做管理方面的工作。
____ H. 我想做醫療保健方面的工作。／我想做医疗保健方面的工作。
____ I. 我想做美術設計方面的工作。／我想做美术设计方面的工作。
____ J. 我想做法律方面的工作。
____ K. 我想做工程與建築方面的工作。／我想做工程与建筑方面的工作。

35.7 ***Pair work:*** *Talk to a partner and find out about his or her career experiences or aspirations. Ask,* 你做甚麼樣的職業？你想做甚麼樣的職業？／你做什么样的职业？你想做什么样的职业？

Respond by using as much as you can of the language in Exercises 35.5 and 35.6. Take notes in the space provided below. Report on what your partner tells you to someone else or to the class as a whole.

35.8 ***Mingling:*** *Walk around and speak in Chinese for as long as you can to as many of your classmates as possible in the time allocated. Talk about your current career or future career aspirations. If your class wishes to, compile everyone's information and make a physical chart to post on the wall or a digital chart to post online.*

Encounter 2 Interviewing for a job

35.9 *Fang Lan calls on Chen Feng to interview for an internship.* 請把中文跟英文對上。／请把中文跟英文对上。

____ a. zǒngcái 總裁／总裁	1. *interview*
____ b. miànshóu 面熟	2. *assessment, evaluation*
____ c. miànshì 面試／面试	3. *CEO*
____ d. jiǎnlì 簡歷／简历	4. *settle, fix*
____ e. tuījiànxìn 推薦信／推荐信	5. *special characteristics*
____ f. píngjià 評價／评价	6. *experience*
____ g. yōudiǎn 優點／优点	7. *weaknesses, weak points*
____ h. quēdiǎn 缺點／缺点	8. *look familiar*
____ i. tèdiǎn 特點／特点	9. *résumé*
____ j. shìchǎng 市場／市场	10. *market*
____ k. jīngyàn 經驗／经验	11. *strengths, strong points*
____ l. shuōdìng 說定／说定	12. *letter of recommendation*

35.10 *View Episode 35, Vignette 2. Indicate whether Fang Lan, Chen Feng, or Xiao Fei makes each of the following statements (given in the order they were made).*

i.

ii.

iii.

_____ a. This way, please come in!

_____ b. Haven't we met somewhere before? You look familiar.

_____ c. Welcome to our firm for this interview.

_____ d. I've read your résumé.

_____ e. Your professor wrote you a really good letter of recommendation.

_____ f. He rates you highly.

_____ g. What can I do for you here?

_____ h. Let's not talk about what you will be doing yet.

_____ i. I'd like to know more about you.

_____ j. I'm a rather open-minded person.

_____ k. I would generally do well in any job that involves communicating with people.

_____ l. We need some market surveys done.

_____ m. Do you have any experience with marketing?

_____ n. I'll pour you another cup. You talk.

_____ o. I hope to learn a lot more at your firm.

_____ p. That's settled, then.

35.11 請把下面的拼音和上面的英文對上。／请把下面的拼音和上面的英文对上。

_____ 1. Wǒ xiǎng gèng duō de liǎojiě yì xiē nǐ.

_____ 2. Nǐ de jiàoshòu gěi nǐ xiě le yí fèn fēicháng hǎo de tuījiànxìn.

_____ 3. Wǒ zhèi ge rén bǐjiào kāilǎng.

_____ 4. Tā duì nǐ de píngjià hěn gāo.

_____ 5. Wǒ dào zhèr lái néng wèi nín zuò xiē shénme ne?

_____ 6. Wǒ zài gěi nǐmen dào yì bēi, nǐmen liáo.

_____ 7. Yìbān yǔ rén gōutōng de gōngzuò wǒ dōu néng shèngrèn.

_____ 8. Wǒmen xūyào yǒu yì xiē shìchǎng fāngmiàn de diàochá.

_____ 9. Nǐ yǒu méiyǒu zuò shìchǎng yíngxiāo fāngmiàn de jīngyàn ne?

____ 10. Wǒ xīwàng dào le gōngsī yǐhòu kěyǐ xuédào gèng duō de dōngxi.

____ 11. Nà jiù shuōdìng le.

____ 12. Lái, lǐbiānr qǐng.

____ 13. Zánmen shìbushì zài nǎr jiànguo ya? Hěn miànshóu.

____ 14. Huānyíng nǐ lái wǒmen gōngsī miànshì.

____ 15. Xiān bù tí zuò shénme.

____ 16. Nǐ de jiǎnlì wǒ kànguo.

35.12 請把下面的漢字和上面的拼音對上。／请把下面的汉字和上面的拼音对上。

____ A. 你有沒有做市場營銷方面的經驗呢？／你有没有做市场营销方面的经验呢？

____ B. 他對你的評價很高。／他对你的评价很高。

____ C. 那就說定了。／那就说定了。

____ D. 我這個人比較開朗。／我这个人比较开朗。

____ E. 我想更多地了解一些你。

____ F. 我希望到了公司以後可以學到更多的東西。／我希望到了公司以后可以学到更多的东西。

____ G. 我再給你們倒一杯，你們聊。／我再给你们倒一杯，你们聊。

____ H. 歡迎你來我們公司面試。／欢迎你来我们公司面试。

____ I. 你的教授給你寫了一份非常好的推薦信。／你的教授给你写了一份非常好的推荐信。

____ J. 咱們是不是在哪兒見過呀？很面熟。／咱们是不是在哪儿见过呀？很面熟。

____ K. 我到這兒來能為您做些甚麼呢？／我到这儿来能为您做些什么呢？

____ L. 我們需要有一些市場方面的調查。／我们需要有一些市场方面的调查。

____ M. 一般與人溝通的工作我都能勝任。／一般与人沟通的工作我都能胜任。

____ N. 先不提做甚麼。／先不提做什么。

____ O. 來，裡邊兒請。／来，里边儿请。

____ P. 你的簡歷我看過。／你的简历我看过。

35.13 ***Pair work:*** *Work with a partner to carry out the interview below. Switch roles if there is time. Pinyin equivalents for the terms in red are provided for your convenience.*

[1]miànshì	[2]gōngsī	[3]jiǎnlì	[4]shōudào
[5]tuījiànxìn	[6]píngjià hěn gāo	[7]yōudiǎn	[8]kāilǎng
[9]shìchǎng yíngxiāo	[10]jīngyàn	[11]Nà jiù shuōdìng le.	

Interviewer	Interviewee
Greet your partner. Thank him/her for coming to this interview[1].	Thank your partner. Tell him/her you've heard a lot about this company[2].
Say you've read your partner's résumé[3] and that it's very good.	Say thank you. Ask if your partner has received[4] the letter of recommendation[5] sent by your professor.
Say you have and that it rated (your partner) very highly[6]. Ask what your partner's strong points[7] are.	Say 2–3 things about what you think your strong points are. Include that you are an open-minded[8] person.
Say that the job your partner is interviewing for has to do with marketing[9]. Ask if your partner has experience[10] in this area.	Say that you are very interested in this job and that yes, you have some experience. Describe what it is (make up some experience if you don't actually have any).
Indicate that you are pleased. Ask when your partner would be able to begin work.	Say that you could start next Monday morning.
Say "That settles it, then."[11] Close down the interview and take leave of your partner.	Say thank you to your partner, indicate how happy you are, and take your leave.

35.14 *Since Fang Lan and Chen Feng are discussing an internship, the issue of a salary never comes up. Most interviews, however, will touch on the issue of salary.*
把英語與中文對上。／把英语与中文对上。

6 a. *salary*	1. niánxīn 年薪
2 b. *monthly salary*	2. yuèxīn 月薪
1 c. *annual salary*	3. fúlì 福利
3 d. *benefits*	4. yīliáo bǎoxiǎn 醫療保險／医疗保险
5 e. *sick leave*	5. bìngjià 病假
7 f. *paid vacation*	6. xīnshuǐ 薪水
4 g. *health care*	7. dàixīn jiàqī 帶薪假期／带薪假期

35.15 *Match the statements below to the topics.*

____ a. niánxīn	1. 這份工作薪水很高。／这份工作薪水很高。
____ b. yuèxīn	2. 福利也很好。
____ c. fúlì	3. 年薪是五萬五。／年薪是五万五。
____ d. yīliáo bǎoxiǎn	4. 月薪超過五千五。／月薪超过五千五。
____ e. bìngjià	5. 每年有兩週帶薪假期。／每年有两周带薪假期。
____ f. xīnshuǐ	6. 你也可以申請病假。／你也可以申请病假。
____ g. dàixīn jiàqī	7. 病了有醫療保險。／病了有医疗保险。

35.16 ***Pair work:*** *In pinyin or characters, fill in the blanks below using your own information. Then exchange information by having a conversation with a partner. If there is time, switch partners and repeat. If your class prefers, turn this into a mingling activity and take a class survey. Remember, 10,000 =* wàn 萬／万.

a. 我是（將來想當）／我是（将来想当）____________________。

(Fill in your current or future profession.)

b. 我理想 (lǐxiǎng) 的年薪是 ____________________。

(Fill in an amount for an ideal salary.)

c. 我實際 (shíjì) 的年薪是／我实际 (shíjì) 的年薪是 ________________。

(Fill in a realistic amount for your salary.)

d. 我每年希望有 ________________ 的帶薪假期／带薪假期。

(Fill in a length of vacation time.)

e. 我每年希望有 ________________ 的病假。

(Fill in a length of sick leave.)

35.17 ***Pair work:*** *Have a brief conversation in Chinese with a partner about your hopes for the salary and benefits of your future (or present) job.*

Encounter 3 Reading and writing

Reading real-life texts

35.18 *58.com* (http://58.com/job) *is a Chinese site that lists jobs in 58 cities in China. Following is a sceenshot of its home page.*

58.com

58同城 58.com　58同城找工作　请输入职位或公司名称　搜职位　发布招聘 »　登记简历 »

系统提示：系统判断您来自 美国，推荐您到 美国全职招聘 频道看看　不自动跳转

城市：北京　广州　天津　深圳　上海　成都　杭州　合肥　武汉　西安　郑州　哈尔滨　长春　长沙　大连　福州　济南　兰州　南京　宁波　青岛　沈阳　石家庄　苏州　重庆　东莞　佛山　南宁　太原　无锡　海口　贵阳　泉州　唐山　包头　鞍山　常州　呼和浩特　济宁　更多»

销售(356257)　普工(10682)　房产经纪人(97632)　保险经纪人(28585)　会计(37878)　网站编辑(72242)
服务员(3194)　厨师(194)　配菜/打荷(5194)　收银员(97177)　发型师(53506)　美容师(53506)
推拿按摩(53506)　足疗保健(53506)　店长/卖场经理(97177)　客服(143852)　前台/接待(236648)　文员(236648)
促销/导购员(97177)　营业员(97177)　司机(109947)　保洁(32724)　保安(95049)　快递员(91225)

求职助手
自我介绍 | 求职信 | 简历范文 | 简历模板 | 半年工作总结 | 银行招聘 | 互联网招聘

普工/技工/工人
普工 | 电工 | 制冷/水暖工 | 切割/焊工 | 钣金工 | 缝纫工 | 装卸/搬运工

人事/行政/后勤
前台/接待 | 文员 | 经理助理/秘书 | 人事经理/主管 | 行政专员/助理 | 人事专员/助理

酒店/餐饮/旅游
服务员 | 厨师 | 配菜/打荷 | 面点师 | 后厨 | 大堂经理/领班 | 传菜员 | 迎宾/接待

美容/美发/保健/健身
发型师 | 美发助理/学徒 | 美容师 | 美容助理/学徒 | 化妆师 | 美甲师 | 推拿按摩

计算机/网络/通信
网站编辑 | 网页设计/制作 | 产品经理/专员 | 网络管理员 | 硬件工程师 | 软件工程师 | 测试

建筑/房产/装修/物业
建筑师 | 造价师/预算师 | 工程项目管理 | 房地产开发/策划 | 施工员 | 工程监理

客服
客服专员/助理 | 客服经理/主管 | 电话客服 | 售前/售后服务 | 客户关系管理

市场营销/公关媒介
市场专员/助理 | 市场拓展 | 市场调研 | 品牌经理 | 市场策划/企划 | 公关媒介专员/经理

a *The search window at the top of the page is labeled* 搜职位 sōu zhíwèi. *What does it mean?*

寫英文／写英文：________________

b *What do the two buttons on the top-right corner mean?* 把中文和英文對上。／把中文和英文对上。

____ 1. fābù zhāopìn 发布招聘　　A. *register a résumé*

____ 2. dēngjì jiǎnlì 登记简历　　B. *publish a job ad*

c *The two lines of blue text below the banner list some of the 58 cities serviced by this website. Write the characters for the following cities (given out of order).*

1. Běijīng	4. Shànghǎi	7. Héféi	10. Xī'an	13. Chángchūn	16. Guǎngzhōu
________	________	________	________	________	________
2. Jǐnán	5. Nánjīng	8. Shíjiāzhuāng	11. Chóngqìng	14. Shěnyáng	17. Hángzhōu
________	________	________	________	________	________
3. Tiānjīn	6. Chéngdū	9. Wǔhàn	12. Hā'ěrbīn	15. Hǎikǒu	18. Fúzhōu
________	________	________	________	________	________

d *Write the number of each of the cities listed above on the map below.*

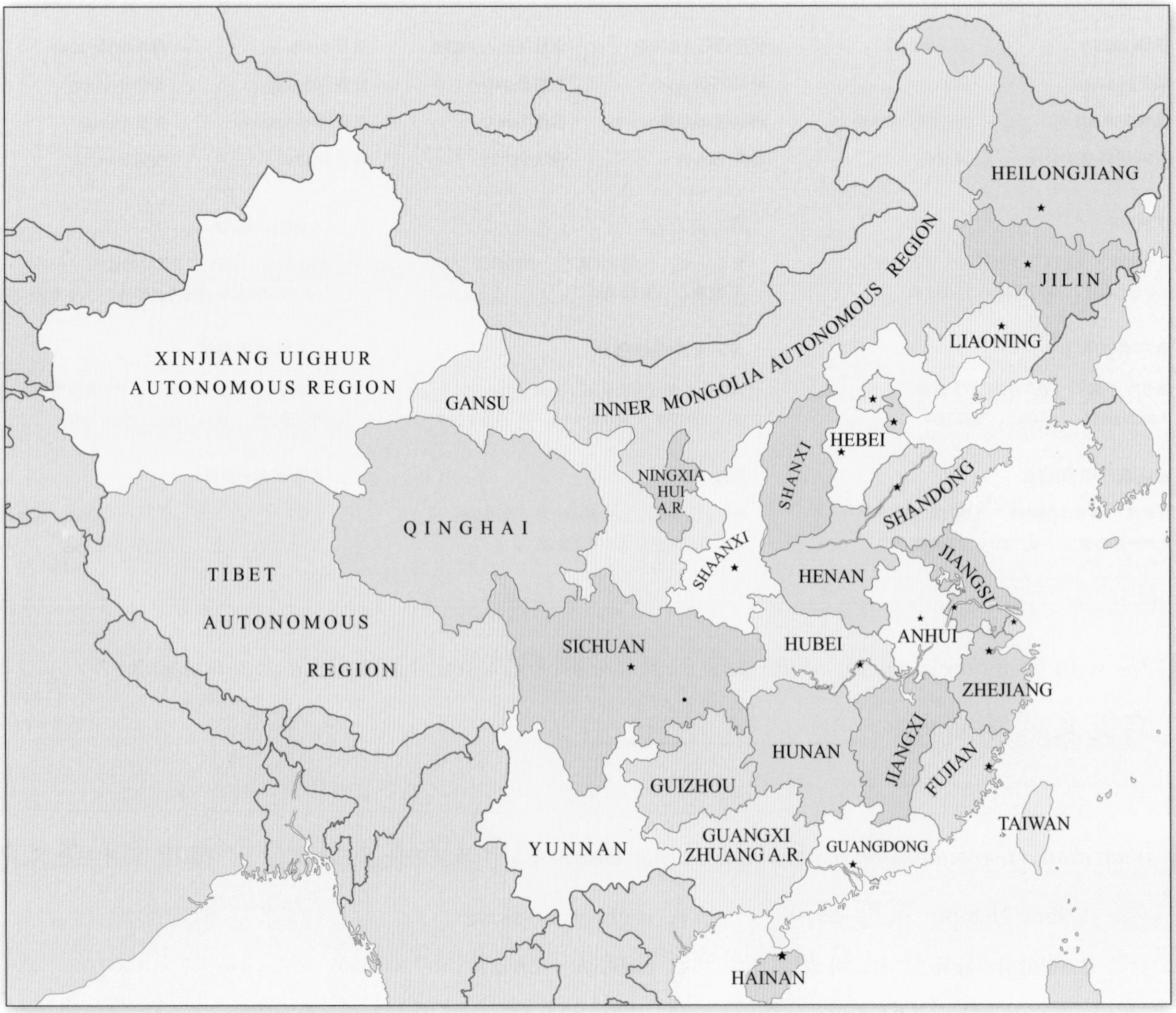

e *The final term in the city listing is* 更多》. *Write the English equivalent:* ____________________

f *The next listing of terms on the home page (in six columns of four rows) is of occupations, for which job ads are available on this site. Match the characters for these occupations with their pinyin and English equivalents.*

a. 銷售／销售	1. bǎoxiǎn jīngjìrén	A. *real-estate agent*
b. 普工	2. kèfú	B. *server*
c. 房產經紀人／房产经纪人	3. pèicài; dǎhé	C. *accountant*
d. 保險經紀人／保险经纪人	4. wǎngzhàn biānjí	D. *massage therapist*
e. 會計／会计	5. diàn zhǎng; màichǎng jīnglǐ	E. *customer service*
f. 網站編輯／网站编辑	6. fàxíngshī	F. *general workers*
g. 服務員／服务员	7. cùxiāo; dǎogòuyuán	G. *front desk, receptionist*
h. 廚師／厨师	8. fángchǎn jīngjìrén	H. *beautician*
i. 配菜; 打荷	9. sījī	I. *cashier*
j. 收銀員／收银员	10. tuīná ànmó	J. *sales*
k. 髮型師／发型师	11. yíngyèyuán	K. *office clerk*
l. 美容師／美容师	12. fúwùyuán	L. *salesperson*
m. 推拿按摩	13. bǎo'ān	M. *chef, cook*
n. 足療保健／足疗保健	14. shōuyínyuán	N. *promotions, buyer*
o. 店長; 賣場經理／店长; 卖场经理	15. bǎojié	O. *insurance agent*
p. 客服	16. xiāoshòu	P. *cleaning staff, janitor*
q. 前台; 接待	17. zúliáo bǎojiàn	Q. *store manager*
r. 文員／文员	18. chúshī	R. *sous-chef*
s. 促銷; 導購員／促销; 导购员	19. qiántái; jiēdài	S. *security guard*
t. 營業員／营业员	20. pǔgōng	T. *website editor*
u. 司機／司机	21. kuàidìyuán	U. *messenger, courier*
v. 保潔／保洁	22. měiróngshī	V. *foot care, reflexologist*
w. 保安	23. kuàijì	W. *driver, chauffeur*
x. 快遞員／快递员	24. wényuán	X. *hairdresser*

g *The first category in this listing of occupations is "sales." If you click on this, you'll see a listing of specific jobs (see the list on the left in the image below). If you click on any specific item, the details of the listing will appear (see the box on the right in the image below). Look at the specifics of this job description and fill in the blanks.*

- ☐ 高薪诚聘投资理财顾问 [1图]
- ☐ 500 强名企高薪＋旅游！聘销售 [1图]
- ☐ 搜狗｜高薪急聘销售精英＋高提成 [8图]
- ☐ 高薪诚聘销售！不悔的选择 [1图]
- ☐ 无责底薪三千＋高提成销售包住宿 [1图]
- ☐ 高端销售顾问＋储备经理 [8图]
- ☐ 电话销售无责3000双休 [8图]
- ☐ 月薪一万双休五险金融顾问 [1图]

综合金融理财中心 先赔保障

招聘职位：销售　　招聘人数：10人

工作经验：不限，可接收应届毕业生　　学历要求：大专

转正工资：8000 - 12000元

五险一金	周末双休	年底双薪	话补	交通补助	饭补	加班补助

薪资福利：工资无责底薪5000－8000（每季度享有一次晋级加薪机会）＋个人提成（5－50的业绩提成）＋个人绩效＋团队奖金＋定期旅游＋年终奖人均月收入8000－25000元上不封顶！本岗为公司直招，薪资福利待遇全部属实，绝无虚假不实信息！1、一经录用，即可享受带薪专业培训！2、一经录用，为员工缴纳五险一金！3、一经录用，公司具备良好的员工关怀体 …

Comprehensive financial and wealth management center **protection guaranteed**

Position offered: ______________　　Number of employees sought: ________

Work experience: None required, new graduates acceptable　　Education required: Associate's degree

Post-probationary salary: ____________________ [per month]

Benefits*	Weekends off	1 month bonus salary at year end	Cost-of-living allowance	Transportation allowance	Overtime allowance

Compensation and benefits: Wages and base salary 5,000–8,000 (each quarter you will have an opportunity to be promoted and raise your ___________) + personal commission (5–50% of sales commission based on performance) + individual performance bonus + team ___________ + regular ___________ + end-of-year bonus. Average monthly income ¥ 8,000–25,000 with no limit! This position is being filled directly by the company; all information about the salary and benefits are reliable, none of it is false! 1. Once you are hired, you will enjoy paid, on-the-job training! 2. Once you are hired, we will pay for benefits. 3. _______________, the company will provide excellent support . . .

The Chinese for this paragraph appears on the next page.

*五险一金 wǔ xiǎn yì jīn *literally means "five policies for one payment." These include policies covering pension, medical insurance, unemployment insurance, maternity leave, workers' compensation insurance, and a general pension fund. The single payment may be made by the individual, by the company, or by both.*

薪资福利：工资无责底薪5000－8000（每季度享有一次晋级加薪机会）＋个人提成（5－50的业绩提成）＋个人绩效＋团队奖金＋定期旅游＋年终奖人均月收入8000－25000元上不封顶！本岗为公司直招，薪资福利待遇全部属实，绝无虚假不实信息！1、一经录用，即可享受带薪专业培训！2、一经录用，为员工缴纳五险一金！3、一经录用，公司具备良好的员工关怀体……

h *Go to* www.58.com/job *and explore. Click on a city, then click on an occupation, and then click on a job posting and do a screen capture. See what you can decipher of the text. Share your screen capture and notes with your class.*

Reading a story

35.19 故事 *Find the following terms in either the traditional or simplified text and circle them. Write in the accompanying number.*

Robin Williams

A scene from the movie *Dead Poets Society*

1. xǐjù yǎnyuán *comedian*
2. Luóbīn Wēiliánmǔsī *Robin Williams*
3. Fútè gōngsī *Ford Motor Company*
4. bùmén *department*
5. zǒngcái *CEO*
6. mótè *model*
7. fùyù *wealthy*
8. bǎomǔ *nanny*
9. dài dà *bring up, raise*
10. dǐnglóu *attic*
11. wánjù *toy*
12. píngkōng *out of nothing*
13. biān chū *make up*
14. juésè *character*

15. wàijiāoguān *diplomat*
16. fānyì *translator*
17. jíxìng biǎoyǎn kè *improvisation class*
18. tūrán *suddenly*
19. yǒu tiānfù *gifted*
20. guānzhòng *viewers, audience*
21. hāhā dà xiào *laugh out loud*
22. bànyǎn *portray*
23. kǒuyīn *accent*
24. jiāoqì *dainty, feminine*
25. cāngying *fly*
26. Sūgélán *Scotland*

27. wàixīngrén *extraterrestrial*
28. shuǐshǒu *sailor*
29. qìchē xiāoshòu yuán *car salesperson*
30. rěrén xǐ'ài *lovable*
31. jīnglíng *genie*
32. zhèngmiàn *positive*
33. fùmiàn *negative*
34. xiàng *(measure word for awards)*
35. jiǎng *award*
36. Àosīkǎ *Oscar*
37. Géláiměi *Grammy*
38. Àiměi *Emmy*
39. Jīnqiú *Golden Globe*

40. dòngdǔxiào *stand-up comedy*
41. chūchǎng *appear onstage*
42. gǔzhǎng *applaud*
43. zǒngtǒng *president*
44. guówáng *king*
45. pǔtōng de lǎobǎixìng *ordinary people*
46. céngjīng *already*
47. xīnshǎng *appreciate, enjoy*
48. kuángzào xǐjù *manic comedy*

49. búxìng *unfortunately*
50. yíbèizi *all one's life*
51. huànyǒu *suffer from*
52. yìyùzhèng *depression*
53. zìshā shēnwáng *commit suicide*
54. shìshì *pass away*
55. biǎoshì *express*
56. chéntòng *deep, sorrowful*
57. āidào *condolences*
58. Bǎilǎohuì *Broadway*
59. tóngyī shíkè *at the same moment*
60. ànxiàle dēngguāng *dimmed their lights*
61. dàoniàn *mourn*
62. chéngbǎishàngqiān *hundreds and thousands*
63. chū *(measure word for an act)*
64. shēngqián *while he was alive*
65. xiàoshēng *laughter*
66. xiāotuì *fade away*

美國有一個著名的喜劇演員叫羅賓•威廉姆斯。他的父親是福特公司的一個部門的總裁，媽媽是模特。他在一個富裕的家庭裡長大，住在一棟有40個房間的大房子裡。因為他是獨生子，父母又很忙，所以他是保姆帶大的。不過大多數時間他只是一個人在家裡的頂樓玩玩具。在這些時間裡他憑空編出了很多角色當做自己的朋友，然後想出了很多關於這些角色的有趣的故事。他母親回家以後，他就演一些角色給媽媽看，媽媽就會大笑。所以他演的角色越來越搞笑。

美国有一个著名的喜剧演员叫罗宾•威廉姆斯。他的父亲是福特公司的一个部门的总裁，妈妈是模特。他在一个富裕的家庭里长大，住在一栋有40个房间的大房子里。因为他是独生子，父母又很忙，所以他是保姆带大的。不过大多数时间他只是一个人在家里的顶楼玩玩具。在这些时间里他凭空编出了很多角色当做自己的朋友，然后想出了很多关于这些角色的有趣的故事。他母亲回家以后，他就演一些角色给妈妈看，妈妈就会大笑。所以他演的角色越来越搞笑。

他上大學的時候本來想學政治和法語，去當外交官或者翻譯。但是自從他上了一門即興表演課以後，他就突然發現自己在即興表演方面非常有天賦。他把以前演給媽媽看的角色都拿出來表演，總

他上大学的时候本来想学政治和法语，去当外交官或者翻译。但是自从他上了一门即兴表演课以后，他就突然发现自己在即兴表演方面非常有天赋。他把以前演给妈妈看的角色都拿出来表演，总

會讓觀眾哈哈大笑。他扮演這些角色的時候，會用不同的人的聲音和口音來説話，比如老人、孩子、男子漢、嬌氣的女人、美國黑人，甚至狗呀、貓呀，還有蒼蠅。他也經常學其他國家的人説英語，比如蘇格蘭人、俄國人、法國人、印度人、中國人。

会让观众哈哈大笑。他扮演这些角色的时候，会用不同的人的声音和口音来说话，比如老人、孩子、男子汉、娇气的女人、美国黑人，甚至狗呀、猫呀，还有苍蝇。他也经常学其他国家的人说英语，比如苏格兰人、俄国人、法国人、印度人、中国人。

後來羅賓・威廉姆斯成了一個有名的電視演員，也成了一位非常成功的電影演員。他成名的第一個角色是在一部電視劇裡演一個可愛的外星人。後來他在電影裡扮演了很多不同的角色，包括水手、作家、音樂家、售貨員、文學老師、汽車銷售員、醫生、教授、心理醫生，還有一個非常惹人喜愛的精靈。他演的角色大多數是正面的，有幾個是負面的。他一生得過16項獎，包括奥斯卡、格萊美、艾美和金球獎。

后来罗宾・威廉姆斯成了一个有名的电视演员，也成了一位非常成功的电影演员。他成名的第一个角色是在一部电视剧里演一个可爱的外星人。后来他在电影里扮演了很多不同的角色，包括水手、作家、音乐家、售货员、文学老师、汽车销售员、医生、教授、心理医生，还有一个非常惹人喜爱的精灵。他演的角色大多数是正面的，有几个是负面的。他一生得过16项奖，包括奥斯卡、格莱美、艾美和金球奖。

除了演電影以外，他還常常參加脱口秀節目，或者演棟篤笑節目。他一出場，多到兩萬人的觀眾都會起來鼓掌歡迎。總統、國王、普通的老百姓，都曾經欣賞過他的狂躁喜劇。

除了演电影以外，他还常常参加脱口秀节目，或者演栋笃笑节目。他一出场，多到两万人的观众都会起来鼓掌欢迎。总统、国王、普通的老百姓，都曾经欣赏过他的狂躁喜剧。

羅賓・威廉姆斯結過三次婚，有三個漂亮能幹的孩子，可不幸的是他本人一輩子都患有抑鬱症。2014 年，他在自己的家裡自殺身亡了。他才63歲。世界各地無數的粉絲對他的逝世表示了沉痛哀悼。紐約百老匯所有的劇院也在同一時刻暗下了燈光來悼念他。不過在互聯網上還可以看到成百上千齣他生前演的戲。笑聲是不會消退的。

罗宾・威廉姆斯结过三次婚，有三个漂亮能干的孩子，可不幸的是他本人一辈子都患有抑郁症。2014 年，他在自己的家里自杀身亡了。他才63岁。世界各地无数的粉丝对他的逝世表示了沉痛哀悼。纽约百老汇所有的剧院也在同一时刻暗下了灯光来悼念他。不过在互联网上还可以看到成百上千齣他生前演的戏。笑声是不会消退的。

35.20 *Do you have a favorite act or portrayal by Robin Williams or by another actor or comedian? Whom were they portraying? Write a brief summary in Chinese.*

Encounter 4 Extension: Cultural mini-documentary

View the cultural mini-documentary for this unit and complete the exercises that follow.

35.21 *People talking about their past jobs don't always use an exact title. Instead, they may say things such as, "I used to be in finance." This series of video interviews may help you learn to do the same and also name some items commonly found on a résumé. Listen to the first part of the interview (0:00–2:36). Match a selection of past occupations mentioned with their English equivalents.*

a *The first few interviewees mention jobs related to finance and administration.* 請把中文跟英文對上。／请把中文跟英文对上。

____ 1. jùzǔ de cáiwù gōngzuò
劇組的財務工作／剧组的财务工作

____ 2. wàimào jìnchūkǒu de gōngzuò
外貿進出口的工作／外贸进出口的工作

____ 3. zǒngjīnglǐ mìshu
總經理秘書／总经理秘书

____ 4. xíngzhèng fāngmiàn de gōngzuò
行政方面的工作／行政方面的工作

A. *secretary to a CEO*

B. *doing receipts and payments*

C. *administrative-type work*

D. *worker for the local government*

____ 5. dāngdì zhèngfǔ de gōngzuò rényuán
當地政府的工作人員／当地政府的工作人员

E. *fiscal work for the production team (of a film)*

____ 6. zài yínháng zuò jīnróng
在銀行做金融／在银行做金融

F. *doing finance in a bank*

____ 7. zuò chūnà de
做出納的／做出纳的

G. *doing foreign trade / import-export*

b *Several interviewees mention opening or working in restaurants. Circle the three words for restaurant that you hear.*

fàndiàn 飯店／饭店

fàntīng 飯廳／饭厅

jiǔlóu 酒樓／酒楼

jiǔjiā 酒家

cāntīng 餐廳／餐厅

cānguǎn 餐館／餐馆

c *Quite a few interviewees mention jobs in entertainment and the arts.* 請把中文跟英文對上。／请把中文跟英文对上。

____ 1. zài diànshìtái zuò yì míng shèxiàngshī
在電視台做一名攝像師／在电视台做一名摄像师

A. *talent (actors') agent*

____ 2. dònghuà gōngzuòshì
動畫工作室／动画工作室

B. *martial-arts coach*

____ 3. yuèduì jīngjìrén
樂隊經紀人／乐队经纪人

C. *martial-arts stunt double*

____ 4. wǔshù jiàoliàn
武術教練／武术教练

D. *be a cinematographer at a television station*

____ 5. wǔshù tìshēn
武術替身／武术替身

E. *actor/talent*

____ 6. yǎnyuán
演員／演员

F. *animation studio*

____ 7. yǎnyì jīngjì
演藝經紀／演艺经纪

G. *music (band) agent*

d *Here are a few miscellaneous phrases used by interviewees about their past jobs.* 請把中文跟英文對上。／请把中文跟英文对上。

____ 1. zìjǐ yě kāi guò xiǎo de gōngsī
自己也開過小的公司／
自己也开过小的公司

____ 2. méiyǒu guò zhèngshì de gōngzuò jīnglì
没有過正式的工作經歷／
没有过正式的工作经历

____ 3. huàhuàr de
畫畫兒的／
画画儿的

____ 4. shèyǐng jìzhě
攝影記者／
摄影记者

____ 5. xiāoshòu, mài dōngxi de, mài yīfu de
銷售，賣東西的，賣衣服的／
销售，卖东西的，卖衣服的

____ 6. chéngxù de kāifā
程序的開發／
程序的开发

____ 7. zhuāngshì gōngsī
裝飾公司／
装饰公司

A. *sales, selling stuff, selling clothes*

B. *also opened my own small company*

C. *developing [software] programs*

D. *have never had any formal work experience*

E. *someone who paints*

F. *interior decoration company*

G. *photojournalist*

e *Here are some important time words and connecting phrases used by the interviewees.* 請把中文跟英文對上。／请把中文跟英文对上。

____ 1. wǒ zuò guò hěn duō zhǒng gōngzuò, shuō shíhuà
我做過很多種工作，説實話／
我做过很多种工作，说实话

____ 2. qǐchū . . .
起初……

A. *at the very beginning I was . . .*

B. *so before I was in the occupation I am in now . . .*

____ 3. wǒ zài zuò xiànzài de zhè fèn zhíyè zhīqián de huà ne . . .
我在做現在的這份職業之前的話呢……／
我在做现在的这份职业之前的话呢……

____ 4. wǒ zuì kāishǐ shì . . .
我最開始是……／
我最开始是……

____ 5. zuò le hǎo duō nián
做了好多年

____ 6. wǒ céngjīng zuò guò . . .
我曾經做過……／
我曾经做过……

____ 7. yìzhí jīběnshang zuò dào xiànzài
一直基本上做到現在／
一直基本上做到现在

C. *in the beginning . . .*

D. *in the past, I did/was . . .*

E. *did it for many years*

F. *basically have been doing it all the way up to now*

G. *to be honest, I have done many different kinds of work*

35.22 *Now listen to the next part of the interview (2:40–end) and see how much you can understand. For each of the following terms that are mentioned, place a check mark in the second column if you would also include that kind of information on your personal résumé* (個人簡歷／个人简历 gèrén jiǎnlì).

Item	On your résumé?
jīběn de gèrén xìnxī 基本的個人信息／基本的个人信息 *basic personal information*	☐
shēngrì 生日 *birthday*	☐
zhùzhǐ 住址 *residential address*	☐
liánxì fāngshì 聯繫方式／联系方式 *contact information*	☐
zhīqián de gōngzuò (zhíyè) jīnglì 之前的工作（職業）經歷／之前的工作（职业）经历 *prior work (occupational) experience*	☐
jiàoyù bèijǐng (xuélì) 教育背景（學歷）／教育背景（学历） *educational background (schooling)*	☐
shíxí de jīnglì 實習的經歷／实习的经历 *internship experience*	☐

xìngqù àihào 興趣愛好／兴趣爱好 *interests and hobbies*	☐
shēngāo, tǐzhòng 身高、體重／身高、体重 *height, weight*	☐
niánlíng 年齡／年龄 *age*	☐
qǔdé de chéngjì 取得的成績／取得的成绩 *successes achieved [e.g., test scores]*	☐
qīwàng de zhíyè 期望的職業／期望的职业 *hoped-for occupation / career goal*	☐
qīwàng de xīnzī 期望的薪資／期望的薪资 *hoped-for compensation / salary target*	☐
qiúzhí yìxiàng 求職意向／求职意向 *intent in seeking employment / statement of purpose*	☐
yǔyán nénglì 語言能力／语言能力 *language proficiency*	☐
jìsuànjī nénglì 計算機能力／计算机能力 *computer proficiency*	☐

35.23 *Now jot down a few sentences in pinyin or characters to explain the differences between your résumé and those of the interviewees. Share your statements with your classmates.*

Recap

Grammar

China is changing, as is Chinese—Look out for what's happening with 的

China has changed, and so has its language. You've already learned that the character set has been simplified. 中國 is now 中国 and 裡邊 is now 里边 in the PRC, for example. Beyond how characters look, another fundamental change involves how text is constructed. In the past, traditional *báihuà* 白話／白话 "vernacular" writing tended to feature text written in short sentences, primarily because of its attachment to actual speech. Simply put, people wrote as they spoke. Nowadays, however, increasingly longer sentences are becoming more commonplace in Chinese writing. In part, this is because of the amount of translation into Chinese from other languages. Long and complex modifiers in English, especially, can produce many skewed 的 modifications in Chinese. This poses a greater challenge to second learners of Chinese, because short bursts of thought punctuated by periods are much easier to understand than sentences with long and complex modifiers connected to an ultimate 的, or several intermediate 的s, and finally that welcome period.

The process began in the 1920s and has now become common for Chinese writing*. The characters have been simplified, true, but the unsimplified ones remain, and the burden is on learners of Chinese to learn both. Written texts have changed in the opposite direction: from the simple to the more complex. Therefore, our strong advice is, when reading, look for the 的. It will surely be followed by something crucial to your understanding of the text. Do that and your Chinese life will be easier.

Here are some examples of the shift, drawn from texts you have already read. The text in black is adapted from one of your earlier readings, whereas the text in red exemplifies the shift described here.

1. The first example is about Zhang Yimou, the famous Chinese movie director. First, review the black text (the original) and then read the one in red, which is the text as revised. Do the same for the second example. Each short sentence in the original is lettered, which should help clearly link to pieces of the more complex sentence in red. The first example is presented in traditional characters, and the second is in simplified.

(a) 張導演第一次出國是1985年。(b) 那時他去夏威夷參加國際電影節。(c) 他當時還沒有出名。(d) 他在夏威夷的時候也還不會説英文。(e) 所以他很難跟別人溝通。

(a) 1985年第一次出國 (b)去夏威夷參加國際電影節, (c) 那時還是没有出名 (d) 而且一點英文不會説的張藝謀發現: (e) 跟別人溝通很難。

See the difference: five short sentences boiled down into one long, complex sentence. Basically, in the complex sentence, what comes after 的 is the main thought: (e) Zhang Yimou found it hard to communicate with others. All of the other segments tell a little more about the subject, namely Zhang Yimou, who (a) left the country for the first time in 1985, (b) went to take part in the Hawaii International Film Festival, (c) had not become famous yet, and (d) could not speak English at all.

2. The second example is about Larry Page, one of the cofounders of Google.

(a) 佩奇是一个美国人。(b) 他从小就对计算机特别感兴趣。(c) 他只有六岁的时候，他父亲就给他买了一台计算机。(d) 后来他上了密歇根大学读计算机工程。(e) 毕业以后，他做了几年计算机技术方面的工作。(f) 24岁那年，他决定去斯坦福大学学习计算机科学。

(b) 从小就对计算机特别感兴趣，(c) 六岁时候就从父亲那里得到一台计算机，(d) 后来又从密歇根大学计算机工程专业毕业的 (a) 美国人佩奇，(e) 在做了几年计算机技术方面的工作以后，(f) 24岁那年，决定去斯坦福大学学习计算机科学。

Again, what comes after 的 is the main thought: (a) The American Page, (e) after working in computer technology for a few years, (f) decided to attend Stanford University to study computer science at the age of 24.

*This discussion is inspired by an excellent source, *Modern Chinese: History and Sociolinguistics*, by Ping Chen, Cambridge University Press, 1999.

What comes before is further information about the subject, Larry Page, who (b) had been interested in computers since he was small, (c) received a computer from his father at age 6, and (d) graduated in computer engineering from the University of Michigan.

3. Here's another example drawn from a column written by David Brooks of the *New York Times* and published in the Chinese version of the *Times* on January 12, 2015. (By the way, the Chinese version of the *Times* is published daily at cn.nytimes.com, where both versions can be viewed side by side. It's great fun to read, even though some native Chinese have complained that the translations produce stilted sentences in Chinese.) Notice how the text flows right to a final 的.

Not long ago, a friend sent me a speech that the great civil rights leader John Gardner gave to the Stanford Alumni Association 61 years after he graduated from that college.

不久前，一位朋友给我发来伟大的民权领袖约翰·加德纳 (John Gardner) 从斯坦福 (Stanford) 毕业61年后给校友会所做的演讲。

Note that much of what comes before the 的 modifies what comes after. Thus, (a) 伟大的民权领袖约翰·加德纳 *wěidà de mínquán lǐngxiù Yuēhàn Jiādénà;* (b) 从斯坦福 (Stanford) 毕业61年后 *cóng Sītǎnfú bìyè 61 nián hòu;* and (c) 给校友会所做 *gěi xiàoyǒuhuì suǒ zuò* all describe 演讲 *yǎnjiǎng*. Namely, the speech was (a) given by the great civil rights leader John Gardner, (b) 61 years after he graduated from Stanford, (c) to the alumni association.

And the basic information is "Not long ago, a friend sent me a speech."

的 is the most commonly used Chinese character. It is also, in our view, the most important, and now we know why. Make friends with 的!

Vocabulary

Please refer to page R-2 for a list of grammatical abbreviations used throughout this book.

ànmó 按摩 massage N/V

bǎo'ān 保安 security guard N; ensure public security VO

bàofù 抱負／抱负 aspiration; ambition N

bǎojié 保潔／保洁 janitor N; do sanitation work VO

bǎoxiǎn 保險／保险 insurance N; insure; be insured V

biānjí 編輯／编辑 editor; compiler N; edit; compile V

bìngjià 病假 sick leave N

chuánméi 傳媒／传媒 (communication) media N

chúshī 廚師／厨师 cook; chef N

cùxiāo 促銷／促销 sales promotion N/V

dǎhé 打荷 tournant *(person who does chores in a professional kitchen)* N

dàixīn jiàqī 帶薪假期／带薪假期 paid vacation N

dào 倒 pour V

dàochá 倒茶 pour tea VO

dǎogòuyuán 導購員／导购员 promotions; buyer N

dēngjì 登記／登记 register; check in *(at a hotel, etc.)* V

diànzhǎng 店長／店长 manager of a shop N

fābù 發布／发布 issue; announce; release V

fǎlǜ 法律 law N

fángchǎn jīngjìrén 房產經紀人／房产经纪人 real-estate agent N

fàxíngshī 髮型師／发型师 hairdresser; hair stylist N

fúlì 福利 benefits; welfare N

fúwùyuán 服務員／服务员 server; attendant N

gōngchéng 工程 engineering N

gōngzī 工資／工资 salary; wages; pay N

gōutōng 溝通／沟通 link up; communicate RV

guǎnlǐ 管理 manage; supervise V; management; administration N

hétong 合同 contract; agreement N

jiǎnlì 簡歷／简历 résumé; curriculum vitae N

jiànzhù 建築／建筑 build; construct V; building; edifice; architecture N

jiāoliú 交流 exchange; interchange V

jiàoyù 教育 education N; teach; educate V

jiè 界 circles; group; "world" BF

jiēdài 接待 admit/receive a guest V; reception; front desk N

jīliè 激烈 intense; fierce; acute; sharp SV

jìnéng 技能 skills; technique N

jīngjìrén 經紀人／经纪人 broker; middleman; agent N

jīngyàn 經驗／经验 experience N; go through; experience V

jìngzhēng 競爭／竞争 compete; competition V/N

jīnróng 金融 finance; banking N

kāilǎng 開朗／开朗 sanguine; optimistic; open-minded SV

kèfú 客服 customer service N

kuàidìyuán 快遞員／快递员 messenger; courier N

kuàijì 會計／会计 bookkeeper; accountant N

lèi 類／类 kind; type; class; category N

liáo 聊 chat V

liǎojiě 了解 understand; comprehend V; comprehension; understanding N

lǐxiǎng 理想 ideal(s) N

màichǎng jīnglǐ 賣場經理／卖场经理 store manager N

mǎnyì 滿意／满意 satisfied; pleased SV

měiróngshī 美容師／美容师 beautician N

měishù shèjì 美術設計／美术设计 graphic design N

méitǐ 媒體／媒体 media; information N

miànshì 面試／面试 interview; audition VO/V

miànshóu *(also pronounced* **miànshú***)* 面熟 familiar-looking SV

niánxīn 年薪 annual salary N

pèicài 配菜 sous-chef *(assistant to the cook)* N

péixùn 培訓／培训 training N; cultivate; train V

píngjià 評價／评价 assessment; evaluation; appraisal N; evaluate V

pǔgōng 普工 ordinary worker N

qiántái 前台 front/reception desk N

qīxiàn 期限 time limit; deadline N

quēdiǎn 缺點／缺点 shortcoming; defect; disadvantage N

shāngwù 商務／商务 business; business affairs N

shāo 稍 slightly A

shèngrèn 勝任／胜任 be qualified for; be competent; be up to the task V

shìchǎng 市場／市场 market; marketplace; bazaar N

shìchǎng yíngxiāo 市場營銷／市场营销 marketing N

shíxí 實習／实习 practice; intern; do fieldwork N/V

shōuyínyuán 收銀員／收银员 cashier N

shuōdìng 說定／说定 settle; agree on V/RV

sījī 司機／司机 driver; chauffeur N

tèdiǎn 特點／特点 characteristic; trait; peculiarity N

tuījiànxìn 推薦信／推荐信 letter of recommendation N

tuīná 推拿 massage therapy N

wǎngzhàn 網站／网站 website N

wèishēng bǎojiàn 衛生保健／卫生保健 healthcare provisions N

wěndìng 穩定／稳定 stable; steady SV; stabilize V

wényuán 文員／文员 office worker; clerk N

xiànjīn liú 現金流／现金流 cash flow N

xiāoshòu 銷售／销售 sell; market V; sales; marketing N

xīnshuǐ 薪水 salary; pay; wages N

xìnxī jìshù 信息技術／信息技术 information technology N

yèyú 業餘／业余 spare time; after hours N

yīliáo bǎojiàn 醫療保健／医疗保健 medical care N

yíngxiāo 營銷／营销 marketing N

yíngyèyuán 營業員／营业员 shop/business staff N

yōudiǎn 優點／优点 merit; strong/good point; advantage N

yǒuyìyì 有意義／有意义 have meaning; have significance V/VO

yuèxīn 月薪 monthly salary N

zhǎng 長／长 grow; increase V

zhāopìn 招聘 invite applications for a job N

zhǐdǎo 指導／指导 guidance; direction; supervision N; guide; supervise V

zhíjiē 直接 direct; immediate SV; directly A

zhīshi 知識／知识 knowledge N

zhíyè 職業／职业 occupation; profession; vocation N; professional ATTR

zhuānyè 專業／专业 specialized field of research; specialty N

zǒngcái 總裁／总裁 CEO; president N

zúliáo bǎojiàn 足療保健／足疗保健 foot care; reflexology N

Checklist of "can do" statements

After completing this unit, you should be able to perform each of the following tasks:

Listening and speaking

- ☐ Describe any work you did in the past or that you do now.
- ☐ Talk about what you like and dislike about your work.
- ☐ Describe your ideal career.
- ☐ Discuss what you would hope to have in terms of salary and benefits.

Reading and writing

- ☐ Decipher some details on a Chinese employment website.
- ☐ Comprehend a short description of the life of a famous comedian and actor.
- ☐ Write a short description of the professional life of someone well known.

Understanding culture

- ☐ Make several accurate statements about common Chinese careers.
- ☐ Make several accurate statements about what should appear on a Chinese résumé.

UNIT

36

"Beauty is in the eye of the beholder"*

情人眼裡出西施

Qíngrén yǎnli chū Xīshī

The ideal life partner

In this unit, you will learn how to:

- talk about characteristics of your ideal romantic partner.
- describe people with whom you have had a close relationship in the past.
- describe a key relationship between two people you know.
- discuss differences in marriage expectations between the East and West or between the past and present.
- decipher some items on pages of a Chinese dating website.
- read a story about the relationship between two people.
- write an ending to a story.
- comment on some Chinese people's views on ideal romantic partners.

*Literally, this idiom states, "A Xishi appears in the eyes of her lover," which is to say, to her lover, every woman is as beautiful as the legendary Xishi, one of the Four Great Beauties of ancient China. In 490 BCE, the minister of her home state of Yue gave Xishi to the king of the rival state of Wu. Bewitched by her beauty, that besotted man was the ruin of his own kingdom.

Encounter 1 Discussing characteristics of an ideal life partner

36.1 *Chen Feng, Xiao Fei, and Fang Lan are discussing a dating website they are designing.* 請把中文跟英文對上。／请把中文跟英文对上。

____ a. shèjiāo wǎngzhàn 社交網站／社交网站	1. *ideal life partner*
____ b. shìchǎng diàochá 市場調查／市场调查	2. *educational background*
____ c. lǐxiǎng duìxiàng 理想對象／理想对象	3. *survey questionnaire*
____ d. yāoqiú 要求	4. *social networking website*
____ e. diàochá wènjuàn 調查問卷／调查问卷	5. *prince on a white horse*
____ f. xiàndài de niánqīngrén 現代的年輕人／现代的年轻人	6. *living conditions*
____ g. xuélì 學歷／学历	7. *young people nowadays*
____ h. zhíyè 職業／职业	8. *market survey*
____ i. zhùfáng zhuàngkuàng 住房狀況／住房状况	9. *profession*
____ j. báimǎ wángzǐ 白馬王子／白马王子	10. *requirements*

36.2 *View Episode 36, Vignette 1. Chen Feng, Xiao Fei, and Fang Lan are discussing details of their proposed website and how to design it. Indicate who says each of the following sentences.* 請注明這話是誰說的？／请注明这话是谁说的？

	陳峰／陈峰	小飛／小飞	方蘭／方兰
a. We hope to combine modern social networking with traditional customs of matchmaking to expand people's social circles.	☐	☐	☐
b. The questions could be about different types of relationships, about heterosexual love, for example, or even homosexual love.	☐	☐	☐
c. I think we should concentrate on understanding what modern young people are looking for in an ideal companion.	☐	☐	☐
d. We'll include physical characteristics, such as height, weight, and body type, and maybe even face shape.	☐	☐	☐
e. Then we can put in personality characteristics as well.	☐	☐	☐

f. I think we should include educational background on our survey questionnaire—whether someone has graduated with a high school, college, or graduate degree.	☐	☐	☐
g. Then we should also include position and occupation, for example, whether a person has a freelance job, is working in the state civil service, or has a specialization.	☐	☐	☐
h. I think we can also include something about your current type of housing. For example, whether someone is a landlord or a tenant or has been living with parents all along.	☐	☐	☐
i. I've come to see that young people like you are very different from how we used to be. You can be this specific about what you want in an ideal mate.	☐	☐	☐
j. Not all young people are so focused on material requirements.	☐	☐	☐

36.3 請把下面的拼音跟上面的英文對上。／请把下面的拼音跟上面的英文对上。

____ 1.Wǒ juéde zánmen de zhòngdiǎn shì yào liǎojiě xiàndài de niánqīngrén duì zìjǐ lǐxiǎng zhōng de bànlǚ, tā yǒu shénmeyàng de tiáojiàn.

____ 2. Xìnggé tèzhēng yě kěyǐ fàng jìnqu.

____ 3. Wǒ juéde xuélì yě yào liè dào wǒmen zhè ge diàochá wènjuàn shang, gāozhōng, dàxué háishi yánjiūshēng bìyè, dōu yào liè shàngqu.

____ 4. Wèntí kěnéng shèjí dào gèzhǒng bùtóng xíngtài de liǎngxìng guānxi, bǐfāng shuō yìxìng liàn, shènzhì yú tóngxìngliàn, zánmen dōu yào bāokuò zài nèi.

____ 5. Zánmen kěyǐ bǎ zhùfáng zhuàngkuàng yě fàng jìnqu. Bǐfāngshuō nǐ shì fángdōng a, háishi zūhù a, háishi qìjīnwéizhǐ yìzhí gēn fùmǔ zhù.

____ 6. Wǒmen shì xīwàng bǎ xiàndài de shèjiāo wǎnglùo gēn chuántǒng de xiāngqīn xísú lái jiéhé, lái bāngzhù rénmen kuòzhǎn shèjiāo quān.

____ 7. Búshì suǒyǒu niánqīngrén dōu nàme zhùzhòng wùzhì tiáojiàn de.

____ 8. Tǐmào tèzhēng yě luóliè jìnqu, lìrú shēngāo, tǐzhòng, shēnxíng, shènzhìyú liǎnxíng dōu kěyǐ fàng shàngqu.

____ 9. Dìwèi hé zhíyè yě yīnggāi fàng jìnqu, bǐrú shuō zhè ge rén, tā shì zìyóu zhíyè ne, guójiā gōngwùyuán ne, háishi shénme zhuānyè rénshì.

____ 10. Wǒ fāxiàn nǐmen xiànzài de niánqīngrén hé wǒmen dāngshí hái zhēn de shì bù yíyàng. Nǐmen kěyǐ bǎ zhè zhǒng lǐxiǎng zhōng de bànlǚ de tiáojiàn jùhuà dào rúcǐ dìbù.

36.4 請把下面的漢字跟上面的拼音對上。／请把下面的汉字跟上面的拼音对上。

____A. 問題可能涉及到各種不同形態的兩性關係，比方說異性戀，甚至於同性戀，咱們都要包括在內。／问题可能涉及到各种不同形态的两性关系，比方说异性恋，甚至于同性恋，咱们都要包括在内。

____B. 性格特徵也可以放進去。／性格特征也可以放进去。

____C. 我們是希望把現代的社交網絡跟傳統的相親習俗來結合，來幫助人們擴展社交圈。／我们是希望把现代的社交网络跟传统的相亲习俗来结合，来帮助人们扩展社交圈。

____D. 地位和職業也應該放進去，比如說這個人，他是自由職業呢、國家公務員呢，還是甚麼專業人士。／地位和职业也应该放进去，比如说这个人，他是自由职业呢、国家公务员呢，还是什么专业人士。

____E. 咱們可以把住房狀況也放進去。比方說你是房東啊，還是租戶啊，還是迄今為止一直跟父母住。／咱们可以把住房状况也放进去。比方说你是房东啊，还是租户啊，还是迄今为止一直跟父母住。

____F. 我覺得咱們的重點是要了解現代的年輕人對自己理想中的伴侶，他有甚麼樣的條件。／我觉得咱们的重点是要了解现代的年轻人对自己理想中的伴侣，他有什么样的条件。

____G. 不是所有年輕人都那麼注重物質條件的。／不是所有年轻人都那么注重物质条件的。

____H. 體貌特徵也羅列進去，例如身高、體重、身形、甚至於臉型都可以放上去。／体貌特征也罗列进去，例如身高、体重、身形、甚至于脸型都可以放上去。

____I. 我發現你們現在的年輕人和我們當時還真的是不一樣。你們可以把這種理想中的伴侶的條件具化到如此地步。／我发现你们现在的年轻人和我们当时还真的是不一样。你们可以把这种理想中的伴侣的条件具化到如此地步。

____J. 我覺得學歷也要列到我們這個調查問卷上，高中、大學還是研究生畢業，都要列上去。／我觉得学历也要列到我们这个调查问卷上，高中、大学还是研究生毕业，都要列上去。

36.5 *What are you looking for in a life partner? Rank the following characteristics from 1 (most important) to 5 (least important).*

____ xìnggé tèzhēng 性格特徵／性格特征

____ xuélì 學歷／学历

____ tǐmào tèzhēng 體貌特徵／体貌特征

____ zhùfáng zhuàngkuàng 住房狀況／住房状况

____ dìwèi hé zhíyè 地位和職業／地位和职业

36.6 *Categorize the terms in the first column.*

	性格特徵／性格特征	學歷／学历	體貌特徵／体貌特征	住房狀況／住房状况	地位和職業／地位和职业
a. shì fángdōng 是房東／是房东	☐	☐	☐	☐	☐
b. rén tèbié hǎo 人特別好／人特别好	☐	☐	☐	☐	☐
c. yánjiūshēng bìyè 研究生畢業／研究生毕业	☐	☐	☐	☐	☐
d. yì mǐ bā 一米八	☐	☐	☐	☐	☐
e. liǎn hěn yuán 臉很圓／脸很圆	☐	☐	☐	☐	☐
f. gāozhōng bìyè 高中畢業／高中毕业	☐	☐	☐	☐	☐
g. tóufa shì hēisè de 頭髮是黑色的／头发是黑色的	☐	☐	☐	☐	☐
h. hěn kěkào 很可靠	☐	☐	☐	☐	☐
i. yìzhí gēn fùmǔ zhù 一直跟父母住	☐	☐	☐	☐	☐
j. shì guójiā gōngwùyuán 是國家公務員／是国家公务员	☐	☐	☐	☐	☐
k. dàxué bìyè 大學畢業／大学毕业	☐	☐	☐	☐	☐
l. shì zūhù 是租戶／是租户	☐	☐	☐	☐	☐
m. yì bǎi wǔshí bàng 一百五十磅	☐	☐	☐	☐	☐
n. shì zìyóu zhíyè 是自由職業／是自由职业	☐	☐	☐	☐	☐
o. fēicháng yǒushàn 非常友善	☐	☐	☐	☐	☐

36.7 ***Pair work:*** *Have a conversation in Chinese with a partner about what you are looking for in a life partner. Discuss the characteristics that are important to you and give specific examples of each. Ask,* 你理想中的伴侶要有甚麼樣的條件？／你理想中的伴侣要有什么样的条件？ *Respond by using as much as you can of the language in Exercise 36.6. Take at least 5–6 turns each. If there is time, switch to another partner.*

36.8 *Xiao Fei says that the planned website will be inclusive, and he gives the following example:* 請用英文填空。／请用英文填空。

Bǐfāng shuō yìxìngliàn, shènzhì yú tóngxìngliàn, zánmen dōu yào bāokuò zài nèi.

比方說異性戀，甚至於同性戀，咱們都要包括在內。／
比方说异性恋，甚至于同性恋，咱们都要包括在内。

For example, ____________________, and even ______________________, we want to include both.

36.9 *Fang Lan speaks about the characteristics she is looking for in a life partner. Categorize these as* 正面 zhèngmiàn *(positive) or* 負面／负面 fùmiàn *(negative), in Fang Lan's opinion.*

	正面	負面／负面
a. xūwěi	☐	☐
b. qínfèn	☐	☐
c. kěkào	☐	☐
d. yánsù	☐	☐
e. zhēnchéng	☐	☐
f. jījí	☐	☐
g. fúkuā	☐	☐
h. nèixiàng	☐	☐
i. lèguān	☐	☐
j. lǎnduò	☐	☐
k. zhēnshí	☐	☐
l. jǐnshèn	☐	☐

36.10 請把拼音和英文對上。／请把拼音和英文对上。

____ a. Wǒ bú yào yí ge fúkuā de rén. 1. *He is serious.*

____ b. Tā zǒng shì hěn kěkào. 2. *She is hardworking.*

____ c. Tā hěn qínfèn. 3. *They are both very positive.*

____ d. Tā yǒushíhou hǎoxiàng tèbié zhēnshí. 4. *I want someone who is sincere.*

____ e. Tā hěn yánsù. 5. *I don't want someone who is pompous.*

____ f. Wǒ juéde tā hěn xūwěi. 6. *He is always optimistic.*

____ g. Tāmen liǎ dōu hěn jījí. 7. *She is always reliable.*

____ h. Nǐ yīngdāng jǐnshèn yìdiǎn. 8. *She is sometimes a little lazy.*

____ i. Tā bǐjiào nèixiàng. 9. *He sometimes seems very real.*

____ j. Wǒ yào yí ge zhēnchéng de rén. 10. *I find him insincere.*

____ k. Tā yǒu de shíhou yǒu yìdiǎn lǎnduò. 11. *You should be more cautious.*

____ l. Tā zǒng shì hěn lèguān. 12. *He is rather introverted.*

36.11 請把下面的漢字和上面的拼音對上。／请把下面的汉字和上面的拼音对上。

____ 1. 她很勤奮。／她很勤奋。

____ 2. 他比較內向。／他比较内向。

____ 3. 我不要一個浮誇的人。／我不要一个浮夸的人。

____ 4. 他很嚴肅。／他很严肃。

____ 5. 她總是很可靠。／她总是很可靠。

____ 6. 他總是很樂觀。／他总是很乐观。

____ 7. 他有時候好像特別真實。／他有时候好像特别真实。

____ 8. 她有的時候有一點懶惰。／她有的时候有一点懒惰。

____ 9. 他們倆都很積極。／他们俩都很积极。

____ 10. 你應當謹慎一點。／你应当谨慎一点。

____ 11. 我要一個真誠的人。／我要一个真诚的人。

____ 12. 我覺得他很虛偽。／我觉得他很虚伪。

36.12 *Fang Lan says that she is looking for a serious, introverted person to balance her, because she herself is too "wacky and easygoing" (*fēngfengdiāndiān, dàdaliēliē 瘋瘋癲癲、大大咧咧／疯疯癫癫、大大咧咧*).*

Her full statement is: "I'm normally too wacky and easygoing." 請寫拼音或者漢字。／请写拼音或者汉字。

____

____

36.13 ***Pair work:*** *Talk to a partner about the characteristics of your ideal life partner.*

36.14 ***Mingling:*** *Walk around and speak in Chinese for as long as you can to as many of your classmates as possible in the time allocated. Talk about the hopes you have for your life partner. If your class wishes to, compile everyone's information and make a physical chart to post on the wall or a digital chart to post online.*

Encounter 2 Discussing courtship and marriage

36.15 *Fang Lan's parents describe the matchmaking process in their day and their own relationship.* 請把中文和英文對上。／请把中文和英文对上。

___ a. kào shúrén jièshào 靠熟人介紹／靠熟人介绍	1. *reconstituted household*
___ b. qīnqi péngyou 親戚朋友／亲戚朋友	2. *the two parties, both sides*
___ c. méiren 媒人	3. *matchmaker, go-between*
___ d. jièshào duìxiàng 介紹對象／介绍对象	4. *two people who love each other*
___ e. shuāngfāng 雙方／双方	5. *rely on introductions by acquaintances*
___ f. jiātíng bèijǐng 家庭背景	6. *impression of her is just so-so*
___ g. jiàn le miàn 見了面／见了面	7. *whether or not they can get along*
___ h. néng bùnéng tándelái 能不能談得來／能不能谈得来	8. *friends and relatives*
___ i. yǒu méiyǒu gǎnjué 有沒有感覺／有没有感觉	9. *introduce a potential life partner*
___ j. duì tā yìnxiàng yìbān 對她印象一般／对她印象一般	10. *after having met*
___ k. liǎng ge xiāng'ài de rén 兩個相愛的人／两个相爱的人	11. *whether or not they have feelings (for each other)*
___ l. chóngzǔ jiātíng 重組家庭／重组家庭	12. *family backgrounds*

36.16 *View Episode 36, Vignette 2. Indicate whether Fang Lan, Emma, Lao Fang, or Zhang Suyun makes each of the following statements (given in the order they were made).*

i.

ii.

iii.

iv.

_____ a. What are you so busy doing? You don't even have time for dinner.

_____ b. During our time, we had to rely on people we knew to introduce us to candidates for marriage, either friends and relatives or matchmakers.

_____ c. To make a match between two people, first you had to look at the couple's family backgrounds, whether or not they were evenly matched.

____ d. Some people even had to check to see whether the horoscopes of the couple were compatible.

____ e. Naturally, it depended on whether they got along and had any feelings for each other.

____ f. I thought she was too ferocious—not the image of the virtuous wife and loving mother.

____ g. He was honest and straightforward and down-to-earth; he made me feel safe.

____ h. Marriage, that's just two people who love each other getting together, raising children, supporting each other, taking care of each other's old folks, and when we get old ourselves, keeping each other company.

____ i. Do you think there is a difference in perspective on love and marriage between Westerners and Chinese?

____ j. Ideal partners are two people who find each other attractive and who make each other happy—who are able to grow together.

____ k. It doesn't matter whether it's East or West. I think aspirations for love, marriage, and family are the same; everyone hopes to be happy.

36.17 請把下面的拼音和上面的英文對上。／请把下面的拼音和上面的英文对上。

____ 1. Jièshào duìxiàng ne, shǒuxiān yào kànkan shuāngfāng de zhè ge jiātíng bèijǐng, kànkan shìbushì méndānghùduì.

____ 2. Zìrán'érrán yào kàn liǎng ge rén néng bùnéng tándelái le, yǒu méiyǒu gǎnjué le.

____ 3. Bùguǎn shì dōngfāng háishi xīfāng, wǒ xiǎng tāmen duì àiqíng, hūnyīn, jiātíng de kěwàng dōu shì yíyàng de, dōu xīwàng néng xìngfú.

____ 4. Wǒmen nà huǐr ya, tán liàn'ài dōu děi kào shúrén jièshào, yào bù qīnqi péngyou, yào bù ne jiùshì méiren.

____ 5. Nǐ máng shénme ne? Fàn dōu gùbushàng chī.

____ 6. Wǒ juéde tā tài lìhai le, búshì wǒ xīnmù zhōng de xiánqīliángmǔ de xíngxiàng.

____ 7. Nǐ juéde xīfāngrén de hūnyīn hé liàn'àiguān hé wǒmen Zhōngguórén yǒu shénme qūbié ma?

____ 8. Jiéhūn ma, jiùshì liǎng ge xiāng'ài de rén zài yìqǐ, shēng'éryùnǚ, hùxiāng zhīchí, zhàogu shuāngfāng de lǎorén, děng yǐhòu wǒmen dōu lǎo le zài hùxiāng péibàn.

____ 9. Lǐxiǎng de bànlǚ shì shuāngfāng néng hùxiāng xīyǐn, yíkuàir gǎndào kuàilè, yìqǐ chéngzhǎng.

____ 10. Yǒu de rén ne, hái děi suànsuan liǎng ge nánnǚ zài yíkuài a, shìbushì shēngchén bāzì, néng bùnéng pèideshàng.

____ 11. Tā rén tèbié hānhou, lǎoshi, shízài, yǒu ānquángǎn.

36.18 請把下面的漢字和上面的拼音對上。／请把下面的汉字和上面的拼音对上。

___A. 我覺得她太厲害了，不是我心目中的賢妻良母的形象。／我觉得她太厉害了，不是我心目中的贤妻良母的形象。

___B. 結婚嘛，就是兩個相愛的人在一起，生兒育女，互相支持，照顧雙方的老人，等以後我們都老了再互相陪伴。／结婚嘛，就是两个相爱的人在一起，生儿育女，互相支持，照顾双方的老人，等以后我们都老了再互相陪伴。

___C. 理想的伴侶是雙方能互相吸引，一塊兒感到快樂，一起成長。／理想的伴侣是双方能互相吸引，一块儿感到快乐，一起成长。

___D. 介紹對象呢，首先要看看雙方的這個家庭背景，看看是不是門當戶對。／介绍对象呢，首先要看看双方的这个家庭背景，看看是不是门当户对。

___E. 你覺得西方人的婚姻和戀愛觀和我們中國人有甚麼區別嗎？／你觉得西方人的婚姻和恋爱观和我们中国人有什么区别吗？

___F. 你忙甚麼呢？飯都顧不上吃。／你忙什么呢？饭都顾不上吃。

___G. 自然而然要看兩個人能不能談得來了，有沒有感覺了。／自然而然要看两个人能不能谈得来了，有没有感觉了。

___H. 我們那會兒呀，談戀愛都得靠熟人介紹，要不親戚朋友，要不呢就是媒人。／我们那会儿呀，谈恋爱都得靠熟人介绍，要不亲戚朋友，要不呢就是媒人。

___I. 不管是東方還是西方，我想他們對愛情、婚姻、家庭的渴望都是一樣的，都希望能幸福。／不管是东方还是西方，我想他们对爱情、婚姻、家庭的渴望都是一样的，都希望能幸福。

___J. 有的人呢，還得算算兩個男女在一塊啊，是不是生辰八字，能不能配得上。／有的人呢，还得算算两个男女在一块啊，是不是生辰八字，能不能配得上 。

___K. 他人特別憨厚、老實、實在，有安全感。／他人特别憨厚、老实、实在，有安全感。

36.19 ***Pair work:*** *Work with a partner to discuss in Chinese whether you think there is a difference in views on courtship and marriage expectations between the past and the present, or between the East and West. Go into detail as much as you can. Take notes on your discussion, and write several statements expressing your views.* 請寫拼音或者漢字。／请写拼音或者汉字。

Encounter 3 Reading and writing

Reading real-life texts

36.20 Baihe.com *is a popular Chinese dating website.*

百合 baihe.com 实名婚恋网开创者

a *What do you think* Bǎihé *means?*

____

b 实名婚恋网开创者 = *"pioneer of dating networks with real names"* 請對上英語和中文。／请对上英语和中文。

____ 1. shímíng 實名／实名 — A. *pioneer*

____ 2. hūnliànwǎng 婚戀網／婚恋网 — B. *real names*

____ 3. kāichuàngzhě 開創者／开创者 — C. *dating network*

c 每天上千对牵手幸福！ 請對上英語和中文。／请对上英语和中文。

____ 1. měi tiān 每天 — A. *up to 1,000 pairs*

____ 2. shàngqiān duì 上千對／上千对 — B. *happy, happiness*

____ 3. qiānshǒu 牽手／牵手 — C. *every day*

____ 4. xìngfú 幸福 — D. *hold hands*

Now write out a catchy translation of this statement:

____

36.21 *Following is the registration area of Baihe's homepage.*

百合 baihe.com 实名婚恋网开创者

8500万会员 | 实名婚恋网开创者 | 每天上千对牵手幸福！

账号信息

注册方式 手机号注册 邮箱注册

帐号

验证码 免费获取验证码

收不到短信？使用语音验证码。

密码

完善资料

昵称

性别 我是男生 我是女生 * 注册后不可更改

生日 请选择 请选择 请选择

地区 请选择 请选择 请选择

身高 175 学历 本科

收入 4000-5000 婚姻 未婚

已经阅读并同意百合服务条款

注册完成

a Zhànghào xìnxī *means "account information." Write the characters for this term:*

________ ________ ________ ________

b *There are two ways to register (*注册 zhùcè*). What are they?* 請勾選。／请勾选。

☐ *with a cell phone number*

☐ *with a username and password*

☐ *with your e-mail address*

c 验证码 yànzhèng mǎ *means "verification number." The little gray box next to it states, "Obtain a verification number at no cost." Circle and label the following terms:*

____ 1. huòqǔ *obtain*

____ 2. miǎnfèi *for free*

d *The little message beneath the gray box states,* 收不到短信？使用语音验证码。 *The question asks (select one choice):*

Can't receive ☐ *e-mails?*

☐ *text messages?*

e *What do you put in the* 密码 mìmǎ *box?* 請勾選。／请勾选。

☐ *password*

☐ *username*

f Wánshàn zīliào *means "complete materials." Write the characters for this term:*

_______ _______ _______ _______

g *The first piece of information the site seeks in this area is your* nìchēng *nickname. Write the characters for this term:*

_______ _______

h *Next the site seeks to know your gender. What does the asterisked warning* (Zhùcè hòu bù kě gēnggǎi) *state?* 請填空。／请填空。

____________________________, no changes possible.

i *What follows are your birthdate and home region. You are instructed to select from a pull-down menu. Write the characters for "Please select"* (Qǐng xuǎnzé)*:*

_______ _______ _______

j *Finally, in what order does the site request the following information?*

____ *marital status*

____ *income*

____ *height*

____ *educational background*

Note that the default information states "not married," "4,000–5,000 RMB/month," "175 cm," and "college degree."

k *The little box to check is to affirm, "*已经阅读并同意百合服务条款.*" Number the following in the correct order to produce this sentence.*

____ fúwù *service*

____ bìng *also*

____ tiáokuǎn *terms*

____ tóngyì *agree to*

____ yuèdú *read*

____ Bǎihé *Baihe*

____ yǐjing *already*

l *By clicking the big orange box, you "Complete registration" (*zhùcè wánchéng*). Write the characters for this:*

______ ______ ______ ______

36.22 *Following is a testimonial by two satisfied clients.*

对的时间遇到对的人
关键词：
一见钟情
夫妻相

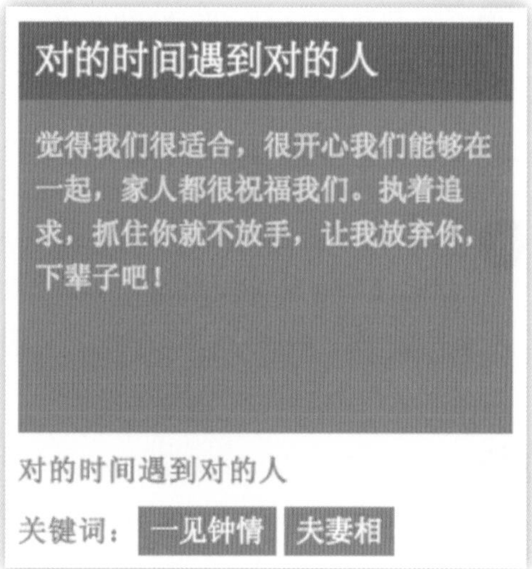
对的时间遇到对的人
觉得我们很适合，很开心我们能够在一起，家人都很祝福我们。执着追求，抓住你就不放手，让我放弃你，下辈子吧！
对的时间遇到对的人
关键词：
一见钟情
夫妻相

a *The text in orange is the same below both images.*

Line 1: Dùi de shíjiān yùdào duì de rén.
Yùdào *means "to meet."*
這句話甚麼意思？請寫英文。／
这句话什么意思？请写英文。

____

Line 2: Guānjiàn cí: Yījiànzhōngqíng Fūqīxiàng
Guānjiàn cí *means "tag words." Please write the characters for the following:*

Looks like a couple: ______________

Love at first sight: ______________

b *The image on the right is a testimonial by the couple. The title is the same as Line 1 below the images. The rest of the statement is as follows.* 請用拼音和英文填空。／请用拼音和英文填空。

觉得我们很适合，很开心我们能够在一起，家人都很祝福我们。执着追求，抓住你就不放手，让我放弃你，下辈子吧！

________ wǒmen hěn __________, hěn __________ wǒmen __________ zài __________, ________ dōu hěn zhùfú wǒmen. Zhízhuó zhuīqiú, zhuāzhù nǐ jiù bú __________, ràng wǒ fàngqì nǐ, xià bèizi ba!

I feel we are very ____________. *I'm very* ___________ *we can be together. Both our* ____________ *wish us happiness. After a dedicated pursuit, I have caught you and will not let go. If you tell me to give you up, how about in the next lifetime!*

Reading a story

36.23 故事 *Find the following terms in either the traditional or simplified text and circle them. Write in the accompanying number.*

1. shànyú *be good at*
2. qíguài *strange*
3. lǐngzhe *leading*
4. xuékē nèiróng *subject content*
5. qīngsōng *relaxed*
6. dòu tā wán *teases him*
7. rě tā xiào *makes him laugh*
8. xīxihāhā *laughing out loud*
9. lègebùtíng *laughing nonstop*
10. zài tā shēnbiān *be by her side*
11. gǎnjǐn *quickly*
12. tán liàn'ài *dating*
13. kǎolǜ *consider, think over*

14. gèzì *each*
15. shìyìng *adapt to*
16. jù *get together*
17. shuōchángdàoduǎn *talk about all topics (literally, speak of the long and talk of the short)*
18. sùkǔbàolè *tell of hardships and joys*

19. jiànjiàn de *gradually*
20. chéngjiā āndìng xiàlai *become a family and settle down*
21. duìxiàng *romantic partner*
22. chūyú wúnài *out of desperation*
23. guāiguāi *obediently, cooperatively*
24. xiāngqīn duìxiàng *blind date*
25. gǎnkuài *quickly, in a hurry*
26. bàogào *report*
27. zhè chǎng xì yǎn de zěnmeyàng *how we performed the play*
28. yíduàn shíjiān *a period of time*
29. dùjì *jealousy*
30. huìmiàn *meet*
31. mòshēngrén *stranger*
32. cóngxīn *anew*
33. gǎnqíng *feeling*
34. yǒuqíng *friendship*
35. àiqíng *love*
36. jīqíng *passion*

37. hùxiāng zūnjìng *mutual respect*
38. xiāngyù *encounters*
39. yìxiǎngbúdào *unexpected*
40. rénshēng tǐyàn *life experiences*
41. yóuyù *hesitant*
42. jiūjié *conflicted*

43. gāncuì yuēdìng *simply promise*
44. móshì *mode*
45. shēngmìng *lifetime*
46. lìng yí bàn *other half*
47. zhùfú *give best wishes*
48. yíbèizi *lifelong*
49. "hóngyán zhījǐ" *"red confidant" = female confidant*
50. "lányán zhījǐ" *"blue confidant" = male confidant*
51. dānshēn *single*

小王和小劉是同學。小王很外向，大大咧咧，喜歡戶外活動，善於交朋友。小劉比較內向，學習很認真，做事很謹慎。奇怪的是，他們兩個人雖然個性很不一樣，但特別談得來。下課以後，小劉領著小王一起做作業，上網查信息，討論新的學科內容。完了以後小王帶著小劉去咖啡館聊天、去附近的小公園散步、去購物中心逛街。小劉不愛說話，可是他和小王在一起的時候感覺很輕鬆，很快樂。小王常逗他玩，惹他笑。小王喜歡搞笑，總是嘻嘻哈哈，樂個不停。小劉在她身邊讓她有一種安全感。朋友們問他們："你們將來會結婚嗎？"他們就趕緊回答，"不，我們不在談戀愛，我們只是普通的朋友。考慮婚姻的事還早著呢。以後再說吧！"

小王和小刘是同学。小王很外向，大大咧咧，喜欢户外活动，善于交朋友。小刘比较内向，学习很认真，做事很谨慎。奇怪的是，他们两个人虽然个性很不一样，但特别谈得来。下课以后，小刘领着小王一起做作业，上网查信息，讨论新的学科内容。完了以后小王带着小刘去咖啡馆聊天、去附近的小公园散步、去购物中心逛街。小刘不爱说话，可是他和小王在一起的时候感觉很轻松，很快乐。小王常逗他玩，惹他笑。小王喜欢搞笑，总是嘻嘻哈哈，乐个不停。小刘在她身边让她有一种安全感。朋友们问他们："你们将来会结婚吗？"他们就赶紧回答，"不，我们不在谈恋爱，我们只是普通的朋友。考虑婚姻的事还早着呢。以后再说吧！"

大學畢業以後，他們各自找到了一份工作。為了適應新的職業，兩個人都變得很忙。有的時候到了周末都沒有時間再聚了，不過他們還是經常會通過電話或者微信聯系，說長道短，訴苦報樂。

大学毕业以后，他们各自找到了一份工作。为了适应新的职业，两个人都变得很忙。有的时候到了周末都没有时间再聚了，不过他们还是经常会通过电话或者微信联系，说长道短，诉苦报乐。

漸漸地，兩家父母開始著急了，希望自己孩子早一點成家安定下來。所以兩邊親戚朋友都開始給小王和小劉介紹對象了。出於無奈，他們兩個都乖乖去跟各自的相親對象見面、吃飯、看電影、散步。可是回

渐渐地，两家父母开始着急了，希望自己孩子早一点成家安定下来。所以两边亲戚朋友都开始给小王和小刘介绍对象了。出于无奈，他们两个都乖乖去跟各自的相亲对象见面、吃饭、看电影、散步。可是回

家以後他們就趕快互相打電話報告，今天這場戲演得怎麼樣？過了一段時間他們發現自己有一種新的感覺，奇怪，這是妒忌嗎？小劉和別人會面的時候，小王很難過。小王見個陌生人的時候，小劉很不安心。怎麼辦？他們開始從新考慮兩人之間的感情：這是友情還是愛情？愛情難道不應該更有激情嗎？他們可以靠著現有的感情成為男女朋友，將來結婚嗎？

家以后他们就赶快互相打电话报告，今天这场戏演得怎么样？过了一段时间他们发现自己有一种新的感觉，奇怪，这是妒忌吗？小刘和别人会面的时候，小王很难过。小王见个陌生人的时候，小刘很不安心。怎么办？他们开始从新考虑两人之间的感情：这是友情还是爱情？爱情难道不应该更有激情吗？他们可以靠着现有的感情成为男女朋友，将来结婚吗？

父母說，婚姻就這麼簡單。兩個相愛，互相尊敬的人生活在一起，互相支持，生兒育女，照顧老人，然後自己老了以後，互相陪伴。這就是愛情，這就是人生。可是年輕人心裡想，沒那麼簡單。世界變大了。可去的地方還多著呢，可做的事情還多著呢，可認識的人也還多著呢。如果現在就結婚定下來，那麼一切就都完了，新的相遇，意想不到的人生體驗就都沒了。兩個人很猶豫，很糾結，不知道該怎麼辦。

父母说，婚姻就这么简单。两个相爱，互相尊敬的人生活在一起，互相支持，生儿育女，照顾老人，然后自己老了以后，互相陪伴。这就是爱情，这就是人生。可是年轻人心里想，没那么简单。世界变大了。可去的地方还多着呢，可做的事情还多着呢，可认识的人也还多着呢。如果现在就结婚定下来，那么一切就都完了，新的相遇，意想不到的人生体验就都没了。两个人很犹豫，很纠结，不知道该怎么办。

How do you think this story might end? Read Ending 1, and write an alternative ending.

Ending 1:

後來兩人乾脆約定：還是保持現在的朋友相處模式；如果今後雙方遇到了彼此生命中更合適的另一半，就互相祝福，做一輩子的“紅顏知己”和“藍顏知己”；如果兩人三十歲之前都還單身，也沒有遇到更合適的結婚對象，那麼兩個人就在一起吧！

后来两人干脆约定：还是保持现在的朋友相处模式；如果今后双方遇到了彼此生命中更合适的另一半，就互相祝福，做一辈子的“红颜知己”和“蓝颜知己”；如果两人三十岁之前都还单身，也没有遇到更合适的结婚对象，那么两个人就在一起吧！

Ending 2:

Encounter 4 Extension: Cultural mini-documentary

View the cultural mini-documentary for this unit and complete the exercises that follow.

36.24 *This video introduces several people's thoughts about what makes for an ideal romantic partner or potential spouse. For each speaker, fill in the blanks with pinyin.*

a.

這個問題就是不好答了，找伴侶這個，它跟找職業還不太一樣，你可以很明確地告訴別人你喜歡甚麼職業，不喜歡甚麼職業，因為那個職業不管你喜不喜歡，它就是那個樣子，但是伴侶呢，她是一個活人，所以呢你得去適應她，你除了喜歡她你還得要適應她，她還得要適應你。所以我覺得這個挺難的。／

这个问题就是不好答了，找伴侣这个，它跟找职业还不太一样，你可以很明确地告诉别人你喜欢什么职业，不喜欢什么职业，因为那个职业不管你喜不喜欢，它就是那个样子，但是伴侣呢，她是一个活人，所以呢你得去适应她，你除了喜欢她你还得要适应她，她还得要适应你。所以我觉得这个挺难的。

Zhège wèntí jiùshì bù hǎo dá le, zhǎo bànlǚ zhèi ge, tā gēn zhǎo zhíyè hái bú tài yíyàng, nǐ kěyǐ ____________________ gàosu biéren nǐ xǐhuan shénme zhíyè, bù xǐhuan shénme zhíyè, yīnwèi nèi ge zhíyè ___________ nǐ xǐ bu xǐhuan, tā jiùshì nèi ge yàngzi, dànshì bànlǚ ne, tā shì yí ge ____________, suǒyǐ ne nǐ děi qù shìyìng tā, nǐ ___________ xǐhuan tā nǐ hái děi yào shìyìng tā, tā hái děi yào shìyìng nǐ. Suǒyǐ wǒ juéde zhèi ge __________ de.

*That's really a tough question to answer. Finding a partner, that's . . . it's really not the same as finding a career. You can **very clearly** tell someone what careers you like and don't like, because a career is what it is **no matter** whether you like it or not, but a companion is a **living person**, so you have to adapt to her—**aside from** liking her, you have to adapt to her, and she has to adapt to you. So I think this is **quite difficult.***

b.

我心目中理想的伴侶，我認為首要的一點就是責任心是最首要的，然後另外第二點我也覺得我們應該可以能成為朋友，意思就是我們能夠足夠地了解對方，傾聽對方，無話不談。／

我心目中理想的伴侣，我认为首要的一点就是责任心是最首要的，然后另外第二点我也觉得我们应该可以能成为朋友，意思就是我们能够足够地了解对方，倾听对方，无话不谈。

Wǒ ____________ lǐxiǎng de bànlǚ, wǒ rènwéi shǒuyào de yì diǎn jiùshì __________ shì zuì shǒuyào de, ránhòu lìngwài dì’èr diǎn wǒ yě juéde wǒmen yīnggāi kěyǐ néng __________ péngyou, yìsi jiùshì wǒmen nénggòu __________ liǎojiě duìfāng, qīngtīng duìfāng, wú huà bù tán.

The ideal companion ***in my mind****, I think the most important thing—a* ***sense of responsibility*** *is the most important, and then the second thing, I also feel we should be able* ***to become*** *friends, and by that I mean that we are able to* ***sufficiently*** *understand the other person and listen to the other person, so that there’s no subject we can’t talk about.*

c.

我是一個比較重感情的人，我覺得就是反正我的另一半吧，就是我會努力地去讀懂她，當然我也希望她能讀懂我。／

我是一个比较重感情的人，我觉得就是反正我的另一半吧，就是我会努力地去读懂她，当然我也希望她能读懂我。

Wǒ shì yí ge bǐjiào ________________ de rén, wǒ juéde jiùshì fǎnzhèng ____________________ ba, jiùshì wǒ huì nǔlì de qù dúdǒng tā, dāngrán wǒ yě __________ tā néng dúdǒng wǒ.

I’m the kind of guy who ***places great emphasis on emotions****. So I think, anyway, when it comes to* ***my other half****, I’ll work hard to read her emotions, and of course* ***I hope*** *that she can read mine.*

d.

我覺得就是他要有，非常大度的人，因為過日子嘛，就是很，平平淡淡的，也許你可以談一場很轟轟烈烈的戀愛，但是過日子是需要就是互相包容的，就是不管你長得有多好看，你總有老的一天，就不管你現在是多麼牛，也許你過兩年就不行啦，不是不行啦，就是走下坡路了，就是要不管甚麼時候這個人都有一個很大的包容度，可以就是兩個人互相彼此支撐，走到最後。／

我觉得就是他要有，非常大度的人，因为过日子嘛，就是很，平平淡淡的，也许你可以谈一场很轰轰烈烈的恋爱，但是过日子是需要就是互相包容的，就是不管你长得有多好看，你总有老的一天，就不管你现在是多么牛，也许你过两年就不行啦，不是不行啦，就是走下坡路了，就是要不管什么时候这个人都有一个很大的包容度，可以就是两个人互相彼此支撑，走到最后。

Wǒ juéde jiùshì tā yào yǒu, fēicháng dàdù de rén, yīnwèi guòrìzi ma, jiùshì hěn, ________________ de, yěxǔ nǐ kěyǐ tán yì chǎng hěn ________________ de liàn’ài, dànshì guòrìzi shì xūyào jiùshì ______________ de, jiùshì bùguǎn nǐ zhǎng de yǒu duō hǎokàn, nǐ __________ lǎo de yìtiān, jiù bùguǎn nǐ xiànzài shì duōme _____, _______ nǐ guò liǎng nián jiù bùxíng la, búshì bùxíng la, jiùshì zǒu xiàpōlù le, jiùshì yào bùguǎn shénme shíhou zhège rén dōu yǒu yí ge hěn dà de bāoróngdù, kěyǐ jiùshì liǎng ge rén hùxiāng ________ zhīchēng, zǒu dào zuìhòu.

I feel, you know, he's got to have, got to be a very open-minded person, because living life, you know, it's very ***normal and boring****. Maybe you've had a very* ***passionate*** *affair, but when it comes to living life, what is needed is* ***mutual tolerance****. I mean, no matter how good-looking you may be,* ***there will always be*** *that day when you'll grow old. I mean, no matter how* ***awesome*** *you may be now,* ***maybe*** *after a few years you'll be all washed up. Well, not all washed up—I mean, on a downward trajectory. So what's needed is, no matter when, this person will have a lot of tolerance, so that you can, you know, the two of you* ***mutually*** *support each other all the way to the end.*

e.

每個人的想法不一樣，理念不一樣，我覺得我理想中的未來的老婆，她要懂得，懂我，首先她要懂得我，二呢，她要會心疼我，因為這個當然了也是相互的，我也要懂她，我也要會心疼她，但是呢，在中國人的傳統的理念當中呢，女人最大的好處呢，就是說就是善良、懂事兒、然後她對你好，這是中國男人需要的。／

每个人的想法不一样，理念不一样，我觉得我理想中的未来的老婆，她要懂得，懂我，首先她要懂得我，二呢，她要会心疼我，因为这个当然了也是相互的，我也要懂她，我也要会心疼她，但是呢，在中国人的传统的理念当中呢，女人最大的好处呢，就是说就是善良、懂事儿、然后她对你好，这是中国男人需要的。

Měi ge rén de xiǎngfǎ bù yíyàng, _________ bù yíyàng, wǒ juéde wǒ lǐxiǎng zhōng de wèilái de lǎopo, tā yào dǒngde, dǒng wǒ, __________ tā yào dǒngde wǒ, èr ne, tā yào huì _________ wǒ, yīnwèi zhège dāngrán le yěshì xiānghù de, wǒ yě yào dǒng tā, wǒ yě yào huì xīnténg tā, dànshì ne, zài Zhōngguórén de chuántǒng de lǐniàn dāngzhōng ne, nǚrén zuìdà de hǎochù ne, jiùshì shuō jiùshì __________, dǒngshìr, ránhòu tā duì nǐ hǎo, zhè shì Zhōngguó nánrén _______ de.

Each person will have a different idea, a different ***concept****. I guess my ideal future wife, she needs to understand . . . understand me.* ***First of all****, she needs to understand me. And second, she should* ***cherish*** *me, because . . . of course this is a mutual thing, I need to understand her too, and cherish her, but in the traditional Chinese concept, a woman's strongest point is that, you know, she is* ***kindhearted*** *and understanding, and she's good to you. That's what a Chinese man* ***needs****.*

f.

我認為適合自己的伴侶首先要跟自己有共同的語言，還有共同的興趣愛好，至少我們的性格不會太突兀，不會經常就是有那個叫甚麼，對，經常有摩擦，或者經常有不同的意見，會吵架，我覺得這樣就不是理想中的伴侶。／

我认为适合自己的伴侣首先要跟自己有共同的语言，还有共同的兴趣爱好，至少我们的性格不会太突兀，不会经常就是有那个叫什么，对，经常有摩擦，或者经常有不同的意见，会吵架，我觉得这样就不是理想中的伴侣。

Wǒ rènwéi shìhé zìjǐ de bànlǚ shǒuxiān yào gēn zìjǐ yǒu _________________________, hái yǒu gòngtóng de xìngqù àihào, zhìshǎo wǒmen de __________ bú huì tài tūwù, bú huì jīngcháng jiùshì yǒu nà ge jiào shénme, duì, jīngcháng yǒu ______, huòzhě jīngcháng yǒu bùtóng de ________, huì _________, wǒ juéde zhèyàng jiù búshì lǐxiǎng zhōng de bànlǚ.

The way I see it, a companion that suits me first of all needs to have ***a common language*** *with me, as well as common interests and hobbies. At a minimum, our* ***personalities*** *should not be too much in conflict, so that there's not frequently, whatchacallit, right, there's frequently* ***friction****, and differing* ***opinions****, and we frequently* ***quarrel****. I feel that this is not what I would call an ideal partner.*

g.

然後有共同的朋友圈，我可以去跟她的朋友圈玩兒，她也可以和我的朋友圈玩兒，然後對雙方的，對我的父母也很好，然後我們有很多一樣的愛好，比如說音樂呀，比如說都喜歡看甚麼樣兒的電影呀，還有一些在衣服上的一些觀點，就說她不會覺得我土，我也不會覺得她土。／

然后有共同的朋友圈，我可以去跟她的朋友圈玩儿，她也可以和我的朋友圈玩儿，然后对双方的，对我的父母也很好，然后我们有很多一样的爱好，比如说音乐呀，比如说都喜欢看什么样儿的电影呀，还有一些在衣服上的一些观点，就说她不会觉得我土，我也不会觉得她土。

Ránhòu yǒu gòngtóng de péngyou quān, wǒ kěyǐ qù gēn tā de péngyou quān wánr, tā yě kěyǐ hé wǒ de péngyou quān wánr, ránhòu ________________ de, duì wǒ de fùmǔ yě hěn hǎo, ránhòu wǒmen yǒu ____________________ àihào, bǐrú shuō yīnyuè ya, bǐrú shuō dōu xǐhuan kàn ________________ diànyǐng ya, hái yǒu yìxiē ________________ yìxiē guāndiǎn, _________ tā bú huì juéde wǒ tǔ, wǒ yě bú huì juéde tā tǔ.

And . . . if there is a common circle of friends, I can hang out with her group of friends, she can hang out with my group of friends, and ***each of us toward the other's*** *[parents] . . . she's good to my parents, and . . . if we have* ***a lot of the same*** *interests, such as music or* ***what kinds of*** *movies we both like to watch and some opinions* ***on clothing, I mean****, she won't think I'm a hick and I won't think she's a hick.*

h.

我對男朋友的要求就是一定要人好，其次呢就是他經濟上怎麼樣我不太關注，但是一定要人好，一定要孝順父母。／

我对男朋友的要求就是一定要人好，其次呢就是他经济上怎么样我不太关注，但是一定要人好，一定要孝顺父母。

Wǒ duì nánpéngyou de ________ jiùshì yídìng yào _________, qícì ne jiùshì tā jīngjì shang zěnmeyàng wǒ _________________, dànshì yídìng yào rén hǎo, yídìng yào __________ fùmǔ.

What I'm looking for *in a boyfriend is that he's got* ***to be a good person****, and beyond that,* ***I won't pay much attention*** *to his economic circumstances, but he's got to be a good person. He's got to* ***care for*** *his parents.*

i.

我呢算是比較傳統的中國人，想起一句話就是夫唱婦隨，嫁雞隨雞，嫁狗隨狗，這是我的觀點，就是稍微有一點大男子主義吧，就是女人嘛就是聽男人的，讓你幹嘛你幹嘛就是了，比較傳統算是就是。／

我呢算是比较传统的中国人，想起一句话就是夫唱妇随，嫁鸡随鸡，嫁狗随狗，这是我的观点，就是稍微有一点大男子主义吧，就是女人嘛就是听男人的，让你干嘛你干嘛就是了，比较传统算是就是。

Wǒ ne _______ bǐjiào chuántǒng de Zhōngguórén, xiǎngqǐ yí jù huà jiùshì fūchàng-fùsuí, jià jī suí jī, jià gǒu suí gǒu, zhè shì wǒ de __________, jiùshì ____________________ dà nánzǐ zhǔyì ba, jiùshì nǚrén ma jiùshì _______________, ràng nǐ gànmá nǐ gànmá jiùshì le, bǐjiào chuántǒng suànshì jiùshì.

I guess ***I would count*** *as a more traditional Chinese. I'm thinking of a saying: "The husband sings and the wife follows. If you're married to a chicken, follow the chicken; if you're married to a dog, follow the dog." That's my* ***viewpoint****; it's . . .* ***got a tiny bit of*** *male chauvinist in it, that is, women should* ***do what men say****, whatever I ask you to do, you do it and that's all, kind of traditional, you might say.*

j.

因為呢兩個人在一起嘛，關鍵就是看感情，感情有了甚麼都好說。／

因为呢两个人在一起嘛，关键就是看感情，感情有了什么都好说。

Yīnwèi ne liǎng ge rén zài yìqǐ ma, __________ jiùshì kàn gǎnqíng, gǎnqíng yǒule shénme dōu hǎoshuō.

Because when it's the two of you together, you know, ***the important thing*** *is feeling. If you've got that connection, you can handle anything.*

k.

別打別鬧，倆人掙錢多少無所謂，只要互相恩愛是最好的。／

别打别闹，俩人挣钱多少无所谓，只要互相恩爱是最好的。

Bié dǎ bié nào, liǎ rén zhèng qián duōshao ___________, zhǐyào hùxiāng ______ shì zuì hǎo de.

Don't fight and fuss. However much the two of you earn ***isn't important****. The best is when you* ***love and care*** *for each other.*

l.

我跟我老公兩個就是順其自然認識的，然後最主要不分物質最主要還是感情，就是你喜歡我，我喜歡你就夠了，不要求任何，就是呀長相呀、物質呀甚麼都不重要，最主要是感覺，是吧？／

我跟我老公两个就是顺其自然认识的，然后最主要不分物质最主要还是感情，就是你喜欢我，我喜欢你就够了，不要求任何，就是呀长相呀、物质呀什么都不重要，最主要是感觉，是吧？

Wǒ gēn wǒ lǎogōng liǎng ge jiùshì shùn qí zìrán rènshi de, ránhòu zuì zhǔyào bù fēn wùzhì zuì zhǔyào háishi gǎnqíng, jiùshì nǐ xǐhuan wǒ, wǒ xǐhuan nǐ jiù ______, bù yāoqiú ______, jiùshì ya _________ ya, wùzhì ya shénme dōu bú zhòngyào, zuì zhǔyào shì ______, shì ba?

My man and I, the two of us met just sort of naturally, and . . . the most important thing is feelings and not material things. I mean, if we like each other, ***it's enough****. I wouldn't demand* ***any*** *. . . you know,* ***looks****, material things, none of that's important—what's important is* ***the feeling****, right?*

36.25 上面這些人的看法，你跟哪一個最一致？跟哪一個看法最不同？把兩個人的照片都圈起來 *(circle)*，然後在下邊寫幾句 *(several sentences)* 關於你找理想伴侶的想法。／上面这些人的看法，你跟哪一个最一致？跟哪一个看法最不同？把两个人的照片都圈起来 *(circle)*，然后在下边写几句 *(several sentences)* 关于你找理想伴侣的想法。

Shàngmian zhè xiē rén de kànfǎ, nǐ gēn nǎ yí ge zuì yízhì? Gēn nǎ yí ge kànfǎ zuì bùtóng? Bǎ liǎng ge rén de zhàopiàn dōu quān qǐlai, ránhòu zài xiàbian xiě jǐ jù guānyú nǐ zhǎo lǐxiǎng bànlǚ de xiǎngfǎ:

Recap

Grammar

What? Chinese has prefixes and suffixes too?

Yes, indeed. And you've already learned quite a few.

Examples:

~子: *as in* 妻子 qīzǐ, 身子 shēnzi, 孩子 háizi, 房子 fángzi

~人: *as in* 熟人 shúrén, 媒人 méiren, 介紹人／介绍人 jièshàorén

~們／们: *as in* 他們／他们 tāmen, 朋友們／朋友们 péngyou men, 孩子們／孩子们 háizimen, 咱們／咱们 zánmen

~學／学: *as in* 歷史學／历史学 lìshǐxué, 地理學／地理学 dìlǐxué, 社會學／社会学 shèhuìxué

~家: *as in* 歷史學家／历史学家 lìshǐxuéjiā, 科學家／科学家 kēxuéjiā, 專家／专家 zhuānjiā

~員／员: *as in* 服務員／服务员 fúwùyuán, 售票員／售票员 shòupiàoyuán, 公務員／公务员 gōngwùyuán

~觀／观: *as in* 價值觀／价值观 jiàzhíguān, 戀愛觀／恋爱观 liàn'àiguān, 世界觀／世界观 shìjièguān (*world view*)

~面: *as in* 方面 fāngmiàn, 裡面／里面 lǐmiàn, 前面 qiánmiàn, 正面 zhèngmiàn, 反面 fǎnmiàn

~方: *as in* 雙方／双方 shuāngfāng (*both sides*), 我方 wǒfāng (*our side*), 對方／对方 duìfāng (*the other side*)

可~: *as in* 可說／可说 kě shuō, 可笑 kě xiào, 可愛／可爱 kě'ài

重~ (chóng~) *translates as "re- + verb" so* 重組家庭／重组家庭 chóngzǔ jiātíng *means "a reconstituted family"*

Some of these prefixes and suffixes have been in use in Chinese for centuries, whereas others have been drawn into new language uses largely by contact with European languages, especially when there was a need to translate Western words and concepts into Chinese. Native Chinese words were used to express such English prefixes and suffixes as *non-, -ness, -tion, -ize, -ity,* and so on.

Such "innovations" evolved within the limitations of existing Chinese grammar and involved extending the reach of existing Chinese words and expressions.

The proliferation of these forms since the early years of the 20th century, which continues today, is an example of how Chinese has changed under the influence of European languages.

Here are some other examples:

非 fēi *translates as "non-" or "un-"*: 非法 fēifǎ *illegal*

性 xìng *translates as "-ity" or "-ness"*: 競爭性／竞争性 jìngzhēngxìng *competitiveness*

化 huà *translates as "-ize"*: 西化 xīhuà *Westernize*

主義／主义 zhǔyì *translates as "-ism"*: 社會主義／社会主义 shèhuìzhǔyì *Socialism*

Exercise: Can you figure out the meaning of these terms? 用英文填空。

現代／现代 xiàndài *modern* + 化 huà *-ization*
= 現代化／现代化 ____________

複雜／复杂 fùzá *complex* + 性 xìng *-ity, -ness*
= 複雜性／复杂性 ____________

美國／美国 Měiguó *preceded by* 非 fēi *non-, un-*
= 非美國的／非美国的 ____________

女性 nǚxìng *female* + 主義／主义 zhǔyì *-ism*
= 女性主義／女性主义 ____________

Chinese, like all languages, is changing, and rapidly so—it is responding to the needs of its users. For more on this topic, see *Modern Chinese: History and Sociolinguistics* by Ping Chen (Cambridge University Press, 1999), from which some of the examples above were drawn. Also, for a more comprehensive treatment, see *The Chinese Lexicon: A Comprehensive Survey* by Yip Po-Ching (Routledge, 2000).

Vocabulary

Please refer to page R-2 for a list of grammatical abbreviations used throughout this book.

ānquángǎn 安全感 sense of security N

báimǎ wángzǐ 白馬王子／白马王子 knight in shining armor; prince on a white horse N

bànlǚ 伴侶／伴侣 companion; mate; partner N

bèijǐng 背景 background; backdrop N

bǐrú shuō 比如説／比如说 for example; for instance VP

chéngzhǎng 成長／成长 grow up; mature V

chóngzǔ 重組／重组 reorganization N; reorganize V

chuántǒng 傳統／传统 tradition; convention N

dàdaliēliē 大大咧咧 careless; casual RF

diàochá 調查／调查 investigate; survey N/V

dìbù 地步 extent; condition; state N

dìwèi 地位 position; status N

fángdōng 房東／房东 landlord N

fàng jìnqu 放進去／放进去 put in; include; add RV

fēngfengdiāndiān 瘋瘋癲癲／疯疯癫癫 flighty; erratic RF

fúkuā 浮誇／浮夸 be pompous; boast; exaggerate SV/V

fùmiàn 負面／负面 negative side; negative N

gǎnjué 感覺／感觉 feel; perceived; become aware of V; feeling; sensation N

gōngwùyuán 公務員／公务员 government employee N

gùbushàng 顧不上／顾不上 cannot manage/attend to RV

hānhou 憨厚 simple and honest; straightforward SV

huìr 會兒／会儿 moment; time N

hùxiāng 互相 mutually; each other A

jiéhé 結合／结合 combine; integrate; join V

jījí 積極／积极 positive; active; energetic; vigorous; dynamic SV

jǐnshèn 謹慎／谨慎 cautions; prudent SV

jù(tǐ)huà 具(體)化／具(体)化 specify V

kào 靠 depend on; rely on V

kěkào 可靠 reliable; trustworthy SV

kěwàng 渴望 thirst for; long for V

kuòzhǎn 擴展／扩展 expand; spread; extend V; expansion N

lǎnduò 懶惰／懒惰 lazy; indolent SV

lǎoshi 老實／老实 honest; frank SV

lèguān 樂觀／乐观 optimistic; hopeful SV

liàn'àiguān 戀愛觀／恋爱观 feelings about love; perspectives about love N

liǎngxìng 兩性／两性 both sexes N

liǎnxíng 臉形／脸形 shape of one's face N

liè(shàngqu) 列(上去) list RV

lìhai 厲害／厉害 difficult to deal with SV

lìrú 例如 for instance; for example; such as C

lǐxiǎng 理想 ideal N/SV

luóliè 羅列／罗列 enumerate; set out; spread out V

méiren 媒人 matchmaker; go-between N

méndānghùduì 門當戶對／门当户对 be well-matched in social and economic status *(for marriage)* IE

nèixiàng 內向／内向 introverted SV

péibàn 陪伴 keep somebody company; accompany V

pèideshàng 配得上 be able to match RV

qìjīn wéizhǐ 迄今為止／迄今为止 until now; so far IE

qínfèn 勤奮／勤奋 diligent; assiduous SV

quān 圈 circle; ring N

rúcǐ 如此 thus; like this; such VP

shèjí 涉及 involve; touch upon V

shèjiāo 社交 social contact/interaction/life N

shēngāo 身高 height *(of a person)* N

shēngchénbāzì 生辰八字 one's birth data for astrological/marriage purposes IE

shēng'éryùnǚ 生兒育女／生儿育女 bear and raise children IE

shēnxíng 身形 figure; physical build N

shènzhì 甚至 even (to the point of) C

shènzhì yú 甚至於／甚至于 even to the point of; so much so that C

shízài 實在／实在 honest; dependable SV

shuāngfāng 雙方／双方 both sides; two parties N

shúrén *(also pronounced* **shóurén***)* 熟人 acquaintance; friend N

tándelái 談得來／谈得来 get along well; be congenial RV

(tā) rén hǎo (他／她)人好 he/she is a good person PH

tèzhēng 特徵／特征 trait; characteristic; distinctive feature N

tiáojiàn 條件／条件 requirement; condition; factor; term N

tǐmào 體貌／体貌 figure and appearance N

tǐzhòng 體重／体重 (body) weight N

tóngxìngliàn 同性戀／同性恋 homosexuality; homosexual N

wènjuàn 問卷／问卷 questionnaire N

wùzhì 物質／物质 material; matter; substance N

xiāng'ài 相愛／相爱 love each other V

xiāngqīn 相親／相亲 go on a blind date; meet a prospective spouse VP

xiánqīliángmǔ 賢妻良母／贤妻良母 a good wife and a good mother IE

xìngfú 幸福 happiness N; happy SV

xìnggé 性格 nature; disposition; temperament N

xíngtài 形態／形态 form; shape; style; pattern; type N

xíngxiàng 形象 image N

xīnmù zhōng 心目中 in one's heart/mind N

xísú 習俗／习俗 custom; convention N

xīyǐn 吸引 attract; draw; fascinate V

xuélì 學歷／学历 record of formal schooling; educational background N

xūwěi 虛偽／虚伪 hypocritical; false; insincere SV

yánsù 嚴肅／严肃 serious; solemn SV

yāoqiú 要求 demand; request; requirement N/V

yìbān 一般 ordinary; common; average SV

yìnxiàng 印象 impression N

yìxìngliàn 異性戀／异性恋 heterosexuality; heterosexual N

yǒushàn 友善 friendly; amicable SV

zài nèi 在內／在内 be included; including VO

zhàogu 照顧／照顾 look after; care for; attend to V

zhēnchéng 真誠／真诚 truthful; genuine; sincere SV

zhèngmiàn 正面 positive side; positive N

zhēnshí 真實／真实 true; real; authentic SV

zhīchí 支持 support; stand by; back V

zhíyè 職業／职业 occupation; profession; vocation N

zhòngdiǎn 重點／重点 key point; focal point; emphasis N

zhuàngkuàng 狀況／状况 condition; situation N

zhuānyè rénshì 專業人士／专业人士 professionals; personnel in a specific field N

zhùfáng 住房 housing N

zhùzhòng 注重 lay stress on; pay attention to V

zìrán'érrán 自然而然 naturally; automatically; spontaneously IE

zìyóu zhíyè 自由職業／自由职业 self-employment; freelance profession N

zūhù 租戶／租户 tenant N

Checklist of "can do" statements

After completing this unit, you should be able to perform each of the following tasks:

Listening and speaking

- ☐ Converse about the characteristics of your ideal romantic partner.
- ☐ Describe people with whom you have had a close relationship in the past.
- ☐ Describe a key relationship between two people you know.
- ☐ Talk about what you perceive as differences in marriage expectations between the East and West or between the past and present.

Reading and writing

- ☐ Decipher some items on the pages of a Chinese dating website.
- ☐ Comprehend a short story about the relationship between two people.
- ☐ Write an ending to a short story about the relationship between two people.

Understanding culture

- ☐ Make several accurate statements about the views of some Chinese people on ideal romantic partners.

UNIT 37

"A paradise on earth"

世外桃源

Shìwàitáoyuán

The ideal place to live

In this unit, you will learn how to:

- talk about characteristics of an ideal place to live.
- specify what you are looking for in a house or an apartment.
- specify what services you would like to have available in your community.
- specify desired details in the layout and furnishings within your home.
- comprehend details in e-mail ads about housing, home furnishings, and community facilities.
- read a story about housing choices.
- write a story about housing choices.

Encounter 1 Discussing types of places to live

37.1 *Xiao Mao, Luo Xueting, and Mick give advice to Tang Yuan and A-Juan on where to look for a place to live.* 請把中文跟英文對上。／请把中文跟英文对上。

____ a. sìhéyuàn 四合院
____ b. shēnghuó shèshī 生活設施／生活设施
____ c. huáiyùn 懷孕／怀孕
____ d. gāocéng lóufáng 高層樓房／高层楼房
____ e. xiǎoqū 小區／小区
____ f. gōngyùlóu 公寓樓／公寓楼
____ g. gōnggòng fúwù 公共服務／公共服务
____ h. píngfáng 平房
____ i. fángdìchǎn jīngjìrén 房地產經紀人／房地产经纪人
____ j. fángwū zūlìn de zhōngjiè 房屋租賃的中介／房屋租赁的中介

1. *pregnant*
2. *apartment building*
3. *multistory building*
4. *public services*
5. *courtyard dwelling*
6. *residential community*
7. *single-story house*
8. *living facilities*
9. *rental agent*
10. *real-estate broker*

37.2 *View Episode 37, Vignette 1. Xiao Mao, Luo Xueting, and Mick discuss various kinds of housing in Beijing. Below are statements about each type of dwelling they mention, plus one that they don't mention. Please classify each statement by checking the correct column.*

	四合院	高層公寓樓／高层公寓楼	平房
a. Děi yòng diàntī shàng gāocéng.	☐	☐	☐
b. Tōngcháng yǒu zìjǐ de qiányuàn hé hòuyuàn.	☐	☐	☐
c. Gèzhǒng shèshī qíquán.	☐	☐	☐
d. Hěn yǒu lǎo Běijīng de tèsè.	☐	☐	☐
e. Zhǐyǒu gōnggòng cèsuǒ.	☐	☐	☐
f. Tōngcháng zhǐ zhù yì jiā rén.	☐	☐	☐
g. Dōngtiān bǐjiào lěng, kěyǐ shāoméi huòzhě yòng diàn qǔnuǎn.	☐	☐	☐
h. Tōngcháng kào gōnggòng qǔnuǎn shèshī.	☐	☐	☐

37.3 請把下面的漢字跟上面的拼音對上。／请把下面的汉字跟上面的拼音对上。

____ 1. 很有老北京的特色。

____ 2. 通常只住一家人。

____ 3. 得用電梯上高層。／得用电梯上高层。

____ 4. 通常靠公共取暖設施。／通常靠公共取暖设施。

____ 5. 只有公共廁所。／只有公共厕所。

____ 6. 通常有自己的前院和後院。／通常有自己的前院和后院。

____ 7. 各種設施齊全。／各种设施齐全。

____ 8. 冬天比較冷，可以燒煤或者用電取暖。／冬天比较冷，可以烧煤或者用电取暖。

37.4 請把下面的英文跟上面的漢字對上。／请把下面的英文跟上面的汉字对上。

____ A. It generally relies on public heating facilities.

____ B. All the facilities are complete and available.

____ C. You generally have your own front yard and backyard.

____ D. It really has the feeling of old Beijing.

____ E. It generally only houses one family.

____ F. You need an elevator to get to the higher floors.

____ G. It's cold in winter. You can burn coal or use electricity for heat.

____ H. There's only a public toilet.

37.5 ***Pair work:*** *Talk briefly with a partner about whether you prefer to live in a house or an apartment, or if you'd like to try a Beijing-style courtyard dwelling. You will have an opportunity to talk more in depth about housing in Encounter 2.*

37.6 *Available public facilities are often a deciding factor for where people choose to live. Luo Xueting mentions several; many communities have access to even more facilities.* 請把中文跟英文對上。／请把中文跟英文对上。

____ a. chāoshì 超市	1. *restaurant*
____ b. gòuwù zhōngxīn 購物中心／购物中心	2. *hospital*
____ c. fànguǎn 飯館／饭馆	3. *drugstore*
____ d. gānxǐdiàn 乾洗店／干洗店	4. *library*
____ e. yàodiàn 藥店／药店	5. *fire station*
____ f. diànyǐngyuàn 電影院／电影院	6. *supermarket*
____ g. xuéxiào 學校／学校	7. *park*
____ h. yīyuàn 醫院／医院	8. *train station*
____ i. gōngyuán 公園／公园	9. *public parking*
____ j. gōnggòng qìchēzhàn 公共汽車站／公共汽车站	10. *dry cleaners*
____ k. dìtiězhàn 地鐵站／地铁站	11. *subway station*
____ l. túshūguǎn 圖書館／图书馆	12. *shopping center*
____ m. huǒchēzhàn 火車站／火车站	13. *gas station*
____ n. jiāyóuzhàn 加油站	14. *police station*
____ o. xiāofángzhàn 消防站	15. *cinema / movie theater*
____ p. jǐngchájú 警察局	16. *bus stop*
____ q. yóujú 郵局／邮局	17. *post office*
____ r. gōnggòng tíngchēchǎng 公共停車場／公共停车场	18. *school*

37.7 ***Pair work:*** *What kinds of facilities are there within a mile of where you live? Interview a partner.*

你住的地方一里以內都有甚麼？有____嗎？／你住的地方一里以内都有什么？有_____吗？

	你	你的夥伴／你的伙伴
超市		
購物中心／购物中心		
飯館／饭馆		
乾洗店／干洗店		
藥店／药店		
電影院／电影院		

	你	你的夥伴／你的伙伴
學校／学校		
醫院／医院		
公園／公园		
公共汽車站／公共汽车站		
地鐵站／地铁站		
圖書館／图书馆		
火車站／火车站		
加油站		
消防站		
警察局		
郵局／邮局		
公共停車場／公共停车场		

37.8 *Based on your answers in Exercise 37.7, compose a narrative about your neighborhood, as in the model below. Take notes below. Then present your statement to a partner, a small group, or the class. As you listen to your classmate describe the area in which she or he lives, try to guess where it is.*

我住的地區很方便。我家對面就是公園，再過去就有一個圖書館。從我家走路五分鐘就有一個小小的購物區，有個小超市，兩個小飯館，一個藥店。還有一個乾洗店。購物區那兒有公共汽車站，對面就是消防站。要是你想去大一點的購物中心或者電影院的話，那就得開車。我住的城市没有地鐵或火車。／我住的地区很方便。我家对面就是公园，再过去就有一个图书馆。从我家走路五分钟就有一个小小的购物区，有个小超市，两个小饭馆，一个药店。还有一个干洗店。购物区那儿有公共汽车站，对面就是消防站。要是你想去大一点的购物中心或者电影院的话，那就得开车。我住的城市没有地铁或火车。

Encounter 2 Discussing the location and layout of a housing unit

37.9 *Zhang Suyun shows an apartment to A-Juan and Tang Yuan.* 請把中文跟英文對上。／请把中文跟英文对上。

____ a. zhè tào fángzi 這套房子／这套房子
____ b. jiāotōng tèbié fādá 交通特別發達／交通特别发达
____ c. tíngchēwèi 停車位／停车位
____ d. ānquán 安全
____ e. liǎng shì yì tīng liǎng wèi 兩室一廳兩衛／两室一厅两卫
____ f. chúfáng 廚房／厨房
____ g. tǐng fāngbiàn de 挺方便的
____ h. wèishēngjiān 衛生間／卫生间
____ i. tàiyángnéng 太陽能／太阳能
____ j. fēngjǐng tǐng měi de 風景挺美的／风景挺美的
____ k. yángtái 陽台／阳台

1. *with developed (convenient) transportation*
2. *two bedrooms, a living room / dining room, two bathrooms*
3. *this apartment (suite of rooms)*
4. *it's very convenient*
5. *parking space*
6. *bathroom*
7. *safe*
8. *porch, balcony*
9. *the scenery is quite beautiful*
10. *solar energy*
11. *kitchen*

37.10 *View Episode 37, Vignette 2. Indicate whether the speakers are talking about space inside (*內／内 nèi*) or outside (*外 wài*) the apartment, or if they are talking about the apartment itself (*房 fáng*). (Statements might be slightly adjusted but are given in the order they were made.)*

	內／内	外	房
a. Zhè tào fángzi shì gāng tuīchū de.	☐	☐	☐
b. Zhè biān jiùshì dìtiězhàn, zǒuguòqu bú dào wǔ fēnzhōng shíjiān.	☐	☐	☐

	內／内	外	房
c. Zhèlǐ de dìlǐ wèizhi búcuò.	☐	☐	☐
d. Xiǎoqū de lǜhuà tǐng hǎo de.	☐	☐	☐
e. Yǒu dìxià liǎng céng chēkù.	☐	☐	☐
f. Zhè shì wǒmen dàtáng.	☐	☐	☐
g. Zhè xiǎoqū tèbié ānquán.	☐	☐	☐
h. Zhè fángzi zuò běi cháo nán, cháoxiàng tèbié de hǎo.	☐	☐	☐
i. Zhè biānr shì chúfáng.	☐	☐	☐
j. Cìwò jiù xiān zuò wǒ de gōngzuòjiān ba.	☐	☐	☐
k. Zhǔwò lǐbian dài yǒu wèishēngjiān.	☐	☐	☐
l. Wèishēngjiān lǐbianr shèbèi qíquán.	☐	☐	☐
m. Zhè huāyuán tè piàoliang, kōngqì yě hǎo.	☐	☐	☐

37.11 請把下面的漢字跟上面的拼音對上。／请把下面的汉字跟上面的拼音对上。

____ 1. 這裡的地理位置不錯。／这里的地理位置不错。
____ 2. 有地下兩層車庫。／有地下两层车库。
____ 3. 這套房子是剛推出的。／这套房子是刚推出的 。
____ 4. 這邊兒是廚房。／这边儿是厨房。
____ 5. 衛生間裡邊兒設備齊全。／卫生间里边儿设备齐全。
____ 6. 小區的綠化挺好的。／小区的绿化挺好的。
____ 7. 主臥裡邊帶有衛生間。／主卧里边带有卫生间。
____ 8. 這花園特漂亮，空氣也好。／这花园特漂亮，空气也好。
____ 9. 次臥就先做我的工作間吧。／次卧就先做我的工作间吧。
____ 10. 這邊就是地鐵站，走過去不到五分鐘時間。／这边就是地铁站，走过去不到五分钟时间。
____ 11. 這是我們大堂。／这是我们大堂。
____ 12. 這小區特別安全。／这小区特别安全。
____ 13. 這房子坐北朝南，朝向特別的好。／这房子坐北朝南，朝向特别的好。

37.12 請把下面的英文跟上面的漢字對上。／请把下面的英文跟上面的汉字对上。

____ A. *There are two underground parking levels.*

____ B. *The location here is pretty good.*

____ C. *The apartment faces south, which is really good.*

____ D. *The garden is really beautiful, and the air is good.*

____ E. *This apartment just came on the market.*

____ F. *The facilities in the bathroom are complete.*

____ G. *This community is really safe.*

____ H. *This is our lobby.*

____ I. *Let's use the second bedroom as my workroom for the moment.*

____ J. *Over this way is the subway station; it's less than a five-minute walk away.*

____ K. *There's a bathroom in the master bedroom.*

____ L. *The "greenification" [planting of green life] in this community is pretty good.*

____ M. *This way is the kitchen.*

37.13 *What are you looking for in a housing unit? Rank the following characteristics from 1 (most important) to 14 (least important).*

____ Dilǐ wèizhi hǎo, jiāotōng fādá 地理位置好，交通發達／地理位置好，交通发达

____ Dilǐ wèizhi hěn ānquán 地理位置很安全

____ Huánjìng hěn měi 環境很美／环境很美

____ Cháoxiàng tèbié hǎo 朝向特別好／朝向特别好

____ Yǒu tíngchēwèi 有停車位／有停车位

____ Yǒu chúfáng 有廚房／有厨房

____ Shèbèi qíquán, jiājù hěn xīn 設備齊全，傢俱很新／设备齐全，家具很新

____ Yǒu yángtái 有陽台／有阳台

____ Zūjīn huò jiàqián bú tài gāo 租金或價錢不太高／租金或价钱不太高

____ Shēnghuó shèshī wánshàn 生活設施完善／生活设施完善

____ Lǜhuà hěn hǎo 綠化很好／绿化很好

____ Yǒu zìjǐ de qiányuàn hé hòuyuàn 有自己的前院和後院／有自己的前院和后院

____ Yuànzi lǐ yǒu shù 院子裡有樹／院子里有树

____ Gōnggòng fúwù hǎo 公共服務好／公共服务好

37.14 ***Pair work:*** *Work with a partner to discuss in Chinese what you seek in your ideal housing arrangement. Go into detail as much as you can. Take notes from your discussion, and write several statements expessing your views.* 請寫拼音或者漢字。／请写拼音或者汉字。

37.15 *Classify each term below by checking the correct room.*

	廚房／厨房	衛生間／卫生间	客廳／客厅
a. diànbīngxiāng 電冰箱／电冰箱	☐	☐	☐
b. línyùfáng 淋浴房	☐	☐	☐
c. xiǎochúbǎo 小廚寶／小厨宝	☐	☐	☐
d. méiqìzào 煤氣灶／煤气灶	☐	☐	☐
e. luòdìchuānghu 落地窗戶／落地窗户	☐	☐	☐
f. táidēng 檯燈／台灯	☐	☐	☐
g. xǐwǎnjī 洗碗機／洗碗机	☐	☐	☐
h. diànshì 電視／电视	☐	☐	☐
i. tàiyángnéng rèshuǐqì 太陽能熱水器／太阳能热水器	☐	☐	☐
j. wēibōlú 微波爐／微波炉	☐	☐	☐
k. yùgāng 浴缸	☐	☐	☐
l. shūzhuō 書桌／书桌	☐	☐	☐
m. chōushuǐmǎtǒng 抽水馬桶／抽水马桶	☐	☐	☐
n. chōuyóuyānjī 抽油煙機／抽油烟机	☐	☐	☐
o. xǐshǒutái 洗手台	☐	☐	☐

37.16 *Now match the terms in Exercise 37.15 with the images below.*

microwave oven
1. ____

gas range
2. ____

vanity (for sink)
3. ____

refrigerator
4. ____

TV set
5. ____

French window
6. ____

shower stall
7. ____

flush toilet
8. ____

desk lamp
9. ____

desk
10. ____

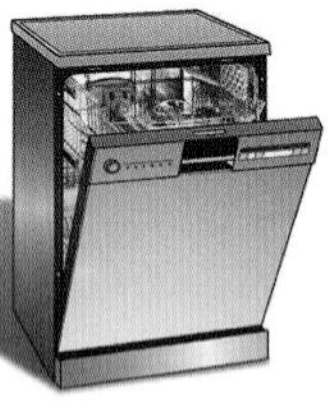

dishwasher
11. ____

solar water heater
12. ____

bathtub
13. ____

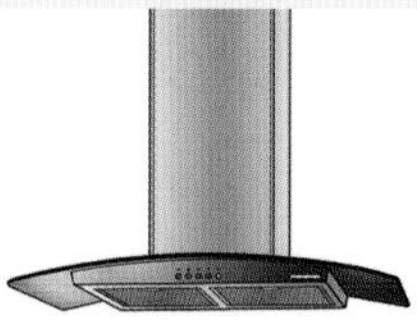

kitchen ventilator
14. ____

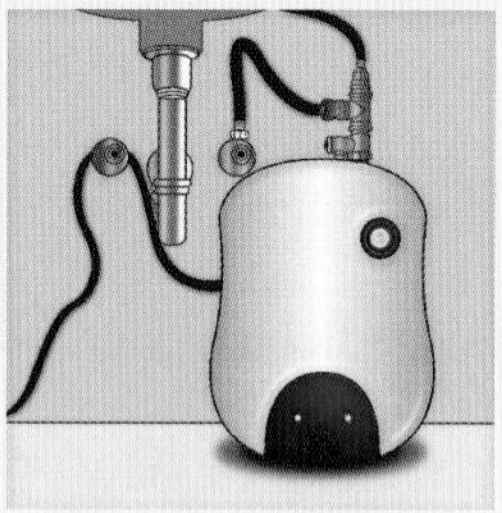

water heater (for kitchen sink)
15. ____

37.17 ***Pair work:*** *Describe the furnishings/accoutrements of the living room, bathroom, and kitchen where you live (or of your ideal living space). Is your refrigerator a Chinese brand (*Zhōngguó páizi 中國牌子／中国牌子*), for example? Do you have a separate bathtub and shower stall in your bathroom? As your partner speaks, try to write down the details or, if you like, sketch out the room being described.*

Encounter 3 Reading and writing

Reading real-life texts

37.18 *Following are a series of e-mails from University of Hawaii Chinese graduate students to a listserv of faculty and students from the PRC.*

a *Write the Chinese characters next to the terms below, based on the e-mail.*

Save　Send

-----原始邮件-----

主题：

发件人: XX <XX13210@yahoo.com>

发送时间: 2014年9月18日 星期一

收件人: [listserv]

抄送: XX <XX@nju.edu.cn>

----original message---- ______________________

Topic: ______________________

Sender: ______________________

Time sent: ______________________

Recipient: ______________________

Copy to: ______________________

b *There are six messages about wide-ranging topics. Match the English to their topics.*

____ 1. *renting a room*　A. 主题：找公交车月票

____ 2. *bus pass*　B. 主题：需要买床

____ 3. *short-term rental*　C. 主题：需要租房

____ 4. *buying a bed*　D. 主题：没有 Costco 卡，但是想去 Costco 购物的朋友

____ 5. *roommate*　E. 主题：急求现在开始之短期租

____ 6. *membership card*　F. 主题：寻室友

C 請用英文填空。／请用英文填空。

■ 邮件一

主题：找公交车月票

大家好！我是新到夏威夷大学的访问学者！

想请教大家一个问题，夏威夷大学能给访问学者办理公交车月票吗？

非常感谢！

Topic: Looking for a ____________________

Hello everyone! I am a visiting scholar who has ____________________ ____________*! I'd like to ask everyone a question: Can the University of Hawaii arrange a bus pass for* ____________________*?*

Thank you very much!

■ 邮件二

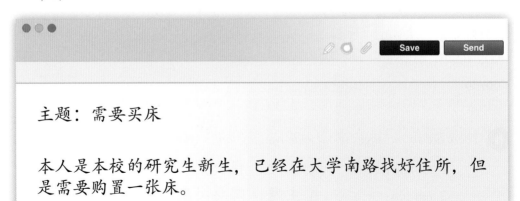

主题：需要买床

本人是本校的研究生新生，已经在大学南路找好住所，但是需要购置一张床。

对床有两点要求：

1.单人或双人床 （房间空间较小）

2.使用期一年以内，卫生情况较好（害怕臭虫）

本人将于8月15日早上抵达夏威夷，如果有朋友有合适的床转让给我，或有好的建议，请有劳联系我的 e-mail：xxx123@gmail.com

初次赴美，诸多方面有待学习，敬请各位指导帮助，万分感谢！

Topic: ____________________

I am a new ____________________ in this school. I've already found a place to live on South ______________ Avenue, but I need to purchase a bed.

I have two requirements for a bed:

1. ____________________ or ____________________ bed (the space in the room is rather small)

2. used for less than ____________________, comparatively clean (I'm afraid of bedbugs)

I will arrive in Hawaii on the ___________ of August 15. If someone has an appropriate bed for me, or any good suggestions, may I bother you to contact me at my e-mail: xxx123@gmail.com

This is my first time to ____________________, and there is a lot I have to learn. I hope you will all afford me advice and help. Thank you so very much!

■ 邮件三

Save Send

主题：需要租房

你好。

我是在夏大读政治的本科生，20号会来到火奴鲁鲁，现需租一房间（有个人单间最好，但跟人合住一房也可以考虑）。

要求：价格合理，干净卫生

本人22岁，男，无不良爱好，现在在加州打工中。

之前在校园里是住 Gateway House 的，现在退掉了所以要重新租房，如果有校内的朋友需要室友也可以跟我联系。

qq：1074xxxxxx

电话：1-808-xxx-xxxx

谢谢大家的帮助

Topic: ______________________

Hello.

I am an ______________________ *studying* ____________ *at the University of Hawaii. I will arrive in Honolulu on the 20th and need to rent a room (a* ____________ *room would be best, but I will also consider* ____________ ____________*).*

Requirements: reasonable cost, clean, and hygienic

I am ____________, ________, *with no bad* ____________. *Now I am in* ____________ *in the middle of a job.*

I used to live in the Gateway House on campus, but I moved out and now need to start over. If you're a student in the university and ______________________, you can also contact me.

qq: 1074xxxxxx

phone: 1-808-xxx-xxxx

Thanks to everyone for your help.

■ 邮件四

Save Send

主题：没有 Costco 卡，但是想去 Costco 购物的朋友

(Costco 简介：Costco 是一家大型会员制超市，购物需持卡方可进入，或有持卡的朋友陪你进店。店内所售商品种类很多，相对价格是很低的。)

8月4日左右办理了一张 Costco 卡，办理费约55美元。

Costco 政策是允许一个帐号下面有两张卡，即你我可以各持一张卡，各自独立购物。

(Costco 购物最好使用现金或者信用卡，Debit 卡似乎也可以用。此外，持 Costco 卡可以在 Costco 名下加油站加油，油费比较便宜。)

为了降低办卡成本，希望找朋友合享该卡，合享方式如下：你出25美元，即可拥有自己名下一张 Costco 卡。

如果有住校内或者附近的朋友，不想办卡，但是希望经常去 Costco 购物，也可以把联系方式告诉我。我可以偶尔开车载你去 Costco。我住处离学校不远。

Topic: Someone who ____________________________ but would like to ________ ________________________

(Short intro to Costco: Costco is a large-sized membership supermarket. In order to _________, you have to enter with a card, or you can enter the store with a _____________________________. In the store, there is a wide variety of merchandise on sale, and their prices are very _____________.)

Around August 4, I signed up for a Costco card. _____________________________ __________________.

Costco policy is that each account can have ________________, so that you and I can each have a card, and we can ______________________________.

(To shop at Costco, it's best to use _______________ or credit card. I think you can use a debit card too. In addition, if you have a Costco card, you can get gas at the Costco gas station, where the ____________________________________.)

In order to reduce the cost of the card, I hope to find a friend to share it in the following fashion: ____________________________, and you can immediately have your own Costco card.

If you live on campus or nearby, and if you ____________________________ but ____, you can also let me have your contact information. I can occasionally drive you to Costco. I live off campus _____ ________________________________.

■ 邮件五

主题：急求现在开始之短期租

Hi,

我是天文学研究所新生

男性

因计划有变

希望找可以住一星期的地方

客厅亦可

能睡就好(自己有睡袋)

请回信 xxxxx@gmail.com

或留言(xxx-xxx-xxxx)

万分感谢!!

Topic: Urgently seeking a short-term rental starting immediately

Hi,

I am a new graduate student at the Institute for Astronomy.

____

Because plans have changed, ______________________________________.

A living room would be OK too, as long as ______________________. *(I have my own sleeping bag.)*

________________________ *xxxxx@gmail.com*

or ___________________________ *(xxx-xxx-xxxx)*

Thank you so much!

■ 邮件六

Save Send

主题：寻室友

抱歉打扰，我有一个公寓房间可以分租。如有女性朋友寻找室友，请与我联系。手机： XXX-XXX-XXXX

祝愉快！

Topic: Seeking a ______________

Sorry to disturb you. I ____________________________ *for rent. If you're* ____________________________, *please* ____________________.

______________: *xxx-xxx-xxxx*

Wishing you happiness!

Reading a story

37.19 故事 *Find the following terms in either the traditional or simplified text and circle them. Write in the accompanying number.*

1. Zhào Hóng *Zhao Hong*
2. shěng *save (on an expense)*
3. fángzū *rent*
4. cún qǐlai *put in savings*
5. jiāoqū *suburbs*
6. dìxiàshì *basement*
7. qǐmǎ *at least*
8. kuānchǎng *spacious*
9. guǒyuán *orchard*
10. shǒufù *down payment*
11. zǎn *save up*
12. fēnqī fùkuǎn *pay in installments*
13. lìxī *interest*
14. fángkuǎn *cost of the house*
15. fùqīng *pay up*
16. xīnkǔ *toil, work hard*
17. fángdài *house mortgage*

18. Mǎlì Bùlǎng *Mary Brown*
19. hézū *rent together*
20. pǔputōngtōng *very ordinary*
21. gōngyòng *share*
22. mǎnyì *be satisfied*
23. wěndìng *stable*
24. qíngkuàng *situation*
25. biàn *change*
26. suǒwèi *so-called*
27. wēixiǎo zhùfáng *micro-housing, "tiny home"*
28. píngfāng chǐ *square meter*
29. zhùzhái *residence*
30. wēixíng *miniaturized*
31. jiēdài *to host*
32. jùhuì *get together*
33. jiāshàng lúnzi *put on wheels*
34. biànyú *be convenient to*
35. yídòng *shift, move*
36. bānjiā *move home*
37. zhěngge *entire*
38. qùchù *destination*
39. yì kǒuqì *in one breath, in one fell swoop*
40. zìyóu *free*
41. qīngsōng *relaxed*

---

42. gèng xiàng *more like*
43. xiànshí *realistic*

趙洪今年大學畢業了。過了半年他找到一份非常好的工作。為了省房租，他決定先不搬出父母的家，把自己的薪水存起來以後再去買郊區的房子。他希望買一棟比較大的房子，有上下兩層，最好還要有地下室和頂樓。房間麼，越多越好。他起碼要四間臥室、四間衛生間、還要有客廳、飯廳、書房和廚房—廚房一定要很寬敞。還要有個雙車位的車庫。當然也要前後院。另外，要是能有一個小果園就更好了。他住的城市房價不低，所以必須先把首付攢出來，然後準備分期付款，每個月付一筆利息，總共得付三十年才能把房款付清。所以趙洪做好準備了，他得要辛苦一輩子來還這筆房貸。

赵洪今年大学毕业了。过了半年他找到一份非常好的工作。为了省房租，他决定先不搬出父母的家，把自己的薪水存起来以后再去买郊区的房子。他希望买一栋比较大的房子，有上下两层，最好还要有地下室和顶楼。房间么，越多越好。他起码要四间卧室、四间卫生间、还要有客厅、饭厅、书房和厨房—厨房一定要很宽敞。还要有个双车位的车库。当然也要前后院。另外，要是能有一个小果园就更好了。他住的城市房价不低，所以必须先把首付攒出来，然后准备分期付款，每个月付一笔利息，总共得付三十年才能把房款付清。所以赵洪做好准备了，他得要辛苦一辈子来还这笔房贷。

瑪麗・布朗也是今年畢業的，畢業不久她也找到了一份挺不錯的工作。可是她

玛丽・布朗也是今年毕业的，毕业不久她也找到了一份挺不错的工作。可是她

和趙洪不同，她不願意留在家裡和父母一起住。她先找了兩個朋友，三個人合租了一套普普通通的房子，三間臥室，客廳、飯廳、廚房和衛生間都是公用。他們都沒有車，不是騎自行車就是坐公交車或者走路上班。瑪麗很滿意他們公寓的位置，就在市中心，去哪兒都很方便。可是她覺得現在這樣不是很穩定，因為萬一她的同屋有一個人要搬走，大家的情况就都得變。她也不願意付一輩子的房租。所以瑪麗看上了所謂"微小住房"，就是可能只有一到兩百平方尺的小住宅，裡頭所有的設施都是微型的。家裡沒有地方接待朋友也沒有關係，大家可以到咖啡館或餐廳去聚會。有些微小住房甚至可以加上輪子，便於移動，需要搬家的時候可以把整個小房子搬到新的去處。這種小房子，瑪麗可以一口氣把房款付清，不用分期付款。她覺得這樣會更自由，更輕鬆。

那麼你呢？你覺得你更像趙洪，還是更像瑪麗·布朗？你最理想，但也是最現實的房子，會是甚麼樣的？

和赵洪不同，她不愿意留在家里和父母一起住。她先找了两个朋友，三个人合租了一套普普通通的房子，三间卧室，客厅、饭厅、厨房和卫生间都是公用。他们都没有车，不是骑自行车就是坐公交车或者走路上班。玛丽很满意他们公寓的位置，就在市中心，去哪儿都很方便。可是她觉得现在这样不是很稳定，因为万一她的同屋有一个人要搬走，大家的情况就都得变。她也不愿意付一辈子的房租。所以玛丽看上了所谓"微小住房"，就是可能只有一到两百平方尺的小住宅，里头所有的设施都是微型的。家里没有地方接待朋友也没有关系，大家可以到咖啡馆或餐厅去聚会。有些微小住房甚至可以加上轮子，便于移动，需要搬家的时候可以把整个小房子搬到新的去处。这种小房子，玛丽可以一口气把房款付清，不用分期付款。她觉得这样会更自由，更轻松。

那么你呢？你觉得你更像赵洪，还是更像玛丽·布朗？你最理想，但也是最现实的房子，会是什么样的？

37.20 *Write a response to the question posed in the story.* 請寫漢字。／请写汉字。

Encounter 4 Extension: Cultural mini-documentary

View the cultural mini-documentary for this unit and complete the exercises that follow.

37.21 *As you might imagine, real estate is hot property in the booming city of Beijing. Folks looking for properties to rent or buy can visit any of a multitude of real estate agencies, most of which are chains. You will notice that the words used for "real estate" vary: we have* 地產／地产 dìchǎn, 房產／房产 fángchǎn, *and* 不動產／不动产 búdòngchǎn. *There's also an agency called 5i5j, meant to sound like* 我愛我家／我爱我家wǒ'àiwǒjiā *when read aloud. Using an agency means paying a fee, but it also usually comes with greater sense of confidence in the reliability of the transaction. After watching this video, you may feel a bit more ready for what you'll find when you go looking for a rental property in China yourself. First, warm up by matching some key words to their English translations.*

____ a. yèzhǔ, fángzhǔ 業主，房主／业主，房主	1. *electrical appliances*
____ b. fángzū, zūjīn 房租，租金	2. *property owner, landlord*
____ c. fùkuǎn fāngshì 付款方式	3. *suite, apartment*
____ d. jiājù 傢俱／家具	4. *payment method*
____ e. diànqì 電器／电器	5. *utilities (fees)*
____ f. shuǐdiànfèi 水電費／水电费	6. *rent (money)*
____ g. yí tào fángzi 一套房子	7. *rental contract*
____ h. zūfáng hétong 租房合同	8. *furniture*

37.22 *From 0:20 through 4:15, an agent from Beijing Centaline Property Agency, Ltd., answers a number of questions. For each question, find the English summary that answers the question. Write the summary's letter next to the appropriate question. Not all of the summaries will be used. Please note that the speaker's regional accent makes words with* z-, *such as* 租賃／租赁 zūlìn *(rent), sound more like they begin with* zh-.

____ 1. Nǐ guòqù yǒu guo wàiguó kèhù ma? 你過去有過外國客戶嗎？／你过去有过外国客户吗？

____ 2. Tāmen huì zhíjiē shàng nǐmen diànshang lái ne, háishi yǒu biéren tì tāmen bàn? 他們會直接上你們店上來呢，還是有別人替他們辦？／他们会直接上你们店上来呢，还是有别人替他们办？

____ 3. Dāng yí ge rén kànzhòng le yí ge fángzi, nàme tā zū fángzi de guòchéng shì shénmeyàng de? 當一個人看中了一個房子，那麼他租房子的過程是甚麼樣的？／当一个人看中了一个房子，那么他租房子的过程是什么样的？

____ 4. Yǒu jǐ zhǒng zhǒnglèi de zūfáng hétong? 有幾種種類的租房合同？／有几种种类的租房合同？

____ 5. Fángzi shìbushì yǒu dài jiājù hé bú dài jiājù de? 房子是不是有帶傢俱和不帶傢俱的？／房子是不是有带家具和不带家具的？

____ 6. Fángzū bāo bù bāokuò shuǐdiàn? 房租包不包括水電？／房租包不包括水电？

____ 7. Fángzū fēn nǎ jǐ zhǒng fùkuǎn fāngshì? 房租分哪幾種付款方式？／房租分哪几种付款方式？

____ 8. Jùtǐ jiāoqián de fāngshì shì shénme? 具體交錢的方式是甚麼？／具体交钱的方式是什么？

____ 9. Zài kèhù kàn bùtóng de fángzi (shí), nǎxiē yīnsù shì zuì zhòngyào de? 在客戶看不同的房子（時），哪些因素是最重要的？／在客户看不同的房子（时），哪些因素是最重要的？

a *It's not included. Rent is just the rent that the owner nets; all other charges are the responsibility of the renter, for example, the water bill, power bill, gas bill, the charge for a parking space, and the sanitation bill; typically all of these are paid by the renter. As for property fees, only in residential rentals are they paid by the property owner. If it's a commercial rental, the renter will pay them.*

b *I'm from Beijing Centaline Property Agency, Ltd. As our main business, we handle the rental market and sales in the surrounding area.*

c *Right, this is usually according to the renters' needs, and we'll find the housing stock for them. Typically, here in Beijing, most places are rented with furniture and electrical appliances. I mean, all of them include a TV, washing machine, and all of the electrical appliances, and then the furniture—the bed, sofas, wardrobes—they're all complete. One more kind is for these things to be ordered according to the needs of the customer. It can be negotiated with the owner. For example, I need this thing, can you put it there for me? or, I don't want this thing, can you take it away?*

d *Typically, in choosing a place, the first might be based on the position of the place within the housing estate—is it a unit with a view, or on a certain floor? Because some people, for example younger people, may prefer relatively higher floors, because the view from higher floors, the vista, and the light, may all be a little bit better than on lower floors; that's one aspect. The second aspect is in line with the way the unit is decorated and what furniture and appliances it has, because the vast majority of renters all want furniture and appliances, complete, so they can move in, just carrying their bags. For renters, that may save more time and energy on setting the place in order; so typically, these are the two most common factors.*

e *Typically, there are several ways. The first kind is when companies introduce us—that's the most common. It may be that a company has a dedicated person who is in charge of coming around to look for housing, and when they find a place, if the company people feel it's nice, then the person who's going to live there will come and have a look. The second type of situation is individuals renting housing—that is, individuals who show up at our office looking for housing, and then we'll take them to look at places.*

f *Typically, there are three types of payment methods. The one used by most is a single month's [rent as] deposit, plus the first three months of rent; that's the first method. The second kind is one month's deposit plus six months' rent. The third payment method is one month's deposit plus twelve months of rent, because typically, commonly, when we sign a contract, it's usually for a full year.*

g *Typically, there are two kinds. The first kind is when several people who know one another all rent an apartment together. Sometimes it's several people who don't know one another but whom we introduce to one another, and then they all rent an apartment together; we usually refer to this as "sharing a table." One more type is the whole rental—one person rents the whole place as a residence for a family or for several friends living together.*

h *Typically, there are two methods. For places that are rentals, cash is relatively more common. The second method is through a bank transfer method where the money is transferred to the property owner, because when the contract is signed we'll have the two sides meet.*

i *Uh-huh, yes, we've made deals with quite a few foreign customers.*

j *We'll give them some consultation based on their needs, and then, [depending on] how many bedrooms it is, based on their needs, we'll match them to our housing stock.*

37.23 *From 4:15 through the end, the agent is showing us a typical apartment available for rent. Based on the lettered quotes from her description, mark each statement* T *(true) or* F *(false) and write the letter of the relevant quote in the box.*

Statement	T/F	Letter
1. The apartment doesn't get very much light.		
2. This is a three-bedroom unit.		
3. The toilet and shower facilities are combined in a single bathroom.		
4. The agency's fee is typically split between the renter and the landlord.		
5. The dining room and living room are combined into one.		
6. The bathroom is quite large.		
7. The unit is tucked off in a corner of the housing estate.		
8. The agency's fee is based on one month's rent at the agreed-upon rental rate.		

a Zhèi ge fángzi zhěngge shì yī jūshì, yí shì yì tīng yì chú yí wèi.
這個房子整個是一居室，一室一廳一廚一衛。／这个房子整个是一居室，一室一厅一厨一卫。

b Yùshì hé wèishēngjiān shì zài yìqǐ de.
浴室和衛生間是在一起的。／浴室和卫生间是在一起的。

c Zhěngge wèishēngjiān kōngjiān hěn dà.
整個衛生間空間很大。／整个卫生间空间很大。

d Zhèi ge lóu de wèizhi hěn hǎo, tā shì zài yuánqū de yí ge zuì zhōngxīn de wèizhi.
這個樓的位置很好，它是在園區的一個最中心的位置。／这个楼的位置很好，它是在园区的一个最中心的位置。

e Yīnwèi tā shì shǔyú zhōngjiān céng, zhào jìnlai de tàiyáng (yángguāng) huì hěn duō.
因為它是屬於中間層，照進來的太陽（陽光）會很多。／因为它是属于中间层，照进来的太阳（阳光）会很多。

f Yǒu liǎng ge tīng, kètīng jí qí cāntīng.
有兩個廳，客廳及其餐廳。／有两个厅，客厅及其餐厅。

g Yìbān de zhè zhǒng qíngkuàng xià de huà shì zūfāng hé fángzhǔ yìrén-yíbànr lái chéngdān.
一般的這種情況下的話是租方和房主一人一半兒來承擔。／一般的这种情况下的话是租方和房主一人一半儿来承担。

h Wǒmen de shōufèi biāozhǔn jiùshì chéngjiāo jià de yuèzūjīn.
我們的收費標準就是成交價的月租金。／我们的收费标准就是成交价的月租金。

Recap

Grammar

Modern written Chinese: Chinese on a diet

In all languages, writing differs from speech. Speech forms change rapidly, sometimes even daily. Written language displays slower and less sweeping changes, likely because written language is more formal and more prestigious than spoken and is therefore more resistant to change. In Chinese, differences between the spoken and written are especially marked and can present a significant challenge for the language learner.

Here are a few of the more salient points of difference:

1. In the spoken language, words are generally composed of two or more characters to disambiguate those that sound alike. In the formal written language, however, one character suffices to convey a precise meaning.
2. Unlike the spoken language, where the words used are a part of the common, widely used, and more easily understood everyday language, written language vocabulary is more formal, literary, and elevated. In U.S. culture, think of the difference between the *New York Daily News* and the *New York Times*.
3. Unlike the spoken language, the written, formal style will often use allusions drawn from the vast, classical tradition of Chinese literature—allusions that are apt to be familiar to the educated elite but less so to others (and to the language learner). Such phrases are often in the form of 四字成語／四字成语 or "four-character phrases," which can convey thoughts compactly, economically, and forcefully.
4. Unlike the spoken language, which can be messy and full of interruptions, corrections, incomplete sentences, or repetitions, the written language is far less so; it is compact and says a lot in much fewer words—truly Chinese on a diet. The spoken language is language in casual garb, language in your Saturday morning, slightly soiled jeans and old pullover, whereas the written is often "dressed to kill." Jeans versus tuxedo.
5. Some grammatical constructions are only used in writing and rarely, if ever, spoken—except, perhaps, for formal addresses. Spoken sentences tend to be shorter and more repetitive, whereas in the written style, sentences are more complex and have many subordinate clauses. Thus, they pose particular challenges for learners.

Exercise: Below, we have reproduced the text of the fourth e-mail from Exercise 37.18 as an example of some of the points made here. On the next page, you'll find a list of the more literary vocabulary items of this text on the left and their rough spoken equivalents on the right.

With a classmate, read the text once again and substitute the spoken words for the more written-style words. The words that need substitution are in red in the text.

主题：没有Costco卡，但是想去Costco 购物的朋友

(Costco 简介：Costco 是一家大型会员制超市，购物需持卡方可进入，或有持卡的朋友陪你进店。店内所售商品种类很多，相对价格是很低的。)

8月4日左右办理了一张 Costco 卡，办理费约55美元。

Costco 政策是允许一个帐号下面有两张卡，即你我可以各持一张卡，各自独立购物。

(Costco 购物最好使用现金或者信用卡，Debit 卡似乎也可以用。此外，持 Costco 卡可以在 Costco 名下加油站加油，油费比较便宜。)

为了降低办卡成本，希望找朋友合享该卡，合享方式如下：你出25美元，即可拥有自己名下一张 Costco 卡。

如果有住校内或者附近的朋友，不想办卡，但是希望经常去Costco 购物，也可以把联系方式告诉我。我可以偶尔开车载你去 Costco。我住处离学校不远。

gòuwù 購物／购物	mǎi dōngxi 買東西／买东西
xū 需	xūyào 需要
chí 持	yǒu, chíyǒu 有，持有
fāng 方	cái 才
kě 可	néng, kěyǐ 能，可以
huò 或	huòshì 或是
shòu 售	mài de 賣的／卖的
yuē 約／约	chàbuduō 差不多
jí 即	jiùshì, jiùshì shuō 就是, 就是説／就是, 就是说
cǐwài 此外	chúle zhèxiē yǐwài 除了這些以外／除了这些以外
gāi 該／该	zhèi ge 這個／这个
rúxià 如下	shì zhèyàng 是這樣／是这样
jí kě 即可	jiù kěyǐ 就可以
zài nǐ qù 載你去／载你去	sòng nǐ qù 送你去

Vocabulary

Please refer to page R-2 for a list of grammatical abbreviations used throughout this book.

àihào 愛好／爱好 interests; hobby/hobbies N

ānquán 安全 safe; secure SV; security; safety N

bànlǐ 辦理／办理 handle; conduct; transact V

bàoqiàn dǎrǎo 抱歉打擾／抱歉打扰 sorry to trouble you IE

běnkē 本科 undergraduate course of studies N

běnkēshēng 本科生 undergraduate student N

běnrén 本人 me; myself; oneself; in person N

běnxiào 本校 this/our school N

céng 層／层 story; level M

chāoshì 超市 supermarket N

chāosòng 抄送 make a copy for; send a duplicate to V

cháoxiàng 朝向 orientation N

chēkù 車庫／车库 garage N

chéngběn 成本 (net) cost N

chóngxīn 重新 again; anew; afresh A

chòuchóng 臭蟲／臭虫 bedbug N

chōushuǐmǎtǒng 抽水馬桶／抽水马桶 flush toilet N

chōuyóuyānjī 抽油煙機／抽油烟机 kitchen ventilator; exhaust hood N

chūcì 初次 for the first time A

cǐwài 此外 besides; in addition; moreover C

cìwò 次臥／次卧 second/secondary bedroom N

dānrén 單人／单人 single person N

dàtáng 大堂 lobby; hall N

dàxíng 大型 large size/scale ATTR

diànbīngxiāng 電冰箱／电冰箱 refrigerator N

diàntī 電梯／电梯 elevator N

diànyǐngyuàn 電影院／电影院 cinema; movie theater N

dǐdá 抵達／抵达 reach; arrive at V

dìlǐ wèizhi 地理位置 geographical location; location N

dìtiězhàn 地鐵站／地铁站 subway station N

dìxià 地下 underground ATTR

duǎnqī 短期 short time/period/term N

dúlì 獨立／独立 independently A

fādá 發達／发达 developed; flourishing SV

fājiànrén 發件人／发件人 sender of mail; From: *(e-mail header)* N

fāng 方 then and only then *(written style for* 才 **cái***)* A

fángdìchǎn 房地產／房地产 real estate N

fāngshì 方式 way; method N

fànguǎn 飯館／饭馆 restaurant N

fǎngwèn xuézhě 訪問學者／访问学者 visiting scholar N

fāsòng shíjiān 發送時間／发送时间 time sent N

fèi 費／费 cost; charge *(written style for* 費用／费用 **fèiyong**) BF/S

fù 赴 go to *(written style)* V

fúwù 服務／服务 service(s) N

gāi 該／该 above-mentioned; that; this PR

gānjìng wèishēng 乾淨衛生／干净卫生 clean and hygienic VP

gānxǐdiàn 乾洗店／干洗店 dry cleaners N

gāocéng 高層／高层 high-rise ATTR

gè 各 each PR

gèwèi 各位 you all; everybody N

gèzì 各自 each (of us) PR

gōnggòng qìchēzhàn 公共汽車站／公共汽车站 bus stop N

gōnggòng tíngchēchǎng 公共停車場／公共停车场 public parking N

gōngjiāochē 公交車／公交车 commuter bus N

gōngyuán 公園／公园 park N

gōngyùlóu 公寓樓／公寓楼 apartment building N

gōngzuòjiān 工作間／工作间 workroom N

gòuwù 購物／购物 go shopping VO; shopping N

gòuwù zhōngxīn 購物中心／购物中心 shopping center N

gòuzhì 購置／购置 purchase *(durable goods)* V

hàipà 害怕 fear; be afraid/scared V

hé xiǎng 合享 both (of us) can enjoy VP

hélǐ 合理 reasonable; equitable SV

hézhù 合住 share a room/lodging RV

hòuyuàn 後院／后院 backyard N

huáiyùn 懷孕／怀孕 be pregnant VO

huánjìng 環境／环境 environment; surroundings; situation N

huìyuánzhì 會員制／会员制 membership (system) N

huǒchēzhàn 火車站／火车站 train station N

Huǒnúlǔlǔ 火奴魯魯／火奴鲁鲁 Honolulu PW

jí 即 namely *(equivalent here to spoken* 就是 **jiùshì***)* A

jiàngdī 降低 reduce; cut down; drop lower RV

jiǎnjiè 簡介／简介 brief introduction; synopsis N

jiāyóuzhàn 加油站 gas station N

jiēshōu 接收 accept V

jìhuà 計劃／计划 plan; project; program N/V

jìng qǐng 敬請／敬请 respectfully invite V

jǐngchájú 警察局 police station N

jīngjìrén 經紀人／经纪人 agent; broker N

jíqiú 急求 urgently seek VP

kǎ 卡 card *(credit card, membership card, etc.)* N

kào 靠 depend on; rely on V

kǎolǜ 考慮／考虑 think over; consider V

kě 可 can; may *(written style for* 可以 **kěyǐ***)* AV

kōngjiān 空間／空间 space; open area N

kōngqì 空氣／空气 air; atmosphere N

liánxì 聯繫／联系 get in touch with V

línyù 淋浴 shower; shower bath N/V

línyùfáng 淋浴房 shower stall N

liúyán 留言 leave a message VO

lóufáng 樓房／楼房 building of two or more stories N

lǜhuà 綠化／绿化 make a place green V; greening; greenification N

luòdìchuāng(hu) 落地窗(戶)／落地窗(户) French window N

méiqìzào 煤氣灶／煤气灶 gas range/stove N

míngxià 名下 belonging to somebody; under one's own name/account N

páizi 牌子 brand; trademark N

píngfáng 平房 single-story house N

qiányuàn 前院 front yard N

qǐng yǒuláo 請有勞／请有劳 please do me a favor and . . . IE

qǐngjiào 請教／请教 seek advice IE

qíquán 齊全／齐全 complete; all in readiness SV

qǔnuǎn 取暖 warm oneself VO

rèshuǐqì 熱水器／热水器 hot water heater N

rúxià 如下 as follows IE

shāoméi 燒煤／烧煤 burn coal VO

shèshī 設施／设施 facilities N

shì 室 *(for* **wòshì** 臥室／卧室 *– bedroom)* ABBR

shǐyòng 使用 use; employ; apply V

shǐyòngqī 使用期 time of use N

shìyǒu 室友 roommate N

shòu 售 sell V

shōujiànrén 收件人 recipient *(of message, mail)* N

shuāngrén chuáng 雙人床／双人床 double bed N

shuìdài 睡袋 sleeping bag N

sìhéyuàn 四合院 compound with surrounding houses typical of traditional Beijing architecture N

tàiyángnéng 太陽能／太阳能 solar energy N

tào 套 *(for sets/series/suites, etc.)* M

tè 特 especially A

tèsè 特色 distinguishing feature/quality N/SV

tiānwénxué 天文學／天文学 astronomy N

tīng 廳／厅 *(for* **kètīng** 客廳／客厅 *– living room)* ABBR

tíngchēwèi 停車位／停车位 parking space/place N

tōngcháng 通常 usually; normally A

tuīchū 推出 present to the public; come on the market RV

túshūguǎn 圖書館／图书馆 library N

wànfēn 萬分／万分 extremely A

wánshàn 完善 complete; perfect SV

wèi 衛／卫 *(for* **wèishēngjiān** 衛生間／卫生间 – toilet*)* ABBR

wēibōlú 微波爐／微波炉 microwave oven N

Xiàdà 夏大 *(for* **Xiàwēiyí Dàxué** 夏威夷大學／夏威夷大学 – University of Hawaii*)* N/ABBR

xiǎochúbǎo 小廚寶／小厨宝 water heater *(for kitchen sink)* N

xiāofángzhàn 消防站 fire station N

xiàonèi 校內／校内 inside/within the school PW/ATTR

xiǎoqū 小區／小区 residential area; city or town district N

xiàoyuán 校園／校园 campus; school yard PW

Xiàwēiyí 夏威夷 Hawaii PW

xīn dào 新到 have just arrived V

xīnshēng 新生 new student N

xǐshǒutái 洗手台 vanity *(for sink)* N

xǐwǎnjī 洗碗機／洗碗机 dishwasher N

xū chí 需持 must possess VP

xuéxiào 學校／学校 school N

xún 尋／寻 seek; search V

yángtái 陽台／阳台 balcony, terrace, deck N

yàodiàn 藥店／药店 drugstore N

yāoqiú 要求 requirement; demand; request N/V

yì 亦 *(written style for* 也 **yě***)* A

yǐnèi 以內／以内 within S

yīyuàn 醫院／医院 hospital N

yōngyǒu 擁有／拥有 possess; have; own V

yǒu biàn 有變／有变 undergo a change VO

yǒudài 有待 remain (to be done) V

yóujiàn 郵件／邮件 mail N

yóujú 郵局／邮局 post office N

yuánshǐ 原始 original SV

yuē 約／约 about; around; approximately *(written style for* 大約／大约 **dà yuē***)* A

yuèpiào 月票 monthly bus pass N

yùgāng 浴缸 bathtub N

yǔnxǔ 允許／允许 permit; allow V

zài 載／载 transport V

zhànghào 帳號／帐号 account number *(of a bank, store, etc.)* N

zhèngcè 政策 policy N

zhèngzhì 政治 politics; political affairs N

zhǐdǎo bāngzhù 指導幫助／指导帮助 give advice and help IE

zhōngjiè 中介 intermediary; broker N

zhù yúkuài 祝愉快 Wishing you happiness IE

zhuǎnràng 轉讓／转让 transfer possession (to somebody) V

zhùchù 住處／住处 residence; lodgings; quarters N

zhūduō 諸多／诸多 a great deal of; a lot of *(written style)* ATTR

zhùsuǒ 住所 residence N

zhǔtí 主題／主题 topic; theme; subject N

zhǔwò 主臥／主卧 main/master bedroom N

zū 租 rent/rental BF

zūjīn 租金 rent; rental N

zūlìn 租賃／租赁 rent; lease; hire V

zuòběicháonán 坐北朝南 face south with back to north IE

Checklist of "can do" statements

After completing this unit, you should be able to perform each of the following tasks:

Listening and speaking

- ☐ Describe characteristics of an ideal place to live.
- ☐ Talk about what you are looking for in a house or an apartment.
- ☐ Describe what services you would like to have available in your community.
- ☐ Specify desired details in the layout and furnishings within your home.

Reading and writing

- ☐ Decipher some details in e-mail ads about housing, home furnishings, and community facilities.
- ☐ Comprehend a short story involving housing choices.
- ☐ Write a short story of your own.

Understanding culture

- ☐ Make several accurate statements about finding housing through a rental agency in China.

UNIT

38

"No attachments, no worries—happy and free"

無牽無掛樂逍遙

Wúqiānwúguà lè xiāoyáo

The ideal lifestyle

In this unit, you will learn how to:

- talk about your thoughts on an ideal lifestyle.
- describe what you wish for your own future lifestyle.
- talk about what you most appreciate about your current life.
- describe what you hope for in an overseas study program.
- decipher the main ideas of an online discussion about studying abroad.
- read a brief autobiography.
- write a brief autobiography.

Encounter 1 Discussing an ideal future lifestyle

38.1 *Emma and Fang Lan are home with Fang Lan's parents, chatting about lifestyles.* 請把中文跟英文對上。／请把中文跟英文对上。

____ a. lìhai 厲害／厉害	1. *peanuts*
____ b. xiàohua 笑話／笑话	2. *lifestyle*
____ c. huāshēngmǐ 花生米	3. *satisfied, contented*
____ d. xìngfú 幸福	4. *powerful, formidable*
____ e. mǎnzú 滿足／满足	5. *make a toast to life*
____ f. lǐxiǎng de 理想的	6. *joke*
____ g. shēnghuó fāngshì 生活方式	7. *ideal*
____ h. wèi shēnghuó gānbēi 為生活乾杯／为生活干杯	8. *happy*

38.2 *View Episode 38, Vignette 1. Emma and Fang Lan's family are chatting around the dinner table. Indicate who says each of the following sentences (presented in the order in which they appear).* 請注明這話是誰說的。／请注明这话是谁说的。

	方蘭／方兰	父親／父亲	母親／母亲	艾瑪／艾玛
a. Lái, wǒmen gōngxǐ māma.	☐	☐	☐	☐
b. Yòu zhuàn le hǎo duō qián!	☐	☐	☐	☐
c. Nǐ mā lìhai ba!	☐	☐	☐	☐
d. Wǒ tīngdào le yí ge fēicháng hǎoxiào de xiàohua.	☐	☐	☐	☐
e. Wǒmen yǒu xuǎnzé de quánlì ma?	☐	☐	☐	☐
f. Wǒ shì kāi ge wánxiào.	☐	☐	☐	☐
g. Zhēn xiànmù nǐ.	☐	☐	☐	☐
h. Nǐmen zhēn xìngfú!	☐	☐	☐	☐
i. Wèi háizimen de wèilái, gānbēi!	☐	☐	☐	☐

	方蘭／方兰	父親／父亲	母親／母亲	艾瑪／艾玛
j. Shǎo hē diǎnr.	☐	☐	☐	☐
k. Niánqīng de shíhou zánmen fēnjū liǎngdì.	☐	☐	☐	☐
l. Nǐ kàn wǒmen xiànzài de shēnghuó búshì hěn hǎo ma?	☐	☐	☐	☐
m. Wǒ zhēn xiànmù nǐmen de shēnghuó fāngshì.	☐	☐	☐	☐
n. Lái, wèi shēnghuó gānbēi!	☐	☐	☐	☐

38.3 請把下面的漢字跟上面的拼音對上。／请把下面的汉字跟上面的拼音对上。

____ 1. 你媽厲害吧！／你妈厉害吧！

____ 2. 我們有選擇的權利嗎？／我们有选择的权利吗？

____ 3. 我是開個玩笑。／我是开个玩笑。

____ 4. 來，我們恭喜媽媽。／来，我们恭喜妈妈。

____ 5. 來，為生活乾杯！／来，为生活干杯！

____ 6. 又賺了好多錢！／又赚了好多钱！

____ 7. 你看我們現在的生活不是很好嗎？／你看我们现在的生活不是很好吗？

____ 8. 我聽到了一個非常好笑的笑話。／我听到了一个非常好笑的笑话。

____ 9. 年輕的時候咱們分居兩地。／年轻的时候咱们分居两地。

____ 10. 你們真幸福！／你们真幸福！

____ 11. 少喝點兒。／少喝点儿。

____ 12. 我真羨慕你們的生活方式。／我真羡慕你们的生活方式。

____ 13. 真羨慕你。／真羡慕你。

____ 14. 為孩子們的未來，乾杯！／为孩子们的未来，干杯！

38.4 請把下面的英文跟上面的漢字對上。／请把下面的英文跟上面的汉字对上。

____ A. You've made a lot of money again!

____ B. You're really happy!

____ C. Do we have the right to choose?

____ D. I really envy you.

____ E. Your mom's really something, right?

____ F. I'm teasing you.

____ G. Come, let's make a toast to life!

____ H. I really envy your lifestyle.

____ I. Come, let's congratulate Mom.

____ J. Let's make a toast to our children's futures.

____ K. When we were young, we were living separately.

____ L. I heard a really funny joke.

____ M. Don't drink so much.

____ N. See, isn't our life pretty good now?

38.5 *Did you understand Emma's joke? Work it out below.* 請用英文填空。／请用英文填空。

Q: Shéi shì mǐ de māma? 誰是米的媽媽？／谁是米的妈妈？
Who is the mother of rice?

A: Huā. Yīnwèi huā shēng mǐ. 花。因為花生米。／花。因为花生米。
Flowers. Because flowers give birth to rice.

[Huā shēng mǐ is *a pun for* huāshēngmǐ, *meaning* ____________________.]

38.6 *As Fang Lan's father enters, bearing a plate of peanuts, he hears the mention of* huāshēngmǐ *and says, "Speak of the devil and here he is."* 請用拼音填空。／请用拼音填空。

說曹操，曹操到。／说曹操，曹操到。

Shuō ______________, ________________ dào.

(literally, Speak of Cao Cao and Cao Cao arrives.)

FYI 供你参考

Speak of the devil

Cao Cao (*Cáo Cāo* 曹操; 155–220 CE) was the warlord of the region that became the State of Wei during China's Three Kingdoms period (220–280 CE). He's famous for fighting, albeit unsuccessfully, against the generals Liu Bei and Sun Quan at the Battle of the Red Cliffs. The history of the period inspired the classic novel *Sānguó Yǎnyì* 三國演義／三国演义 *Romance of the Three Kingdoms*—one of the four great classical novels discussed in Unit 31—which has been dramatized in many folk operas, movies, and TV dramas. But his popularity among China's youth derives primarily from the video game series called *Romance of the Three Kingdoms*, published by the Japanese Koei Company.

How did Cao Cao become the subject of this widely used saying? According to a popular theory, he was very suspicious and untrusting by nature, and given the tensions that surrounded him, he resorted to employing a small army of spies to gather information and spy on people. These spies were ubiquitous and mobile; they could suddenly appear out of nowhere. This phrase was coined to remind people to watch what they said and did because danger lurked everywhere—one small misstep could land you in trouble with Cao Cao!

38.7 *Fang Lan's father comes across as a wonderful person in this vignette.* 請把中文跟英文對上。／请把中文跟英文对上。

____ a. zhème bàng de lǎogōng 這麼棒的老公／这么棒的老公	1. *has a good character*
____ b. yòu huì chàngxì yòu huì zuòfàn 又會唱戲又會做飯／又会唱戏又会做饭	2. *can both sing and cook*
____ c. xǐhuan gěi nǚ'ér hé lǎopo mánghuo 喜歡給女兒和老婆忙活／喜欢给女儿和老婆忙活	3. *is talented*
____ d. rénpǐn hǎo 人品好	4. *is such a great husband*
____ e. yǒu cáihuá 有才華／有才华	5. *likes to busy himself for his wife and daughter*

38.8 *Emma thinks she knows what she wants out of life.* 請用英文填空。／请用英文填空。

Yǐhòu wǒ yě xiǎng zhèyàng, yǒu ge wěndìng de gōngzuò, yí ge wēnnuǎn de jiā.

以後我也想這樣，有個穩定的工作，一個溫暖的家。／
以后我也想这样，有个稳定的工作，一个温暖的家。

In the future I want to have this too—a stable ___________ *and a*

_______________________.

Fang Lan, however, says she hasn't made up her mind about her ideal lifestyle. 請用英文填空。／请用英文填空。

Wǒ hái méiyǒu xiǎngguo wǒ lǐxiǎng de shēnghuó fāngshì dàodǐ shì shénme yàngzi de, zùihǎo shì qù quán shìjiè zǒu yi zǒu, làngjì tiānyá.

我還沒有想過我理想的生活方式到底是甚麼樣子的，最好是去全世界走一走，浪跡天涯。／

我还没有想过我理想的生活方式到底是什么样子的，最好是去全世界走一走，浪迹天涯。

I haven't thought about what __________________ *would be like yet. Maybe I'd like to* _________________________*, becoming a wanderer.*

38.9 ***Pair work:*** *Talk with a partner about what your ideal future lifestyle would be like. Are you looking for what Emma wants? A spouse like Fang Lan's father? Or are you like Fang Lan? Or something else? Write several sentences below. Repeat with a different partner if there is time.*

Encounter 2 Discussing your present lifestyle

38.10 *Fang Lan and Emma reminisce about the past year and chat about the near future.* 請把中文跟英文對上。／请把中文跟英文对上。

____ a. yǒu yí ge lǐwù yào sòng gěi nǐ 有一個禮物要送給你／有一个礼物要送给你	1. *I'm sad about losing you*
____ b. néng xiǎngqǐ wǒ 能想起我	2. *memories*
____ c. huíyì 回憶／回忆	3. *must look forward to your returning home*
____ d. nǐ péizhe wǒ jīnglì le nàme duō 你陪著我經歷了那麼多／你陪着我经历了那么多	4. *have a gift to give you*
____ e. wǒ shěbude nǐ 我捨不得你／我舍不得你	5. *now the world is flat*
____ f. huì hěn gūdú de 會很孤獨的／会很孤独的	6. *miss you very much*
____ g. xiànzài shìjiè shì píng de 現在世界是平的/现在世界是平的	7. *you'll think of me*
____ h. yídìng fēicháng pànwàng nǐ huí jiā 一定非常盼望你回家	8. *will be very lonely*
____ i. hěn xiǎng nǐ 很想你	9. *you were with me in experiencing so much*

38.11 *View Episode 38, Vignette 2. Indicate whether the speakers are talking about their experiences during the past year or about their future lives.*

	過去／过去	未來／未来
a. Nǐ gěi wǒ de huíyì jiùshì zuì hǎo de lǐwù le.	☐	☐
b. Wǒ yìzhí bǎ nǐ dàngchéng qīn mèimei yíyàng.	☐	☐
c. Wǒ jìde nǐ dài wǒ kànbìng.	☐	☐
d. Nǐ lái Měiguó liúxué, kěyǐ zhù wǒ jiā, zhè yàng wǒmen jiù kěyǐ yòu zài yìqǐ le.	☐	☐
e. Wǒ shìbushì hái kěyǐ qù Hǎoláiwū chuǎngdàng chuǎngdàng?	☐	☐
f. Wǒ tèbié xǐhuan gēn nǐmen quánjiā zài yìqǐ.	☐	☐
g. Wǒmen xíguàn le zhè zhǒng shēnghuó fāngshì, měitiān yìqǐ shàngxué, yìqǐ zuò zuòyè, yìqǐ chīfàn, hái yìqǐ chūqu jùhuì.	☐	☐
h. Nǐ zǒu le, wǒ yí ge rén huì hěn gūdú de.	☐	☐
i. Wǒ huì xiǎngniàn gěi zánmen quānzili de péngyoumen fā duǎnxìn.	☐	☐
j. Wǒ xiǎngzhe qù gōngyuán wán huábǎn.	☐	☐
k. Wǒ yì huíqu jiù děi zhǎo fángzi.	☐	☐
l. Wǒ yào zhǔnbèi zàicì guò yí ge rén de shēnghuó.	☐	☐
m. Nǐ kěyǐ lái kànkan wǒ, wǒ huì gěi nǐ jièshào wǒ nàlǐ de shēnghuó.	☐	☐

38.12 請把下面的漢字跟上面的拼音對上。／请把下面的汉字跟上面的拼音对上。

____ 1. 你來美國留學，可以住我家，這樣我們就可以又在一起了。／你来美国留学，可以住我家，这样我们就可以又在一起了。

____ 2. 我想著去公園玩滑板。／我想着去公园玩滑板。

____ 3. 我一直把你當成親妹妹一樣。／我一直把你当成亲妹妹一样。

____ 4. 你可以來看看我，我會給你介紹我那裡的生活。／你可以来看看我，我会给你介绍我那里的生活。

____ 5. 我們習慣了這種生活方式，每天一起上學，一起做作業，一起吃飯，還一起出去聚會。／我们习惯了这种生活方式，每天一起上学，一起做作业，一起吃饭，还一起出去聚会。

____ 6. 我記得你帶我看病。／我记得你带我看病。

____ 7. 我要準備再次過一個人的生活。／我要准备再次过一个人的生活。

____ 8. 我是不是還可以去好莱塢闖蕩闖蕩？／我是不是还可以去好莱坞闯荡闯荡？

____ 9. 我會想念給咱們圈子裡的朋友們發短信。／我会想念给咱们圈子里的朋友们发短信。

____ 10. 你給我的回憶就是最好的禮物了。／你给我的回忆就是最好的礼物了。

____ 11. 我一回去就得找房子。

____ 12. 你走了，我一個人會很孤獨的。／你走了，我一个人会很孤独的。

____ 13. 我特別喜歡跟你們全家在一起。／我特别喜欢跟你们全家在一起。

38.13 請把下面的英文跟上面的漢字對上。／请把下面的英文跟上面的汉字对上。

____ A. I've always treated you like my own younger sister.

____ B. I'll miss sending texts to the friends in our circle.

____ C. We've gotten used to this lifestyle: every day we go to school together, do our homework together, eat together, and even meet up with friends together.

____ D. I'm looking forward to skateboarding in the park.

____ E. Can I go to Hollywood and try to make my way there?

____ F. After you leave, I'll feel lonely all by myself.

____ G. The memories you've given me are the best present.

____ H. I remember you took me to the doctor.

____ I. I really like being together with your whole family.

____ J. Come study in the United States, and you can live with me. Then we can be together again.

____ K. You can come visit me; I'll show you the lifestyle there.

____ L. I have to get ready to live all alone again.

____ M. As soon as I get back, I have to look for a place to live.

38.14 *If you were to leave in a month to study in China for a year, what would you hate most to leave behind? What would you look forward to most? Write at least three statements in each category. Write in pinyin or characters.*

Wǒ zuì shěbude . . . 我最捨不得……／我最舍不得……

Wǒ zuì pànwàngzhe . . . 我最盼望著……／我最盼望着……

Try to link your sentences together with a connector such as 雖然……可是……／虽然……可是…… suīrán . . . kěshì *(although . . . still). For example:*

Wǒ suīrán hěn shěbude líkāi jiā, kěshì wǒ hěn pànwàngzhe qù Běijīng pá Chángchéng.

我雖然很捨不得離開家，可是我很盼望著去北京爬長城。／我虽然很舍不得离开家，可是我很盼望着去北京爬长城。

Although I'm sad to be leaving home, I'm also looking forward to going to Beijing to climb the Great Wall.

38.15 ***Pair work:*** *Work with a partner to discuss in Chinese what you wrote in Exercise 38.14. Ask each other,* 你要是去中國留學一年，你會捨不得甚麼？你最盼望著甚麼？／你要是去中国留学一年，你会舍不得什么？你最盼望着什么？ (Nǐ yàoshi qù Zhōngguó liúxué yì nián, nǐ huì shěbude shénme? Nǐ zuì pànwàngzhe shénme?) *Go into detail as much as you can and extend the conversation as far as you can. Use some of your "linked sentences" from Exercise 38.14. If there is time, have a conversation on the same topic with a different partner.*

Encounter 3 Reading and writing

Reading real-life texts

38.16 *If you search for* 去中国留学 *on* www.baidu.com, *you might be redirected to* http://zhidao.baidu.com, *where something like the following question and answer might appear.*

关于到中国留学的问题~~

提问者悬赏：5分 | fjkl446 | 分类：出国/留学 | 浏览77次 2015-05-13 12:48

你好 我是外国留学生 请问 在中国读高中再留学进中国大学和在国外读高中再留学进中国 哪一个比较好？？？ 哪一个对我有利一点呢？

Guānyú dào Zhōngguó liúxué de wèntí~~
Nǐ hǎo Wǒ shì wàiguó liúxuéshēng Qǐngwèn zài Zhōngguó dú gāozhōng zài liúxué jìn Zhōngguó dàxué hé zài guówài dú gāozhōng zài liúxué jìn Zhōngguó Nǎ yí ge bǐjiào hǎo??? Nǎ yí ge duì wǒ yǒulì yìdiǎn ne?

网友采纳

2015-05-13 22:16

如果在中国读高中的话，你会给自己打下一个非常扎实的基础。举个简单的例子，GRE数学部分中国人大部分不低于700，美国人的分数，一般来说再除以2吧。

在国外读高中再来中国读大学的话，你进校的途径应该不太一样，属于留学生那一批，首先要过语言考试一类的，比较麻烦。

推荐你可以先联系几所大学询问一下具体的政策再做决定比较好。

Wǎngyǒu cǎinà
Rúguǒ zài Zhōngguó dú gāozhōng de huà, nǐ huì gěi zìjǐ dǎxià yí ge fēicháng zhāshi de jīchǔ. Jǔ ge jiǎndān de lìzi, GRE shùxué bùfen Zhōngguórén dàbùfen bù dī yú 700, Měiguórén de fēnshù, yìbānláishuō zài chúyǐ 2 ba.
Zài guówài dú gāozhōng zài lái Zhōngguó dú dàxué de huà, nǐ jìn xiào de tújìng yīnggāi bú tài yíyàng, shǔyú liúxuéshēng nèi yì pī, shǒuxiān yào guò yǔyán kǎoshì yí lèi de, bǐjiào máfan.
Tuījiàn nǐ kěyǐ xiān liánxì jǐ suǒ dàxué xúnwèn yíxià jùtǐ de zhèngcè zài zuò juédìng bǐjiào hǎo.

a *The topic of the question is "Questions about Foreign Students Studying in China."* 請用英文填空。／请用英文填空。

Hello. I am a ______________. May I ask which is better: ______________________ in China and then going on to attend a Chinese universiy, or ______________________ and then coming to China to attend university? Which would be more beneficial to me?

b *The title of the answer is "Reader's Choice"* (wǎngyǒu cǎinà). 請用英文填空。／请用英文填空。

If you ______________________, you will establish an extremely solid foundation for yourself. To give you a simple example: Chinese people generally will not score lower than 700 on the ____________ portion of the GRE, whereas the scores of Americans are generally about __________ of that, right?

If you ______________________________, your path to admission will likely be somewhat different. You'll be one of a group of foreign students, so first, you have to ______________________ and the like. It's more cumbersome.

I recommend you first ______________________ to make some inquiries about specific policies, __________________. That would be better.

c *If you have a question about studying in China, what would it be?* 請寫漢字。／请写汉字。

____

____

____

d *Try entering your question on* www.baidu.com *and see if you can find anything useful in the results. Enter your notes below.* 請寫英文。／请写英文。

38.17 *The search described in Exercise 38.16 will also lead to information for Chinese students seeking to study overseas. For example, you might find the advertisement provided below at this website:* http://www.wiseway.com.cn/zhuanti/cglx/?baidu-jiaoyu.

首页 | 英国 | 美国 | 澳洲 | 加拿大 | 德国 | 荷兰 | 瑞士 | 日本 | 韩国 | 中国香港 | 新加坡 | 爱尔兰 | 马来西亚 | 意大利 | 俄罗斯 | 法国 | 西班牙

a *Across the top of the ad, there is a banner listing countries where information about their programs can be found on the site:* 英国、美国、澳洲、加拿大、德国、荷兰、瑞士、日本、韩国 、中国香港、新加坡、爱尔兰、马来西亚、意大利、俄罗斯、法国、西班牙. *Using the banner as a guide, write the Chinese terms for the following countries.* 請寫漢字。／请写汉字。

Germany	________	*Canada*	________	*Spain*	________
Ireland	________	*Malaysia*	________	*Japan*	________
Australia	________	*United States*	________	*South Korea*	________
France	________	*Switzerland*	________	*Italy*	________
Holland	________	*Russia*	________	*Singapore*	________
England	________	*Hong Kong (in China)*	________		

b *The ad is simple and direct. Please write characters for the English below.*

1. *Whether you have money or not, just follow your impulses!*

____

2. *Studying abroad will give you*

____

3. *Study abroad: if you want to go, go!*

____

4. *Enrich your life experiences*

____

5. *Improve your personal overall capacity*

____

6. *Excellent teaching resources*

____

C 把下面的拼音跟你上面寫的漢字對上。／把下面的拼音跟你上面写的汉字对上。

____ Yǒu qián méi qián, jiùshì zhènme rènxìng!!!

____ Chūguó liúxué xiǎngqù jiù qù

____ Chūguó liúxué nín jiāng dédào

____ Yōuzhì jiàoxué zīyuán

____ Gèrén zōnghé nénglì tíshēng

____ Fēngfù rénshēng jiǎnlì

38.18 *Write a note introducing this "study abroad" website to a friend. Note a few things it offers; also note anything you find lacking.* 請寫漢字。／请写汉字。

Reading a story

38.19 故事 *Find the following terms in either the traditional or simplified text and circle them. Write in the accompanying number.*

Shanghai after a Japanese air attack

At home in Lahore, Pakistan. Author is the 5-year-old girl in the middle.

1. láizì *come from*
2. Fúzhōu *Fuzhou (city)*
3. Fújiànshěng *Fujian Province*
4. shěnghuì *provincial capital*
5. xiāngcūn *village*
6. jiāzú *clan*
7. dà yuànzi *big courtyard*
8. dà-xiǎobiàn *defecate and urinate*
9. tiándì *fields*
10. sēnlín *woods*
11. fāngbiàn *relieve oneself*
12. yuánlái *originally*
13. bān *move (home)*
14. dìngjū *settle down*
15. tǒngzhì *govern*
16. jièshào *introduce*
17. qíshí *actually*
18. yīxuéyuàn *medical school*
19. búxìng de shì *what was unfortunate*
20. Dì-èr cì shìjiè dàzhàn *World War II*
21. duǒbì *evade, escape from*
22. zhànzhēng *war*
23. qiān *relocate*
24. nèidì *interior of the country*
25. Chóngqìng *Chongqing (city)*
26. mòshēng *strange, unfamiliar*
27. yóuqí *especially*
28. guójiā *the country, the nation*
29. wěndìng *stable*
30. zhǎngbèimen *elders*
31. gǎnjǐn *hurriedly*

32. sān, sìshí niándài *the 1930s and 1940s*
33. wēixiǎn *dangerous*
34. zhànlǐng *occupied by*
35. nào nèizhàn *suffering a civil war*
36. duǒ *escape*
37. luàn *in upheaval*
38. shúrén *acquaintances*
39. Bājīsītǎn *Pakistan*
40. gōngchǎng *factory*
41. shǒuxí gōngchéngshī *chief engineer*

42. shēchǐ *luxurious*
43. gài *build, erect*
44. wéizhe *surrounded by*
45. wéiqiáng *surrounding wall*
46. dài suǒ *with a lock*
47. tiěmén *iron gate*
48. gù *hire*
49. yòngren *household servants*
50. qízhōng yí ge *one among these*
51. zhuānmén *specially, exclusively*
52. fùzé *be responsible for*
53. sòng *escort*
54. lìng *other*
55. què *but, however*
56. jiānkǔ *hard, difficult*
57. xìnfèng *believe, adhere to*
58. Yīsīlánjiào *Islam*
59. nánshòu *hard to bear*
60. huáshì *Fahrenheit*
61. hǎozài *fortunately*
62. shànliáng *kind-hearted*
63. yǒuhǎo *friendly*
64. huíyì *memories*
65. wēnnuǎn *warm*

66. yí ge jiē yí ge *one by one*
67. shèng *leave behind*
68. yuè lái yuè *more and more*
69. gūdú *lonely*
70. míngquè *clear*
71. mùbiāo *goal*
72. zhōngyú *finally*
73. yímín *immigrate*

---

74. yìnxiàng *impression*
75. xíngrén *pedestrian*
76. xiāofèizhě *consumer*
77. dádào *attain*
78. jìxù *continue*
79. wǎng xià *onward*
80. shěbude *feel reluctant*
81. liúxiàlai *stay on*
82. xìngfú *happy*
83. zēngzhǎng *increase, add to*
84. zhīshi *knowledge*

我來自一個中國家庭，我父母都是福州人。福州是福建省的省會。我父親是在福州鄉下的小鄉村出生的。他的家族裡有幾十個人，都住在一個大院子裡。那時房子裡頭沒有廁所，要大小便的時候，得跑到田地或者森林裡去方便。我爸爸到了上學的年齡，就被送到福州城裡的一所小學去上學。我媽媽的家人原來也是從福州來的，不過他們後來搬到香港定居了。因為香港那時候是英國人統治的，所以她家兄弟姐妹到了上學的年齡的時候，我外公外婆就讓孩子們回福州去上學了。後來，在福州，親戚把我媽介紹給我爸了。其實，我媽那時還不想結婚，她希望到上海去上醫學院，她很想成為醫生。可不幸的是，第二次世界大戰開始了，她的醫學院為了躲避戰爭，遷到內地的重慶去了。我外公外婆不願意讓女兒一個人跟著學校去那麼遠，到一個陌生的地方，尤其那時候國家還那麼不穩定。所以長輩們就決定讓我父母趕緊結婚，定居在上海。

我来自一个中国家庭，我父母都是福州人。福州是福建省的省会。我父亲是在福州乡下的小乡村出生的。他的家族里有几十个人，都住在一个大院子里。那时房子里头没有厕所，要大小便的时候，得跑到田地或者森林里去方便。我爸爸到了上学的年龄，就被送到福州城里的一所小学去上学。我妈妈的家人原来也是从福州来的，不过他们后来搬到香港定居了。因为香港那时候是英国人统治的，所以她家兄弟姐妹到了上学的年龄的时候，我外公外婆就让孩子们回福州去上学了。后来，在福州，亲戚把我妈介绍给我爸了。其实，我妈那时还不想结婚，她希望到上海去上医学院，她很想成为医生。可不幸的是，第二次世界大战开始了，她的医学院为了躲避战争，迁到内地的重庆去了。我外公外婆不愿意让女儿一个人跟着学校去那么远，到一个陌生的地方，尤其那时候国家还那么不稳定。所以长辈们就决定让我父母赶紧结婚，定居在上海。

可是上海在三、四十年代也很危險—被日本佔領了，又鬧內戰。我父母就躲到香港去了。可是香港也很亂，我父親又找不到工作。因為他是工程師，所以就有熟人給他介紹了一份工作，在巴基斯坦的一個工廠裡當首席工程師。後來他們一家人都去了巴基斯坦。我就是在那兒出生的。

可是上海在三、四十年代也很危险—被日本占领了，又闹内战。我父母就躲到香港去了。可是香港也很乱，我父亲又找不到工作。因为他是工程师，所以就有熟人给他介绍了一份工作，在巴基斯坦的一个工厂里当首席工程师。后来他们一家人都去了巴基斯坦。我就是在那儿出生的。

在巴基斯坦，我們的生活在一些方面過得很奢侈：父親的工廠給我們蓋了一棟很漂亮的大房子，圍著圍牆，有一個帶鎖的鐵門。我們家還雇了三個傭人，其中一個專門負責送我上城裡的一所英國學校。可是在另一些方面我們卻過得很艱苦：巴基斯坦人因為信奉伊斯蘭教，所以不吃豬肉。但中國人没有豬肉吃一般都會覺得很難受。還有，巴基斯坦夏天會熱到華氏120度，特別難受。好在巴基斯坦人比較善良、友好。所以我的回憶還是很溫暖的。

在巴基斯坦，我们的生活在一些方面过得很奢侈：父亲的工厂给我们盖了一栋很漂亮的大房子，围着围墙，有一个带锁的铁门。我们家还雇了三个佣人，其中一个专门负责送我上城里的一所英国学校。可是在另一些方面我们却过得很艰苦：巴基斯坦人因为信奉伊斯兰教，所以不吃猪肉。但中国人没有猪肉吃一般都会觉得很难受。还有，巴基斯坦夏天会热到华氏120度，特别难受。好在巴基斯坦人比较善良、友好。所以我的回忆还是很温暖的。

我有兩個哥哥，一個姐姐。可是從我五歲開始，他們都一個接一個地到美國去留學了，只剩我一個人在家裡。我覺得越來越孤獨。從那以後我心裡就有了一

我有两个哥哥，一个姐姐。可是从我五岁开始，他们都一个接一个地到美国去留学了，只剩我一个人在家里。我觉得越来越孤独。从那以后我心里就有了一

個很明確的目標，那就是我也要到美國去上大學。在我14歲那年，父母和我終於也移民美國了。

个很明确的目标，那就是我也要到美国去上大学。在我14岁那年，父母和我终于也移民美国了。

我對美國的第一個印象是：怎麼街上都沒人？能看到的人也都在汽車裡，行人特別少。美國難道真的沒多少人嗎？可是到了購物中心一看就明白了：哦，原來大家都躲在商店裡。美國果然是個消費者的國家！過了三年，我也上大學了，達到了小時候的目標！能走進美國的大學很不容易，所以我讀完四年大學以後決定繼續往下讀，一直讀到博士畢業了還捨不得走。所以我就留下來當老師了。大學裡的生活特別幸福：可以一輩子跟年輕人在一起，不停地增長知識。

我对美国的第一个印象是：怎么街上都没人？能看到的人也都在汽车里，行人特别少。美国难道真的没多少人吗？可是到了购物中心一看就明白了：哦，原来大家都躲在商店里。美国果然是个消费者的国家！过了三年，我也上大学了，达到了小时候的目标！能走进美国的大学很不容易，所以我读完四年大学以后决定继续往下读，一直读到博士毕业了还舍不得走。所以我就留下来当老师了。大学里的生活特别幸福：可以一辈子跟年轻人在一起，不停地增长知识。

38.20 *Write a brief autobiography or a story about the life of someone in your family.*
請寫漢字。／请写汉字。

Encounter 4 Extension: Cultural mini-documentary

View the cultural mini-documentary for this unit and complete the exercises that follow.

38.21 *The speakers in the video were asked to talk about the vast and rapid changes in China with regard to basic living conditions. For the first two minutes or so, the speakers address food, clothing, transportation, and shelter. For each speaker, fill in the blanks with pinyin. (Before you begin, note that 140 square meters is about 1,500 square feet, and 9 square meters is just under 100 square feet, or 10'x10'.)*

a.

我覺得中國從這幾十年來變化巨大。可以用一個“巨大”的詞兒來形容，確實是。／

我觉得中国从这几十年来变化巨大。可以用一个“巨大”的词儿来形容，确实是。

Wǒ juéde Zhōngguó cóng zhè jǐshí nián lái __________ jùdà. Kěyǐ _____ yí ge “jùdà” de cír lái _____________, quèshí shì.

*I think that in the past few decades China's **changes** have been colossal. Really, you can **use** the word "colossal" to **describe** them.*

b.

在這十年，或者二十年來，我整個的生活習慣有，其實是，確實是有很多方面的改變，包括衣、食、住、行，這些方面都有非常明顯的改觀。／

在这十年，或者二十年来，我整个的生活习惯有，其实是，确实是有很多方面的改变，包括衣、食、住、行，这些方面都有非常明显的改观。

Zài zhè shí nián, huòzhě èrshínián lái, wǒ __________ de shēnghuó xíguàn yǒu, qíshí shì, ________ shì yǒu hěn duō fāngmiàn de __________, bāokuò yī, shí, zhù, xíng, zhèxiē fāngmiàn dōu yǒu fēicháng __________ de gǎiguān.

*During the last ten or twenty years, my **entire** lifestyle has, actually, **indeed** undergone **changes** in so many ways, including clothing, food, shelter, and transportation—there has been a **clear** shift in all of these aspects.*

c.

確實變化比較快。從我個人來講，我覺得從住的方面，我住上了大房子，面積大了；從吃的方面，我可以吃到中國以外世界各地的美食。／

确实变化比较快。从我个人来讲，我觉得从住的方面，我住上了大房子，面积大了；从吃的方面，我可以吃到中国以外世界各地的美食。

Quèshí biànhuà bǐjiào kuài. Cóng wǒ _______ lái jiǎng, wǒ juéde cóng zhù de _____________, wǒ zhù shangle dà fángzi, _______ dà le; cóng chī de fāngmiàn, wǒ kěyǐ chī dào Zhōngguó yǐwài shìjiè _____ de měishí.

*Truly, the changes have been quite fast. From my **individual** viewpoint, **as far** as shelter **goes**, I've moved into a big place—the **area** is bigger; as far as eating goes, I can eat delicacies from **all kinds of places** in the world beyond China.*

d.

過去吃的，一年四季到冬天，六到七個月没有菜吃。一直就是這個樣子，没有菜，吃甚麼呀？吃豆子，當菜，一是豆腐，二是豆芽兒。現在，菜市場的菜，我不説您也知道，琳琅滿目，甚麼菜都有，反季的菜你也能吃得到。／

过去吃的，一年四季到冬天，六到七个月没有菜吃。一直就是这个样子，没有菜，吃什么呀？吃豆子，当菜，一是豆腐，二是豆芽儿。现在，菜市场的菜，我不说您也知道，琳琅满目，什么菜都有，反季的菜你也能吃得到。

Guòqù chī de, yì nián sìjì dào __________, liù dào qī ge yuè méiyǒu cài chī. Yìzhí jiùshì __________________, méiyǒu cài, chī shénme ya? Chī dòuzi, dàng cài, yī shì dòufu, èr shì ________. Xiànzài, càishìchǎng de cài, wǒ bù shuō nín yě zhīdào, ___________________, shénme cài dōu yǒu, ________ de cài nǐ yě néng chī de dào.

*Food in the past, when the season rolled around to **winter**, for six or seven months there were no vegetables to eat. It was **this way** for all that time—no vegetables, so what did we eat? We ate beans, as vegetables—first, as tofu, and second, as **bean sprouts**. Nowadays, the vegetables at the market, you know, without me telling you, there's **a dazzling array**, every kind of vegetable, and you can even have vegetables **out of season**.*

e.

就像穿著打扮這樣的一些方面吧。就像以前的話，可能會更在乎一些外表的一些東西，但現在可能不會。／

就像穿着打扮这样的一些方面吧。就像以前的话，可能会更在乎一些外表的一些东西，但现在可能不会。

Jiù xiàng ___________ dǎbàn zhèyàng de yìxiē fāngmiàn ba. Jiù xiàng yǐqián de huà, kěnéng huì gèng ________ yìxiē wàibiǎo de yìxiē dōngxi, ____ xiànzài kěnéng bú huì.

*Like, as far as **clothing** and grooming and stuff like that are concerned; the way it was before, I might have **cared** a lot more about things on the surface, **but** now I probably wouldn't.*

f.

穿的，現在人都不講究了，我撿孩子剩下的都撿不過來了，歲數也到了，也没甚麼可置備的了。在以前，穿一件滌卡都已經炫耀得不行了。戴一塊兒上海錶，都覺得非常了不起了。／

穿的，现在人都不讲究了，我捡孩子剩下的都捡不过来了，岁数也到了，也没什么可置备的了。在以前，穿一件涤卡都已经炫耀得不行了。戴一块儿上海表，都觉得非常了不起了。

Chuān de, xiànzài rén dōu bù jiǎngjiu le, wǒ jiǎn háizi _____________ dōu jiǎn bú guòlái le, ________ yě dàole, yě méi shénme kě zhìbèi de le. Zài ________, chuān yí jiàn díkǎ dōu yǐjing ___________ de bùxíng le. Dài yíkuàir Shànghǎi _____, dōu juéde fēicháng liǎobuqǐ le.

*Clothes—now nobody takes too much care about them. Picking up my kids' **castoffs**, I can't even keep up. I'm at an **age** now where I don't really need to be buying things. In **the past**, if we wore something made of Dacron it was like totally **showing off**. And wearing a Shanghai **watch** you felt on top of the world.*

g.

那麼出行也非常方便。我每年都會安排假期，這個是以前做不到的。／

那么出行也非常方便。我每年都会安排假期，这个是以前做不到的。

Nàme chūxíng yě fēicháng __________. Wǒ měinián dōu huì _______ jiàqī, zhèi ge shì yǐqián ___________ de.

*So traveling is also really **convenient**. Every year, I **arrange** to have a vacation. That's something you **couldn't do** before.*

h.

行。我自己現在，我根本想不到我自己還能買上車，我都買了十年了。我可以説提前步入小康了。／

行。我自己现在，我根本想不到我自己还能买上车，我都买了十年了。我可以说提前步入小康了。

Xíng. __________ xiànzài, wǒ gēnběn xiǎngbudào wǒ zìjǐ hái néng mǎi shang chē, wǒ dōu mǎi le _______ le. Wǒ kěyǐ shuō ________ bùrù xiǎokāng le.

*Talk about transportation. **Myself**, now, I could never have imagined I could manage to buy a car, but here I've already owned one for **ten years**! You could say I stepped into the middle class **ahead of schedule**.*

i.

還有就是購物方面，也是非常方便。我能買到很多的東西，在國內，可以買到國外很多東西。／

还有就是购物方面，也是非常方便。我能买到很多的东西，在国内，可以买到国外很多东西。

Hái yǒu jiùshì ________ fāngmiàn, yě shì fēicháng fāngbiàn. Wǒ néng mǎi dào hěn duō de dōngxi, zài ________, kěyǐ mǎi dào ________ hěn duō dōngxi.

*And then there's **shopping**; that's really convenient too. I can buy all kinds of stuff. Here **in China** I can buy all kinds of things from **abroad**.*

j.

還有一個，住，衣食住嘛。這個住的方面更不用説了。以前，就是幾家住在一個九平米的房子，十平米的房子，就是這個樣子。現在我有一個三居室，一百四十多平。我姑娘還有一個別墅，我這邊兒還有一套四合院兒。非常非常幸福。／

还有一个，住，衣食住嘛。这个住的方面更不用说了。以前，就是几家住在一个九平米的房子，十平米的房子，就是这个样子。现在我有一个三居室，一百四十多平。我姑娘还有一个别墅，我这边儿还有一套四合院儿。非常非常幸福。

Hái yǒu yí ge, ____, yī shí zhù ma. Zhèi ge zhù de fāngmiàn gèng _______________ le. Yǐqián, jiùshì _________ zhù zài yí ge jiǔ píngmǐ de fángzi, shí píngmǐ de fángzi, jiùshì zhèi ge yàngzi. Xiànzài wǒ yǒu yí ge _____________, yìbǎi sìshí duō píng. Wǒ __________ hái yǒu yí ge biéshù, wǒ zhèi biānr hái yǒu yí tào sìhéyuànr. Fēicháng fēicháng ________.

*There's one more thing: shelter. You know, clothing, food, **shelter**. With this one, shelter, it's even more **self-evident**. In the past, **several families** would live in a 9- or 10-square-meter unit. That's just how it was. Now I have a **three-bedroom**, and it's over 140 square meters. And my **daughter** has a villa, and here I have a traditional courtyard home. I'm really, really **happy**.*

38.22 *Starting at about 2:07, one of the speakers addresses changes in communication. In a slip of the tongue, he changes the name of the popular microblogging service* Wēixìn 微信, *known in the United States as WeChat, to* Fēixìn 飛信／飞信, *but then self-corrects when he refers to it the second time. Using this small glossary as a guide, can you figure out what he is saying? Write numbers in the blanks to put the six English summaries in the correct order.*

yóuqí 尤其 *especially*
biànhuà 變化／变化 *change*
gōutōng de fāngshì 溝通的方式／沟通的方式 *modes of communication, ways of staying in touch*
rén yǔ rén zhījiān 人與人之間／人与人之间 *between people*
lián diànhuà dōu méiyǒu 連電話都沒有／连电话都没有 *didn't even have a telephone*
suǒyǒu de zhè zhǒng 所有的這種／所有的这种 *all these kinds of*
gānggāng dé dào 剛剛得到／刚刚得到 *just obtained*
shùzì 數字／数字 *number, figure, statistic*
quán shìjiè 全世界 *the entire world*
mùqián 目前 *at present*
yònghù 用戶／用户 *users, subscribers*
xiǎngxiàng 想像／想象 *imagine*
bùdéliǎo 不得了 *impressive, awesome*
gèngjiā 更加 *even more*
tōngguò Wēixìn 通過微信／通过微信 *via WeChat*
jíshí 及時／及时 *in good time, promptly*
liǎojiě 了解 *get to know a lot about*
zhěngtǐ lái shuō 整體來說／整体来说 *on the whole, overall*
míngxiǎn 明顯／明显 *clear, obvious*

____ *All these modes of communication—the convenience is just hard for us to imagine. When we had just started to have Weibo, we thought Weibo was all that, Weibo was just . . . now we find that WeChat is even more convenient, even faster.*

____ *First there was QQ, and Skype, all of these kinds of . . . And today, now that it's all developed—I just got a statistic the other day. They say now there are 90,000,000 WeChat users in the world, of whom 50,000,000 are in China, and they say there are 30,000,000 users in the United States. Of course, in the United States, it's not called Wēixìn; it's called WeChat.*

____ *In the past, maybe, take us for instance. When I began my studies, back then—forget about cell phones; we didn't even have telephones. And look, now we've gone from having phones to having cell phones, and finally the Internet.*

____ *I think this is just so very very . . . overall, I think that in China, especially in China, this can be seen just so very, very clearly. The changes over the past ten years have been really, really fast.*

____ *Just look at our whole film crew: All of our communications, our keeping in touch, is all through our WeChat. Even before the American side arrived, we did it all through WeChat, efficiently and quickly getting in touch, right on time, about the things we needed to know about, and getting to know about them in time.*

____ *There's one more thing. I feel that in the past ten years, in particular in the last ten years, I think one place in which the changes have been really, really big is in modes of communication. People's ways of staying in touch have undergone a huge change.*

38.23 *Finally, starting at 3:36, one of the speakers offers a summary. Read the text and translation, and then move on to the next exercise.*

我覺得確實是天翻地覆的變化。我從六十年代下鄉，一直到現在。從回到北京，改革開放，這麼多年一直到現在，變成現在這個樣子，根本你想不到。不是我想不到，我覺得每一個中國人都想不到，確實變化太大。／

我觉得确实是天翻地覆的变化。我从六十年代下乡，一直到现在。从回到北京，改革开放，这么多年一直到现在，变成现在这个样子，根本你想不到。不是我想不到，我觉得每一个中国人都想不到，确实变化太大。

Wǒ juéde quèshí shì tiānfān-dìfù de biànhuà. Wǒ cóng liùshí niándài xià xiāng, yìzhí dào xiànzài. Cóng huí dào Běijīng, gǎigé kāifàng, zhème duō nián yìzhí dào xiànzài, biànchéng xiànzài zhèi ge yàngzi, gēnběn nǐ xiǎngbudào. Bú shì wǒ xiǎngbudào, wǒ juéde měi yí ge Zhōngguórén dōu xiǎngbudào, quèshí biànhuà tài dà.

I feel it truly is a sea change. From being sent down to the countryside in the 1960s, up until now. Since I returned to Beijing, the reform and opening, all these years up until now, for it to have changed into the way it is now, you totally couldn't have imagined it. I'm not just saying I personally couldn't have imagined it; I don't think any Chinese person could have imagined it. Really, the changes have been just too great.

38.24 *In the space below, write one statement in Chinese based on what you have heard and what you find most striking about the changes in China over the last few decades.*

Recap

Grammar

Connecting thoughts within sentences

With a classmate, read the grammar notes below and then imagine you are to leave in a month to study in China for a year.

Nǐ líkāi Měiguó zuì shěbude shénme?
你離開美國最捨不得甚麼？／你离开美国最舍不得什么？
What would you most hate to leave behind?

Nǐ qù Zhōngguó zuì pànwàngzhe shénme?
你去中國最盼望著甚麼？／你去中国最盼望着什么？
What would you most look forward to?

Write at least three statements in each category and try to link your thoughts together with connectors such as those used in the following examples.

■ **Showing contrast**

suīrán . . . kěshì . . .
雖然……可是……／虽然……可是……
although . . . still . . .

Wǒ suīrán hěn shěbude líkāi jiā, kěshì wǒ hěn pànwàngzhe qù Běijīng pá Chángchéng.
我雖然很捨不得離開家，可是我很盼望著去北京爬長城。／
我虽然很舍不得离开家，可是我很盼望着去北京爬长城。
Although I feel bad about leaving home, still, I'm looking forward to going to Beijing to climb the Great Wall.

Suīrán zhèlǐ de shēnghuó hěn shūfu, kěshì wǒ háishì hěn xiǎngjiā, xiǎngniàn wǒ jiāli de qīnqi péngyou.
雖然這裡的生活很舒服，可是我還是很想家，想念我家裡的親戚朋友。／
虽然这里的生活很舒服，可是我还是很想家，想念我家里的亲戚朋友。
Although life here is very comfortable, still, I miss home a lot. I miss my friends and my family.

■ **Giving a reason**

yīnwèi . . . suǒyǐ . . .
因為……所以……／因为……所以……
since/because . . . therefore . . .

Yīnwèi xiànzài shìjiè shì píng de, suǒyǐ suǒyǒu de rén dōu yǒu jīhuì guò yí ge hǎo yìdiǎnr de shēnghuó.
因為現在世界是平的，所以所有的人都有機會過一個好一點兒的生活。／
因为现在世界是平的，所以所有的人都有机会过一个好一点儿的生活。
Because the world is flat nowadays, everyone will have the opportunity to live a better life.

■ **"If-ing" (Just suppose . . .)**

yàoshi . . . jiù . . .
要是……就……
if . . . (then) . . .

Wǒ yàoshi néng xiàng nǐ yíyàng cōngmíng, jiù huì hěn gāoxìng.
我要是能像你一樣聰明，就會很高興。／
我要是能像你一样聪明，就会很高兴。
If I could be as smart as you, I'd be very happy.

rúguǒ . . . jiù . . .
如果……就……
if . . . (then) . . .

Rúguǒ nénggòu gēn nǐmen shēnghuó zài yìqǐ, wǒ jiù huì guò hǎorìzi.
如果能夠跟你們生活在一起，我就會過好日子。／
如果能够跟你们生活在一起，我就会过好日子。
If I could live with you all, I would have a good life.

rúguǒ . . . de huà
如果……話／如果……的话
if . . .

Rúguǒ nǐ bú qù de huà, wǒ yě bú qù.
如果你不去的話，我也不去。／
如果你不去的话，我也不去。
If you don't go, I won't go either.

Hedging your bet or expressing a condition

zhǐyǒu . . . cái
只有……才
only when . . . (then)

Zhǐyǒu wǒ bàmā zài wǒ shēnbiānr, wǒ cái néng guò yí ge lǐxiǎng de shēnghuó.
只有我爸媽在我身邊兒，我才能過一個理想的生活。／
只有我爸妈在我身边儿，我才能过一个理想的生活。
I can only live an ideal lifestyle if my parents are by my side.

zhǐyào . . . jiù
只要……就
as long as . . . (then)

Nǐ zhǐyào nǔlì, jiù huì jìnbù.
你只要努力，就會進步 。／
你只要努力，就会进步。
As long as you work hard, you will make progress.

zhǐyǒu . . . cái
只有……才
only if . . . (then)

Zhǐyǒu yǒu jìnbù, cáinéng mǎnzú fùmǔ duì nǐ de qīwàng.
只有有進步，才能滿足父母對你的期望。／
只有有进步，才能满足父母对你的期望。
Only if you make progress will you satisfy your parents' expectations.

Stressing purpose

wèile . . .
為了……／为了……
for the purpose of . . .; for . . .

Wèile háizi de wèilái, hǎo fùmǔ chángcháng huì xīshēng yíqiè.
為了孩子的未來，好父母常常會犧牲一切。／
为了孩子的未来，好父母常常会牺牲一切。
Good parents will often sacrifice everything for the sake of their children.

Expressing sequential actions

xiān . . . ránhòu . . .
先……然後……／先……然后……
first . . . then . . .

Nǐ xiān děi zhǎodào yí ge wěndìng de gōngzuò, zhuàn diǎnr qián, ránhòu cái hǎo zhǎo duìxiàng.
你先得找到一個穩定的工作，賺點兒錢，然後才好找對象。／
你先得找到一个稳定的工作，赚点儿钱，然后才好找对象。
First you have to find a stable job and earn some money, and then you can look for a life partner.

yī . . . jiù . . .
一……就……
as soon as . . . (then) . . .

Zhōngguórén cháng shuō, Cáo Cāo hěn lìhai, nǐ yì shuō tā, tā jiù huì chūxiàn zài nǐ shēnbiān, zhǔnbèi shā nǐ!
中國人常說，曹操很厲害，你一說他，他就會出現在你身邊，準備殺你！／
中国人常说，曹操很厉害，你一说他，他就会出现在你身边，准备杀你！
Chinese people often say that Cao Cao is really something. As soon as you mention him, he'll appear by your side, ready to kill you!

Expressing "no matter what"

wúlùn . . . háishì . . .
無論……還是……／
无论……还是……
bùguǎn . . . háishì . . .
不管……還是……／
不管……还是……
No matter how/what . . .

Bùguǎn wǒ yǒu duō máng, yàoshi fùmǔ xūyào wǒ bāngmáng, wǒ háishì huì qù de.
不管我有多忙，要是父母需要我幫忙，我還是會去的。／
不管我有多忙，要是父母需要我帮忙，我还是会去的。
No matter how busy I am, if my parents need my help, I will still go.

■ **Listing**

yòu . . . yòu . . .
又……又……
Both . . . and . . .

Nǐ bàba zhēn bàng, yòu huì chàngxì yòu huì zuò fàn.
你爸爸真棒，又會唱戲又會做飯。／
你爸爸真棒，又会唱戏又会做饭。
Your father is really great. He can both sing opera and cook.

■ **Expressing alternatives/choices**

shì . . . háishì . . .
是……還是……／是……还是……
. . . or . . .

Nǐ dàxué bìyè hòu shì yào zhǎo gōngzuò háishì jìxù dúshū?
你大學畢業後是要找工作還是繼續讀書？／
你大学毕业后是要找工作还是继续读书？
After you graduate, do you want to look for a job or keep on studying?

■ **"Since-ing" (making an inference)**

jìrán . . . jiù . . .
既然……就……
Since . . . (then) . . .

Nǐ jìrán yǐjing juédìng guò yí ge rén de shēnghuó, wǒ yǐhòu jiù bú zài lǐ nǐ le.
你既然已經決定過一個人的生活，我以後就不再理你了。／
你既然已经决定过一个人的生活，我以后就不再理你了。
Since you've already decided to live alone, I won't pay any more attention to you then.

■ **Excepting/excluding**

chúle . . . yǐwài
除了……以外
chúle . . . zhīwai
除了……之外
Apart from . . .

Chúle gěi tā fā le jǐ ge duǎnxìn yǐwài, wǒ gēn tā méiyǒu shénme zhíjiē de liánxì.
除了給他發了幾個短信以外，我跟他沒有甚麼直接的聯繫。／
除了给他发了几个短信以外，我跟他没有什么直接的联系。
Apart from sending him a few text messages, I haven't had much direct contact with him.

(For more on connecting thoughts within sentences, see *Chinese: A Comprehensive Grammar,* by Yip and Rimmington, Routledge, London and New York, 2004, pp. 330–346.)

Vocabulary

Please refer to page R-2 for a list of grammatical abbreviations used throughout this book.

àihào 愛好／爱好 interests; hobby/hobbies N

bàng 棒 good; fine; great SV

bù dī yú 不低於／不低于 not lower than VP

cáihuá 才華／才华 literary/artistic talent N

cǎinà 採納／采纳 accept; adopt *(suggestions, etc.)* V

Cáo Cāo 曹操 celebrated general (155–220 CE) of the Three Kingdoms period N

céng 層／层 *(for stories of a building, floors)* M

chàngxì 唱戲／唱戏 perform in a traditional opera VO

chuǎngdàng 闖蕩／闯荡 make an itinerant living V

chúyǐ 除以 *(a number)* to be divided by VP

dǎ jīchǔ 打基礎／打基础 lay a foundation VO

dàbùfen 大部分 major part N

dáfù 答覆／答复 answer; reply V

dàngchéng 當成／当成 regard; consider as VP

dàodǐ 到底 at last; in the end; finally A

dáyí 答疑 answer questions; clarify matters VO

diǎnjī 點擊／点击 press; hit; strike; click *(a keyboard)* V

fā duǎnxìn 發短信／发短信 send a text message VP

fāngshì 方式 way; pattern; fashion N

fēngfù 豐富／丰富 enrich V; rich, abundant, plentiful SV

fēnjū liǎngdì 分居兩地／分居两地 live in separate locations; live apart IE

fēnshù 分數／分数 grade; mark N

gānbēi 乾杯／干杯 drink a toast VO; Cheers! Bottoms up! IE

gèrén 個人／个人 personal N/ATTR

gōngxǐ 恭喜 congratulations N/IE

gūdú 孤獨／孤独 lonely; lonesome SV

guò 過／过 undergo; go through V

Hǎoláiwū 好萊塢／好莱坞 Hollywood PW

huāshēngmǐ 花生米 shelled peanut N

huíyì 回憶／回忆 recollect; recall V; memories N

huòdé 獲得／获得 gain; acquire; get; achieve V

jiǎnlì 簡歷／简历 résumé; curriculum vitae N

jiàoxué 教學／教学 teaching; education(al) N/ATTR

jìn xiào 進校／进校 enter school VO

jīnglì 經歷／经历 experience N; go through V

jùhuì 聚會／聚会 get together N/V

jùtǐ 具體／具体 concrete; specific SV

kànbìng 看病 see a doctor VO

làngjì tiānyá 浪跡天涯／浪迹天涯 roam all over IE

lǎogōng 老公 husband N

lèi 類／类 class; type N

liánxì 聯繫／联系 link up with; get in touch with V

lìhai 厲害／厉害 tough; capable; sharp; terrific SV

liúxué 留學／留学 study abroad V

lǐxiǎng 理想 ideal N; ideal SV

mánghuo 忙活 be busy/swamped VO

mǎnzú 滿足／满足 be satisfied/contented SV

mǐ 米 rice N

miǎnfèi 免費／免费 be free of charge VO

pá Chángchéng 爬長城／爬长城 climb the Great Wall VP

pànwàng 盼望 hope/long for; look forward to V

péi 陪 accompany; join in with V

píng 平 flat; level; even SV

pínggū 評估／评估 assessment, evaluation N; evaluate V

qū 區／区 district N

quán shìjiè 全世界 the entire world N

quánjiā 全家 the whole family N

quánlì 權利／权利 right; privilege N

quānzi 圈子 circle; ring; clique N

rénpǐn 人品 quality of someone's character N

rénshēng 人生 (human) life N

rénshēng jiǎnlì 人生簡歷／人生简历 life experiences N

rènxìng 任性 willful; headstrong SV

rúguǒ . . . de huà 如果……的話／如果……的话 if . . . C

Sānguó Yǎnyì 三國演義／三国演义 *Romance of the Three Kingdoms (novel)* N

shěbude 捨不得／舍不得 be loathe to part with RV

shǒuxiān 首先 first A

shǔyú 屬於／属于 belong to; be a part of V

tíshēng 提升 promote; elevate RV

tuījiàn 推薦／推荐 recommend V

tújìng 途徑／途径 way; channel N

wán huábǎn 玩滑板 (go) skateboarding VP

wǎngyǒu 網友／网友 netizens N

wèi 為／为 for; to CV

wèilái 未來／未来 future; time to come N

wěndìng 穩定／稳定 stable, steady SV; stabilize V

wēnnuǎn 溫暖／温暖 warm SV

xiǎng 想 remember with longing; miss V

xiǎngqǐ 想起 think of; remember; recall RV

xiànmù 羨慕／羡慕 admire; envy V

xíguàn 習慣／习惯 be accustomed/used to V; habit N

xìngfú 幸福 happy SV; happiness N

xuǎnzé 選擇／选择 select; choose V; choice; alternative N

xúnwèn 詢問／询问 *(formally)* inquire V

yìbānláishuō 一般來説／一般来说 generally speaking VP

yìzhí 一直 always; all along A

yōuzhì 優質／优质 high/top quality/grade ATTR

zàixiàn 在線／在线 be online VO

zhāshi 扎實／扎实 solid; sound SV

zhuàn 賺／赚 earn; make a profit; gain V

zīyuán 資源／资源 resources; natural resources N

zōnghé 綜合／综合 comprehensive ATTR

Checklist of "can do" statements

After completing this unit, you should be able to perform each of the following tasks:

Listening and speaking

- ☐ Describe your thoughts on an ideal lifestyle.
- ☐ Talk about your hopes for your own future lifestyle.
- ☐ Describe what you most appreciate about your current life.
- ☐ Describe what you hope for in an overseas study program.

Reading and writing

- ☐ Decipher the main ideas of an online discussion about studying abroad.
- ☐ Comprehend a brief autobiography.
- ☐ Write a brief autobiography of your own.

Understanding culture

- ☐ Make several accurate statements about changing lifestyles in China.

UNIT

39

"If you believe, it will work"

心誠則靈

Xīnchéngzélíng

Spiritual practices

In this unit, you will learn how to:

- talk about some aspects of your spiritual practices.
- have a conversation about practices in some key world religions.
- discuss ways to celebrate a holiday or festival.
- decipher some entries on a list of national holidays in China.
- read a legend about the Boddhisattva Guanyin.
- write a short story about a religious figure.
- comment on some common practices in celebrating the Dragon Boat Festival.

Encounter 1 Discussing religious practices

39.1 *Emma and Fang Lan observe Fang Lan's mother, Zhang Suyun, burning incense in the morning.* 請把中文跟英文對上。／请把中文跟英文对上。

____ a. shāo yí zhù xiāng 燒一炷香／烧一炷香	1. *protect the whole family*
____ b. bǎoyòu quánjiā 保佑全家	2. *believe in a religion*
____ c. bài Fó 拜佛	3. *church (the building)*
____ d. jìzǔ 祭祖	4. *mosque*
____ e. Dàojiào 道教	5. *make offerings to the ancestors*
____ f. xìn jiào 信教	6. *Daoism*
____ g. Jīdūjiào 基督教	7. *(a) Catholic (person)*
____ h. Tiānzhǔjiào 天主教	8. *burn a stick of incense*
____ i. Tiānzhǔjiàotú 天主教徒	9. *Catholicism*
____ j. jiàotáng 教堂	10. *Muslim*
____ k. Mùsīlín 穆斯林	11. *Islam*
____ l. Yīsīlánjiào 伊斯蘭教／伊斯兰教	12. *worship the Buddha*
____ m. qīngzhēnsì 清真寺	13. *Christianity*
____ n. zuò lǐbài 做禮拜／做礼拜	14. *attend religious service*

39.2 *View Episode 39, Vignette 1. Zhang Suyun, Fang Lan, and Emma are talking about various religious practices. Indicate which belief system they refer to when they make the remarks below. Note that they could be referring to more than one system.*

	祭祖	道教	佛教	基督教	天主教	伊斯蘭教／伊斯兰教
a. měitiān zǎoshang qǐlai shāo zhù xiāng	☐	☐	☐	☐	☐	☐
b. gǎnxiè tāmen bǎoyòu wǒmen quánjiā píng'ān	☐	☐	☐	☐	☐	☐
c. zuò mísa	☐	☐	☐	☐	☐	☐
d. zuò mísa de shíhou shāoxiāng	☐	☐	☐	☐	☐	☐
e. zài jiāli shāoxiāng	☐	☐	☐	☐	☐	☐

	祭祖	道教	佛教	基督教	天主教	伊斯蘭教／伊斯兰教
f. yì tiān zuò wǔ cì dǎogào	☐	☐	☐	☐	☐	☐
g. (nǚrén) měitiān dài tóujīn	☐	☐	☐	☐	☐	☐
h. cónglái bù chī zhūròu	☐	☐	☐	☐	☐	☐
i. xíngshàn, jīdé, zuò hǎorén	☐	☐	☐	☐	☐	☐

39.3 請把下面的英文跟上面的拼音對上。／请把下面的英文跟上面的拼音对上。

____ 1. burn incense at home

____ 2. never eat pork

____ 3. burn incense during Mass

____ 4. burn a stick of incense upon awakening every day

____ 5. pray five times a day

____ 6. do good, accumulate merit, be a kind person

____ 7. go to Mass

____ 8. (women) wear a head scarf every day

____ 9. thank them for keeping our whole family safe

39.4 請把下面的漢字跟上面的英語對上。／ 请把下面的汉字跟上面的英语对上。

____ A. 做彌撒的時候燒香／做弥撒的时候烧香

____ B. 每天早上起來燒炷香／每天早上起来烧炷香

____ C. （女人）每天戴頭巾／（女人）每天戴头巾

____ D. 感謝他們保佑我們全家平安／感谢他们保佑我们全家平安

____ E. 從來不吃豬肉／从来不吃猪肉

____ F. 在家裡燒香／在家里烧香

____ G. 行善，積德，做好人／行善，积德，做好人

____ H. 做彌撒／做弥撒

____ I. 一天做五次禱告／一天做五次祷告

39.5 *What are the places of worship for the various religions called?* 請用下面的詞彙填空。／请用下面的词汇填空。

qīngzhēnsì 清真寺 sìmiào 寺廟／寺庙 jiàotáng 教堂

a. Wǒ shì Fójiàotú. Wǒ xìn Fójiào. Wǒ cháng dào ____________ lǐ qù bài Fó.

我是佛教徒。我信佛教。我常到 ____________ 裡去拜佛。／
我是佛教徒。我信佛教。我常到 ____________ 里去拜佛。

b. Wǒ shì Jīdūjiàotú. Wǒ xìn Jīdūjiào. Wǒ měi Xīngqītiān shàng ____________ qù zuò lǐbài.

我是基督教徒。我信基督教。我每星期天上 ____________ 去做禮拜。／
我是基督教徒。我信基督教。我每星期天上 ____________ 去做礼拜。

c. Wǒ shì Mùsīlín. Wǒ xìn Yīsīlánjiào. Wǒ měi Xīngqīwǔ shàng ____________ qù zuò lǐbài.

我是穆斯林。我信伊斯蘭教。我每星期五上 ____________ 去做禮拜。／
我是穆斯林。我信伊斯兰教。我每星期五上 ____________ 去做礼拜。

39.6 *In this vignette, the characters also discuss not adhering to a religious belief. They begin their discussion with a joke.*

Àimǎ: Nǐ ne? Nǐ gēn nǐ bàba nǐmen xìn shénme jiào?
Fāng Lán: Wǒ bà ya, zhǐ xìn shuìjiào.

a. *Circle the two characters pronounced* jiào*, which make this pun possible. One has to do with faith and the other with sleeping.*

艾瑪／艾玛: 你呢？你跟你爸爸你們信甚麼教？／
你呢？你跟你爸爸你们信什么教？
方蘭／方兰: 我爸呀，只信睡覺。／我爸呀，只信睡觉。

b. *If you want to use humor to say that you don't have a religious belief, you could do so in several ways—one humorous and the others "straight." Check the one you prefer.*

Q: Nǐ xìn jiào ma?

A: ☐ Wǒ bú xìn jiào.
☐ Wǒ shénme jiào dōu bú xìn.
☐ Wǒ zhǐ xìn shuìjiào.

c. *Write the characters for the question and answers given on page 206.*

Q: ______________________________

A: ______________________________

____

____

39.7 *The characters then talk about other quasi-spiritual practices that are not linked to religion. Please fill in the blanks with the correct terms.* 請用拼音填空。／请用拼音填空。*Some terms may be used more than once. (If necessary, view the last segment of the vignette again to refresh your memory.)*

zōngjiào *religion*	xìnyǎng *religious belief*	shàngtiān(táng) *go to Heaven*
duànliàn shēntǐ *work out your body*	yújiā *yoga*	míngxiǎng *meditate*

Àimǎ: Wǒ yǒuxiē péngyou tāmen suīrán méiyǒu _______, kěshì měitiān sāncì _______, ránhòu hái zuò yújiā.

艾瑪／艾玛: 我有些朋友他們雖然没有信仰，可是每天三次冥想，然後還做瑜伽。／
我有些朋友他们虽然没有信仰，可是每天三次冥想，然后还做瑜伽。

Fāng Lán: Zuò _________, nà hěn nán de! Dànshì zhè yīnggāi hé _________ méiyǒu shénme guānxi ba?

方蘭／方兰: 做瑜伽，那很難的！但是這應該和宗教没有甚麼關係吧？／
做瑜伽，那很难的！但是这应该和宗教没有什么关系吧？

Àimǎ: Wǒ yě zuò yújiā. Wǒ tǐng xǐhuan yújiā! Dànshì duì wǒ lái shuō zhè zhǐshì yìzhǒng ____________ de huódòng, búshì zōngjiào.

艾瑪／艾玛: 我也做瑜伽。我挺喜歡瑜伽！但是對我來説這只是一種鍛煉身體的活動，不是宗教。／
我也做瑜伽。我挺喜欢瑜伽！但是对我来说这只是一种锻炼身体的活动，不是宗教。

Fāng Lán: Qíshí jiù xiàng wǒ mā shuō de yíyàng, bùguǎn nǐ yǒu méiyǒu _________, bùguǎn nǐ xìn shénme, wǒmen dōu yīnggāi zuò gè hǎorén. Zhè yàng cái yǒu kěnéng yǒu jīhuì __________!

方蘭／方兰:	其實就像我媽說的一樣，不管你有沒有信仰，不管你信甚麼，我們都應該做個好人。這樣才有可能有機會上天！／其实就像我妈说的一样，不管你有没有信仰，不管你信什么，我们都应该做个好人。这样才有可能有机会上天！
Zhāng Sūyún:	Bié shàngtiān shàngtiān de, kuài chīfàn!
張蘇雲／张苏云:	別上天上天的，快吃飯！／别上天上天的，快吃饭！

39.8 ***Pair work:*** *Have a conversation in Chinese with a partner about your religious beliefs and practices. Begin by asking,* 你信教嗎？／你信教吗？ Nǐ xìn jiào ma? *Respond by using as much as you can of the language in the previous exercises. Provide some details of your beliefs and practices. If there is time, switch to another partner.*

39.9 ***Mingling:*** *Walk around and speak in Chinese for as long as you can to as many of your classmates as possible about your religious beliefs and practices. If your class wishes to, compile everyone's information and make a physical chart to post on the wall or a digital chart to post online.*

39.10 *When Emma and Zhang Suyun are at the altar, Emma comments that Fang Lan looks like her paternal grandmother—to which Zhang Suyun responds that her personality is more like her paternal grandfather's. Please fill in the blanks with the correct terms.* 請用拼音填空。／请用拼音填空。 *(If necessary, view the beginning segment of the vignette again to refresh your memory.)*

jiānchí yuánzé *insist on principles*	gùzhi *stubborn*
xìnggé *personality*	juè *pig-headed*

Àimǎ:	Lánlan, wǒ juéde nǐ zhǎng de hǎo xiàng nǎinai.
艾瑪／艾玛:	蘭蘭，我覺得你長得好像奶奶。／兰兰，我觉得你长得好像奶奶。
Zhāng Sūyún:	Kěshì Lánlan de _____ ya xiàng tā de yéye——______, _______.
張蘇雲／张苏云:	可是蘭蘭的性格呀像她的爺爺——倔,固執。／可是兰兰的性格呀像她的爷爷——倔,固执。
Fāng Lán:	Wǒ zhè cái búshì gùzhi ne, wǒ zhè jiào _______________.
方蘭／方兰:	我這才不是固執呢，我這叫堅持原則。／我这才不是固执呢，我这叫坚持原则。

39.11 ***Pair work:*** *Whom do you resemble—in looks and personality? Talk to a partner. Ask,* 你像誰？你外表像誰，性格像誰？／你像谁？你外表像谁，性格像谁？ Nǐ xiàng shéi? Nǐ wàibiǎo xiàng shéi, xìnggé xiàng shéi? *Give some details. Some useful vocabulary is provided for your convenience. If there is time, switch to another partner.*

wàibiǎo 外表 *external appearance*	wàixiàng 外向 *extroverted*
nèixiàng 內向／内向 *introverted*	kāilǎng 開朗／开朗 *open-minded*
huópō 活潑／活泼 *lively*	gùzhi 固執／固执 *stubborn*
dúlì 獨立／独立 *independent*	píqi hǎo 脾氣好／脾气好 *good-tempered*
píqi huài 脾氣壞／脾气坏 *bad-tempered*	suíhe 隨和／随和 *easygoing*

39.12 ***Mingling:*** *Walk around and speak in Chinese for as long as you can to as many of your classmates as possible about whom they resemble, both physically and in terms of personality. Obtain details. Take notes on a blank class roster.*

Encounter 2 Discussing the celebration of a festival

39.13 *Fang Lan's family is preparing to celebrate the Double Fifth Festival, also called the Dragon Boat Festival. (See Unit 29 in Book 3 for a discussion of key Chinese festivals.)* 請把中文和英文對上。／请把中文和英文对上。

____ a. àicǎo 艾草	1. *race dragon boats*
____ b. zhāofú qūxié 招福驅邪／招福驱邪	2. *legend*
____ c. zòngzi 粽子	3. *Asiatic wormwood leaves*
____ d. sài lóngzhōu 賽龍舟／赛龙舟	4. *celebrate a holiday*
____ e. Duānwǔjié 端午節／端午节	5. *summon blessings and drive out evil*
____ f. chuánshuō 傳說／传说	6. *Double Fifth Festival*
____ g. Wǔyuè chūwǔ 五月初五	7. *filled rice dumplings wrapped in bamboo leaves*
____ h. jiérì 節日／节日	8. *fifth day of the fifth month*
____ i. chuántǒng de nónglì 傳統的農曆／传统的农历	9. *festival*
____ j. guòjié 過節／过节	10. *all get together*
____ k. tuánjù zài yìqǐ 團聚在一起／团聚在一起	11. *traditional lunar (agricultural) calendar*

39.14 *View Episode 39, Vignette 2. Indicate whether Fang Lan, Emma, Lao Fang, or Zhang Suyun make each of the following statements (given in the order they are made).*

i.

ii.

iii.

iv.

_____ a. Where should I hang these Asiatic wormwood leaves?

_____ b. Attach them to the door.

_____ c. They can bring blessings and expel evil and disease.

_____ d. I've bought zongzi!

_____ e. There's date filling, red bean filling, five-grain filling, and the meat and saltwater filling that you like.

_____ f. Isn't Double Fifth the festival when they race dragon boats?

_____ g. Is it that the more you eat, the faster you row?

_____ h. On the fifth day of the fifth month of the lunar calendar, which is today, the custom of wrapping and eating zongzi still holds for all of us.

_____ i. When we were little, every family wrapped its own zongzi.

_____ j. We'd make a huge heap and cook up a huge pot.

_____ k. Nowadays, living conditions are better, so we don't make them anymore; we go out and buy them.

_____ l. It seems that Chinese festivals are all about eating!

_____ m. In the traditional Chinese calendar, every month has a festival!

_____ n. On the eve of Chinese New Year, people in the north eat jiaozi, whereas people in the south eat soup rice balls.

_____ o. For Thanksgiving, there's a big turkey meal. For Halloween, we eat candy and chocolate.

_____ p. So even though the two countries have festivals that can be the same or different, one thing is exactly the same—and that is that we all get together with family and friends!

39.15 請把下面的拼音和上面的英文對上。／请把下面的拼音和上面的英文对上。

_____ 1. Měi yì nián nónglì de Wǔyuè chūwǔ, jiùshì jīntiān, wǒmen dàhuǒr bāo zòngzi chī zòngzi de zhè zhǒng chuántǒng xísú yìzhí liúchuán dào jīntiān.

_____ 2. Xiànzài tiáojiàn hǎo le, wǒmen dōu bù bāo le, dōu shàngjiē mǎi.

_____ 3. Jiùshì liǎng ge guójiā de jiérì yǒu xiāngtóng yě yǒu bùtóng, dànshì (yǒu) yì diǎn shì yīmóyīyàng de, nà jiùshì yào gēn jiārén hé péngyoumen tuánjù zài yìqǐ!

_____ 4. Zhè ge àicǎo yīnggāi guà nǎr?

_____ 5. Wǒmen xiǎo de shíhou, dōu shì jiājiāhùhù zìjǐ bāo zòngzi.

_____ 6. Zhōngguórén de jiérì hǎoxiàng dōu shì hé chī yǒuguān!

_____ 7. Jiùshì bǎ fú zhāo jìnlai, bǎ xié'è a bìngmó a qūzhú chūqu.

_____ 8. Duānwǔjié búshì sài lóngzhōu de jiérì ma?

_____ 9. Gǎn'ēnjié de shíhou chī huǒjī dàcān, Wànshèngjié de shíhou chī tángguǒ qiǎokèlì.

_____ 10. Bǎ tā tiē zài ménshang.

_____ 11. Yǒu hóngzǎo de, yǒu hóngdòu de, yǒu wǔgǔ de, yǒu nǐ ài chī de ròuzòng, hái yǒu nǐ ài chī de xiánshuǐzòng!

_____ 12. Zhōngguó zhèi ge chuántǒng de nónglì ya, měi ge yuè dōu yǒu jiérì!

_____ 13. Zòngzi mǎi huílai la!

_____ 14. Bāo yí dà duī, zhǔ yí dà guō.

_____ 15. Dànián sānshí de shíhou, běifāng chī de shì jiǎozi, nánfāng chī de shì tāngyuánr.

_____ 16. Nándào chīde yuèduō huáde yuèkuài?

39.16 請把下面的漢字和上面的拼音對上。／请把下面的汉字和上面的拼音对上。

_____ A. 難道吃得越多划得越快？／难道吃得越多划得越快？

_____ B. 中國人的節日好像都是和吃有關！／中国人的节日好像都是和吃有关！

_____ C. 這個艾草應該掛哪兒？／这个艾草应该挂哪儿？

_____ D. 現在條件好了，我們都不包了，都上街買。/ 现在条件好了，我们都不包了，都上街买。

_____ E. 我們小的時候，都是家家戶戶自己包粽子。／我们小的时候，都是家家户户自己包粽子。

_____ F. 就是把福招進來，把邪惡啊、病魔啊驅逐出去。／就是把福招进来，把邪恶啊、病魔啊驱逐出去。

_____ G. 大年三十的時候，北方吃的是餃子，南方吃的是湯圓兒。／大年三十的时候，北方吃的是饺子，南方吃的是汤圆儿。

_____ H. 粽子買回來啦！／粽子买回来啦！

_____ I. 包一大堆，煮一大鍋。／包一大堆，煮一大锅。

____ J. 端午節不是賽龍舟的節日嗎？／端午节不是赛龙舟的节日吗？

____ K. 感恩節的時候吃火雞大餐，萬聖節的時候吃糖果巧克力。／感恩节的时候吃火鸡大餐，万圣节的时候吃糖果巧克力。

____ L. 把它貼在門上。／把它贴在门上。

____ M. 就是兩個國家的節日有相同也有不同，但是(有)一點是一模一樣的，那就是要跟家人和朋友們團聚在一起！／就是两个国家的节日有相同也有不同，但是(有)一点是一模一样的，那就是要跟家人和朋友们团聚在一起。

____ N. 每一年農曆的五月初五，就是今天，我們大伙兒包粽子吃粽子的這種傳統習俗一直流傳到今天。／每一年农历的五月初五，就是今天，我们大伙儿包粽子吃粽子的这种传统习俗一直流传到今天。

____ O. 中國這個傳統的農曆呀，每個月都有節日！／中国这个传统的农历呀，每个月都有节日！

____ P. 有紅棗的、有紅豆的、有五穀的，有你愛吃的肉粽，還有你愛吃的鹹水粽！／有红枣的、有红豆的、有五谷的，有你爱吃的肉粽，还有你爱吃的咸水粽！

39.17 ***Pair work:*** *Work with a partner to discuss in Chinese (1) how the Double Fifth (Dragon Boat) Festival is celebrated and (2) how a festival with which you are familiar is celebrated. Go into detail as much as you can. Take notes on your discussion, and write several statements from your descriptions.* 請寫拼音或者漢字。／请写拼音或者汉字。

FYI 供你参考

Qu Yuan—Poet and patriot

Qu Yuan (*Qū Yuán* 屈原) was a poet who lived around 300 BCE, during the Warring States period. He is credited with having written or inspired the verses collected in the *Chǔ Cí* 楚辭／楚辞 *Songs of the South.* This ancient anthology includes the famous poem *Lí Sāo* 離騷／离骚 *Encountering Sorrow*, an epic poem about the travails of the poet over the course of his life.

Qu Yuan lived in the southern state of Chu, which is in modern-day Hubei Province. He served as a minister in the government but was slandered, and he eventually became so depressed about the political corruption around him that he committed ritual suicide by drowning himself in the Miluo River. Legend has it that the common people, who loved and admired him, then searched the river in boats, hoping to save him. Failing to do so, they threw offerings into the water to keep fish and shrimp from consuming his body. The Dragon Boat races are said to commemorate that ancient search.

39.18 *Zhang Suyun tells the story behind the Dragon Boat Festival. Using the information from the FYI about Qu Yuan, fill in the blanks with terms from the box.* 請用拼音填空。／请用拼音填空。

lǎobǎixìng *common people*	shīrén *poet*	mǐtuán *rice ball*
shītǐ *corpse*	tóu jiāng *throw himself into the river*	wèi *feed*

Duānwǔjié ya, shì wèi le jìniàn wǒmen gǔdài de àiguó de ______, Qū Yuán. Jùshuō tā dāngnián ______ yǐhòu a, dāngdì _______ mǎshàng huáchuán qù zhǎo, zhǎo le hǎo jǐ tiān dōu méi zhǎozháo. Tāmen hàipà Qū Yuán de ________ bèi yú ya xiā a gěi chī le zěnme bàn ya, jiù xiǎng bànfǎ, jiù yòng _______ zòngyè bāoguǒ tóu dào jiāng lǐbianr _______yú wèi xiā chī.

端午節呀，是為了紀念我們古代的愛國的詩人，屈原。據説他當年投江以後啊，當地老百姓馬上划船去找，找了好幾天都没找著。他們害怕屈原的屍體被魚呀蝦啊給吃了怎麼辦呀，就想辦法，就用米糰粽葉包裹投到江裡邊兒餵魚餵蝦吃。／

端午节呀，是为了纪念我们古代的爱国的诗人，屈原。据说他当年投江以后啊，当地老百姓马上划船去找，找了好几天都没找着。他们害怕屈原的尸体被鱼呀虾啊给吃了怎么办呀，就想办法，就用米团粽叶包裹投到江里边儿喂鱼喂虾吃。

39.19 *In Chinese, tell the story behind a holiday (the term comes from "holy day") with which you are familiar, such as Christmas, Passover, Thanksgiving, Ramadan, or perhaps Martin Luther King, Jr. Day. Look up vocabulary using Internet resources or by asking your teacher. After you have your story corrected, share it with your classmates, on a class website, or in a class scrapbook.*

Encounter 3 Reading and writing

Reading real-life texts

39.20 *Below is a complete list of holidays for a specific year from* www.baidu.com. *Based on this list, fill in the dates in the table that follows.*

一月	1月1日	元旦	1月26日	腊八节[农历十二月初八]
	1月28日	国际麻风节[一月的最后一个星期日]		
二月	2月2日	世界湿地日	2月11日	小年[农历十二月二十三]
	2月14日	情人节	2月17日	除夕[农历年的最后一天]
	2月18日	春节[农历年的第一天]	2月19日	苗族花山节[农历正月初二至初七]
三月	3月1日	国际海豹日	3月3日	全国爱耳日
	3月4日	木脑纵歌[农历正月十五]	3月4日	元宵节[农历正月十五日]
	3月5日	学习雷锋纪念日	3月8日	国际劳动妇女节
	3月11日	国际尊严尊敬日	3月12日	中国植树节
	3月14日	国际警察日	3月15日	国际消费者权益日
	3月16日	手拉手情系贫困小伙伴全国统一行动日	3月19日	中和节(太阳生日)[农历二月初一]
	3月20日	阿露窝罗节	3月20日	龙抬头节[农历二月初二]
	3月21日	世界森林日	3月21日	世界儿歌日
	3月21日	国际消除种族歧视日	3月21日	世界睡眠日
	3月22日	世界水日	3月23日	世界气象日
	3月24日	世界防治结核病日	3月25日	中小学生安全教育日
	3月25日	春社日[立春后第五个戊日]	3月26日	白族三月街[农历三月十日至二十一]
	3月30日	花朝节(花神节)[农历二月十二]	3月30日	耶稣受难日[复活节前的星期五]

四月	4月1日	国际愚人节	4月4日	寒食节[冬至日后105日清明前一日]
	4月5日	清明节	4月6日	复活节[春分月圆后第一个星期日]
	4月6日	观音菩萨生日[农历二月十九]	4月7日	世界卫生日
	4月11日	世界帕金森病日	4月13日	傣族泼水节[阳历4月13日至4月15日间]
	4月19日	上巳节（女儿节）[农历三月初三]	4月21日	全国企业家活动日
	4月22日	世界地球日	4月22日	世界儿童日[第四个星期日]
	4月23日	世界图书和版权日	4月25日	全国预防接种宣传节日
	4月26日	国际秘书日	4月26日	世界知识产权日
五月	5月1日	国际劳动节	5月4日	中国青年节
	5月5日	全国碘缺乏病宣传日	5月5日	全国爱眼日
	5月8日	世界红十字日	5月8日	世界哮喘日[第二周的周二]
	5月12日	国际护士节	5月13日	母亲节[第二个星期天]
	5月15日	国际家庭日	5月15日	国际牛奶日[第三个星期二]
	5月17日	世界电信日	5月18日	国际博物馆日
	5月20日	全国助残日[第三个星期日]	5月20日	中国学生营养日
	5月20日	全国母乳喂养宣传日	5月22日	国际生物多样性日
	5月24日	佛诞节[农历四月初八]	5月31日	世界无烟日
六月	6月1日	国际儿童节	6月5日	世界环境日
	6月6日	全国爱眼日	6月9日	中国文化遗产日[6月的第二个星期六]
	6月17日	世界防治荒漠化和干旱日	6月17日	父亲节[第三个星期日]
	6月19日	端午节[农历五月初五]	6月20日	世界难民日
	6月23日	国际奥林匹克日	6月25日	全国土地日
	6月26日	国际禁毒日	6月26日	联合国宪章日
七月	7月1日	香港回归纪念日	7月1日	中共建党节
	7月7日	国际合作社日[第一个星期六]	7月7日	中国人民抗日战争纪念日
	7月11日	世界人口日	7月11日	世界海事日
	7月26日	世界语(言)创立日		
八月	8月1日	观音成道日[农历六月十九]	8月1日	中国人民解放军建军节
	8月6日	哈尼族苦扎扎节[农历六月二十四]	8月6日	观莲节(莲花生日)[农历六月二十四]
	8月6日	苗族吃新节	8月6日	火把节[农历六月二十四]
	8月19日	七夕情人节[农历七月初七]	8月27日	中元节[鬼节][农历七月十五]
九月	9月3日	抗日战争胜利纪念日	9月8日	国际扫盲日
	9月10日	中国教师节	9月10日	地藏节[农历七月三十]
	9月10日	世界预防自杀日	9月16日	国际臭氧层保护日
	9月18日	中国国耻日	9月20日	全国爱牙日
	9月20日	全国公民道德宣传日	9月22日	无车日
	9月21日	国际和平日	9月27日	世界旅游日
	9月25日	中秋节[农历八月十五]	9月30日	国际聋人节[最后一个星期日]
	9月28日	世界教师节(孔子诞辰)		
十月	10月1日	世界建筑日[第一个星期一]	10月1日	国际住房日(人居日)[第一个星期一]
	10月1日	国庆节	10月1日	国际老人节
	10月4日	世界动物日	10月8日	全国高血压日
	10月9日	世界邮政日	10月10日	国际减灾日[第二个星期三]
	10月10日	世界精神卫生日	10月11日	世界视觉日[第二个星期四]
	10月13日	世界保健日	10月13日	中国少年先锋队诞辰日
	10月14日	国际音乐节[10月中旬]	10月14日	世界标准日
	10月15日	国际盲人节	10月16日	世界粮食日
	10月17日	国际消除贫困日	10月18日	重阳节[敬老节][农历九月初九]
	10月18日	世界传统医药日	10月24日	联合国日
	10月28日	全国男性健康日	10月29日	观音出家日[农历九月十九]
	10月31日	万圣节		

十一月	11月7日	十月革命纪念日	11月8日	中国记者节
	11月9日	中国消防宣传日	11月10日	世界青年节
	11月10日	祭祖节[农历十月初一]	11月11日	光棍节
	11月11日	国际科学与和平周[11日所属一周]	11月14日	世界糖尿病日
	11月17日	国际大学生节	11月22日	感恩节[第四个星期四]
	11月25日	国际消除对妇女的暴力日		
十二月	12月1日	世界艾滋病日	12月3日	国际残疾人日
	12月4日	中国法制宣传日	12月5日	国际志愿人员日
	12月7日	国际民航日	12月9日	世界足球日
	12月9日	国际儿童广播电视日[第二个星期日]	12月10日	世界人权日
	12月13日	南京大屠杀纪念日	12月20日	澳门回归纪念日
	12月20日	闹时节	12月21日	国际篮球日
	12月22日	冬至节	12月24日	平安夜
	12月25日	圣诞节		

January	_____ Yuándàn *New Year's Day*	_____ Guójì Máfēng Jié (Yīyuè de zuìhòu yí ge Xīngqīrì) *World Leprosy Day (last Sunday in January)*
February	_____ Shìjiè Shīdì Rì *World Wetlands Day* _____ Chúxī *Chinese New Year's Eve (last day of the lunar calendar)*	_____ Qíngrén Jié *Valentine's Day* _____ Chūnjié *Spring Festival (Chinese New Year)*
March	_____ Guójì Hǎibào Rì *International Seal Day* _____ Quánguó Àiʼěr Rì *National Ear Care Day* _____ Yuánxiāo Jié *Lantern Festival* _____ Guójì Láodòng Fùnǚ Jié *International Women's (Labor) Day* _____ Zhōngguó Zhíshù Jié *Chinese Tree-planting (Arbor) Day* _____ Guójì Xiāofèizhě Quányì Rì *World Consumer Rights Day* _____ Shìjiè Sēnlín Rì *World Forests Day* _____ Guójì Xiāochú Zhǒngzúqíshì Rì *International Day for the Elimination of Racial Discrimination*	_____ Xuéxí Léi Fēng Jìniàn Rì *Learn from Léi Fēng Memorial Day* _____ Guójì Zūnyán Zūnjìng Rì *International Day of Respect for Dignity* _____ Guójì Jǐngchá Rì *International Police Day* _____ Shǒulāshǒu Qíngxì Pínkùn Xiǎohuǒbàn Quánguó Tǒngyī Xíngdòng Rì *Hand-in-hand in Commiseration with Our Poorer Companions National Day of Action* _____ Shìjiè Shuìmián Rì *World Sleep Day* _____ Shìjiè Shuǐ Rì *World Water Day* _____ Zhōng-xiǎoxuésheng Ānquán Jiàoyù Rì *Primary and Secondary Safety Education Day* _____ Yēsū Shòunàn Rì (Fùhuójié qián de Xīngqīwǔ) *Good Friday (Friday before Easter)* _____ Huāzhāojié *Flower Festival*
April	_____ Guójì Yúrén Jié *April Fool's Day* _____ Qīngmíng Jié *Qingming Festival; Chinese Tomb-sweeping Day* _____ Guānyīn Púsà Shēngrì (Nónglì Èryuè shíjiǔ) *Birthday of Guanyin, Goddess of Mercy (nineteenth day of the second month in the lunar calendar)* _____ Guójì Mìshū Rì *International Secretary's Day*	_____ Hánshí Jié (Dōngzhì rì hòu 105 rì Qīngmíng qián 1 rì) *Cold Food Festival (105 days after the winter solstice, 1 day before Qingming)* _____ Fùhuó Jié *Easter ("Return to Life Day")* _____ Shìjiè Wèishēng Rì *World Health Day* _____ Quánguó Qǐyèjiā Huódòng Rì *National Entrepreneur's Day* _____ Shìjiè Dìqiú Rì *World Earth Day* _____ Shìjiè Értóng Rì (dì-sì ge Xīngqīrì) *World Children's Day (fourth Sunday)*

May	_____ Guójì Láodòng Jié *International Labor Day* _____ Mǔqīn Jié (dì-èr ge Xīngqītiān) *Mother's Day (second Sunday)* _____ Shìjiè Diànxìn Rì *World Telecommunications Day* _____ Fódàn Jié (Nónglì Sìyuè chūbā) *Buddha's Birthday (eighth day of the fourth month, lunar calendar)*	_____ Zhōngguó Qīngnián Jié *Chinese Youth Day* _____ Shìjiè Hóngshízì Rì *World Red Cross Day* _____ Guójì Jiātíng Rì *International Day of Families* _____ Guójì Niúnǎi Rì (dì-sān ge Xīngqī'èr) *International Milk Day (third Tuesday)* _____ Shìjiè Wúyān Rì *World No-smoking Day*
June	_____ Guójì Értóng Jié *International Children's Day* _____ Quánguó Àiyǎn Rì *National Eye Care Day* _____ Shìjiè Fángzhì Huāngmòhuà hé Gānhàn Rì *World Day to Combat Desertification and Drought* _____ Duānwǔ Jié (Nónglì Wǔyuè Chūwǔ) *Double Fifth (Dragon Boat) Festival (fifth day of the fifth month in the lunar calendar)*	_____ Shìjiè Huánjìng Rì *World Environment Day* _____ Zhōngguó Wénhuà Yíchǎn Rì (Liùyuè de dì-èr ge Xīngqīliù) *Chinese Cultural Heritage Day (second Saturday in June)* _____ Fùqīn Jié (dì-san ge Xīngqīrì) *Father's Day (third Sunday)* _____ Shìjiè Nànmín Rì *World Refugee Day* _____ Quánguó Tǔdì Rì *National Land Day* _____ Guójì Jìndú Rì *International Day Against Drug Abuse*
July	_____ Xiānggǎng Huíguī Jìniànrì *Anniversary of the Return of Hong Kong* _____ Zhōngguó Rénmín Kàng Rì Zhànzhēng Jìniànrì *Memorial Day of the Chinese People's War Against Japan*	_____ Zhōnggòng Jiàndǎng Jié *Chinese Communist Party Founding Day* _____ Shìjiè Rénkǒu Rì *World Population Day* _____ Shìjièyǔ(yán) Chuànglìrì *Establishment of Esperanto Day*
August	_____ Zhōngguó Rénmín Jiěfàngjūn Jiànjūn Jié *People's Liberation Army Founding Day* _____ Zhōngyuán Jié (Guǐ Jié) (Nónglì Qīyuè 15 rì) *Hungry Ghost Festival (fifteenth day of the seventh month in the lunar calendar)*	_____ Qīxī Qíngrén Jié (Nónglì Qīyuè chūqī) *Tanabata Festival, Qixi Festival, Festival of the Cowherd and Weaving Maid (seventh day of the seventh month in the lunar calendar)*
September	_____ Kàng Rì Zhànzhēng Shènglì Jìniànrì *Commemoration Day of Victory in the War Against Japan* _____ Shìjiè Yùfáng Zìshā Rì *World Suicide Prevention Day* _____ Zhōngguó Guóchǐ Rì *China's Day of National Humiliation* _____ Quánguó Àiyá Rì *National Teeth Care Day* _____ Wúchē Rì *Car Free Day* _____ Shìjiè Jiàoshī Jié (Kǒngzǐ Dànchén) *World Teachers' Day (Birthday of Confucius)*	_____ Guójì Sǎománg Rì *International Literacy Day* _____ Zhōngguó Jiàoshī Jié *Chinese Teachers' Day* _____ Guójì Chòuyǎngcéng Bǎohù Rì *International Day for the Protection of the Ozone Layer* _____ Guójì Hépíng Rì *International Peace Day* _____ Zhōngqiū Jié (Nónglì Bāyuè 15 rì) *Mid-Autumn Festival (fifteenth day of the eighth month in the lunar calendar)* _____ Shìjiè Lǚyóu Rì *World Tourism Day* _____ Guójì Lóngrén Jié (zuìhòu yí ge Xīngqīrì) *International Day of the Deaf (last Sunday)*

October	_____ Guóqìngjié *National Day* _____ Guójì Lǎorén Jié *International Day for Older Persons* _____ Quánguó Gāoxuèyā Rì *National Hypertension Day* _____ Shìjiè Bǎojiàn Rì *World Health Day* _____ Shìjiè Biāozhǔn Rì *World Standards Day* _____ Guójì Mángrén Jié *World Sight Day* _____ Shìjiè Chuántǒng Yīyào Rì *World Traditional Medicine Day* _____ Liánhéguó Rì *United Nations Day* _____ Quánguó Nánxìng Jiànkāng Rì *National Men's Health Day*	_____ Guójì Zhùfáng Rì (Rénjū Rì) (dì-yī ge Xīngqīyī) *International Housing Day (Habitat Day) (first Monday)* _____ Shìjiè Dòngwù Rì *World Animal Day* _____ Shìjiè Jīngshén Wèishēng Rì *World Mental Health Day* _____ Guójì Yīnyuèjié (Shíyuè zhōngxún) *International Music Festival (mid-October)* _____ Shìjiè Liángshí Rì *World Food Day* _____ Guójì Xiāochú Pínkùn Rì *International Day for the Eradication of Poverty* _____ Chóngyáng Jié (Jìnglǎo Jié) (Nónglì Jiǔyuè chūjiǔ) *Double Ninth Festival (Senior Citizen's Day) (ninth day of the ninth month in the lunar calendar)* _____ Wànshèng Jié *Halloween*
November	_____ Shíyuè Gémìng Jìniànrì *Anniversary of the October Revolution* _____ Zhōngguó Xiāofáng Xuānchuán Rì *China Fire Awareness Day* _____ Shìjiè Tángniàobìng Rì *World Diabetes Day* _____ Guójì Dàxuéshēng Jié *International College Students Day* _____ Gǎn'ēnjié (dì-sì ge Xīngqīsì) *Thanksgiving Day (fourth Thursday)*	_____ Zhōngguó Jìzhě Jié *China Correspondent Festival* _____ Shìjiè Qīngnián Jié *World Youth Day* _____ Jìzǔ Jié (Nónglì Shíyuè chūyī) *Ancestral Worship Festival (first day of the tenth month in the lunar calendar)* _____ Guānggùn Jié *Singles Day* _____ Guójì Xiāochú duì Fùnǚ de Bàolì Rì *International Day for the Elimination of Violence Against Women*
December	_____ Shìjiè Àizībìng Rì *World AIDS Day* _____ Zhōngguó Fǎzhì Xuānchuán Rì *Chinese Legal Awareness Day* _____ Shìjiè Zúqiú Rì *World Football Day* _____ Nánjīng Dàtúshā Jìniànrì *Anniversary of the Nanjing Massacre* _____ Àomén Huíguī Jìniànrì *Anniversary of the Return of Macau* _____ Píng'ānyè *Christmas Eve* _____ Shèngdànjié *Christmas Day*	_____ Guójì Cánjírén Rì *International Day of Disabled Persons* _____ Guójì Zhìyuànrényuán Rì *International Volunteer Day* _____ Shìjiè Rénquán Rì *World Human Rights Day* _____ Guójì Lánqiú Rì *International Basketball Day* _____ Dōngzhì Jié *Winter Solstice Festival*

Reading a story

39.21 故事 *Find the following terms in either the traditional or simplified text and circle them. Write in the accompanying number.*

1. Fójiàotú *followers of Buddhism*
2. xìnfèng *believe in*
3. Guānyīn Púsà *the Boddhisattva Guanyin, Goddess of Mercy*
4. guānyú *concerning, about*
5. chuánshuō *legends*
6. qízhōng *among these*
7. Miàoshàn gōngzhǔ *the princess Miaoshan ("The Good")*
8. jùshuō *it is said*
9. guówáng *king*
10. jiānchí bú jià *insist on not marrying*
11. jiějué *solve, resolve*
12. rénshēng *human life*
13. tòngkǔ *suffering*
14. fāhuǒ *fly into a rage*
15. dàshēng hǎn *shouted loudly*
16. kěn *be willing*
17. ràngbù *give way*
18. guānzhù *care about, pay attention to*
19. rénshēng dàshì *the key issues of human life*
20. jiéhūn *marriage*

21. bànfǎ *way, means*
22. bī *force, coerce*
23. chūjià *give herself in marriage*
24. guānjìn *lock into*
25. dāying *agree*
26. yuèláiyuèshòu *thinner and thinner*
27. shēntǐ *body*
28. yuèláiyuèruò *weaker and weaker*
29. shěbude *not bear to*
30. shòuzuì *suffer pain*
31. tōutōude *secretly*
32. jiùchūlái *rescue*
33. ràng tā *allow her*
34. táozǒu le *run away*
35. yízuò miào *a temple*
36. chūjiā *take religious vows*
37. liú zài miàoli *stay in the temple*
38. xiūdào *follow a monastic life*
39. zǎoqǐ *rise early*
40. báikāishuǐ *plain boiled water*
41. cūliáng *coarse grains*
42. báitiān *during the day*
43. kǔ gàn *work bitterly hard*
44. niànjīng *study the scriptures*
45. rènwéi *consider*
46. jiānkǔ *hardship*
47. fǎn'ér *on the contrary*
48. shūxīn *enjoyable*
49. yǒu yìyì *be meaningful*
50. zhōngyú *finally*

51. cángshēnchù *hiding place*
52. fāxiàn *discover*
53. wánghòu *queen*
54. qīnzì *in person*
55. kǔkǔ quànshuō *plead rigorously with*
56. sǐhuó bù kěn *refuse staunchly (refuse, whether she is to live or die)*
57. jiānchí *insist*
58. pò miào *broken-down temple*
59. rě de *incite*
60. qì fēng *become mad with rage*
61. yúshì *thereupon*
62. diǎn qǐ yì bǎ huǒ *lit a fire*
63. shāohuǐ *burn down, destroy by fire*
64. qíguài *strange*
65. huǒ miè le *fire went out*
66. huó bújiàn rén sǐ bújiàn shī *couldn't find her, living or dead ("if living, not see the person; if dead, not see the body")*
67. xiāoshī *disappear*
68. jīngxǐng guòlai *shocked to his senses*
69. yìshi *realize*
70. bǎobèi *precious*
71. zuìzhōng *ultimately*
72. bēishāng chéng jí *sickened by grief*

73. yuǎndào ér lái *come from far away*
74. chuáng qián *by his bedside*
75. jiǎnchá *examine*
76. jiù huó *save his life*
77. bìxū *must*
78. xīngānqíngyuàn *of one's own free will*
79. shěqì *sacrifice*
80. huīfù jiànkāng *recover health*
81. fǒuzé *or else*
82. méijiù le *there is nothing more to be done*
83. xiāoxi *news*
84. huīxīn *despondent, despairing*
85. yíjù huà *one sentence*

86. kāngfù *be healed*
87. tūrán *suddenly*
88. biàn le yàngzi *changed her appearance*
89. yǎnkànzhe *in front of his eyes*
90. huàchéng *be transformed into*
91. Qiānshǒu Qiānyǎn Guānyīn Púsà *The Boddhisattva Guanyin with 1,000 Arms and 1,000 Eyes (all-seeing, all-powerful)*

中國的佛教徒大多都信奉觀音菩薩。

關於觀音菩薩有很多傳説。其中一個是講一個叫妙善公主的故事。據説，妙善的父親是一個國王。他想讓他女兒嫁給另外一個國王的兒子，可是妙善堅持不嫁。她問父親：結婚能解決人生最大的問題嗎？父親問：甚麼問題？妙善説：人病了的痛苦、人老了的痛苦、人死了的痛苦。她父親聽見發火了，大聲喊：這種問題是能解決的嗎？可是妙善不肯讓步，因為她心裡關注的是人生大事，所以對結婚一點興趣都沒有。

中国的佛教徒大多都信奉观音菩萨。

关于观音菩萨有很多传说。其中一个是讲一个叫妙善公主的故事。据说，妙善的父亲是一个国王。他想让他女儿嫁给另外一个国王的儿子，可是妙善坚持不嫁。她问父亲：结婚能解决人生最大的问题吗？父亲问：什么问题？妙善说：人病了的痛苦、人老了的痛苦、人死了的痛苦。她父亲听见发火了，大声喊：这种问题是能解决的吗？可是妙善不肯让步，因为她心里关注的是人生大事，所以对结婚一点兴趣都没有。

國王想找辦法逼他女兒出嫁，就把她關進她自己的房間裡，説她要是不答應結婚，就不給水喝或飯吃。這樣過了好幾天，女兒變得越來越瘦，身體也越來越弱。妙善的母親捨不得讓孩子這樣受罪，就偷偷地把她救出來，讓她逃走了。

她逃到了一座廟裡，然後出家了。

国王想找办法逼他女儿出嫁，就把她关进她自己的房间里，说她要是不答应结婚，就不给水喝或饭吃。这样过了好几天，女儿变得越来越瘦，身体也越来越弱。妙善的母亲舍不得让孩子这样受罪，就偷偷地把她救出来，让她逃走了。

她逃到了一座庙里，然后出家了。

妙善公主留在廟裡修道：早起、喝白開水、吃粗糧、白天苦幹、夜裡念經。可是她不認為這種生活很艱苦，反而覺得特別舒心。她覺得這種生活才有意義，自己終於到家了。

妙善公主留在庙里修道：早起、喝白开水、吃粗粮、白天苦干、夜里念经。可是她不认为这种生活很艰苦，反而觉得特别舒心。她觉得这种生活才有意义，自己终于到家了。

可是不久她的藏身處被她父親發現了。國王和王后親自到廟裡去了，苦苦勸説他們女兒回宮。可是女兒死活不肯，堅持留在破廟裡也不回王宮，惹得國王都快氣瘋了。於是他點起一把火把廟給燒毀了。

奇怪的是，火滅了以后，妙善公主活不見人死不見屍，消失了。這時國王才驚醒過來，意識到他的寶貝女兒沒了，最終悲傷成疾。

可是不久她的藏身处被她父亲发现了。国王和王后亲自到庙里去了，苦苦劝说他们女儿回宫。可是女儿死活不肯，坚持留在破庙里也不回王宫，惹得国王都快气疯了。于是他点起一把火把庙给烧毁了。

奇怪的是，火灭了以后，妙善公主活不见人死不见尸，消失了。这时国王才惊醒过来，意识到他的宝贝女儿没了，最终悲伤成疾。

國王病了很久，變得越來越弱。可是請來的醫生沒有一個能治好他。最後，有一個遠道而來的醫生到了他床前，檢查了他的身體，告訴他，只有一個辦法能救活他。他必須找到一個人，心甘情願捨棄自己的一隻眼睛、一隻手，送給他做藥。他只有吃了這個藥才能恢復健康，否則就沒救了。聽了這個消息，國王很灰心，覺得自己沒希望了。到哪兒能找到這樣一個心甘情願捨棄自己的一

国王病了很久，变得越来越弱。可是请来的医生没有一个能治好他。最后，有一个远道而来的医生到了他床前，检查了他的身体，告诉他，只有一个办法能救活他。他必须找到一个人，心甘情愿舍弃自己的一只眼睛、一只手，送给他做药。他只有吃了这个药才能恢复健康，否则就没救了。听了这个消息，国王很灰心，觉得自己没希望了。到哪儿能找到这样一个心甘情愿舍弃自己的一

隻眼睛一隻手給他做藥的人呢?

在這個時候，他看到他女兒妙善公主回來了，口裡只說了一句話：“爸爸，我願意。”

只眼睛一只手给他做药的人呢?

在这个时候，他看到他女儿妙善公主回来了，口里只说了一句话：“爸爸，我愿意。”

女兒的這一句話剛說完，國王的身體馬上就康復了。女兒也突然變了樣子：兩隻手變成了很多手，兩隻眼睛變成了很多眼睛。國王眼看著女兒妙善公主化成了“千手千眼觀音菩薩。”

女儿的这一句话刚说完，国王的身体马上就康复了。女儿也突然变了样子：两只手变成了很多手，两只眼睛变成了很多眼睛。国王眼看着女儿妙善公主化成了“千手千眼观音菩萨。”

39.22 *Write a story about a religious figure of your choice— Moses, Mohammed, Jesus, or Gautama Buddha, for example. Have your story corrected by your teacher or another native speaker; then share your final draft with your classmates. If you can, illustrate your story using images from the Internet or ones that you create. You can take some notes in the space below.*

Encounter 4 Extension: Cultural mini-documentary

View the cultural mini-documentary for this unit and complete the exercises that follow.

39.23 *The Dragon Boat Festival, also known as the Double Fifth or* 端午節／端午节 Duānwǔjié, *marks the time of year when the weather really starts to heat up. Many different traditional folk activities, varying from region to region, are attached to this festival. First, warm up by matching some key words to their English translations.*

____ a. àn nónglì lái suàn de 按農曆來算的／按农历来算的	1. *leaf-wrapped rice dumplings*
____ b. Wǔyuè chū wǔ 五月初五	2. *the Chinese people*
____ c. shīrén 詩人／诗人	3. *paddle dragon boats*
____ d. qùshì 去世	4. *traditional folk customs*
____ e. Zhōnghuá mínzú 中華民族／中华民族	5. *fifth day of the fifth lunar month*
____ f. chuántǒng mínsú 傳統民俗／传统民俗	6. *release floating lanterns*
____ g. huá lóngzhōu 划龍舟／划龙舟	7. *pass away, die*
____ h. fàng hédēng 放河燈／放河灯	8. *lucky, auspicious*
____ i. zòngzi 粽子	9. *poet*
____ j. jíxiáng 吉祥	10. *calculated according to the traditional lunar calendar*

39.24 *In the first 45 seconds or so of the video,* 王老師／王老师 Wáng lǎoshī *places the Dragon Boat Festival in the general context of Chinese festivals. She refers obliquely to a feature of the traditional Chinese lunar calendar—namely, the new moon always falls on* 初一 chūyī *(the first day of the month) and the full moon on the fifteenth. Match some of the expressions used with their English equivalents.*

____ a. zhǔyào yǒu něixiē 主要有哪些	1. *Mid-Autumn Festival*
____ b. Chūnjié 春節／春节	2. *single-day*
____ c. Zhōngqiū 中秋	3. *throw [oneself] into a river*
____ d. tèshū de rìzi 特殊的日子	4. *what are the major ones*
____ e. dān rìzi de 單日子的／单日子的	5. *commemorate Qu Yuan*
____ f. jìniàn Qū Yuán 紀念屈原／纪念屈原	6. *become*
____ g. tóujiāng 投江	7. *Spring Festival*
____ h. chéng 成	8. *special day*

39.25 *Around 1:12, the legend on a display in the park is visible, reading* 北京第六屆龍潭端午文化節／北京第六屆龙潭端午文化节 Běijīng dì-liù jiè Lóngtán Duānwǔ wénhuà jié, *or sixth Annual Longtan [Park] Double-Fifth Cultural Festival, Beijing. Most of the footage in this video was shot at the festival. Based on the lettered quotes from the description of cultural practices associated with the holiday (1:20–2:41), mark each statement* T *(true) or* F *(false), and write the letter of the relevant quote in the box.*

Statement	T/F	Letter
1. Among the various customs associated with the Double Fifth is the tying of a multicolored thread around the wrist.		
2. Among the activities planned for today at the park is the release of floating lanterns.		
3. The dragon boat races are what the man remembers most about the Double Fifth from his childhood.		
4. The kids call the festival the "Dumpling Festival."		
5. Wearing fragrant pouches and burning Asiatic wormwood leaves are supposed to be a symbol of confronting the bad things in your life.		
6. The customs associated with the festival have come into being in the past several hundred years.		
7. These customs are not only about good luck but also about avoiding evil and illness.		

a. Jīntiān de zhǔyào huódòng ne, shì huá lóngzhōu, mínzú jiǎngzuò, háiyǒu zhè ge fàng hédēng de huódòng.
今天的主要活動呢，是划龍舟，民族講座，還有這個放河燈的活動。／今天的主要活动呢，是划龙舟，民族讲座，还有这个放河灯的活动。

b. "Jīntiān shì ge shénme jiérì?" "Zòngzi jié!" "Yòu jiào?" "Duānwǔjié!"
"今天是個甚麼節日？" "粽子節！" "又叫？" "端午節"！／"今天是个什么节日？" "粽子节！" "又叫？" "端午节！"

c. Tí dào Duānwǔjié ne, yǒu hěn duō de mínsú, hé tā de chuánchéng. Dànshì ne, wǒmen yǒu jǐ yàng fēicháng zhòngyào de xísú, shì jǐ qiān nián dōu méiyǒu gǎibiàn de, bǐrú shuō, sài lóngzhōu, chī zòngzi, bāo zòngzi, xì wǔcǎixiàn, dài xiāngbāo, zhè xiē xísú ne, dōu shì fēicháng shēnrù rénxīn.
提到端午節呢，有很多的民俗，和它的傳承。但是呢，我們有幾樣非常重要的習俗，是幾千年都沒有改變的，比如說，賽龍舟、吃粽子、包粽子、繫五彩線、戴香包，這些習俗呢，都是非常深入人心。／提到端午节呢，有很多的民俗，和它的传承。但是呢，我们有几样非常重要的习俗，是几千年都没有改变的，比如说，赛龙舟、吃粽子、包粽子、系五彩线、戴香包，这些习俗呢，都是非常深入人心。

d. Xiǎo shíhou, Duānwǔjié, Duānwǔjié de huà zhǔyào jiù shì chī zòngzi ba.
小時候，端午節，端午節的話主要就是吃粽子吧。／小时候，端午节，端午节的话主要就是吃粽子吧。

e. Wǒmen Duānwǔ yǒushíhou hái yǒu nèi ge xiàn, wǔcǎixiàn, ránhòu guà zài shǒu shang, dàibiǎo yì zhǒng bǎo píng'ān.
我們端午有時候還有那個線，五彩線，然後掛在手上，代表一種保平安。／我们端午有时候还有那个线，五彩线，然后挂在手上，代表一种保平安。

f. Dài xiāngnáng, xūn àicǎo de huà, kěnéng yě jiù shì yì zhǒng, xiàngzhēng yì zhǒng, jiù shì yì zhǒng měihǎo de yuànwàng.
帶香囊、熏艾草的話，可能也就是一種，象徵一種，就是一種美好的願望。／带香囊、熏艾草的话，可能也就是一种，象征一种，就是一种美好的愿望。

g. Zhèi xiē xísú ne, dàibiǎo zhe jíxiáng, yě yǒu qūxié-bìdú de nèihán.
這些習俗呢，代表著吉祥，也有驅邪避毒的內涵。／这些习俗呢，代表着吉祥，也有驱邪避毒的内涵。

39.26 *Based on some further information about the holiday (2:54–3:23), fill in the blanks in the pinyin.*

一提到粽子呢，人們難免想起來古代的屈原。戰國時期呢，屈原大夫懷著悲憤的心情投江自盡了。民眾為了讓他的屍體呢，不被水怪侵害，划著龍舟競相地去打撈他。後來演化了民間賽龍舟這個習俗呢，就在中國的大部分地區，南方北方盛行開來，至今呢，長盛不衰。／

一提到粽子呢，人们难免想起来古代的屈原。战国时期呢，屈原大夫怀着悲愤的心情投江自尽了。民众为了让他的尸体呢，不被水怪侵害，划着龙舟竞相地去打捞他。后来演化了民间赛龙舟这个习俗呢，就在中国的大部分地区，南方北方盛行开来，至今呢，长盛不衰。

Yì tí dào zòngzi ne, rénmen ___________ xiǎng qǐlai gǔdài de Qū Yuán. __________ shíqī ne, Qū Yuán dàfū huáizhe bēifèn de xīnqíng tóu jiāng zìjìn le. Mínzhòng wèile ràng tā de ______ ne, bú bèi shuǐguài qīnhài, huázhe __________ jìngxiāng de qù dǎlāo tā. Hòulái yǎnhuàle mínjiān sài lóngzhōu zhè ge xísú ne, jiù zài Zhōngguó de dàbùfen dìqū, ________ běifāng shèngxíng kāi lái, _______ ne, chángshèng-bùshuāi.

Speaking of rice dumplings wrapped in leaves, people will ***inevitably*** *think of the ancient Qu Yuan. In the* ***Warring States*** *period, Grand Master Qu Yuan, filled with grief, put an end to his life by throwing himself into a river. The people, in order to let his* ***body*** *not be harmed by water creatures, raced* ***dragon boats*** *in a contest to fish his body out of the water. Later, this evolved into the folk custom of racing dragon boats. In most parts of China, in* ***the South*** *and in the North, it has become popular and has survived all the way* ***up to the present****.*

39.27 *Starting at about 3:52, we hear about the custom of releasing floating lanterns. For each question, find the summary in English that answers the question. Write the summary's letter next to its question. Only three of the summaries will match.*

____ 1. Duānwǔjié yǒu duōshao nián de lìshǐ le? 端午節有多少年的歷史了？／端午节有多少年的历史了？

____ 2. Rénmen yìbān zài hédēng shang dōu xiě yìxiē shénme? 人們一般在河燈上都寫一些甚麼？／人们一般在河灯上都写一些什么？

____ 3. Nǐmen jīntiān wǎnshang fàng de hédēng shì shénme xíngzhuàng? 你們今天晚上放的河燈是甚麼形狀？／你们今天晚上放的河灯是什么形状？

a. *This activity of releasing river lanterns—it's a tradition of the Chinese people. For our lanterns this year, we have selected a traditional Chinese form: the form of the lotus. On top there is a candle, and so first we have everybody light the candle, then they wish for good luck—that is, a prayer for security, health, and happiness.*

b. *Releasing river lanterns? It's—it seems to be mainly a way of wishing for luck, because people may write phrases on them that are significant, that are prayers for good luck, and then they put them in the river, and they follow the current down, carrying one's beautiful wishes on down the stream.*

c. *It represents one's beautiful wishes and that one hopes one's wishes can become true.*

d. *I also think it must be a sort of wish, a wish for a new life or whatever.*

e. *A prayer for luck, to keep safe.*

f. *The Double Fifth is a very traditional Chinese festival that already has 2,500 years of history behind it. A festival that has endured more than 1,000 years—it's easy to see that the cultural roots of this festival are deep.*

Recap

Grammar

Presenting thoughts accurately in sentences (1)

In this exercise, you will be given a thought framed within a context; your task is to present that thought accurately by using the proper Chinese sentence type. Write your version on the line provided, and check the end of the Recap for our version and analysis.

1. You want to ask someone, "For how long did you study Chinese?"

____

2. The ticket has already been bought, and your friend knows that fact. He wants to know when you bought the ticket. How would you tell him you bought the ticket yesterday?

____

3. Your friend notices that you're extremely tired today. You explain that you only slept four hours last night. Express that thought.

____

4. You're at a party and offered yet another drink by your host. You politely decline by saying you'll have no more to drink and must leave.

____

5. Your good friend asks if you're sick (不舒服 *bù shūfu*). You reply that you're not but that in the last few days you haven't slept very well.

____

More of this practice is to come in the next unit.

Answers and analysis:

1. Nǐ xué**guo** duō jiǔ de Zhōngwén? 你學過多久的中文？／你学过多久的中文？
   ANALYSIS: The sentence calls for use of the experiential suffix *-guo*, since the time frame is the indefinite past. If, on the other hand, you want to ask, "How long have you been studying Chinese?"—meaning that the person you address is *still* studying Chinese—then you would say, "你學了多久的中文了？／你学了多久的中文了？" *Nǐ xuéle duō jiǔ de Zhōngwén le?*

2. Wǒ **shì** zuótiān xiàwǔ mǎi **de** piào. 我是昨天下午買的票。／我是昨天下午买的票。
   ANALYSIS: In instances such as this one, Chinese highlights the specific circumstances of **past** events with the *shi . . . de* pattern. No *le* here either.

3. Wǒ zuótiān wǎnshang zhǐ shuì **le** sì ge zhōngtóu, suǒyǐ jīntiān fēicháng lèi. 我昨天晚上只睡了四個鐘頭，所以今天非常累。／我昨天晚上只睡了四个钟头，所以今天非常累。
   ANALYSIS: This is an instance of verbal *le* (rather than sentence *le*) since the action took place at a point in the past and the object is specified and delimited (i.e., "four hours").

4. Xièxie nín. Wǒ bù hē **le**, wǒ děi zǒu **le**. 謝謝您。我不喝了，我得走了。／谢谢您。我不喝了，我得走了。
   ANALYSIS: *Le* is used here because you will drink no more. There is clearly a change in state; you were drinking before but no longer want to. The same "change of state" is implied in the second clause; you were not leaving before but are leaving now.

5. Méiyǒu bù shūfu, kěshì zhèi liǎng tiān shuì **de** bú tài hǎo. 没有不舒服，可是這兩天睡得不太好。／没有不舒服，可是这两天睡得不太好。
   ANALYSIS: Here, the thrust of the utterance is to comment on the performance of the action—in this case, sleeping. Thus, the proper form is a complement (不太好 *bú tài hǎo*) linked to the verb with *de*.

Vocabulary

Please refer to page R-2 for a list of grammatical abbreviations used throughout this book.

àicǎo 艾草 Asiatic wormwood leaves N

àiguó 愛國／爱国 patriotic SV

bài 拜 do obeisance to; worship V

bāo 包 wrap V

bāoguǒ 包裹 wrap; bundle V; bundle; package N

bǎoyòu 保佑 bless and protect V

bìngmó 病魔 serious illness N

cái 才 actually A

chuánshuō 傳説／传说 legend; tradition N

dàcān 大餐 sumptuous meal; banquet; feast N

dàhuǒr 大夥兒／大伙儿 we; us; we all; everyone N

dāngdì 當地／当地 locality; the place named/mentioned N

dāngnián 當年／当年 that year; those years N

dǎogào 禱告／祷告 pray V

Dàojiào 道教 Daoism *(as a religion)* N

duànliàn 鍛煉／锻炼 engage in physical exercise V

Duānwǔjié 端午節／端午节 Dragon Boat Festival *(fifth day of the fifth lunar month)* N

duì wǒ lái shuō 對我來說／对我来说 as far as I'm concerned VP

dúlì 獨立／独立 independent SV; independence N

Fó 佛 Buddha N

Fójiào 佛教 Buddhism N

Fójiàotú 佛教徒 followers of Buddhism N

fú 福 good fortune; blessing; happiness N

Gǎn'ēnjié 感恩節／感恩节 Thanksgiving Day N

guà 掛／挂 put up V

gǔdài 古代 ancient times N

guòjié 過節／过节 celebrate a festival/holiday VO

gùzhi 固執／固执 obstinate; stubborn SV

hàipà 害怕 be afraid; scared V

hóngdòu 紅豆／红豆 red bean N

hóngzǎo 紅棗／红枣 red date paste N

huá 划 row V

huáchuán 划船 row/paddle a boat VO

huǒjī 火雞／火鸡 turkey N

huópō 活潑／活泼 lively; vivacious SV

jiājiāhùhù 家家戶戶／家家户户 each and every family RF

jiānchí 堅持／坚持 insist on; persist in V

jiāng 江 river N

jiàotáng 教堂 church; cathedral N

jiǎozi 餃子／饺子 dumplings; Chinese ravioli N

jīdé 積德／积德 accumulate merit by good works VO

Jīdū 基督 Jesus; Christ N

Jīdūjiào 基督教 Christianity N

Jīdūjiàotú 基督教徒 Christian *(person)* N

jiérì 節日／节日 festival; holiday N

jìniàn 紀念／纪念 commemorate V

jìzǔ 祭祖 offer sacrifices to ancestors VO

juè 倔 stubborn; pig-headed SV

jùshuō 據說／据说 it is said that VP

kāilǎng 開朗／开朗 sanguine; optimistic SV

lǎobǎixìng 老百姓 common people; civilians N

liúchuán 流傳／流传 hand down; spread; circulate V

lóngzhōu 龍舟／龙舟 dragon boat N

ménshang 門上／门上 on a door PW

míngxiǎng 冥想 thought; meditation N/V

mǐtuán 米糰／米团 rice ball N

Mùsīlín 穆斯林 Muslim *(loan word)* N/PL

nándào 難道／难道 Is it possible that . . . ? Can it be that . . . ? Do you mean . . . ? *(usually with* **ma** 嗎／吗*?)* VP

nèixiàng 內向／内向 introverted SV

nónglì 農曆／农历 lunar calendar N

ǒu'ěr 偶爾／偶尔 occasionally A

píng'ān 平安 safe and sound; peaceful SV

píqi 脾氣／脾气 temperament; disposition N

píqi hǎo 脾氣好／脾气好 good-tempered VP

píqi huài 脾氣壞／脾氣坏 bad-tempered VP

qiǎokèlì 巧克力 chocolate *(loan word)* N/PL

qīngzhēnsì 清真寺 mosque N

qūxié 驅邪／驱邪 expel evil VO

qūzhú 驅逐／驱逐 expel; get rid of V

ròuzòng 肉粽 glutinous rice dumpling filled with meat N

sài 賽／赛 compete V

shàng tiān(táng) 上天(堂) go to Heaven VO

shàngjiē 上街 go into the street; go shopping VO

shāoxiāng 燒香／烧香 burn incense sticks VO

shīrén 詩人／诗人 poet N

shītǐ 屍體／尸体 corpse N

sìmiào 寺廟／寺庙 temple N

suíhé 隨和／随和 amiable SV

tángguǒ 糖果 sweets; candy N

tāngyuánr 湯圓兒／汤圆儿 glutinous rice dumplings served in soup N

Tiānzhǔ 天主 God *(in Catholicism)* N

Tiānzhǔjiào 天主教 Catholicism N

Tiānzhǔjiàotú 天主教徒 Catholic *(person)* N

tiáojiàn 條件／条件 condition; factor N

tiē 貼／贴 paste/glue/stick to V

tóu 投 throw; toss V

tóujīn 頭巾／头巾 scarf; kerchief; turban N

tú 徒 disciple; pupil; apprentice BF

tuánjù (zài yìqǐ) 團聚(在一起)／团聚(在一起) get together V

wàibiǎo 外表 outward appearance; exterior N

wàixiàng 外向 extroverted SV

Wànshèngjié 萬聖節／万圣节 Halloween; All Saints' Day N

wèi 餵／喂 feed V

wǔgǔ 五穀／五谷 grains; cereals; the five grains N

Wǔyuè chūwǔ 五月初五 fifth day of the fifth lunar month N

xiā 蝦／虾 shrimp N

xiāngtóng 相同 be alike/identical; be equivalent V

xiánshuǐzòng 鹹水粽／咸水粽 saltwater rice dumpling N

xié'è 邪惡／邪恶 evil; evil force SV/N

xìnggé 性格 nature; disposition; temperament N

xíngshàn 行善 do good works VO

xìnjiào 信教 believe/profess a religion VO

xìnyǎng 信仰 belief N; believe V

xísú 習俗／习俗 custom; convention N

yí dà duī 一大堆 a large pile N

yí dà guō 一大鍋／一大锅 a large potful N

yīmóyīyàng 一模一樣／一模一样 be exactly alike IE

Yīsīlánjiào 伊斯蘭教／伊斯兰教 Islam; Islamism *(loan word)* N/PL

yǒuguān 有關／有关 about; concerning VO

yuánzé 原則／原则 principle N

yújiā 瑜伽 yoga *(loan word)* N/PL

zhāofú 招福 elicit blessings VO

zhāojìnlai 招進來／招进来 beckon in; attract into RV

zhǔ 煮 boil; cook V

zhù 炷 stick *(for incense)* M

zōngjiào 宗教 religion N

zòngyè 粽葉／粽叶 bamboo leaves; palm leaves N

zòngzi 粽子 pyramid-shaped dumpling of glutinous rice wrapped in reed leaves N

zuò hǎorén 做好人 be a good person VP

zuò lǐbài 做禮拜／做礼拜 go to church; attend religious service VO

zuò mísa 做彌撒／做弥撒 go to (Catholic) Mass VO

Checklist of "can do" statements

After completing this unit, you should be able to perform each of the following tasks:

Listening and speaking

- ☐ Converse about some aspects of your spiritual practices.
- ☐ Talk about practices in some key world religions.
- ☐ Discuss ways to celebrate a holiday or festival.

Reading and writing

- ☐ Decipher some entries on a list of national holidays in China.
- ☐ Comprehend a short story about the Boddhisattva Guanyin.
- ☐ Write a short story about a religious figure.

Understanding culture

- ☐ Make several accurate statements about some common practices in celebrating the Dragon Boat Festival.

UNIT **40**

"Ascend to a higher level"

更上一層樓

Gèng shàng yì céng lóu

Future language learning plans

In this unit, you will learn how to:

- talk about your own experiences learning Chinese.
- discuss your current proficiency in Chinese.
- talk about some challenges in learning Chinese.
- talk about your past experience with Chinese regional languages.
- compare learning Chinese with learning English.
- discuss activities that might help you gain proficiency in Chinese.
- decipher some key points in an online response to a query about how best to learn English.
- read an autobiographical account of encounters with foreign languages.
- write a brief account about any interesting encounters you have had with foreign languages or speakers of foreign languages.

Encounter 1 Discussing some challenges in learning Chinese

40.1 *Chen Feng and Xiao Mao are visiting Mick at* The Hutong. 請把中文跟英文對上。／请把中文跟英文对上。

____ a. huíguó 回國／回国	1. *connect to; become expert in; an expert*
____ b. hútòng 胡同	2. *dialect*
____ c. tōng 通	3. *skip over*
____ d. shèjì 設計／设计	4. *approve*
____ e. niú 牛	5. *tongue twister*
____ f. ràokǒulìng 繞口令／绕口令	6. *illiterate*
____ g. bàozhǐ 報紙／报纸	7. *design*
____ h. zàntóng 贊同／赞同	8. *return to one's own country*
____ i. dàgài de yìsi 大概的意思	9. *read and understand*
____ j. yuèdú 閱讀／阅读	10. *type*
____ k. cí 詞／词	11. *approximate meaning*
____ l. tiàoguòqu 跳過去／跳过去	12. *vocabulary*
____ m. kànmíngbai 看明白	13. *hot, outstanding, "something" (slang)*
____ n. wényánwén 文言文	14. *TV show*
____ o. kǒuyǔ 口語／口语	15. *Beijing alleyway*
____ p. fāngyán 方言	16. *classical Chinese*
____ q. wénmáng 文盲	17. *speech, oral language*
____ r. dǎzì 打字	18. *newspaper*
____ s. diànshìjù 電視劇／电视剧	19. *read*
____ t. xiūgǎi 修改	20. *revise, modify*

40.2 *View Episode 40, Vignette 1. Chen Feng and Xiao Mao show Mick a flier that Chen Feng's firm has designed for Mick's business,* The Hutong. *In getting his feedback, they chat about Mick's Chinese. Classify the statements below into these categories:*

甲 jiǎ: *general conversation*

乙 yǐ: *discussion of the flier*

丙 bǐng: *discussion of Mick's Chinese*

丁 dīng: *discussion of the nature of Chinese language and language learning in general*

	甲	乙	丙	丁
a. Nǐ lái Zhōngguó duōshao nián le?	☐	☐	☐	☐
b. Nǐ píngcháng huíguó ma?	☐	☐	☐	☐
c. Zhè shì shéi shèjì de?	☐	☐	☐	☐
d. Nǐ kàndedǒng Zhōngwén ma? Zhōngguó Hànzì?	☐	☐	☐	☐
e. Qíshí zài yuèdú de shíhou, yǒu shíhou jiùshì kàn ge dàgài de yìsi.	☐	☐	☐	☐
f. Pèngshang nǐ bù dǒng de nàxiē cí, wánquán kěyǐ tiàoguòqu.	☐	☐	☐	☐
g. Wényánwén hé xiàndài Zhōngwén shì bù yíyàng de.	☐	☐	☐	☐
h. Qíshí, nǐ de kǒuyǔ hěn hǎo.	☐	☐	☐	☐
i. Wǒ shuōbuzhǔn.	☐	☐	☐	☐
j. Zhèxiē huà zánmen dōu tīngbudǒng!	☐	☐	☐	☐
k. Nǐ de Hànzì xiě de zěnmeyàng?	☐	☐	☐	☐
l. Wǒ bú huì xiě, dànshì wǒ huì dǎzì.	☐	☐	☐	☐
m. Wǒ juéde nǐ yào měitiān jiānchí duōduō de liànxí.	☐	☐	☐	☐
n. Méishìr de shíhou, kěyǐ kànyikàn Zhōngguó pāi de diànshìjù.	☐	☐	☐	☐
o. Zhè ge jiùshì wǒmen de shèjì.	☐	☐	☐	☐
p. Nǐ kànkan háiyǒu shénme xūyào xiūgǎi.	☐	☐	☐	☐
q. Hēchá ba, hē kāishuǐ!	☐	☐	☐	☐

40.3 請把下面的英文跟上面的拼音對上。／请把下面的英文跟上面的拼音对上。

____ 1. Who designed this?

____ 2. I can't write, but I can type.

____ 3. When you run into words you don't know, you can absolutely just skip them.

____ 4. Do you go back to your country regularly?

____ 5. My pronunciation is not good. [I don't speak accurately.]

____ 6. So this is our design.

____ 7. Classical Chinese is not the same as modern Chinese.

____ 8. How many years has it been since you came to China?

____ 9. I think you should persist in practicing a lot every day.

____ 10. Have some tea, or some [boiled] water!

____ 11. Actually, you speak quite well.

____ 12. How well do you write Chinese characters?

____ 13. Can you read Chinese characters?

____ 14. When you're not busy, you can watch some Chinese TV shows.

____ 15. Take a look and see if anything needs to be revised.

____ 16. Even we can't understand all those dialects!

____ 17. Actually, in reading, sometimes you just want to get the gist.

40.4 請把下面的漢字跟上面的英語對上。／请把下面的汉字跟上面的英语对上。

____ A. 其實，你的口語很好。／其实，你的口语很好。

____ B. 你看得懂中文嗎？中國漢字？／你看得懂中文吗？中国汉字？

____ C. 喝茶吧，喝開水！／喝茶吧，喝开水！

____ D. 你的漢字寫得怎麼樣？／你的汉字写得怎么样？

____ E. 碰上你不懂的那些詞，完全可以跳過去。／碰上你不懂的那些词，完全可以跳过去。

____ F. 你平常回國嗎？／你平常回国吗？

____ G. 這些話咱們都聽不懂！／这些话咱们都听不懂！

____ H. 我説不準。／我说不准。

____ I. 我覺得你要每天堅持多多地練習。／我觉得你要每天坚持多多地练习。

____ J. 你來中國多少年了？／你来中国多少年了？

____ K. 這個就是我們的設計。／这个就是我们的设计。

____ L. 你看看還有甚麼需要修改。／你看看还有什么需要修改。

____ M. 文言文和現代中文是不一樣的。／文言文和现代中文是不一样的。

____ N. 這是誰設計的？／这是谁设计的？

____ O. 我不會寫，但是我會打字。／我不会写，但是我会打字。

____ P. 其實在閱讀的時候，有時候就是看個大概的意思。／其实在阅读的时候，有时候就是看个大概的意思。

____ Q. 没事兒的時候，可以看一看中國拍的電視劇。／没事儿的时候，可以看一看中国拍的电视剧。

40.5 *Following is the text on the flier, followed by Xiao Mao's explanation of what it means.* 請用英文填空。／请用英文填空。

通胡同，通中国。胡同通，中国通

Tōng Hútòng, tōng Zhōngguó. Hútòng tōng, Zhōngguó tōng.

Xiao Mao explains:

"通過胡同，可以通向中國，那了解了胡同介紹的文化和知識，有可能就會成為一個中國通。／
通过胡同，可以通向中国，那了解了胡同介绍的文化和知识，有可能就会成为一个中国通。"

"Tōngguò hútòng, kěyǐ tōng xiàng Zhōngguó, nà liǎojiě le hútòng jièshào de wénhuà hé zhīshi, yǒu kěnéng jiù huì chéngwéi yí ge Zhōngguótōng."

"Going through __________, you can get to __________. If you understand the _____________ and knowledge The Hutong *introduces to you, you have the capacity to become a China __________."*

40.6 *Mick says that because of his pronunciation problems, he jokingly pretends to be someone from Xinjiang.* 請用英文填空。／请用英文填空。

Wǒ shuōbuzhǔn, wǒ yìbān lái shuō wǒ zìjǐ shì Xīnjiāngrén, kàn, dà bízi, tāmen dōu míngbai le.

我說不準，我一般來說我自己是新疆人，看，大鼻子，他們都明白了。／
我说不准，我一般来说我自己是新疆人，看，大鼻子，他们都明白了。

My pronunciation is not accurate. I generally say ______________________, look, _____________. They all understand this.

Yángròuchuàn! Yángròuchuàn!

羊肉串！羊肉串！

Mutton skewers! Mutton skewers!

Following are some statements about Xinjiang, a Chinese autonomous region, and its people. All are accurate. Check the ones touched upon here. Note: 維吾爾／维吾尔 Wéiwú'ěr Uighur.

☐ a. 新疆在中國西北部。／新疆在中国西北部。

☐ b. 新疆人口百分之四十三是維吾爾人。／新疆人口百分之四十三是维吾尔人。

☐ c. 維吾爾人大多是信奉伊斯蘭教。／维吾尔人大多是信奉伊斯兰教。

☐ d. 維吾爾人看起來像西方人：白皮膚、大眼睛、高鼻子。／维吾尔人看起来象西方人：白皮肤、大眼睛、高鼻子。

☐ e. 維吾爾人吃很多羊肉。／维吾尔人吃很多羊肉。

☐ f. 維吾爾人喜歡把羊肉塊串起來放到火裡去烤。／维吾尔人喜欢把羊肉块串起来放到火里去烤。

☐ g. 維吾爾人有自己的語言，所以他們說中文有一點困難。／维吾尔人有自己的语言，所以他们说中文有一点困难。

40.7 ***Pair work:*** *Have a conversation in Chinese with a partner about your Chinese. Begin by asking,* 你覺得你的中文怎麼樣？／你觉得你的中文怎么样？ *Respond by providing some details of your strengths and weaknesses. Make some suggestions to your partner about what he or she can do to improve. If there is time, switch to another partner.*

FYI 供你参考

Chinese languages

Pǔtōnghuà 普通話／普通话 "Common language"—which is called *Guóyǔ* 國語／国语 "National language" in Taiwan and elsewhere and *Huáyǔ* 華語／华语 "Chinese language" in Chinese communities in Southeast Asia—is the standard form of Chinese and is spoken natively by about 70 percent of the population. In addition, standard Chinese is now familiar to almost everyone in both the PRC and Taiwan. Modern written Chinese is typically based on the vocabulary and grammar of standard Chinese.

Besides standard Chinese, there are six additional families of Chinese languages (by one classification; other linguists distinguish more varieties) spoken throughout the country (see map). These languages are often called dialects, which is misleading, since they are mutually incomprehensible, and are as different from each other as French is from Spanish.

The varieties of Mandarin Chinese indicated here are Northern, Eastern, and Southwestern; the pronunciation may differ enough among and within these regions that you'd have a challenge understanding even common phrases! In addition, the major Chinese language families are:

- **Wu** (吳／吴 *Wú*): The most widely known representative of 吳語／吴语 is Shanghainese 上海話／上海话 *Shànghǎihuà*, although the variety spoken in Suzhou is considered standard for this diverse group of sublanguages. Generalissimo Chiang Kai-shek, who led the Chinese Republican army against the emerging Communist forces, was a Wu speaker.
- **Gan** (贛／赣 *Gàn*): Gan is commonly called 江西話／江西话 *Jiāngxīhuà*, since it is spoken natively by many people in Jiangxi Province and the surrounding areas, including parts of Hunan, Hubei, Anhui, and Fujian.
- **Hakka** (客家 *Kèjiā*): Literally, "guest families" in the Hakka pronunciation. The Hakka peoples are said to have migrated from northern China and now live all over southern China, as well as in well-established communities around the world.
- **Xiang** (湘 *Xiāng*): Xiang is commonly called Hunanese 湖南話／湖南话 *Húnánhuà*. Mao Zedong spoke Hunanese, and his oral addresses were famously challenging to follow.
- **Min** (閩／闽 *Mǐn*): Min is spoken primarily in Fujian Province and in communities where Fujian people have migrated. Hokkien is the subvariety widely spoken in Taiwan, where it's also called Taiwanese. The Fuzhou language is spoken in the provincial capital and by a large community in New York City.
- **Yue** (粵 *Yuè*): Yue is commonly called Cantonese, since it is the variety of the language spoken in the capital city of Guangdong Province (earlier called Canton) and Hong Kong. Yue languages are spoken throughout Guangdong and Guangxi Provinces, as well as in emigrant communities in the United States, Canada, Australia, and Southeast Asia.

Internationally, the best known of the Chinese regional languages are Cantonese, Taiwanese, and Shanghainese. If you search online, you'll hear samples of the Chinese languages. One example: http://intothemiddlekingdom.com/tag/chinese-dialects/

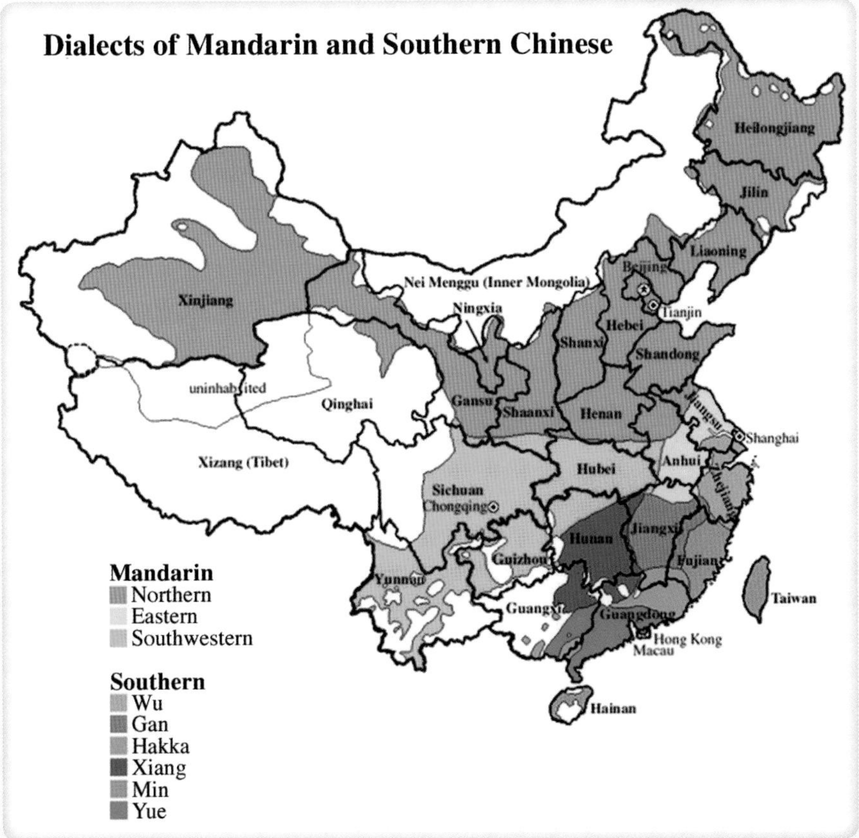

40.8 *In the course of their conversation, Chen Feng, Xiao Mao, and Mick discuss the various Chinese languages. Which of the following did they mention?* 請勾選。／请勾选。

- ☐ 官話／官话 Guānhuà *(literally, "official language")—Mandarin Chinese*
- ☐ 上海話／上海话 Shànghǎihuà
- ☐ 江西話／江西话 Jiāngxīhuà
- ☐ 浙江話／浙江话 Zhèjiānghuà *(a variety of the* Wú *language family)*
- ☐ 客家話／客家话 Kèjiāhuà
- ☐ 閩南話／闽南话 Mǐnnánhuà *(a variety of the* Mǐn *language family)*
- ☐ 福州話／福州话 Fúzhōuhuà
- ☐ 湖南話／湖南话 Húnánhuà

40.9 ***Mingling:*** *Walk around and speak in Chinese for as long as you can to as many of your classmates as possible about your experiences with Mandarin Chinese and any of the other Chinese languages. If your class wishes to, compile everyone's information and make a physical chart to post on the wall or a digital chart to post online. List the Chinese languages and indicate who in your class has heard any of them.*

40.10 *This vignette includes several examples of "clever commentary" that enlivens the conversation.*

a *When Mick bemoans the fact that he cannot read Chinese newspapers, Xiao Mao says wryly:* Qíshí yǒu shíhou kànbudǒng bàozhǐ yě búshì yí jiàn huàishìr, a? 其實有時候看不懂報紙也不是一件壞事兒，啊？／其实有时候看不懂报纸也不是一件坏事儿，啊？

小毛為甚麼這麼說？請勾選一個答案。／小毛为什么这么说？请勾选一个答案。

- ☐ 因為小毛不愛看報紙。／因为小毛不爱看报纸。
- ☐ 因為報紙上的新聞會讓讀者難過。／因为报纸上的新闻会让读者难过。
- ☐ 因為外國人不應該看中文報紙。／因为外国人不应该看中文报纸。

b *A common saying to express the fact that it is hard, even for native speakers, to remember how to write characters is* tíbǐwàngzì 提筆忘字／提笔忘字. 請用英文填空。／请用英文填空。*Literally, this expression means the following:*

When I lift my pen to write, I find that I have ______________________.

c *When Chen Feng criticizes the absent Xiao Fei, he uses the following four-character expression to describe his work ethic:* cūxīndàyì 粗心大意. Cūxīn 粗心, *literally "rough heart," means "careless." Its opposite is* xìxīn 細心／细心, *which literally means "fine heart"—thus, "careful."* Dàyì 大意 *generally means "main idea," but here it means being satisfied with just having a rough idea, rather than* jīngyì 經意／经意—*being mindful of nuances.* 請勾選一個答案。／请勾选一个答案。

The entire phrase means:

☐ *slapdash* ☐ *overly fixated on detail* ☐ *impatient* ☐ *lazy*

d *Finally, when Mick offers his guests the simple but elegant beverages of tea or hot boiled water, Xiao Mao says approvingly:* Jūnzǐ zhī jiāo dàn rú shuǐ. 君子之交淡如水。 *This idiom is taken from the sayings of the Daoist sage Zhuangzi. Literally, it means the following:*

Superior person (君子) + *'s* (之) + *interactions* (交) + *bland, clear* (淡) + *like* (如) + *water* (水)

Thus, "Friendship between persons of high moral cultivation is as plain as water." Further extrapolating, it means "The interactions between cultivated persons are easygoing, unforced, transparent, and without ulterior motives."

By contrast, Zhuangzi continues: Xiǎorén zhī jiāo gān ruò lǐ. 小人之交甘若醴。 *Literally, this means the following:*

Inferior person (小人) + *'s* (之) + *interactions* (交) + *sweet* (甘) + *like* (若) + *liqueur* (醴)

Thus, "Interactions between common persons are as sweet as liqueur." Further extrapolating, it means, "The interactions between common people are sentimental, demanding, cloying, and with ulterior motives."

Which saying do you think reflects Chinese social ideals? 請寫漢字。／请写汉字。

Just for fun, walk around the room. Come up to a classmate and say the adage you wrote above. If your classmate says it to you first, reply with 是啊！ *before moving on. Repeat until you've spoken to everyone in class, including your teacher.*

Encounter 2 Discussing future plans for language study

40.11 *Fang Lan and Emma are preparing for Emma's imminent departure from China.*
請把中文和英文對上。／请把中文和英文对上。

____ a. guāi háizi 乖孩子
____ b. lái Měiguó liúxué 來美國留學／来美国留学
____ c. Yīngyǔ de yǔfǎ 英語的語法／英语的语法
____ d. Yīngyǔ de fāyīn 英語的發音／英语的发音
____ e. tèbié de fùzá 特別的複雜／特别的复杂
____ f. fāyuán bǐjiào duō 發源比較多／发源比较多
____ g. Yīngwén dāncí 英文單詞／英文单词
____ h. luóxuánshàngshēngshì de xuéxí 螺旋上升式的學習／螺旋上升式的学习
____ i. fǎnguòlai 反過來／反过来
____ j. tuìbù 退步
____ k. yǒu dàolǐ 有道理

1. *English pronunciation*
2. *upward-spiraling learning*
3. *obedient, well-behaved children*
4. *English words*
5. *the reverse, the opposite*
6. *has many sources*
7. *come to the United States to study*
8. *extremely complicated*
9. *English grammar*
10. *reasonable, justifiable*
11. *regress*

40.12 *View Episode 40, Vignette 2. Indicate whether Fang Lan or Emma makes each of the following statements (given in the order they are made).*

i.

ii.

____ a. Wǒ shōushi xíngli.
____ b. Nǐ néng bāng wǒ máng ma?
____ c. Wǒ bù xiǎng ràng nǐ zǒu!
____ d. Wǒ xiànzài jiù zài dú nǐ de Yīngwén shū ne!
____ e. Nǐ xué Yīngwén yǒu méiyǒu wǒ xué Zhōngwén zhème nán?
____ f. Wǒ juéde Yīngyǔ de yǔfǎ hé fāyīn tèbié de fùzá.
____ g. Kěnéng shì yīnwèi Yīngyǔ de fāyuán bǐjiào duō.
____ h. Yǒuxiē Yīngwén dāncí hǎoxiàng hái láizì Zhōngwén!
____ i. Nǐ bù shuō wǒ hái bù zhīdào ne.

_____ j. Wǒ xiànzài zuì zhòngyào de jiùshì gēn nǐ yíyàng: Yào liànxí, liànxí zài liànxí.

_____ k. Xué de yuè duō ne, zuò de jiù yuè hǎo; zuò de yuè hǎo, xué de jiù gèng duō.

_____ l. Zhè shì yì zhǒng luóxuánshàngshēngshì de xuéxí.

_____ m. Fǎnguòlai yěshì yíyàng.

_____ n. Rúguǒ tài jiǔ búyòng zhèxiē xué de dōngxi, kěnéng hěn kuài jiù huì tuìbù de.

_____ o. "Nìshuǐxíngzhōu, bújìnzétuì."

_____ p. Tài yǒu dàolǐ le.

_____ q. Hǎohǎo xuéxí, tiāntiān xiàngshàng!

40.13 請把下面的英文和上面的拼音對上。／请把下面的英文和上面的拼音对上。

_____ 1. I'm reading your English book right now!

_____ 2. What I need to do now is be like you: practice, practice, and practice some more.

_____ 3. Maybe it's because English comes from many sources.

_____ 4. It's an upward spiral of learning.

_____ 5. The more you learn, the better you'll do; the better you do, the more you'll learn.

_____ 6. "When paddling against the current, if you stop, you'll go backward." [i.e., Use it or lose it.]

_____ 7. I'm packing.

_____ 8. Is learning English as hard for you as learning Chinese is for me?

_____ 9. Some English words seem to come from Chinese!

_____ 10. That's absolutely right. [That's very reasonable.]

_____ 11. Can you help me?

_____ 12. I think English grammar and pronunciation are especially complicated.

_____ 13. If you hadn't told me, I wouldn't have known.

_____ 14. The reverse is the same.

_____ 15. If you don't use what you've learned, you might quickly regress.

_____ 16. I don't want to let you go!

_____ 17. Study hard and improve every day!

40.14 請把下面的漢字和上面的英文對上。／请把下面的汉字和上面的英文对上。

____ A. 你不說我還不知道呢。／你不说我还不知道呢。

____ B. 我現在就在讀你的英文書呢！／我现在就在读你的英文书呢！

____ C. 學得越多呢，做得就越好；做得越好，學得就更多。／学得越多呢，做得就越好；做得越好，学得就更多。

____ D. 好好學習，天天向上！／好好学习，天天向上！

____ E. 我覺得英語的語法和發音特別的複雜。／我觉得英语的语法和发音特别的复杂。

____ F. 我收拾行李。

____ G. 反過來也是一樣。／反过来也是一样。

____ H. 可能是因為英語的發源比較多。／可能是因为英语的发源比较多。

____ I. "逆水行舟，不進則退。／逆水行舟，不进则退。"

____ J. 你能幫我忙嗎？／你能帮我忙吗？

____ K. 太有道理了。

____ L. 我現在最重要的就是跟你一樣：要練習，練習再練習。／我现在最重要的就是跟你一样：要练习，练习再练习。

____ M. 有些英文單詞好像還來自中文！／有些英文单词好像还来自中文！

____ N. 如果太久不用這些學的東西，可能很快就會退步的。／如果太久不用这些学的东西，可能很快就会退步的。

____ O. 你學英文有沒有我學中文這麼難？／你学英文有没有我学中文这么难？

____ P. 這是一種螺旋上升式的學習。／这是一种螺旋上升式的学习。

____ Q. 我不想讓你走！／我不想让你走！

40.15 *Fang Lan talks about English words of possible Chinese origin. Which of the following does she mention?* 請勾選。／请勾选。

☐ a. brainwashing: *from* 洗腦／洗脑 xǐnǎo *wash brain, used by the Chinese military during the Korean War*

☐ b. chow: *perhaps from* 炒 chǎo, *the most common form of Chinese cooking*

☐ c. ginseng: *from the Hokkien Chinese pronunciation of* 人參／人参 rénshēn

☐ d. gung ho: *from* 共和 gònghé *cooperative*

☐ e. ketchup: *from the Cantonese pronunciation of* 茄汁 qiézhī *tomato sauce*

☐ f. kowtow: *from* 磕頭／磕头 kētóu, *to knock the head on the ground as a gesture of respect*

☐ g. long time no see: *from* 好久不見／好久不见 hǎojiǔbújiàn

☐ h. lychee: *from the Cantonese pronunciation of* 荔枝 lìzhī

☐ i. no can do: *from* 不可以 bù kěyǐ

☐ j. ramen: *from* 拉麵／拉面 lāmiàn *pulled noodles*

☐ k. tea: *from the Amoy pronunciation of* 茶 chá

☐ l. tycoon: *from the Cantonese pronunciation of* 大君 dàjūn *great lord*

☐ m. typhoon: *from* 颱風／台风 táifēng *hurricane*

40.16 ***Pair work:*** *Work with a partner to discuss in Chinese how you think Chinese compares with English. Comment on how persisting in practicing is the key to improving your proficiency. Take notes on what is said.* 請寫拼音或者漢字。／请写拼音或者汉字。

Encounter 3 Reading and writing

Reading real-life texts

40.17 *If you go onto* www.baidu.com *and search for* 怎么学好英语, *one of the suggested links that appears is for a forum at the following address:* http://tieba.baidu.com/p/160611568. *The topic for this discussion board is* 我是怎么从零开始学英语的 Wǒ shì zěnme cóng líng kāishǐ xué Yīngyǔ de *(How I began from zero and learned English). Following is a simulated response based on some real posts.*

大大鱼头

现在有不少人认为学英语没必要死记硬背英文单词，我觉得这并不完全对。语言学习有听说读写四个方面，写作的前提就是必须要有一定的单词量的积累，如果没有一定的单词量，英语的书写能力也不会太好。阅读跟写作不同，看见一个单词，能认读、知道单词的意思就可以了，不需要掌握单词的准确拼写。口语和听力就更不一样了，不会拼写单词、甚至根本不认识单词都没有关系，只要会说、能听懂就行。很多英语国家的人也有一些单词不会拼写或者根本就不认识，但他们都会说英语。所以说，不懂语法、不会拼写单词不会影响人们的沟通和交流。对母语者来说，他们通常不需要刻意去学习语法，就像小孩子自然学会说话一样，他们在学会说话的过程中也自然习得了母语的语法。你要是问一个三岁的美国孩子英语语法的问题，他肯定不知道，但这不会影响他说英语。当然，我觉得，如果我们要跟说英语的外国人沟通，最重要的还是听力，只有听得懂，才能说得好。

a 請用英文填空。／请用英文填空。

Nowadays, quite a few people think that to ____________, you don't have to memorize English words. I don't think that this is entirely right. There are four aspects of learning a foreign language: listening, ______________, reading, and writing. A prerequisite to writing is that you have to have accumulated a requisite number of words. If you don't have the vocabulary, your writing ability in English will ________________. Reading is not the same as writing. If you see a word, and you can read it and know its meaning, then that is enough; you don't have to be able to spell it correctly. ______________ and ______________ are even more different. If you can't spell words, or even if you can't read them, it doesn't matter; as long as you can speak and understand words when you hear them, that is enough. People in many ____________________ find words they cannot spell or maybe can't even read, but they can all speak English. So, if you don't know grammar or spelling, this doesn't influence your ability to communicate and interact. Native speakers normally don't need to learn grammar deliberately. It's like a ______________ naturally learning to speak—in the process of learning to speak, they naturally acquire the grammar of their native language. If you ask a three-year-old American child about ________________________, he will certainly not know, but this does not affect his speaking English. Of course, I think that to communicate with English-speaking foreigners, the most important thing is listening comprehension. Only when you can understand can you speak well.

b *Write the characters for the following:*

1. dāncí *vocabulary word:* ___________
2. zhǔnquè pīnxiě *spell accurately:* ___________
3. kǒuyǔ *speech:* ___________
4. mǔyǔ *native tongue:* ___________
5. yǔfǎ *grammar:* ___________
6. gōutōng *communicate:* ___________
7. tīnglì *listening comprehension:* ___________

Reading a story

40.18 故事 *Find the following terms in either the traditional or simplified text and circle them. Write in the accompanying number.*

1. yǔyán *language*
2. bèijǐng *background*
3. fùzá *complicated*
4. fāngyán *regional language*
5. Mǐndōnghuà *the language of eastern Fujian province*
6. shěnghuì *provincial capital*
7. zhèngmíng *formal name*
8. rénkǒu *population*
9. chéngzhǎng *grow up*
10. guòchéng *course*
11. dāngshí *at the time*
12. Bājīsītǎn *Pakistan*
13. zhōuwéi *surroundings*
14. yí jù *one sentence*
15. Wūěrdūyǔ *Urdu (language)*
16. shuōqǐlái *in speaking*
17. línguó *neighboring country*
18. Yìndìwén *Hindi*
19. wénzì *script, written language*
20. Ālābó *Arabic*
21. guānfāng *official*
22. Fànwén *Devanagari (Hindi script)*
23. zìmǔ *alphabet*
24. chūshēng *birth*
25. ǒu'ěr *occasionally*

26. yīngdāng *ought to*
27. xià diǎn gōngfu *make some effort*
28. hǎo ràng *so that, make it happen that*
29. yì shǒu gē *a song*
30. hé X yǒuguān *have to do with X*
31. gēcí *song lyrics*
32. yóuchāi *postal carrier*
33. sòngxìn *deliver the mail*
34. xīngfèn de *excitedly*
35. ràozhe *circling around*
36. yòu bèng yòu tiào *hopping and jumping*
37. zuǐ lǐ hǎnzhe *yelling*
38. fán *annoyed*
39. gǎn zǒu *shoo away*
40. wěiqu *wronged*
41. huíxiǎng qǐlai *thinking back*
42. fàn cuòwù *make a mistake*

43. gēnjù *according to*
44. Yīsīlánjiào *Islamic religion*
45. chuántǒng *traditions*
46. mǎn jiē pǎo *run around the streets*
47. yǎng chéng X de xíguàn *developed the habit of doing X*
48. yì yǒu kòng *whenever there is free time*
49. duǒ *hide*
50. wūzilǐ *inside the house*
51. xiǎoshuō *novels, fiction*
52. shǔjià *summer vacation*
53. gè zhǒng gè yàng *all different kinds*
54. shuǐpíng *level*
55. yuè lái yuè hǎo *better and better*

56. děngdào *by the time (of something)*
57. yímín *immigrate*
58. yǔwén kè *language arts class*
59. kuā *praise*
60. mǔyǔ *native tongue*
61. bìng *actually, really*
62. chà yuǎnle *not nearly as good*

63. shuō mènghuà *talk in one's sleep*
64. zǒng shì *always, every time*
65. jǐnguǎn *even though*
66. zìcóng *ever since*
67. qùshì *pass away, die*
68. zhǐyào *as long as*
69. hūnhūnchénchén *dazed and groggy*
70. bànmèngbànxǐng *half awake, half asleep*
71. dànǎo *brain*

我學語言的背景很復雜。我們家裡講的是中國的一種方言：福州話，也叫閩東話，因為福州是福建省的省會，而福建省的正名叫“閩”。可是中國只有很少一部分人口說福州話，所以在我成長的過程中，我父母也試著教我一點普通話，或者叫國語。

可是因為當時我爸爸在巴基斯坦工作，所以我們周圍聽到的語言沒有一句是中國話。巴基斯坦人說烏爾都語。這種語言說起來跟鄰國印度的印地文一樣，可是兩個國家用的文字不一樣：巴

我学语言的背景很复杂。我们家里讲的是中国的一种方言：福州话，也叫闽东话，因为福州是福建省的省会，而福建省的正名叫“闽”。可是中国只有很少一部分人口说福州话，所以在我成长的过程中，我父母也试着教我一点普通话，或者叫国语。

可是因为当时我爸爸在巴基斯坦工作，所以我们周围听到的语言没有一句是中国话。巴基斯坦人说乌尔都语。这种语言说起来跟邻国印度的印地文一样，可是两个国家用的文字不一样：巴

基斯坦寫的是阿拉伯文字，而印度的官方語言寫的是梵文字母。

所以我出生以後，在家裡説福州話，偶爾聽到普通話，可是和鄰居小朋友在一起玩的時候説的是烏爾都語。

基斯坦写的是阿拉伯文字，而印度的官方语言写的是梵文字母。

所以我出生以后，在家里说福州话，偶尔听到普通话，可是和邻居小朋友在一起玩的时候说的是乌尔都语。

我到三、四歲的時候，我家人覺得應當下點功夫教我英文，好讓我五歲的時候去上英國人辦的小學。所以我姐姐決定從教我一首英語歌開始。這首歌和我的英文名字有關，叫“Cindy”。歌詞裡面有一句是：“Write me a letter soon”。然後我姐姐告訴我這句話的意思是，“快點給我寫封信”。所以我心裡想，“哦，那麼‘soon’的意思就是‘信’”！可能是因為“soon”跟“信”聽起來有一點像。然後那天下午郵差來送信的時候，我就興奮地繞著他又蹦又跳，嘴裡喊著，“Soon! Soon! Soon!”媽媽聽了不知道我在説甚麼，所以覺得很煩，就把我趕走了。我心裡覺得很委屈，也不明白為甚麼没人聽得懂我的“英語”。後來，一直等到我長大了，學好英語了以後，回想起來，才明白當時自己犯了甚麼錯誤。

我到三、四岁的时候，我家人觉得应当下点功夫教我英文，好让我五岁的时候去上英国人办的小学。所以我姐姐决定从教我一首英语歌开始。这首歌和我的英文名字有关，叫“Cindy”。歌词里面有一句是：“Write me a letter soon”。然后我姐姐告诉我这句话的意思是，“快点给我写封信”。所以我心里想，“哦，那么“soon”的意思就是‘信’”！可能是因为‘soon’跟“信”听起来有一点像。然后那天下午邮差来送信的时候，我就兴奋地绕着他又蹦又跳，嘴里喊着，“Soon! Soon! Soon!”妈妈听了不知道我在说什么，所以觉得很烦，就把我赶走了。我心里觉得很委屈，也不明白为什么没人听得懂我的“英语”。后来，一直等到我长大了，学好英语了以后，回想起来，才明白当时自己犯了什么错误。

因為巴基斯坦天氣很熱，而且根據伊斯蘭教的傳統，女孩子又最好不要滿街跑，所以我養成了一有空就躲在屋子裡看英語小說的習慣。我每年一個暑假下來可以看好幾十本各種各樣的小說。所以我的英文水平越來越好。

因为巴基斯坦天气很热，而且根据伊斯兰教的传统，女孩子又最好不要满街跑，所以我养成了一有空就躲在屋子里看英语小说的习惯。我每年一个暑假下来可以看好几十本各种各样的小说。所以我的英文水平越来越好。

等到我十四歲移民到美國來，在美國的高中上語文課的時候，老師誇我的英語比一般的美國學生還要好。“英語是你的母語嗎？”她問。“不是”，我回答，“我們家裡講的是福州話”。“哦，那你的母語是福州話嗎？”她接著問。“也不算吧，因為我的福州話說得並不是很好，比我的英語差遠了。”“那你的母語是甚麼呢？”我也不知道！很可能我就沒有母語！

等到我十四岁移民到美国来，在美国的高中上语文课的时候，老师夸我的英语比一般的美国学生还要好。“英语是你的母语吗？”她问。“不是”，我回答，“我们家里讲的是福州话”。“哦，那你的母语是福州话吗？”她接着问。“也不算吧，因为我的福州话说得并不是很好，比我的英语差远了。”“那你的母语是什么呢？”我也不知道！很可能我就没有母语！

但奇怪的是，要是我說夢話，說的總是福州話。儘管自從我上了大學，開始工作，一直到父母去世，這中間好幾十年很少說福州話，可是只要我睡得昏昏沉沉，半夢半醒，這個時候說出來的話總是福州話。

人的大腦真的很有意思！

但奇怪的是，要是我说梦话，说的总是福州话。尽管自从我上了大学，开始工作，一直到父母去世，这中间好几十年很少说福州话，可是只要我睡得昏昏沉沉，半梦半醒，这个时候说出来的话总是福州话。

人的大脑真的很有意思！

40.19 *Write a brief account of any interesting contact you have had with foreign languages or speakers of foreign languages (including Chinese or any Chinese regional languages).*

Encounter 4 Extension: Cultural mini-documentary

View the cultural mini-documentary for this unit and complete the exercises that follow.

40.20 *The interviewee featured here, Mark Rowswell—known in China as* 大山 Dàshān*—is without doubt the most famous Chinese-speaking foreigner ever, frequently appearing on Chinese television. His fame is partly due to his skill in the traditional art of* 相聲／相声 xiàngsheng, *traditional comic crosstalk, but also to the excellence of his spoken Chinese. Who knows? If you study hard, you may someday receive the compliment* 哇，你中文說得比大山還好呢！／哇，你中文说得比大山还好呢！ *In the meantime, learn a bit about how he learned Chinese, and take away a few tips!*

In the first part (0:00–0:59), Mark describes his Chinese-learning history up to when he started learning 相聲／相声. *Write the letters in the blanks to match his descriptions. One letter has been filled in for you.*

a. *cassette tapes* 磁帶／磁带 cídài

b. *about seven years* 算七年吧 suàn qīnián ba

c. *twenty-some years* 二十幾年／二十几年 èrshí jǐ nián

d. *totally random reasons* 很偶然的原因 hěn ǒurán de yuányīn

e. *three years* 三年 sānnián

f. *China was in a period of reform and opening* 中國改革開放／中国改革开放 Zhōngguó gǎigékāifàng

g. *a sense of curiosity* 一種好奇心／一种好奇心 yìzhǒng hàoqíxīn

h. *majoring in Chinese* 主修漢語／主修汉语 zhǔxiū Hànyǔ

i. *independent study* 自學／自学 zìxué

j. *studying freely* 自由學習／自由学习 zìyóu xuéxí

k. *studying formally* 正規學習／正规学习 zhèngguī xuéxí

l. *four years* 四年 sìnián

____ 1. approximate length of time he spent formally studying Chinese in school

__*l*__ 2. time spent at the University of Toronto

____ 3. time spent studying at Peking University

____ 4. total time studying Chinese, everything considered

____ 5. his original motivation for studying Chinese

____ 6. the cause of his interest in Chinese in high school

____ 7. one of the reasons he felt that Chinese might be useful in the future

____ 8. a method he used when he was in high school

____ 9. one of the things he bought to help him study

____ 10. what he started to do at the University of Toronto

____ 11. what he did for four years at the University of Toronto

____ 12. how his time at Peking University could be characterized

40.21 *The next section (0:59–1:39) has to do with Mark's motivations for studying* 相聲／相声. *Based on the transcript and what you hear, fill in the missing pinyin.*

我本來就是學中國的語言，相聲是中國語言的藝術，所以我覺得它是一個非常好的學習途徑。來到中國不是為了一種學術研究，是為了深入這裡的社會和這裡的生活，那麼以北京大學作為自己生活的基礎，但是有機會走出去還是很珍惜。因為我覺得如果是純學理論，學書本上的知識，那我還不如去美國去學，那麼到中國來留學主要是要深入這裡的社會，相聲給了我這麼一個窗口，走出去，走進社會，學老百姓的語言，學活生生的中文，所以我覺得也是一種學習方式。／

我本来就是学中国的语言，相声是中国语言的艺术，所以我觉得它是一个非常好的学习途径。来到中国不是为了一种学术研究，是为了深入这里的社会和这里的生活，那么以北京大学作为自己生活的基础，但是有机会走出去还是很珍惜。因为我觉得如果是纯学理论，学书本上的知识，那我还不如去美国去学，那么到中国来留学主要是要深入这里的社会，相声给了我这么一个窗口，走出去，走进社会，学老百姓的语言，学活生生的中文，所以我觉得也是一种学习方式。

Wǒ běnlái jiùshì xué Zhōngguó de yǔyán, xiàngsheng shì Zhōngguó yǔyán de ________, suǒyǐ wǒ juéde tā shì yí ge fēicháng hǎo de xuéxí ________. Lái dào Zhōngguó bú shì wèile yì zhǒng ________ yánjiū, shì wèile ________ zhèlǐ de shèhuì hé zhèlǐ de __________, nàme yǐ Běijīng Dàxué zuòwéi zìjǐ shēnghuó de jīchǔ, dànshì yǒu jīhuì __________ háishì hěn zhēnxī. Yīnwèi wǒ juéde rúguǒ shì chún xué ______, xué shūběn shàng de zhīshi, nà wǒ hái _____ qù Měiguó qù xué, nàme dào Zhōngguó lái liúxué zhǔyào shì yào shēnrù zhèlǐ de shèhuì, xiàngsheng gěile wǒ zhème yí ge __________, zǒu chūqu, zǒu jìn shèhuì, xué __________ de yǔyán, xué huóshēngshēng de Zhōngwén, suǒyǐ wǒ juéde yě shì yì zhǒng xuéxí ________.

I started out learning the Chinese language, and xiangsheng is a Chinese language ***art****, and so I guess I felt it was a very good* ***pathway*** *to learning. I came to China not to do some kind of* ***scholarly*** *research; it was to* ***enter deeply*** *into the society and* ***way of life*** *here, and so I took Peking University as my foundation for living [in Beijing], but at the same time really treasured any opportunity to* ***get out and about****. Because I felt that if I studied only* ***theory****, the knowledge found in books, then I* ***might as well*** *go to the United States for study, so my coming to study in China was mostly about getting deep into Chinese society, and xiangsheng gave me a kind of* ***window*** *into that, to get out there and get into society and learn the language of* ***the common people****, to learn the living language, and so I feel that's one* ***way*** *to study as well.*

40.22 *Next (1:40–2:01), Mark examines the factors that contributed to the achievement of his current skill level. Choose the correct answers.*

a *Among the following, check two reasons he mentions for his success.*

- ☐ *because he had to study for the HSK exam (*漢語水平考試／汉语水平考试 Hànyǔ shuǐpíng kǎoshì*) (Mandarin level exam)*
- ☐ *because he had a personal interest*
- ☐ *because someone pushed him to do it*
- ☐ *because he entered deeply into [social] life*
- ☐ *because he needed to reach a certain level*

b *He is constantly learning through _______.*

- ☐ *frequent review*
- ☐ *the use of a personal tutor*
- ☐ *lots of media*
- ☐ *the process of using the language*

40.23 *Next (2:02–2:16), Mark describes what learning language feels like from the inside. Among the following, check the seven words he uses.*

- ☐ yǒu xìngqù 有興趣／有兴趣 *have interest*
- ☐ gǎnjué dào 感覺到／感觉到 *perceive*
- ☐ jítǐ de 集體的／集体的 *collective, as a group*
- ☐ jìnbù 進步／进步 *progress*
- ☐ chīlì 吃力 *strain to [do something]*
- ☐ nǔlì 努力 *make an effort*
- ☐ hěn jiǔ 很久 *for a long time*
- ☐ tūrán yí xià 突然一下 *all at once, suddenly*
- ☐ jìn jǐ ge yuè 近幾個月／近几个月 *in the past few months*
- ☐ wánquán 完全 *totally*
- ☐ bù yíyàng le 不一樣了／不一样了 *not the same anymore*

40.24 *In the next section (2:17–3:03), Mark describes how he "suddenly became aware of"* (突然意識到／突然意识到 tūrán yìshi dào) *his own progress. Choose the correct answers.*

a *He studied in Taiwan and followed up with a trip to Hong Kong and Mainland China. The season he spent in Taiwan was* ___________.

- ☐ 春天
- ☐ 夏天
- ☐ 秋天
- ☐ 冬天

b *At that point, he had studied Chinese for* _________.

- ☐ 一年
- ☐ 兩年／两年
- ☐ 三年
- ☐ 四年

c *His story about* shǔtiáo 薯條／薯条 *is meant to exemplify* _________.

- ☐ *his learning through navigating daily situations*
- ☐ *his naïveté regarding foreign things in China*
- ☐ *his relief at finding something familiar*
- ☐ *his struggles reading restaurant menus*

d *In describing the difference between his and his classmates' Chinese in a third-year Chinese class, he says it is as if* ___________.

- ☐ *they were from a different university*
- ☐ *they were now moving at different speeds*
- ☐ *they had "given everything back to the teacher"*
- ☐ *a distance had opened up between their levels*

40.25 *Next, Mark tells a story about an incident that brought home to him how much he had learned. Listen and correctly order the Chinese quotes based on the English summary that follows. One number has been supplied for you.*

__6__ 雖然我错了，但是我現在我學中文學到了……／虽然我错了，但是我现在我学中文学到了……

____ 特別生氣，吵來吵去，／特别生气，吵来吵去，

____ 有一次在台北，跟出租司機吵架了，／有一次在台北，跟出租司机吵架了，

____ 所以後來我們那次吵架不了了之，／所以后来我们那次吵架不了了之，

____ 微笑握手。

____ 吵到一半兒的時候我覺得其實他説的有道理，／吵到一半儿的时候我觉得其实他说的有道理，

____ 可能是我理解錯了，／可能是我理解错了，

____ 可以跟出租司機吵架的水平了，／可以跟出租司机吵架的水平了，

____ 但是我心裡特別高興，因為我覺得……／但是我心里特别高兴，因为我觉得……

One time in Taipei I got into a quarrel with a taxi driver. I was so mad, and we argued back and forth, but then when we'd reached about halfway through the argument I felt like what he was saying actually made sense and that maybe it was I who had misunderstood. But I was so happy inside, because I felt that even though I had been wrong, now I had learned Chinese to the level where I could quarrel with a taxi driver! So that argument of ours sort of ended without an ending; we smiled and shook hands.

40.26 *Finally, Mark mentions some differences between first- and second-language learning and offers some points of advice. Match some of the phrases he uses to their English translations.*

____ a. wúlùn . . . háishì . . .
無論……還是……／无论……还是……

____ b. xīnlǐ zhàng'ài
心理障礙／心理障碍

____ c. méiyǒu bìyào de
沒有必要的

____ d. bódà-jīngshēn
博大精深

____ e. xiónghòu de jīchǔ
雄厚的基礎／雄厚的基础

____ f. gēnjù zìjǐ de shuǐpíng
根據自己的水平／根据自己的水平

____ g. bú shì shuō dōu huì zhèxiē
不是説都會這些／不是说都会这些

____ h. guānjiàn de
關鍵的／关键的

1. *unnecessary*
2. *in line with your own level*
3. *a substantial foundation*
4. *mental blocks, psychological obstacles*
5. *essential, the main thing*
6. *may not necessarily know all of this stuff*
7. *no matter whether . . . or . . .*
8. *vast, deep, difficult to understand*

40.27 *Number the following principles 1–4 according to the order in which Mark puts them forward. One is done for you.*

_2_ What you're expressing are your own emotions, your own thoughts—a manifestation of your mental processes.

____ To a certain degree, you've got to break through the feeling that it is a foreign language and that you're learning how Chinese say these things. You've got to gradually make it your own thing, your own language, through the process of learning.

____ Once you've reached a certain level, you should stop thinking of Chinese as a foreign language and start thinking of it as a second language.

____ Even though you may not be a native speaker, the language that you use as a tool to express your own thoughts is your own language.

Recap

Grammar

Presenting thoughts accurately in sentences (2)

In this exercise, you will be given a thought framed within a context; your task is to present that thought accurately by using the proper Chinese sentence type. Write your version on the line provided, and check the end of the Recap for our version and analysis.

1. You can speak some Chinese but really want to improve it. You ask your friend, who is Chinese and has become fluent in English, to tell you about his insights (*xīndé* 心得) into learning English.

____

2. Xiao Mao's birthday is coming up very soon on the calendar. Another friend reminds you of this and asks what you have decided to give him as a present. How does she ask this? (Hint: Use *le*.)

____

3. You arrive at the Beijing airport where your Chinese friend has come to welcome you, but you show up without any luggage. He asks, *Nǐ de xíngli ne?* Express that you can't find it and it was likely taken by mistake by someone.

____

4. You have just come out of Chinese class and your Chinese friend asks you if you wrote down everything the teacher said. Express in Chinese what you friend asks you.

____

5. You've got a problem and your friend asks you if you've figured it out. You answer that just as you were thinking of a solution, the telephone rang.

____

Here are some useful resources for further study of Chinese grammar. The best and most comprehensive source is the title by Charles Li and Sandra Thompson. (This one's a keeper; a treasure for your bookshelf.)

Herzberg, Qin Xue, and Larry Herzberg. *Basic Patterns of Chinese Grammar: A Student's Guide to Correct Structures and Common Errors*. Albany, CA: Stone Bridge Press, 2010.

Li, Charles. N., and Sandra A. Thompson. *Mandarin Chinese: A Functional Reference Grammar*. Oakland, CA: University of California Press, 1989.

Po-Ching, Yip, and Don Rimmington. *Basic Chinese: A Grammar and Workbook.* New York: Routledge, 2009.

Ross, Claudia. *Schaum's Outline of Chinese Grammar (Schaum's Outline Series)*. Columbus, OH: McGraw-Hill Education, 2009.

Answers and analysis:

1. Nǐ kěbu kěyǐ bǎ nǐ xué Yīngwén de xīndé gàosu wǒ? 你可不可以把你學英文的心得告訴我？／你可不可以把你学英文的心得告诉我？
   ANALYSIS: Although there are several ways of getting to this thought, many Chinese will elect to apply the *bǎ* pattern here. Note how the *bǎ* structure can be used for material objects (take the *garbage* out) or for nonmaterial objects (the knowledge you gain from something *xīndé*).

2. Xiǎo Máo de shēngrì kuài dào le, nǐ juédìng sòng tā shénme? 小毛的生日快到了，你決定送他甚麼？／小毛的生日快到了，你决定送他什么？
   ANALYSIS: This application of *le* (among its many) expresses the idea of an imminent action. It is often supported by *kuài* 快, *jiù* 就, *yào* 要, or combinations like *kuài yào* 快要 or *jiù yào* 就要.

3. Zhǎobuzháo. Dàgài bèi shéi gěi ná cuò le. 找不著。大概被誰給拿错了。／找不着。大概被谁给拿错了。
   ANALYSIS: Here, the passive pattern is appropriate—in other words, the one that expresses "by" (*bèi* 被) and is often supported by an accompanying *gěi* 給／给. Also involved in this expression are resultative verb forms *zhǎobuzháo* 找不著／找不着 and *nácuò* 拿錯／拿错.

4. Lǎoshī shuō de huà nǐ dōu xiěxiàlai le ma? 老師説的話你都寫下來了嗎？／老师说的话你都写下来了吗？
   ANALYSIS: In this instance, the verb takes a directional complement: *xiěxiàlai* 寫下來／写下来 (write down). What the teacher said, of course, involves a *de* 的 modifying phrase.

5. Wǒ zhèngzài xiǎngzhe yīnggāi zěnmebàn de shíhou, diànhuàlíng xiǎng le. 我正在想著應該怎麼辦的時候，電話鈴響了。／我正在想着应该怎么办的时候，电话铃响了。
   ANALYSIS: This expression calls for using verb + *zhe*, supported by words such as *zhèngzài* 正在, marking the progressive tense in Chinese.

Vocabulary

Please refer to page R-2 for a list of grammatical abbreviations used throughout this book.

bízi 鼻子 nose N

chuànqǐlai 串起來／串起来 string together V/RV

cí 詞／词 word; term N

cūxīn 粗心 careless SV; carelessness N

cūxīndàyì 粗心大意 careless; negligent; slapdash IE

dàgài 大概 general idea N; probably A

dàn 淡 bland; thin; light; tasteless; weak SV

dāncí 單詞／单词 word; individual word N

dàyì 大意 careless VP

dǎzì 打字 type *(write)*; do typing work VO

diànshìjù 電視劇／电视剧 TV play or drama N

dú 讀／读 read *(usually aloud)* V

fǎnguòlai 反過來／反过来 conversely RV

fāngyán 方言 dialect; topolect; non-Mandarin N

fāyīn 發音／发音 pronounce V; pronunciation N

fāyuán 發源／发源 source, origin N; originate V

fùzá 複雜／复杂 complicated; complex SV

gān 甘 sweet; pleasing; pleasant SV

gāo bízi 高鼻子 high/long-nosed N

guāi 乖 well-behaved; clever SV

hǎohǎo xuéxí tiāntiān xiàngshàng 好好學習天天向上／好好学习天天向上 study hard so that you improve every day IE

hútòng 胡同 lane or alley N

jiānchí 堅持／坚持 persist in; insist on V

jiāo 交 relationships N

jūnzǐ 君子 man of noble character; gentleman N

kàn míngbai 看明白 understand *(by reading or watching)* RV

kǎo 烤 roast; bake; toast V

kǒuyǔ 口語／口语 colloquial speech; spoken/vernacular language N

kùnnán 困難／困难 difficulty; problem N

láizì 來自／来自 come/originate from VP

lǐ 醴 sweet wine, liqueur N

liúxué 留學／留学 study abroad V

luóxuán 螺旋 spiral; helix; screw N

nìshuǐxíngzhōu bújìnzétuì 逆水行舟 不進則退／逆水行舟 不进则退 rowing against the current; if you stop rowing you'll fall back IE

niú 牛 new; hot; cool; outstanding SV

pāi 拍 take pictures; shoot film V

pèngshang 碰上 encounter; run into RV

pífū 皮膚／皮肤 skin N

ràokǒulìng 繞口令／绕口令 tongue twister N

rú 如 be like; measure up to V

ruò 若 as if; seemingly A

shàngshēng 上升 rise V

shèjì 設計／设计 design; plan V/N

shì 式 form; pattern; style BF

shōushi xíngli 收拾行李 pack/ready one's baggage VP

shuōbuzhǔn 說不準／说不准 speak incorrectly; speak unclearly RV

tiàoguò 跳過／跳过 jump over; cross; clear RV

tōng 通 understand thoroughly V; expert S

tuìbù 退步 regress; fall behind; lag behind V

Wéiwú'ěr 維吾爾／维吾尔 Uighur ethnic group of Xinjiang Province N

wénmáng 文盲 an illiterate; illiteracy N; illiterate SV

wényánwén 文言文 classical style of writing; writings in classical Chinese N

xiǎorén 小人 base/mean person; person of low standards N

Xīnjiāng 新疆 Xinjiang *(province in western China)* PW

xiūgǎi 修改 revise; amend; alter; modify V

yángròu 羊肉 mutton N

yángròuchuàn 羊肉串 mutton kebab N

yìbānláishuō 一般來說／一般来 generally A

yǒu dàolǐ 有道理 be reasonable; convincing/plausible SV/VO

yuèdú 閱讀／阅读 read; reading V/N

yǔfǎ 語法／语法 grammar; syntax N

zàntóng 贊同／赞同 approve of; endorse V

Zhōngguótōng 中國通／中国通 a China expert N

Checklist of "can do" statements

After completing this unit, you should be able to perform each of the following tasks:

Listening and speaking

- ☐ Talk about your own experiences learning Chinese.
- ☐ Discuss your current proficiency in Chinese.
- ☐ Talk about some challenges in learning Chinese.
- ☐ Discuss your past experience with Chinese regional languages.
- ☐ Compare learning Chinese with learning English.
- ☐ Discuss activities that might help you gain proficiency in Chinese.

Reading and writing

- ☐ Decipher some key points in an online response to a query about how best to learn English.
- ☐ Read an autobiographical account of encounters with foreign languages.
- ☐ Write an autobiographical account of an encounter with a foreign language.

Understanding culture

- ☐ Make several accurate statements about Chinese regional languages, the Chinese roots of some English words, and the experiences of Mark Rowswell (*Dàshān*) learning Chinese.

REFERENCE

Glossaries

The Chinese-English and English-Chinese glossaries list the words introduced in ***Encounters*** Book 4. Look upon this section as a sort of mini-dictionary. In addition, you may wish to refer to the glossary of measure words starting on page R-29. Traditional characters for each entry are given first, followed by simplified characters. The number refers to the unit in which the word first appears.

The following grammatical abbreviations are used throughout the glossaries:

A	adverb
ATTR	attributive
AV	auxiliary verb
BF	bound form
C	conjunction
CV	coverb
EV	equative verb
I	interjection
IE	idiomatic expression
M	measure word
N	noun
NP	noun phrase
NU	number
P	particle
PH	phrase
PL	phonetic loan
PR	pronoun
PREF	prefix
PREP	preposition
PW	place word
QW	question word
RF	reduplicated form
RV	resultative verb
S	suffix
SP	specifier
SV	stative verb
TW	time word
V	verb
VO	verb object
VP	verbal phrase

Chinese-English Glossary

A

àicǎo 艾草 Asiatic wormwood leaves N, 39
àiguó 愛國／爱国 patriotic SV, 39
àihào 愛好／爱好 interests; hobby/hobbies N, 37
ànmó 按摩 massage N/V, 35
ānquán 安全 safe; secure SV; security; safety N, 37
ānquángǎn 安全感 sense of security N, 36
Àomàn yǔ piānjiàn 傲慢與偏見／傲慢与偏见 *Pride and Prejudice* N, 31
Àoyùnhuì 奧運會／奥运会 *abbr. for* **Àolínpǐkè Yùndònghuì** 奧林匹克運動會／奥林匹克运动会 Olympic Games N, 34

B

bāguà 八卦 gossip (*originally eight trigrams of the* Book of Changes *used in divination*) N, 31
bài 拜 do obeisance to; worship V, 39
bǎikē 百科 encyclopedia N, 33
báimǎ wángzǐ 白馬王子／白马王子 knight in shining armor; prince on a white horse N, 36
bàng 棒 good; fine; great SV, 38
bàngqiú 棒球 baseball N, 34
bànlǐ 辦理／办理 handle; conduct; transact V, 37
bànlǚ 伴侶／伴侣 companion; mate; partner N, 36
bāo 包 wrap V, 39
bǎo'ān 保安 security guard N, 32; ensure public security VO, 35
bàodǎo 報導／报导 report V; information N, 32
bàofù 抱負／抱负 aspiration; ambition N, 35
bāoguǒ 包裹 wrap; bundle V; bundle; package N, 39
bǎojié 保潔／保洁 janitor N; do sanitation work VO, 35
bàoqiàn dǎrǎo 抱歉打擾／抱歉打扰 sorry to trouble you IE, 37
bǎoxiǎn 保險／保险 insurance N; insure; be insured V, 35
bǎoyòu 保佑 bless and protect V, 39
Bāxī 巴西 Brazil PW, 33
bèijǐng 背景 background; backdrop N, 36
běnkē 本科 undergraduate course of studies N, 37
běnkēshēng 本科生 undergraduate student N, 37
běnrén 本人 me; myself; oneself; in person N, 37
běnxiào 本校 this/our school N, 37
biān V1 biān V2 邊V1邊V2／边V1边V2 do V1 and V2 simultaneously C, 34
biānjí 編輯／编辑 editor; compiler N; edit; compile V, 35
biǎoyǎn 表演 performance; exhibition N; perform; act; demonstrate V, 34
bǐcǐ 彼此 each other; one another A, 33
bìngdú 病毒 virus N, 33
bìngjià 病假 sick leave N, 35
bìngmó 病魔 serious illness N, 39
bǐrú shuō 比如說／比如说 for example; for instance VP, 36
bǐsài 比賽／比赛 match; competition N, 34
bìzhǐ 壁紙／壁纸 wallpaper N, 33
bízi 鼻子 nose N, 40
bōchū 播出 broadcast; disseminate RV, 32
bódà 博大 broad; extensive; wide-ranging VP, 34
bù dī yú 不低於／不低于 not lower than VP, 38

C

cái 才 actually A, 39
cǎifǎng 採訪／采访 cover; interview; gather news V, 32
cáihuá 才華／才华 literary/artistic talent N, 38
cǎinà 採納／采纳 accept; adopt *(suggestions, etc.)* V, 38
càiniǎo 菜鳥／菜鸟 beginner; rookie; somebody new to a subject or activity N, 34
Cáo Cāo 曹操 celebrated general (155–220 CE) of the Three Kingdoms period N, 38
céng 層／层 story; level M, 37
chàngxì 唱戲／唱戏 perform in a traditional opera VO, 38
chāoshì 超市 supermarket N, 37
chāosòng 抄送 make a copy for; send a duplicate to V, 37
cháoxiàng 朝向 orientation N, 37
chàyidiǎn 差一點／差一点 almost A, 32
chēkù 車庫／车库 garage N, 37
chéngběn 成本 (net) cost N, 37
chéngzhǎng 成長／成长 grow up; mature V, 36
chōnglàng 衝浪／冲浪 surf VO; surfing N, 34
chōngshàngqu 衝上去／冲上去 charge; rush; dash (over to) RV, 32
chóngxīn 重新 again; anew; afresh A, 37
chóngzǔ 重組／重组 reorganization N; reorganize V, 36
chòuchóng 臭蟲／臭虫 bedbug N, 37
chōushuǐmǎtǒng 抽水馬桶／抽水马桶 flush toilet N, 37

chōuyóuyānjī 抽油煙機／抽油烟机 kitchen ventilator; exhaust hood N, 37
chuánbō(kāi) 傳播(開)／传播(开) disseminate; propagate; spread V, 33
chuǎngdàng 闖蕩／闯荡 make an itinerant living V, 38
chuánméi 傳媒／传媒 (communication) media N, 35
chuànqǐlai 串起來／串起来 string together V/RV, 40
chuánshuō 傳説／传说 legend; tradition N, 39
chuántǒng 傳統／传统 tradition; convention N, 36
chūbǎnshè 出版社 publishing house; publisher; press N, 31
chūcì 初次 for the first time A, 37
chúshī 廚師／厨师 cook; chef N, 35
chūyǎn 出演 play the part of; act; portray VO, 32
chúyǐ 除以 *(a number)* to be divided by VP, 38
cí 詞／词 word; term N, 40
cǐwài 此外 besides; in addition; moreover C, 37
cìwò 次臥／次卧 second/secondary bedroom N, 37
cùxiāo 促銷／促销 sales promotion N/V, 35
cūxīn 粗心 careless SV; carelessness N, 40
cūxīndàyì 粗心大意 careless; negligent; slapdash IE, 40

D

dǎ jīchǔ 打基礎／打基础 lay a foundation VO, 38
dǎ zhāohu 打招呼 say hello to; greet *(somebody)* VO, 32
dàbùfen 大部分 major part N, 38
dàcān 大餐 sumptuous meal; banquet; feast N, 39
dàdaliēliē 大大咧咧 careless; casual RF, 36
dáfù 答覆／答复 answer; reply V, 38
dàgài 大概 general idea N; probably A, 40
dàgāng 大綱／大纲 outline; synopsis; summary N, 32
dǎhé 打荷 tournant *(someone who does chores in a professional kitchen)* N, 35
dàhuǒr 大夥兒／大伙儿 we; us; we all; everyone N, 39
dāi 呆 stay; hang out V, 31
dàixīn jiàqī 帶薪假期／带薪假期 paid vacation N, 35
dàn 淡 bland; thin; light; tasteless; weak SV, 40
dāncí 單詞／单词 word; individual word N, 40
dǎng 擋／挡 get in the way of; block V, 31
dǎng *(also pronounced* **dàng***)* 檔／档 *(for programs and TV series)* M, 32
dāngchéng 當成／当成 regard; consider as VP, 38
dāngdì 當地／当地 locality; the place named/mentioned N, 39
dāngnián 當年／当年 that year; those years N, 39
dānrén 單人／单人 single person N, 37
dào 倒 pour V, 35
dàochá 倒茶 pour tea VO, 35
dàochù (dōu) 到處(都)／到处(都) everywhere; at all places A, 33
dàodǐ 到底 at last; in the end; finally A, 38
dǎogào 禱告／祷告 pray V, 39
dǎogòuyuán 導購員／导购员 promotions; buyer N, 35
Dàojiào 道教 Daoism *(as a religion)* N, 39
dǎoyǎn 導演／导演 director *(of plays, films)* N, 32
dǎrǎo 打擾／打扰 disturb; trouble V, 31
dárén 達人／达人 talent *(loan word from English word talent)* N/PL, 32
dàtáng 大堂 lobby; hall N, 37
dàxíng 大型 large size/scale ATTR, 37
dáyí 答疑 answer questions; clarify matters VO, 38
dàyì 大意 careless VP, 40
dǎzì 打字 type *(write)*; do typing work VO, 40
défēn 得分 score VO, 34
dēngjì 登記／登记 register; check in *(at a hotel, etc.)* V, 35
diànbīngxiāng 電冰箱／电冰箱 refrigerator N, 37
diǎnjī 點擊／点击 press; hit; strike; click *(a keyboard)* V, 38
diǎnjīliàng 點擊量／点击量 click rate; number of "hits" or views N, 33
diànshìjù 電視劇／电视剧 TV play or drama N, 40
diàntī 電梯／电梯 elevator N, 37
diànyǐngyuàn 電影院／电影院 cinema; movie theater N, 37
diànzhǎng 店長／店长 manager of a shop N, 35
diàochá 調查／调查 investigate; survey N/V, 36
dìbù 地步 extent; condition; state N, 36
dǐdá 抵達／抵达 reach; arrive at V, 37
dìlǐ wèizhi 地理位置 geographical location; location N, 37
dīngzhe 盯著／盯着 fix one's eyes on; gaze/stare at V, 33
dìtiězhàn 地鐵站／地铁站 subway station N, 37
dìwèi 地位 position; status N, 36
dìxià 地下 underground ATTR, 37
dòngmàn 動漫／动漫 cartoons; comics; graphic novels N, 33
dòngzuò 動作／动作 movement; motion; action; moves N, 34
dū 都 capital; metropolis BF, 33
dú 讀／读 read *(usually aloud)* V, 40
duànliàn 鍛煉／锻炼 engage in physical exercise V, 39
duǎnqī 短期 short time/period/term N, 37
Duānwǔjié 端午節／端午节 Dragon Boat Festival *(fifth day of the fifth lunar month)* N, 39
duǎnxiǎo 短小 brief VP, 34
duì 隊／队 team N, 34
duì wǒ lái shuō 對我來說／对我来说 as far as I'm concerned VP, 39
duìfāng 對方／对方 adversary; the other side N, 34

duìzhào 對照／对照 contrast; compare; place side by side for comparison *(as parallel texts)* V; **duìzhàobǎn** 對照版／对照版 bilingual edition 31
dújiā 獨家／独家 exclusive; sole ATTR, 32
dúlì 獨立／独立 independently A, 37; independent SV; independence N, 39

F

fā duǎnxìn 發短信／发短信 send a text message VP, 33
fābù 發布／发布 issue; announce; release V, 35
fādá 發達／发达 developed; flourishing SV, 37
fājiànrén 發件人／发件人 sender of mail; From: *(e-mail header)* N, 37
fǎlǜ 法律 law N, 35
fāng 方 then and only then *(written style for 才 cái)* A, 37
fàng jìnqu 放進去／放进去 put in; include; add RV, 36
fángchǎn jīngjìrén 房產經紀人／房产经纪人 real estate agent N, 35
fángdìchǎn 房地產／房地产 real estate N, 37
fángdōng 房東／房东 landlord N, 36
fāngshì 方式 way; fashion; method; means N, 33
fángshǒuqiúyuán 防守球員／防守球员 defensive player N, 34
fànguǎn 飯館／饭馆 restaurant N, 37
fǎnguòlai 反過來／反过来 conversely RV, 40
fǎngwèn xuézhě 訪問學者／访问学者 visiting scholar N, 37
fāngyán 方言 dialect; topolect; non-Mandarin N, 40
fānpāi 翻拍 adapt *(as a movie)* V, 31
fāshēng 發生／发生 happen; occur; take place V, 31
fāsòng shíjiān 發送時間／发送时间 time sent N, 37
fàxíngshī 髮型師／发型师 hairdresser; hair stylist N, 35
fāyīn 發音／发音 pronounce V; pronunciation N, 40
fāyuán 發源／发源 source, origin N; originate V, 40
fèi 費／费 cost; charge *(written style for 費用／费用 fèiyong)* BF/S, 37
fēn 分 divide; separate; allot V, 34
fēngfengdiāndiān 瘋瘋癲癲／疯疯癫癫 flighty; erratic RF, 36
fēngfù 豐富／丰富 rich; plentiful; abundant SV; enrich V, 31
fēngmiàn 封面 cover *(of a publication)* N, 31
fēngōng 分工 division of labor N, 32
fēnjū liǎngdì 分居兩地／分居两地 live in separate locations; live apart IE, 38
fēnshù 分數／分数 grade; mark N, 38
fěnsī 粉絲／粉丝 fan *(loan word)* N/PL, 31
Fó 佛 Buddha N, 39
Fójiào 佛教 Buddhism N, 39
Fójiàotú 佛教徒 followers of Buddhism N, 39
fǒudìng 否定 negate; deny V, 33
fǒurèn 否認／否认 deny; repudiate V, 32
fú 福 good fortune; blessing; happiness N, 39
fù 赴 go to *(written style)* V, 37
fúkuā 浮誇／浮夸 be pompous; boast; exaggerate V, 36
fúlì 福利 benefits; welfare N, 35
fùmiàn 負面／负面 negative side; negative N, 36
fúwù 服務／服务 service(s) N, 37
fúwùyuán 服務員／服务员 server; attendant N, 35
fùyǒu 富有 rich; wealthy SV, 31
fùzá 複雜／复杂 complicated; complex SV, 40

G

gāi 該／该 above-mentioned; that; this PR, 37
gān 甘 sweet; pleasing; pleasant SV, 40
gānbēi 乾杯／干杯 drink a toast VO; Cheers! Bottoms up! IE, 38
Gǎn'ēnjié 感恩節／感恩节 Thanksgiving Day N, 39
gānjìng wèishēng 乾淨衛生／干净卫生 clean and hygienic VP, 37
gǎnjué 感覺／感觉 feel; perceived; become aware of V; feeling; sensation N, 36
gānxǐdiàn 乾洗店／干洗店 dry cleaners N, 37
gāo bízi 高鼻子 high-/long-nosed N, 40
gāocéng 高層／高层 high-rise ATTR, 37
gāo'ěrfūqiú 高爾夫球／高尔夫球 golf *(loan word)* N/PL, 34
gǎoxiào 搞笑 funny SV, 33
gè 各 each PR, 37
gè yì 各異／各异 each different VP, 31
gēn pāi 跟拍 follow somebody with a camera to record an event V, 33
gèrén 個人／个人 personal N/ATTR, 38
gèwèi 各位 you all; everybody N, 37
gèzì 各自 each (of us) PR, 37
gōngchéng 工程 engineering N, 35
gōnggòng qìchēzhàn 公共汽車站／公共汽车站 bus stop N, 37
gōnggòng tíngchēchǎng 公共停車場／公共停车场 public parking N, 37
gōngjiāochē 公交車／公交车 commuter bus N, 37
gōngjùshū 工具書／工具书 reference book N, 31
gōngwùyuán 公務員／公务员 government employee N, 36
gōngxǐ 恭喜 congratulations N/IE, 38
gōngyuán 公園／公园 park N, 37
gōngyùlóu 公寓樓／公寓楼 apartment building N, 37
gōngzī 工資／工资 salary; wages; pay N, 35
gōngzuòjiān 工作間／工作间 workroom N, 37
gòumǎi 購買／购买 purchase; buy V, 33
gōutōng 溝通／沟通 link up; communicate RV, 35
gòuwù 購物／购物 go shopping VO; shopping N, 37

gòuwù zhōngxīn 購物中心／购物中心 shopping center N, 37
gòuzhì 購置／购置 purchase *(durable goods)* V, 37
guà 掛／挂 put up V, 39
guāi 乖 well-behaved; clever SV, 40
guàng 逛 stroll; ramble; roam; browse V, 31
guǎnlǐ 管理 manage; supervise V; management; administration N, 35
guānzhòng 觀眾／观众 spectator; audience N, 31
gùbushàng 顧不上／顾不上 cannot manage/attend to RV, 36
gǔdài 古代 ancient times N, 39
gǔdiǎn 古典 classical ATTR, 32
gūdú 孤獨／孤独 lonely; lonesome SV, 38
guò 過／过 undergo; go through V, 38
guòhuǒ 過火／过火 extreme; going too far SV, 32
guòjié 過節／过节 celebrate a festival/holiday VO, 39
gùzhi 固執／固执 obstinate; stubborn SV, 39

H

hàipà 害怕 fear; be afraid/scared V, 37
hānhou 憨厚 simple and honest; straightforward SV, 36
hǎohǎo xuéxí tiāntiān xiàngshàng 好好學習天天向上／好好学习天天向上 study hard so that you improve every day IE, 40
Hǎoláiwū 好萊塢／好莱坞 Hollywood PW, 38
hé xiǎng 合享 both (of us) can enjoy VP, 37
hé zhāng zhào 合張照／合张照 take a photo together VP, 31
hélǐ 合理 reasonable; equitable SV, 37
hétong 合同 contract; agreement N, 35
hézhù 合住 share a room/lodging RV, 37
Hóng Lóu Mèng 紅樓夢／红楼梦 *Dream of the Red Chamber* N, 31
hóngdòu 紅豆／红豆 red bean N, 39
hóngzǎo 紅棗／红枣 red date paste N, 39
hòuyuàn 後院／后院 backyard N, 37
huá 划 row V, 39
huábǎn 滑板 skateboarding N, 34
huáchuán 划船 row/paddle a boat VO, 39
huáiyùn 懷孕／怀孕 be pregnant VO, 37
huánjìng 環境／环境 environment; surroundings; situation N, 37
huánqiú 環球／环球 the earth; the whole world N; worldwide PREF, 31
huànxiǎng 幻想 fantasy; illusion N/V, 31
huāshēngmǐ 花生米 shelled peanut N, 38
huáxuě 滑雪 skiing N; ski V, 34
huífù 回覆／回复 reply *(to a letter/message)* V; response N, 33
huìr 會兒／会儿 moment; time N, 36
huíyì 回憶／回忆 recollect; recall V; memories N, 38
huìyuánzhì 會員制／会员制 membership (system) N, 37
hūnjià 婚嫁 marriage N; marry V, 33
huǒ 火 hot; popular SV, 32
huǒbào 火爆 explosively popular SV, 33
huǒchēzhàn 火車站／火车站 train station N, 37
huòdé 獲得／获得 gain; acquire; get; achieve V, 38
huǒjī 火雞／火鸡 turkey N, 39
Huǒnúlǔlǔ 火奴魯魯／火奴鲁鲁 Honolulu PW, 37
huópō 活潑／活泼 lively; vivacious SV, 39
hútòng 胡同 lane or alley N, 40
hùxiāng 互相 mutually; each other A, 36

J

jí 集 *(for episodes in a TV series)* M, 32
jí 即 namely *(equivalent here to spoken* 就是 **jiùshì***)* A, 37
jiājiāhùhù 家家戶戶／家家户户 each and every family RF, 39
jiājū 家居 home N, 33
Jiǎn Àosīdīng 簡•奧斯丁／简•奥斯丁 Jane Austen N, 31
jiānchí 堅持／坚持 insist on; persist in V, 39
jiāng 江 river N, 39
jiàngdī 降低 reduce; cut down; drop lower RV, 37
jiǎngpái 獎牌／奖牌 prize medal N, 34
jiǎngshù 講述／讲述 tell about; narrate; relate V, 32
jiāngyào 將要／将要 be going to; will; shall AV, 32
jiǎnjiè 簡介／简介 brief introduction; synopsis N, 37
jiǎnlì 簡歷／简历 résumé; curriculum vitae N, 35
jiànzhù 建築／建筑 build; construct V; building; edifice; architecture N, 35
jiāo 交 relationships N, 40
jiǎofǎ 腳法／脚法 footwork/kicking skill *(in soccer)* N, 34
jiàoliàn 教練／教练 coach; instructor N, 34
jiāoliú 交流 exchange; communicate V; communication N, 33
jiàotáng 教堂 church; cathedral N, 39
jiàoxué 教學／教学 teaching; education(al) N/ATTR, 38
jiàoyù 教育 education N; teach; educate V, 35
jiǎozi 餃子／饺子 dumplings; Chinese ravioli N, 39
jiāshí 加時／加时 overtime *(in sports)* N, 34
jiāyóuzhàn 加油站 gas station N, 37
jīběn 基本 basic; fundamental; elementary SV/N, 34
jīdé 積德／积德 accumulate merit by good works VO, 39
Jīdū 基督 Jesus; Christ N, 39
Jīdūjiào 基督教 Christianity N, 39
Jīdūjiàotú 基督教徒 Christian *(person)* N, 39
jié 節／节 segment; part; period *(in a game)* M, 34
jiè 界 circles; group; "world" BF, 35

jiēdài 接待 admit/receive a guest V; reception; front desk N, 35
jiéhé 結合／结合 fusion; combination N; combine; link; unite V, 34
jiémù 節目／节目 program; item *(on a program)* N, 32
jiérì 節日／节日 festival; holiday N, 39
jiēshōu 接收 accept V, 37
jiēzhù 接住 catch *(something thrown)* RV, 34
jìhuà 計劃／计划 plan; project; program N/V, 37
jījí 積極／积极 positive; active; energetic; vigorous; dynamic SV, 36
jījiàn 擊劍／击剑 fencing *(sport)* N, 34
jīliè 激烈 intense; fierce; acute; sharp SV, 35
jìlùpiān 紀錄片／纪录片 documentary N, 32
jìn xiào 進校／进校 enter school VO, 38
jìnéng 技能 skills; technique N, 35
jìng qǐng 敬請／敬请 respectfully invite V, 37
jīngcǎi 精彩 brilliant; splendid; wonderful; excellent SV, 34
jǐngchájú 警察局 police station N, 37
jīngcháng 經常／经常 often; constantly; frequently; regularly A, 31
jīngdiǎn 經典／经典 classics; scriptures; text N, 31
jīngjì 經濟／经济 economy; financial condition N; **jīngjìxué** 經濟學／经济学 economics *(as a field of study)* 31
jīngjìrén 經紀人／经纪人 broker; middleman; agent N, 35
jīnglì 經歷／经历 experience N; go through V, 38
jìngōngqiúyuán 進攻球員／进攻球员 offensive player N, 34
jīngshēn 精深 profound; penetrating VP, 34
jīngyàn 經驗／经验 experience N; go through; experience V, 35
jīngzhàn 精湛 exquisite; fine SV, 34
jìngzhēng 競爭／竞争 compete; competition V/N, 35
jìniàn 紀念／纪念 commemorate V, 39
jìnliàng 盡量／尽量 to the best of one's ability; as far as possible A, 34
jīnpái 金牌 gold medal N, 34
jìnrénjiēzhī 盡人皆知／尽人皆知 be known to all IE, 33
jīnróng 金融 finance; banking N, 31
jǐnshèn 謹慎／谨慎 cautious; prudent SV, 36
jíqiú 急求 urgently seek VP, 37
jìshù 技術／技术 skill; technique N, 34
jìzhě 記者／记者 reporter N, 32
jìzǔ 祭祖 offer sacrifices to ancestors VO, 39
jù 劇／剧 theatrical work; drama; play N, 32
juè 倔 stubborn; pig-headed SV, 39
juésè 角色 role; part N, 31
jùhuì 聚會／聚会 get together N/V, 38
jūnzǐ 君子 man of noble character; gentleman N, 40
jùshuō 據說／据说 it is said that VP, 39
jùtǐ 具體／具体 concrete; specific SV, 38
jù(tǐ)huà 具(體)化／具(体)化 specify V, 36

K

kǎ 卡 card *(credit card, membership card, etc.)* N, 37
kāilǎng 開朗／开朗 sanguine; optimistic; open-minded SV, 35
kāixīn 開心／开心 feel happy; rejoice V, 31
Kāixīnwǎng 開心網／开心网 Kaixin001 Network *(a Chinese Internet company) (literally, "Happy Net")* N, 33
kàn míngbai 看明白 understand *(by reading or watching)* RV, 40
kàn shìpín 看視頻／看视频 watch videos V, 33
kànbìng 看病 see a doctor VO, 38
káng 扛 carry V, 32
kǎo 烤 roast; bake; toast V, 40
kào 靠 depend on; rely on V, 36
kǎolǜ 考慮／考虑 think over; consider V, 37
kě 可 can; may *(written style for* 可以 **kěyǐ***)* AV, 37
kèfú 客服 customer service N, 35
kējì 科技 science and technology N, 31
kěkào 可靠 reliable; trustworthy SV, 36
kěndìng 肯定 positive; affirmative SV, 33
kěwàng 渴望 thirst for; long for V, 36
kōngjiān 空間／空间 space; open area N, 37
kōngqì 空氣／空气 air; atmosphere N, 37
kǒuyǔ 口語／口语 colloquial speech; spoken/vernacular language N, 40
kuàidìyuán 快遞員／快递员 messenger; courier N, 35
kuàijì 會計／会计 bookkeeper; accountant N, 35
kùnnán 困難／困难 difficulty; problem N, 40
kuòzhǎn 擴展／扩展 expand; spread; extend V; expansion N, 36

L

láizì 來自／来自 come/originate from VP, 40
làn 爛／烂 rotten; really bad *(usually of fruit or other foods, but here denoting lack of skill)* SV, 34
lǎnduò 懶惰／懒惰 lazy; indolent SV, 36
làngjì tiānyá 浪跡天涯／浪迹天涯 roam all over IE, 38
lánkuāng 籃筐／篮筐 basket; rim of a basket N, 34
lánqiú 籃球／篮球 basketball N, 34
lǎobǎixìng 老百姓 common people; civilians N, 39
lǎogōng 老公 husband N, 38
lǎoshi 老實／老实 honest; frank SV, 36
lèguān 樂觀／乐观 optimistic; hopeful SV, 36
lèi 類／类 kind; type; class; category N, 35
lěiqiú 壘球／垒球 softball N, 34
lèixíng 類型／类型 type; category; genre N, 31
lǐ 醴 sweet wine, liqueur N, 40
lì yǔ měi 力與美／力与美 strength and beauty N, 34

liàn'àiguān 戀愛觀／恋爱观 feelings about love; perspectives about love N, 36
liǎngxìng 兩性／两性 both sexes N, 36
liánxì 聯繫／联系 link up with; get in touch with V, 33
liǎnxíng 臉形／脸形 shape of one's face N, 36
liánxù 連續／连续 continuous; successive; running ATTR; continuously; successively; in a row A, 32
liánxùjù 連續劇／连续剧 TV series N, 32
liáo 聊 chat V, 35
liǎojiě 了解 understand; comprehend V; comprehension; understanding N, 35
liè(shàngqu) 列(上去) list RV, 36
lìhai 厲害／厉害 tough; capable; sharp SV, 34
línyù 淋浴 shower; shower bath N/V, 37
línyùfáng 淋浴房 shower stall N, 37
lìrú 例如 for instance; for example; such as C, 36
liúchuán 流傳／流传 hand down; spread; circulate V, 39
liúxué 留學／留学 study abroad V, 40
liúyán 留言 leave a message VO, 37
lǐxiǎng 理想 ideal N/SV, 36
lóngzhōu 龍舟／龙舟 dragon boat N, 39
lóufáng 樓房／楼房 building of two or more stories N, 37
lǜhuà 綠化／绿化 make a place green V; greening; greenification N, 37
Lúndūn 倫敦／伦敦 London PW, 34
luòdìchuāng(hu) 落地窗(戶)／落地窗(户) French window N, 37
luóliè 羅列／罗列 enumerate; set out; spread out V, 36
luóxuán 螺旋 spiral; helix; screw N, 40
lǚyóu 旅遊／旅游 tour V; tourism N, 32

M

màichǎng jīnglǐ 賣場經理／卖场经理 store manager N, 35
mài(ge) guānzi 賣（個）關子／卖（个）关子 hold in suspense *(in storytelling)* VO, 32
mánghuo 忙活 be busy/swamped VO, 38
mànpǎo 慢跑 jog; go jogging N/V, 34
mǎnyì 滿意／满意 satisfied; pleased SV, 35
mǎnzú 滿足／满足 be satisfied/contented SV, 38
màomèi 冒昧 make bold; venture to V, 31
mǎshù 馬術／马术 horsemanship; equestrian arts N, 34
měinǚ 美女 beautiful woman; beauty N, 33
méiqìzào 煤氣灶／煤气灶 gas range/stove N, 37
méiren 媒人 matchmaker; go-between N, 36
měiróngshī 美容師／美容师 beautician N, 35
měishí 美食 gourmet/delicious food N, 33
Měishì zúqiú 美式足球 American football N, 34
měishù shèjì 美術設計／美术设计 graphic design N, 35
méitǐ 媒體／媒体 media; information N, 35
méndānghùduì 門當戶對／门当户对 be well-matched in social and economic status *(for marriage)* IE, 36
ménpài 門派／门派 sect; schools N, 34
ménshang 門上／门上 on a door PW, 39
mǐ 米 rice N, 38
miǎnfèi 免費／免费 be free of charge VO, 38
miànshì 面試／面试 interview; audition VO/V, 35
miànshóu *(also pronounced* **miànshú***)* 面熟 familiar-looking SV, 35
míngxià 名下 belonging to somebody; under one's own name/account N, 37
míngxiǎng 冥想 meditation N/V, 39
míngxīng 明星 (movie/pop) star; celebrity N, 33
mǐtuán 米糰／米团 rice ball N, 39
mùbiāo 目標／目标 goal; target; objective N, 34
Mùsīlín 穆斯林 Muslim *(loan word)* N/PL, 39

N

nándào 難道／难道 Is it possible that . . . ? Can it be that . . . ? Do you mean . . . ? *(usually with* **ma** 嗎／吗?*)* VP, 39
nándù 難度／难度 (degree of) difficulty N, 34
nèiróng 內容／内容 content; substance N, 31
nèixiàng 內向/内向 introverted SV, 36
niánxīn 年薪 annual salary N, 35
nìshuǐxíngzhōu bújìnzétuì 逆水行舟 不進則退／逆水行舟 不进则退 rowing against the current; if you stop rowing you'll fall back IE, 40
niú 牛 hot; cool; outstanding SV, 40
nóng 濃／浓 dense; thick; concentrated; strong; intense SV, 33
nónglì 農曆／农历 lunar calendar N, 39

O

ǒu'ěr 偶爾／偶尔 occasionally A, 39
ǒuxiàng 偶像 idol; image; model N, 31

P

pá Chángchéng 爬長城／爬长城 climb the Great Wall VP, 38
pāi 拍 shoot a movie; take pictures V, 31
páiqiú 排球 volleyball N, 34
páizi 牌子 brand; trademark N, 37
pànwàng 盼望 hope/long for; look forward to V, 38
péi 陪 accompany; keep someone company V, 31
péibàn 陪伴 keep somebody company; accompany V, 36
pèicài 配菜 sous-chef *(assistant to the cook)* N, 35
pèideshàng 配得上 be able to match RV, 36
péixùn 培訓／培训 training N; cultivate; train V, 35
pèng 碰 touch V, 34

pèngshang 碰上 encounter; run into RV, 40
piàofáng 票房 box office N, 32
pífū 皮膚／皮肤 skin N, 40
píng 平 flat; level; even SV, 38
píng'ān 平安 safe and sound; peaceful SV, 39
píngfáng 平房 single-story house N, 37
pínggū 評估／评估 assessment, evaluation N; evaluate V, 38
píngjià 評價／评价 assessment; evaluation; appraisal N; evaluate V, 35
píngjú 平局 draw; tie *(in sports, chess, etc.)* N, 34
píngmù 屏幕 screen *(TV, computer, etc.)* N, 33
pīngpāngqiú 乒乓球 table tennis N, 34
pǐnwèi 品味 taste N; taste; savor VO, 31
píqi 脾氣／脾气 temperament; disposition N, 39
píqi hǎo 脾氣好／脾气好 good-tempered VP, 39
píqi huài 脾氣壞／脾气坏 bad-tempered VP, 39
pò'àn 破案 solve a criminal case VO, 32
pōlà 潑辣／泼辣 bad-tempered; aggressive; fierce and tough SV, 32
pǔgōng 普工 ordinary worker N, 35

Q

qī 期 *(for magazines and periodicals)* M, 32
qí chē 騎車／骑车 bicycling N; ride a bicycle VO, 34
qiáng 強／强 strong; powerful SV, 34
qiántái 前台 front/reception desk N, 35
qiányuàn 前院 front yard N, 37
qiǎokèlì 巧克力 chocolate *(loan word)* N/PL, 33
qiézi 茄子 eggplant (*transliteration of "cheese" when photographing*) N, 31
qìjīn wéizhǐ 迄今為止／迄今为止 until now; so far IE, 36
qīn 親／亲 blood relation N, 33
qínfèn 勤奮／勤奋 diligent; assiduous SV, 36
qíng 情 feelings N, 33
qǐng yǒuláo 請有勞／请有劳 please do me a favor and . . . IE, 37
Qīngcháo 清朝 Qing Dynasty (1644–1911) N, 31
qǐngjiào 請教／请教 seek advice IE, 37
qíngjǐng duǎnjù 情景短劇／情景短剧 sitcom N, 32
qīngzhēnsì 清真寺 mosque N, 39
qīnqiè 親切／亲切 cordial; genial SV, 32
qīnyǎn 親眼／亲眼 with one's own eyes; personally A, 31
qíquán 齊全／齐全 complete; all in readiness SV, 37
qítā 其他 other(s); the rest PR, 34
qiúmén 球門／球门 goal N, 34
qiúyuán 球員／球员 player; team member N, 34
qīxiàn 期限 time limit; deadline N, 35
qū 區／区 district N, 38
qǔ míng 取名 name; christen VO, 31
quān 圈 *(lap around a track)* M, 34; circle; ring N, 36
quán shìjiè 全世界 the entire world N, 38
quánjī 拳擊／拳击 boxing N, 34
quánjiā 全家 the whole family N, 38
quánlì 權利／权利 right; privilege N, 38
quānzi 圈子 circle; ring; clique N, 38
qūbié 區別／区别 difference; distinction N; differentiate V, 34
quēdiǎn 缺點／缺点 shortcoming; defect; disadvantage N, 35
quèdìng 確定／确定 be certain, confirm V, 33
qūgùnqiú 曲棍球 field hockey N, 34
qúnfā 群發／群发 group/mass/multiple mailing V, 33
qǔnuǎn 取暖 warm oneself VO, 37
qūxié 驅邪／驱邪 expel evil VO, 39
qūzhú 驅逐／驱逐 expel; get rid of V, 39

R

ràokǒulìng 繞口令／绕口令 tongue twister N, 31
rè 熱／热 popular SV, 33
(tā) rén hǎo (他／她)人好 he/she is a good person PH, 36
rénpǐn 人品 quality of someone's character N, 38
rénshēng 人生 (human) life N, 38
rénshēng jiǎnlì 人生簡歷／人生简历 life experiences N, 38
rénwù 人物 character; personage N, 31
rènwu 任務／任务 task N, 32
rènxìng 任性 willful; headstrong SV, 38
rèshuǐqì 熱水器／热水器 hot water heater N, 37
róudào 柔道 judo N, 34
ròuzòng 肉粽 glutinous rice dumpling filled with meat N, 39
rú 如 be like; measure up to V, 40
rúcǐ 如此 thus; like this; such VP, 36
rúguǒ . . . de huà 如果……的話／如果……的话 if . . . C, 38
ruò 若 as if; seemingly A, 40
rúxià 如下 as follows IE, 37

S

sài 賽／赛 compete V, 39
Sānguó Yǎnyì 三國演義／三国演义 *Romance of the Three Kingdoms* N, 31
shàng 上 go to V, 34
shàng tiān(táng) 上天(堂) go to Heaven VO, 39
shàngjiē 上街 go into the street; go shopping VO, 39
shàngshēng 上升 rise V, 40
shàng(wǎng) 上(網)／上(网) to go on (the Internet) V, 33
shāngwù 商務／商务 business; business affairs N, 35
shàngyìng 上映 show a film V, 32
shāo 稍 slightly A, 35
Shàolínquán 少林拳 Shaolin form of boxing N, 34

Shàolínsì 少林寺 (Buddhist) Shaolin Temple, Henan Province, China; the cradle of Chinese martial arts PW, 34
shāoméi 燒煤／烧煤 burn coal VO, 37
shāoxiāng 燒香／烧香 burn incense sticks VO, 39
shěbude 捨不得／舍不得 be loathe to part with RV, 38
shèjí 涉及 involve; touch upon V, 36
shèjì 設計／设计 design; plan N/V, 33
shèjiàn 射箭 archery N; shoot arrows VO, 34
shèjiāo 社交 social contact/interaction/life N, 36
shēngāo 身高 height *(of a person)* N, 36
shēngchénbāzì 生辰八字 one's birth data for astrological/marriage purposes IE, 36
shēng'éryùnǚ 生兒育女／生儿育女 bear and raise children IE, 36
shèngrèn 勝任／胜任 be qualified for; competent; be up to the task V, 35
shēnxíng 身形 figure; physical build N, 36
shènzhì 甚至 even (to the point of) C, 36
shènzhì yú 甚至於／甚至于 even to the point of; so much so that C, 36
shèshī 設施／设施 facilities N, 37
shèxiàngjī 攝像機／摄像机 video camera; camcorder N, 32
shèyǐng 攝影／摄影 photography N; take a photograph; shoot a film; film V, 33
shì 室 *(for* **wòshì** 臥室／卧室 *– bedroom)* ABBR, 37
shì 式 form; pattern; style BF, 40
shìchǎng 市場／市场 market; marketplace; bazaar N, 35
shìchǎng yíngxiāo 市場營銷／市场营销 marketing N, 35
shīrén 詩人／诗人 poet N, 39
shītǐ 屍體／尸体 corpse N, 39
shíxí 實習／实习 practice; intern; do fieldwork N/V, 35
shǐyòng 使用 use; emply; apply V, 37
shǐyòngqī 使用期 time of use N, 37
shìyǒu 室友 roommate N, 37
shízài 實在／实在 honest; dependable SV, 36
shòu 售 sell V, 37
shōujiànrén 收件人 recipient *(of message, mail)* N, 37
shōukàn 收看 tune into; watch (TV) V, 32
shǒuményuán 守門員／守门员 goalie; goalkeeper N, 34
shōushi xíngli 收拾行李 pack/ready one's baggage VP, 40
shǒuxiān 首先 first A, 38
shǒuyè 首頁／首页 home page; title page N, 33
shōuyínyuán 收銀員／收银员 cashier N, 35
shuāijiāo 摔跤 wrestling N; wrestle V, 34
shuāngfāng 雙方／双方 both sides; two parties N, 36
shuāngrén chuáng 雙人床／双人床 double bed N, 37
shūchóng 書蟲／书虫 bookworm N, 31
shuìdài 睡袋 sleeping bag N, 37
Shuǐhǔ Zhuàn 水滸傳／水浒传 *Water Margin* N, 31
shuǐjiǎo 水餃／水饺 dumpling N, 32
shuōbuzhǔn 說不準／说不准 speak incorrectly; speak unclearly RV, 40
shuōdìng 說定／说定 settle; agree on V/RV, 35
shúrén (*also pronounced* **shóurén**) 熟人 acquaintance; friend N, 36
shúxī (*also pronounced* **shóuxi**) 熟悉 know something/somebody well SV/V 31
shǔyú 屬於／属于 belong to; be a part of V, 32
sì dà míngzhù 四大名著 four great classical novels (of Chinese literature) N, 31
sìhéyuàn 四合院 compound with surrounding houses typical of traditional Beijing architecture N, 37
sījī 司機／司机 driver; chauffeur N, 35
sìmiào 寺廟／寺庙 temple N, 39
sōu 搜 search; collect; gather V, 33
Sōuhú 搜狐 Sohu *(one of the largest Chinese Internet companies) (literally, "Search-fox")* N, 33
suíhé 隨和／随和 amiable SV, 39

T

tái 台 channel; station N, 32
tàiyángnéng 太陽能／太阳能 solar energy N, 37
tándelái 談得來／谈得来 get along well; be congenial RV, 36
tángguǒ 糖果 sweets; candy N, 39
tāngyuánr 湯圓兒／汤圆儿 glutinous rice dumplings served in soup N, 39
tào 套 *(for sets, series, etc.)* M, 34
tè 特 especially A, 37
tèdiǎn 特點／特点 characteristic; trait; peculiarity N, 35
tèsè 特色 distinguishing feature/quality N/SV, 37
tèzhēng 特徵／特征 trait; characteristic; distinctive feature N, 36
tī jìn 踢進／踢进 kick into RV, 34
tī zúqiú 踢足球 play soccer/football VO, 34
tiānwénxué 天文學／天文学 astronomy N, 37
tiānxià 天下 world; dominion; territory N, 34
Tiānzhǔ 天主 God *(in Catholicism)* N, 39
Tiānzhǔjiào 天主教 Catholicism N, 39
Tiānzhǔjiàotú 天主教徒 Catholic *(person)* N, 39
tiàoguò 跳過／跳过 jump over; cross; clear RV, 40
tiáojiàn 條件／条件 requirement; condition; factor; term N, 36
tiàoshuǐ 跳水 diving N; dive into the water VO, 34
tiǎozhàn 挑戰／挑战 challenge N, 32
tícái 題材／题材 subject matter; theme N, 32
tǐcāo 體操／体操 gymnastics; calisthenics N, 34
tiē 貼／贴 paste/glue/stick to V, 39
tīhuíqu 踢回去 kick back *(in soccer, etc.)* RV, 34
tǐmào 體貌／体貌 figure and appearance N, 36

tīng 廳／厅 *(for* **kètīng** 客廳／客厅 – living room*)* ABBR, 37
tíngchēwèi 停車位／停车位 parking space/place N, 37
tíshēng 提升 promote; elevate RV, 38
tǐyù 體育／体育 physical education/training; sports N, 34
tǐzhòng 體重／体重 (body) weight N, 36
tōng 通 understand thoroughly V; expert S, 40
tōngcháng 通常 usually; normally A, 37
tóngxìngliàn 同性戀／同性恋 homosexuality; homosexual N, 36
tóu 投 throw; toss V, 39
tóu jìn 投進／投进 throw into RV, 34
tóujīn 頭巾／头巾 scarf; kerchief; turban N, 39
tú 徒 disciple; pupil; apprentice BF, 39
tuánduì 團隊／团队 team N, 32
tuánjù (zài yìqǐ) 團聚(在一起)／团聚(在一起) get together V, 39
tuìbù 退步 regress; fall behind; lag behind V, 40
tuīchū 推出 present to the public; come on the market RV, 37
tuījiàn 推薦／推荐 recommend V, 31
tuījiànxìn 推薦信／推荐信 letter of recommendation N, 35
tuīná 推拿 massage therapy N, 35
tújìng 途徑／途径 way; channel N, 38
tuōkǒu xiù 脫口秀 talk show *(loan word)* N/PL, 32
túpiàn 圖片／图片 picture; photograph; images N, 33
túshūguǎn 圖書館／图书馆 library N, 37

W

wàibiǎo 外表 outward appearance; exterior N, 39
wàixiàng 外向 extroverted SV, 39
wán huábǎn 玩滑板 (go) skateboarding VP, 38
wán yóuxì 玩遊戲／玩游戏 play games VP, 33
wànfēn 萬分／万分 extremely A, 37
wǎngqiú 網球／网球 tennis N, 34
Wáng Xīfèng 王熙鳳／王熙凤 Phoenix Wang (a character in *Dream of the Red Chamber*) N, 31
wǎngyè 網頁／网页 Web page N, 33
wǎngyǒu 網友／网友 netizens N, 38
wǎngzhàn 網站／网站 website N, 33
wǎnjiān 晚間／晚间 evening; at night N, 32
wánměi 完美 perfect; consummate SV, 33
wánshàn 完善 complete; perfect SV, 37
Wànshèngjié 萬聖節／万圣节 Halloween; All Saints' Day N, 39
wǎnyuē 婉約／婉约 graceful and restrained ATTR, 32
wèi 味 flavor; taste; smell N, 33
wèi 衛／卫 *(for* **wèishēngjiān** 衛生間／卫生间 – toilet*)* ABBR, 37
wèi 為／为 for; to CV, 38
wèi 餵／喂 feed V, 39
wēibōlú 微波爐／微波炉 microwave oven N, 37
wèilái 未來／未来 future; time to come N, 38
wèishēng bǎojiàn 衛生保健／卫生保健 healthcare provisions N, 35
Wéiwú'ěr 維吾爾／维吾尔 Uighur ethnic group of Xinjiang Province N, 40
wèndá 問答／问答 questions and answers; interrogation N/V, 31
wěndìng 穩定／稳定 stable; steady SV; stabilize V, 35
wènjuàn 問卷／问卷 questionnaire N, 36
wénmáng 文盲 an illiterate; illiteracy N; illiterate SV, 40
wēnnuǎn 溫暖／温暖 warm SV, 38
wēnróu 溫柔 gentle and soft SV, 32
wényánwén 文言文 classical style of writing; writings in classical Chinese N, 40
wényuán 文員／文员 office worker; clerk N, 35
wǔgǔ 五穀／五谷 grains; cereals; the five grains N, 39
wǔshù 武術／武术 martial arts N, 34
Wǔyuè chūwǔ 五月初五 fifth day of the fifth lunar month N, 39
wùzhì 物質／物质 material; matter; substance N, 36

X

Xī Yóu Jì 西遊記／西游记 *Journey to the West* N, 31
xiā 蝦／虾 shrimp N, 39
xià 下 download V, 31
Xiàdà 夏大 *(for* **Xiàwēiyí Dàxué** 夏威夷大學／夏威夷大学 – University of Hawaii*)* N/ABBR, 37
xiàn 限 set a limit; restrict V, 32
xiàn 線／线 line; boundary N, 34
xiǎng 想 remember with longing; miss V, 38
xiàng 像 resemble; take after; be like V, 31
xiàng X yíyàng 像X一樣／像X一样 identical to/very similar to X PH, 33
xiāng'ài 相愛／相爱 love each other V, 36
xiǎngqǐ 想起 think of; remember; recall RV, 38
xiāngqīn 相親／相亲 go on a blind date; meet a prospective spouse VP, 36
xiāngtóng 相同 be alike/identical; equivalent V, 39
xiànjīn liú 現金流／现金流 cash flow N, 35
xiànmù 羨慕／羡慕 admire; envy V, 38
xiánqīliángmǔ 賢妻良母／贤妻良母 a good wife and a good mother IE, 36
xiànshí 現實／现实 practical; pragmatic SV, 32
xiánshuǐzòng 鹹水粽／咸水粽 saltwater rice dumpling N, 39
xiǎo gūniang 小姑娘 young girl/lady N, 31
xiǎochúbǎo 小廚寶／小厨宝 water heater *(for kitchen sink)* N, 37
xiāofángzhàn 消防站 fire station N, 37
xiàonèi 校內／校内 inside/within the school PW/ATTR, 33

xiǎoqū 小區／小区 residential area; city or town district N, 37
xiǎorén 小人 base/mean person; person of low standards N, 40
xiāoshí 消食 help to digest VO, 32
xiāoshòu 銷售／销售 sell; market V; sales; marketing N, 35
xiàoyǒu 校友 alumni; classmates N, 33
xiàoyuán 校園／校园 campus; school yard PW, 37
Xiàwēiyí 夏威夷 Hawaii PW, 37
xié'è 邪惡／邪恶 evil; evil force SV/N, 39
xíguàn 習慣／习惯 be accustomed/used to V; habit N, 38
xìliè 系列 series; set N, 32
xīn dào 新到 have just arrived V, 37
xīnbǎn 新版 new edition; new version N, 31
xìngfú 幸福 happiness N; happy SV, 36
xìnggé 性格 (person's) nature; disposition; temperament N, 31
xíngshàn 行善 do good works VO, 39
xíngtài 形態／形态 form; shape; style; pattern; type N, 36
xíngxiàng 形象 image N, 36
xíngzhēnjù 刑偵劇／刑侦剧 crime investigation show N, 32
Xīnjiāng 新疆 Xinjiang *(province in western China)* PW, 40
xìnjiào 信教 believe/profess a religion VO, 39
xīnmù zhōng 心目中 in one's heart/mind N, 36
xīnshēng 新生 new student N, 37
xīnshuǐ 薪水 salary; pay; wages N, 35
xīnwén 新聞／新闻 news N, 32
xìnxī 信息 information; news; message N, 33
xìnxī jìshù 信息技術／信息技术 information technology N, 35
xìnyǎng 信仰 belief N; believe V, 39
xǐshǒutái 洗手台 vanity *(for sink)* N, 37
xísú 習俗／习俗 custom; convention N, 36
xiù 秀 show *(loan word)* N/PL, 32
xiūgǎi 修改 revise; amend; alter; modify V, 40
xǐwǎnjī 洗碗機／洗碗机 dishwasher N, 37
Xīyǎtú 西雅圖／西雅图 Seattle PW, 33
xīyǐn 吸引 attract; draw; fascinate V, 36
xū chí 需持 must possess VP, 37
xuǎnxiù jiémù 選秀節目／选秀节目 talent show N, 32
xuǎnzé 選擇／选择 select; choose V; choice; alternative N, 38
xuélì 學歷／学历 record of formal schooling; educational background N, 36
xuéxiào 學校／学校 school N, 37
xún 尋／寻 seek; search V, 37
xúnwèn 詢問／询问 *(formally)* inquire V, 38
xūwěi 虛偽／虚伪 hypocritical; false; insincere SV, 36

Y

yǎn 演 perform; play; act; show (a film) V, 31
yángròu 羊肉 mutton N, 40
yángròuchuàn 羊肉串 mutton kebab N, 40
yángtái 陽台／阳台 balcony, terrace, deck N, 37
yánsù 嚴肅／严肃 serious; solemn SV, 36
yǎnyuán 演員／演员 performer; actor; actress N, 31
yàodiàn 藥店／药店 drugstore N, 37
yāoqiú 要求 demand; request; requirement N/V, 36
yǎzhì 雅緻／雅致 refined; tasteful SV; refinement N, 31
yèyú 業餘／业余 spare time; after hours N, 35
yì 亦 *(written style for* 也 **yě***)* A, 37
yí dà duī 一大堆 a large pile N, 39
yí dà guō 一大鍋／一大锅 a large potful N, 39
yǐ lì huán lì 以力還力／以力还力 return **(huán)** force **(lì)** with **(yǐ)** force **(lì)** IE, 34
yǐ sì liǎng bō qiān jīn 以四兩撥千斤／以四两拨千斤 move **(bō)** 1,000 **(qiān)** catties **(jīn)** with **(yǐ)** four **(sì)** ounces **(liǎng)** = Give me a lever and I will move the earth IE, 34
yìbān 一般 generally; ordinarily; usually A, 34; ordinary; common; average SV, 36
yìbānláishuō 一般來說／一般来说 generally speaking VP, 38; generally A, 40
yīliáo bǎojiàn 醫療保健／医疗保健 medical care N, 35
yīmóyīyàng 一模一樣／一模一样 be exactly alike IE, 39
yǐnèi 以內／以内 within S, 37
yíng 贏／赢 win; gain V, 34
yíngxiāo 營銷／营销 marketing N, 35
yíngyèyuán 營業員／营业员 shop/business staff N, 35
yìnxiàng 印象 impression N, 36
Yīsīlánjiào 伊斯蘭教／伊斯兰教 Islam; Islamism *(loan word)* N/PL, 39
yìxìngliàn 異性戀／异性恋 heterosexuality; heterosexual N, 36
yīyuàn 醫院／医院 hospital N, 37
yìzhí 一直 always; all along A, 38
yōngyǒu 擁有／拥有 possess; have; own V, 37
yǒu biàn 有變／有变 undergo a change VO, 37
yǒu dàolǐ 有道理 be reasonable; convincing/plausible SV/VO, 40
yǒudài 有待 remain (to be done) V, 37
yōudiǎn 優點／优点 merit; strong/good point; advantage N, 35
yǒuguān 有關／有关 about; concerning VO, 39
yóujiàn 郵件／邮件 mail N, 37
yōujiǔ 悠久 long in time; long-standing; age-old SV, 34
yóujú 郵局／邮局 post office N, 37
yóuqíshì 尤其是 especially VP, 34
yǒushàn 友善 friendly; amicable SV, 36
Yóutàijiào 猶太教／犹太教 Judaism N, 39

yǒuyìyì 有意義／有意义 have meaning; have significance V/VO, 35
yóuyǒng 游泳 swimming N; swim V, 34
yōuzhì 優質／优质 high/top quality/grade ATTR, 38
yǔ 與／与 and; together with (*used only in written Chinese*) C, 31
yuánshǐ 原始 original SV, 37
yuánzé 原則／原则 principle N, 39
yuánzhù 原著 original work N, 31
yuē 約／约 about; around; approximately (*written style for* 大約／大约 **dà yuē**) A, 37
yuèdú 閱讀／阅读 read; reading V/N, 40
yuèpiào 月票 monthly bus pass N, 37
yuèxīn 月薪 monthly salary N, 35
yǔfǎ 語法／语法 grammar; syntax N, 40
yùgāng 浴缸 bathtub N, 37
yújiā 瑜伽 yoga (*loan word*) N/PL, 39
yúlè 娛樂／娱乐 amusement; entertainment; recreation N, 32
yǔmáoqiú 羽毛球 badminton; feathercock N, 34
yǔnxǔ 允許／允许 permit; allow V, 37

Z

zài 載／载 transport V, 37
zài nèi 在內／在内 be included; including VO, 36
zàixiàn 在線／在线 be online VO, 38
zàntóng 贊同／赞同 approve of; endorse V, 40
zázhì 雜誌／杂志 magazine; journal; periodical N, 31
zhǎng 長／长 grow; increase V, 35
zhànghào 帳號／帐号 account number (*of a bank, store, etc.*) N, 37
zhāofú 招福 elicit blessings VO, 39
zhàogu 照顧／照顾 look after; care for; attend to V, 36
zhāojìnlai 招進來／招进来 beckon in; attract into RV, 39
zhāopìn 招聘 invite applications for a job N, 35
zhāshi 扎實／扎实 solid; sound SV, 38
zhēnchéng 真誠／真诚 truthful; genuine; sincere SV, 36
zhèngcè 政策 policy N, 37
zhèngmiàn 正面 positive side; positive N, 36
zhèngzhì 政治 politics; political affairs N, 37
zhēnrén xiù 真人秀 reality show N, 32
zhēnshí 真實／真实 true; real; authentic SV, 36
zhī lèi 之類／之类 and such/and the like S, 31
zhīchí 支持 support; stand by; back V, 36
zhídǎo 執導／执导 direct (*a film*) V, 32
zhǐdǎo 指導／指导 guidance; direction; supervision N; guide; supervise V, 35
zhǐdǎo bāngzhù 指導幫助／指导帮助 give advice and help IE, 37
zhíjiē 直接 direct; immediate SV; directly A, 35
zhīshi 知識／知识 knowledge N, 35
zhíyè 職業／职业 occupation; profession; vocation N; professional ATTR, 35
zhìzuò 製作／制作 produce V, 32
zhòngdiǎn 重點／重点 key point; focal point; emphasis N, 36
Zhōngguótōng 中國通／中国通 a China expert N, 40
zhōngjiè 中介 intermediary; broker N, 37
zhǔ 煮 boil; cook V, 39
zhù 著 write books, etc. V, 31
zhù 炷 stick (*for incense*) M, 39
zhù yúkuài 祝愉快 Wishing you happiness IE, 37
zhuǎn 轉／转 pass on; transfer V, 33
zhuàn 賺／赚 earn; make a profit; gain V, 38
zhuǎnfā 轉發／转发 forward (*a message, etc*); transmit V, 33
zhuàngjī 撞擊／撞击 dash against; strike (*here: tackle*) V, 34
zhuàngjiàn 撞見／撞见 meet/discover by chance V, 31
zhuàngkuàng 狀況／状况 condition; situation N, 36
zhuàngtài 狀態／状态 state (of affairs); conditions; status N, 33
zhuānlán 專欄／专栏 special column (*in a newspaper, etc.*) N, 31
zhuǎnràng 轉讓／转让 transfer possession (to somebody) V, 37
zhuānyè 專業／专业 specialized field of research; specialty N, 35
zhuānyè rénshì 專業人士／专业人士 professionals; personnel in a specific field N, 36
zhǔchírén 主持人 host; anchor N, 32
zhùchù 住處／住处 residence; lodgings; quarters N, 37
zhūduō 諸多／诸多 a great deal of; a lot of (*written style*) ATTR, 37
zhùfáng 住房 housing N, 36
zhuī 追 chase; pursue; run after V, 34
zhùsuǒ 住所 residence N, 37
zhǔtí 主題／主题 topic; theme; subject N, 37
zhǔwò 主臥／主卧 main/master bedroom N, 37
zhùzhòng 注重 lay stress on; pay attention to V, 36
zìrán'érrán 自然而然 naturally; automatically; spontaneously IE, 36
zìxìn 自信 self-confident; confident V, 33
zìyóu zhíyè 自由職業／自由职业 self-employment; freelance profession N, 36
zīyuán 資源／资源 resources; natural resources N, 38
zǒngcái 總裁／总裁 CEO; president N, 35
zōnghé 綜合／综合 comprehensive ATTR, 38
zōngjiào 宗教 religion N, 39
zòngyè 粽葉／粽叶 bamboo leaves; palm leaves N, 39
zòngzi 粽子 pyramid-shaped dumpling of glutinous rice wrapped in reed leaves N, 39

zū 租 rent/rental BF, 37
zǔ 組／组 section; group N, 33
zūhù 租戶／租户 tenant N, 36
zuìfàn 罪犯 criminal N, 32
zūjīn 租金 rent; rental N, 37
zúliáo bǎojiàn 足療保健／足疗保健 foot care; reflexology N, 35
zūlìn 租賃／租赁 rent; lease; hire V, 37
zuò hǎorén 做好人 be a good person VP, 39
zuò lǐbài 做禮拜／做礼拜 go to church; attend religious service VO, 39
zuò mísa 做彌撒／做弥撒 go to (Catholic) Mass VO, 39
zuò yújiā 做瑜伽 do/perform yoga VO, 34
zuòběicháonán 坐北朝南 face south with back to north IE, 37
zúqiú 足球 football; soccer N, 34
zǔzhī 組織／组织 organize V, 32

English-Chinese Glossary

A

ability: to the best of one's ability jìnliàng 盡量／尽量 A
about yǒuguān 有關／有关 VO; dà yuē 大約／大约 A
above-mentioned gāi 該／该 PR
abundant fēngfù 豐富／丰富 SV
accept cǎinà 採納／采纳; jiēshōu 接收 V
accompany péi; péibàn 陪; 陪伴 V
account number ***(of a bank, store, etc.)*** zhànghào 帳號／帐号 N
accountant kuàijì 會計／会计 N
accumulate merit by good works jīdé 積德／积德 VO
accustomed: be accustomed/used to xíguàn 習慣／习惯 V
achieve huòdé 獲得／获得 V
acquaintance shúrén (shóurén) 熟人 N
acquire huòdé 獲得／获得 V
act biǎoyǎn 表演 V; chūyǎn 出演 VO
active jījí 積極／积极 SV
actor; actress yǎnyuán 演員／演员 N
actually cái 才 A
adapt ***(as a movie)*** fānpāi 翻拍 V
add fàng jìnqu 放進去／放进去 RV
administration guǎnlǐ 管理 N
admire xiànmù 羨慕／羡慕 V
adopt ***(suggestions, etc.)*** cǎinà 採納／采纳 V
advantage yōudiǎn 優點／优点 N
adversary duìfāng 對方／对方 N
advice: give advice and help zhǐdǎo bāngzhù 指導幫助／指导帮助 IE
advice: seek advice qǐngjiào 請教／请教 IE
again; anew; afresh chóngxīn 重新 A
agent jīngjìrén 經紀人／经纪人 N
age-old yōujiǔ 悠久 SV
aggressive pōlà 潑辣／泼辣 SV
agree on shuōdìng 說定／说定 V/RV
agreement hétong 合同 N
air kōngqì 空氣／空气 N
alike: be alike/identical xiāngtóng 相同 V; **be exactly alike** yīmóyīyàng 一模一樣／一模一样 IE
allow yǔnxǔ 允許／允许 V
almost chāyidiǎn 差一點／差一点 A
alter xiūgǎi 修改 V
alternative xuǎnzé 選擇／选择 N
alumnus; alumni xiàoyǒu 校友 N
always; all along yìzhí 一直 A
ambition bàofù 抱負／抱负 N
amend xiūgǎi 修改 V
amiable suíhé 隨和／随和 SV
amicable yǒushàn 友善 SV
amusement yúlè 娛樂／娱乐 N
anchor zhǔchírén 主持人 N
ancient times gǔdài 古代 N
and such/and the like zhī lèi 之類／之类 S
and/together with ***(used only in written Chinese)*** yǔ 與／与 C
announce fābù 發布／发布 V
answer dáfù 答覆／答复 V
answer questions dáyí 答疑 VO
apartment building gōngyùlóu 公寓樓／公寓楼 N
apply shǐyòng 使用 V
apprentice tú 徒 BF
approve of zàntóng 贊同／赞同 V
approximately yuē 約／约 *(written style for* 大約／大约 dà yuē*)* A
archery shèjiàn 射箭 N
architecture jiànzhù 建築／建筑 N
arrive: have just arrived xīn dào 新到 V
arrive at dǐdá 抵達／抵达 V
as follows rúxià 如下 IE
as if ruò 若 A
Asiatic wormwood leaves àicǎo 艾草 N
aspiration bàofù 抱負／抱负 N
assessment pínggū; píngjià 評估／评估; 評價／评价 N
assiduous qínfèn 勤奮／勤奋 SV
astronomy tiānwénxué 天文學／天文学 N
at last dàodǐ 到底 A
atmosphere kōngqì 空氣／空气 N
attendant fúwùyuán 服務員／服务员 N
attention: pay attention to zhùzhòng 注重 V
attract xīyǐn 吸引 V
attract into zhāojìnlai 招進來／招进来 RV
audience guānzhòng 觀眾／观众 N
audition miànshì 面試／面试 VO/V
Austen, Jane Jiǎn Àosīdīng 簡•奧斯丁／简•奥斯丁 N
authentic zhēnshí 真實／真实 SV
automatically zìrán'érrán 自然而然 IE
aware: become aware of gǎnjué 感覺／感觉 V

B

background; backdrop bèijǐng 背景 N
backyard hòuyuàn 後院／后院 N
badminton yǔmáoqiú 羽毛球 N
bad-tempered píqi huài 脾氣壞／脾气坏 VP; pōlà 潑辣／泼辣 SV

bake kǎo 烤 V
balcony yángtái 陽台／阳台 N
bamboo leaves zòngyè 粽葉／粽叶 N
banking jīnróng 金融 N
banquet dàcān 大餐 N
baseball bàngqiú 棒球 N
basic jīběn 基本 SV/N
basket lánkuāng 籃筐／篮筐 N
basketball lánqiú 籃球／篮球 N
bathtub yùgāng 浴缸 N
bazaar shìchǎng 市場／市场 N
bear and raise children shēng'éryùnǚ 生兒育女／生儿育女 IE
beautician měiróngshī 美容師／美容师 N
beauty: beautiful woman měinǚ 美女 N
bedbug chòuchóng 臭蟲／臭虫 N
bedroom: main/master bedroom zhǔwò 主臥／主卧 N
bedroom: second/secondary bedroom cìwò 次臥／次卧 N
beginner càiniǎo 菜鳥／菜鸟 N
belief xìnyǎng 信仰 N
belong to shǔyú 屬於／属于 V
belonging to somebody; under one's own name/account míngxià 名下 N
benefits fúlì 福利 N
besides cǐwài 此外 C
bicycle: ride a bicycle qí chē 騎車／骑车 VO
birth: one's birth data for astrological/marriage purposes shēngchénbāzì 生辰八字 IE
bland dàn 淡 SV
bless and protect bǎoyòu 保佑 V
blessing fú 福 N
blind date xiāngqīn 相親／相亲 VP
block dǎng 擋／挡 V
blood relation qīn 親／亲 N
boast fúkuā 浮誇／浮夸 V
boil zhǔ 煮 V
bookkeeper kuàijì 會計／会计 N
bookworm shūchóng 書蟲／书虫 N
both (of us) can enjoy hé xiǎng 合享 VP
both sexes liǎngxìng 兩性／两性 N
both sides; two parties shuāngfāng 雙方／双方 N
boundary xiàn 線／线 N
boxing quánjī 拳擊／拳击 N
box office piàofáng 票房 N
brand páizi 牌子 N
Brazil Bāxī 巴西 PW
brief duǎnxiǎo 短小 VP
brilliant jīngcǎi 精彩 SV
broad bódà 博大 VP
broadcast bōchū 播出 RV
broker zhōngjiè 中介 N
browse guàng 逛 V
Buddha Fó 佛 N
Buddhism Fójiào 佛教 N
Buddhist *(person)* Fójiàotú 佛教徒 N
build jiànzhù 建築／建筑 V
building of two or more stories lóufáng 樓房／楼房 N
bundle bāoguǒ 包裹 V
burn coal shāoméi 燒煤／烧煤 VO
burn incense sticks shāoxiāng 燒香／烧香 VO
bus: communter bus gōngjiāochē 公交車／公交车 N
bus: monthly bus pass yuèpiào 月票 N
bus stop gōnggòng qìchēzhàn 公共汽車站／公共汽车站 N
business; business affairs shāngwù 商務／商务 N
business staff yíngyèyuán 營業員／营业员 N
busy: be busy/swamped mánghuo 忙活 VO
buy gòumǎi 購買／购买 V

C

calendar: lunar calendar nónglì 農曆／农历 N
calisthenics tǐcāo 體操／体操 N
camcorder shèxiàngjī 攝像機／摄像机 N
campus xiàoyuán 校園／校园 PW
can kě 可 *(written style for* 可以 kěyǐ*)* AV
candy tángguǒ 糖果 N
capable lìhai 厲害／厉害 SV
capital dū 都 BF
card *(credit card, membership card, etc.)* kǎ 卡 N
care for zhàogu 照顧／照顾 V
careless cūxīn 粗心 SV; dàyì 大意 VP; cūxīndàyì 粗心大意 IE
carelessness cūxīn 粗心 N
carry káng 扛 V
cartoons; comics dòngmàn 動漫／动漫 N
cash flow xiànjīn liú 現金流／现金流 N
cashier shōuyínyuán 收銀員／收银员 N
casual dàdaliēliē 大大咧咧 RF
catch *(something thrown)* jiēzhù 接住 RV
category lèi 類／类; lèixíng 類型／类型 N
Catholic *(person)* Tiānzhǔjiàotú 天主教徒 N
Catholicism Tiānzhǔjiào 天主教 N
cautious jǐnshèn 謹慎／谨慎 SV
celebrate a festival/holiday guòjié 過節／过节 VO
celebrity míngxīng 明星 N
CEO zǒngcái 總裁／总裁 N
cereals wǔgǔ 五穀／五谷 N
certain: be certain, confirm quèdìng 確定／确定 V
challenge tiǎozhàn 挑戰／挑战 N
channel tái 台 N
character rénwù 人物 N
characteristic tèdiǎn; tèzhēng 特點／特点; 特徵／特征 N
charge; cost fèi 費／费 BF/S
chase zhuī 追 V

chat liáo 聊 V
chauffeur sījī 司機／司机 N
check in ***(at a hotel, etc.)*** dēngjì 登記／登记 V
Cheers! Bottoms up! gānbēi 乾杯／干杯 IE
chef chúshī 廚師／厨师 N
China expert Zhōngguótōng 中國通／中国通 N
chocolate qiǎokèlì 巧克力 N/PL
choose xuǎnzé 選擇／选择 V
christen qǔ míng 取名 VO
Christian ***(person)*** Jīdūjiàotú 基督教徒 N
Christianity Jīdūjiào 基督教 N
church; cathedral jiàotáng 教堂 N
church: go to church; attend religious service zuò lǐbài 做禮拜／做礼拜 VO
cinema diànyǐngyuàn 電影院／电影院 N
circle quān 圈 N
circles jiè 界 BF
clarify matters dáyí 答疑 VO
classical gǔdiǎn 古典 ATTR
classical style of writing wényánwén 文言文 N
classics jīngdiǎn 經典／经典 N
clean and hygienic gānjìng wèishēng 乾淨衛生／干净卫生 VP
clerk wényuán 文員／文员 N
clever guāi 乖 SV
click ***(a keyboard)*** diǎnjī 點擊／点击 V
click rate diǎnjīliàng 點擊量／点击量 N
climb the Great Wall pá Chángchéng 爬長城／爬长城 VP
clique quānzi 圈子 N
coach jiàoliàn 教練／教练 N
collect sōu 搜 V
combination jiéhé 結合／结合 N
come/originate from láizì 來自／来自 VP
commemorate jìniàn 紀念／纪念 V
common people; civilians lǎobǎixìng 老百姓 N
communicate gōutōng 溝通／沟通 RV
communication jiāoliú 交流 N
commuter bus gōngjiāochē 公交車／公交车 N
companion bànlǚ 伴侶／伴侣 N
company: keep someone company péi; péibàn 陪；陪伴 V
compare duìzhào 對照／对照 V
compete sài 賽／赛; jìngzhēng 競爭／竞争 V
competent shèngrèn 勝任／胜任 V
competition bǐsài 比賽／比赛; jìngzhēng 競爭／竞争 N
compile biānjí 編輯／编辑 V
complete qíquán 齊全／齐全; wánshàn 完善 SV
complex fùzá 複雜／复杂 SV
complicated fùzá 複雜／复杂 SV
comprehend liǎojiě 了解 V
comprehensive zōnghé 綜合／综合 ATTR
concentrated nóng 濃／浓 SV
concerning yǒuguān 有關／有关 VO
condition dìbù 地步; tiáojiàn 條件／条件; zhuàngkuàng 狀況／状况 N
conduct bànlǐ 辦理／办理 V
confident zìxìn 自信 V
congratulations gōngxǐ 恭喜 N/IE
consider kǎolǜ 考慮／考虑 V
consider as dàngchéng 當成／当成 VP
constantly jīngcháng 經常／经常 A
construct jiànzhù 建築／建筑 V
continuous liánxù 連續／连续 ATTR
contract hétong 合同 N
contrast duìzhào 對照／对照 V
conversely fǎnguòlai 反過來／反过来 RV
convincing yǒu dàolǐ 有道理 SV/VO
cook chúshī 廚師／厨师 N; zhǔ 煮 V
copy: make a copy for; send a duplicate to chāosòng 抄送 V
cordial qīnqiè 親切／亲切 SV
corpse shītǐ 屍體／尸体 N
cost; charge fèi 費／费 BF/S
cost (net) chéngběn 成本 N
courier kuàidìyuán 快遞員／快递员 N
cover (of a publication) fēngmiàn 封面 N
crime investigation show xíngzhēnjù 刑偵劇／刑侦剧 N
criminal zuìfàn 罪犯 N
cross tiàoguò 跳過／跳过 RV
cultivate péixùn 培訓／培训 V
curriculum vitae jiǎnlì 簡歷／简历 N
custom xísú 習俗／习俗 N
customer service kèfú 客服 N

D

Daoism Dàojiào 道教 N
deadline qīxiàn 期限 N
defect quēdiǎn 缺點／缺点 N
defensive player fángshǒuqiúyuán 防守球員／防守球员 N
demand yāoqiú 要求 N/V
demonstrate biǎoyǎn 表演 V
dense nóng 濃／浓 SV
deny fǒudìng 否定; fǒurèn 否認／否认 V
depend on kào 靠 V
dependable shízài 實在／实在 SV
design shèjì 設計／设计 N/V
developed fādá 發達／发达 SV
dialect fāngyán 方言 N
difference; distinction qūbié 區別／区别 N
differentiate qūbié 區別／区别 V
difficulty kùnnán 困難／困难 N
difficulty (degree of) nándù 難度／难度 N
digest: help to digest xiāoshí 消食 VO

diligent qínfèn 勤奮／勤奋 SV
direct *(a film)* zhídǎo 執導／执导 V
directly zhíjiē 直接 A
director *(of plays, films)* dǎoyǎn 導演／导演 N
disadvantage quēdiǎn 缺點／缺点 N
disciple tú 徒 BF
dishwasher xǐwǎnjī 洗碗機／洗碗机 N
disposition píqi 脾氣／脾气; xìnggé 性格 N
disseminate bōchū 播出 RV; chuánbō(kāi) 傳播(開)／传播(开) V
distinguishing feature/quality tèsè 特色 N/SV
district qū 區／区 N
disturb dǎrǎo 打擾／打扰 V
divide fēn 分 V
diving tiàoshuǐ 跳水 N
do V1 and V2 simultaneously biān V1 biān V2 邊V1邊V2／边V1边V2 C
documentary jìlùpiān 紀錄片／纪录片 N
dominion tiānxià 天下 N
door: on a door ménshang 門上／门上 PW
double bed shuāngrén chuáng 雙人床／双人床 N
download xià 下 V
dragon boat lóngzhōu 龍舟／龙舟 N
Dragon Boat Festival Duānwǔjié 端午節／端午节 N
drama jù 劇／剧 N
Dream of the Red Chamber Hóng Lóu Mèng 紅樓夢／红楼梦 N
driver sījī 司機／司机 N
drugstore yàodiàn 藥店／药店 N
dry cleaners gānxǐdiàn 乾洗店／干洗店 N
dumpling shuǐjiǎo 水餃／水饺; jiǎozi 餃子／饺子 N

E

each gè 各 PR
each different gè yì 各異／各异 VP
each (of us) gèzì 各自 PR
each other bǐcǐ 彼此; hùxiāng 互相 A
earn zhuàn 賺／赚 V
earth; the whole world huánqiú 環球／环球 N
economics jīngjìxué 經濟學／经济学 N
economy jīngjì 經濟／经济 N
edit biānjí 編輯／编辑 V
editor biānjí 編輯／编辑 N
educate jiàoyù 教育 V
education jiàoyù 教育 N
education: record of formal schooling; educational background xuélì 學歷／学历 N
elementary jīběn 基本 SV/N
elevate tíshēng 提升 RV
elevator diàntī 電梯／电梯 N
elicit blessings zhāofú 招福 VO
emphasis zhòngdiǎn 重點／重点 N
encounter pèngshang 碰上 RV
encyclopedia bǎikē 百科 N
endorse zàntóng 贊同／赞同 V
energetic jījí 積極／积极 SV
engineering gōngchéng 工程 N
enrich fēngfù 豐富／丰富 V
entertainment yúlè 娛樂／娱乐 N
entire world quán shìjiè 全世界 N
enumerate luóliè 羅列／罗列 V
environment huánjìng 環境／环境 N
envy xiànmù 羨慕／羡慕 V
equestrian arts mǎshù 馬術／马术 N
equitable hélǐ 合理 SV
equivalent: be equivalent xiāngtóng 相同 V
erratic fēngfengdiāndiān 瘋瘋癲癲／疯疯癫癫 RF
especially tè 特 A; yóuqíshì 尤其是 VP
evaluate pínggū; píngjià 評估／评估; 評價／评价 V
even píng 平 SV
even (to the point of) shènzhì 甚至 C
evening wǎnjiān 晚間／晚间 N
everybody gèwèi 各位 N
everyone dàhuǒr 大夥兒／大伙儿 N
everywhere dàochù (dōu) 到處(都)／到处(都) A
evil; evil force xié'è 邪惡／邪恶 SV/N
exaggerate fúkuā 浮誇／浮夸 V
example: for example bǐrú shuō 比如說／比如说 VP; lìrú 例如 C
excellent jīngcǎi 精彩 SV
exclusive dújiā 獨家／独家 ATTR
exercise: engage in physical exercise duànliàn 鍛煉／锻炼 V
exhaust hood chōuyóuyānjī 抽油煙機／抽油烟机 N
exhibition biǎoyǎn 表演 N
expand; extend kuòzhǎn 擴展／扩展 V
expansion kuòzhǎn 擴展／扩展 N
expel; get rid of qūzhú 驅逐／驱逐 V
expel evil qūxié 驅邪／驱邪 VO
experience jīnglì 經歷／经历; jīngyàn 經驗／经验 N
exquisite jīngzhàn 精湛 SV
extensive bódà 博大 VP
exterior wàibiǎo 外表 N
extreme guòhuǒ 過火／过火 SV
extremely wànfēn 萬分／万分 A
extroverted wàixiàng 外向 SV
eyes: fix one's eyes on; gaze/stare at dīngzhe 盯著／盯着 V

F

face: shape of one's face liǎnxíng 臉形／脸形 N
face south with back to north zuòběicháonán 坐北朝南 IE
facilities shèshī 設施／设施 N
fall behind tuìbù 退步 V
familiar-looking miànshóu (miànshú) 面熟 SV

family: each and every family jiājiāhùhù 家家戶戶／家家户户 RF
fan fěnsī 粉絲／粉丝 N
fantasy huànxiǎng 幻想 N/V
far: as far as I'm concerned duì wǒ lái shuō 對我來說／对我来说 VP
fascinate xīyǐn 吸引 V
favor: please do me a favor and . . . qǐng yǒuláo 請有勞／请有劳 IE
fear: be afraid/scared hàipà 害怕 V
feast dàcān 大餐 N
feathercock yǔmáoqiú 羽毛球 N
feed wèi 餵／喂 V
feel gǎnjué 感覺／感觉 V
feeling gǎnjué 感覺／感觉 N
feelings qíng 情 N
fencing *(sport)* jījiàn 擊劍／击剑 N
festival jiérì 節日／节日 N
field hockey qūgùnqiú 曲棍球 N
fierce jīliè 激烈 SV
figure *(physical build)* shēnxíng 身形 N
figure and appearance tǐmào 體貌／体貌 N
finally dàodǐ 到底 A
finance jīnróng 金融 N
fine bàng 棒 SV
fire station xiāofángzhàn 消防站 N
first shǒuxiān 首先 A
first: for the first time chūcì 初次 A
flat píng 平 SV
flavor wèi 味 N
flighty fēngfengdiāndiān 瘋瘋癲癲／疯疯癫癫 RF
flourishing fādá 發達／发达 SV
follows: as follows rúxià 如下 IE
food: gourmet/delicious food měishí 美食 N
foot care zúliáo bǎojiàn 足療保健／足疗保健 N
football: American football Měishì zúqiú 美式足球 N
footwork/kicking skill *(in soccer)* jiǎofǎ 腳法／脚法 N
for; to wèi 為／为 CV
for example; for instance bǐrú shuō 比如說／比如说 VP; lìrú 例如 C
fortune: good fortune; blessing; happiness fú 福 N
forward *(a message, etc.)* zhuǎnfā 轉發／转发 V
four great classical novels (of Chinese literature) sì dà míngzhù 四大名著 N
free: be free of charge miǎnfèi 免費／免费 VO
freelance profession zìyóu zhíyè 自由職業／自由职业 N
French window luòdìchuāng(hu) 落地窗(戶)／落地窗(户) N
frequently jīngcháng 經常／经常 A
friendly yǒushàn 友善 SV
front desk jiēdài 接待 N
front yard qiányuàn 前院 N
fundamental jīběn 基本 SV/N
funny gǎoxiào 搞笑 SV
future wèilái 未來／未来 N

G

gain zhuàn 賺／赚 V
garage chēkù 車庫／车库 N
gas range/stove méiqìzào 煤氣灶／煤气灶 N
gas station jiāyóuzhàn 加油站 N
gather sōu 搜 V
generally yìbān 一般 A
generally speaking yìbānláishuō 一般來說／一般来说 VP
genial qīnqiè 親切／亲切 SV
genre lèixíng 類型／类型 N
gentle and soft wēnróu 温柔 SV
gentleman jūnzǐ 君子 N
genuine zhēnchéng 真誠／真诚 SV
get along well tándelái 談得來／谈得来 RV
get in the way of dǎng 擋／挡 V
get together tuánjù (zài yìqǐ) 團聚(在一起)／团聚(在一起) V
girl: young girl/lady xiǎo gūniang 小姑娘 N
glutinous rice dumplings (served in soup) tāngyuánr 湯圓兒／汤圆儿 N
go: be going to jiāngyào 將要／将要 AV
go to shàng 上 V
go to *(written style)* fù 赴 V
goal mùbiāo 目標／目标; qiúmén 球門／球门 N
goalie; goalkeeper shǒuményuán 守門員／守门员 N
God *(in Catholicism)* Tiānzhǔ 天主 N
gold medal jīnpái 金牌 N
golf gāo'ěrfūqiú 高爾夫球／高尔夫球 N/PL
good bàng 棒 SV
good: be a good person zuò hǎorén 做好人 VP
good: do good works xíngshàn 行善 VO
good: he/she is a good person (tā) rén hǎo (他／她)人好 PH
good-tempered píqi hǎo 脾氣好／脾气好 VP
gossip bāguà 八卦 N
government employee gōngwùyuán 公務員／公务员 N
graceful and restrained wǎnyuē 婉約／婉约 ATTR
grade fēnshù 分數／分数 N
grains wǔgǔ 五穀／五谷 N
grammar yǔfǎ 語法／语法 N
graphic design měishù shèjì 美術設計／美术设计 N
graphic novels dòngmàn 動漫／动漫 N
great bàng 棒 SV
great deal of *(written style)* zhūduō 諸多／诸多 ATTR
green: make a place green lǜhuà 綠化／绿化 V
greening; greenification lǜhuà 綠化／绿化 N
greet: say hello to; greet (somebody) dǎ zhāohu 打招呼 VO

group zǔ 組／组 N
group/mass/multiple mailing qúnfā 群發／群发 V
grow zhǎng 長／长 V
grow up chéngzhǎng 成長／成长 V
guidance zhǐdǎo 指導／指导 N
gymnastics tǐcāo 體操／体操 N

H

habit xíguàn 習慣／习惯 N
hairdresser; hair stylist fàxíngshī 髮型師／发型师 N
hall dàtáng 大堂 N
Halloween Wànshèngjié 萬聖節／万圣节 N
handle bànlǐ 辦理／办理 V
happen fāshēng 發生／发生 V
happiness xìngfú 幸福; fú 福 N
happy xìngfú 幸福 SV
happy: feel happy kāixīn 開心／开心 V
Hawaii Xiàwēiyí 夏威夷 PW
headstrong rènxìng 任性 SV
healthcare provisions wèishēng bǎojiàn 衛生保健／卫生保健 N
heart: in one's heart/mind xīnmù zhōng 心目中 N
Heaven: go to Heaven shàng tiān(táng) 上天(堂) VO
height *(of a person)* shēngāo 身高 N
heterosexual; heterosexuality yìxìngliàn 異性戀／异性恋 N
high-rise gāocéng 高層／高层 ATTR
hire zūlìn 租賃／租赁 V
hobby/hobbies àihào 愛好／爱好 N
holiday jiérì 節日／节日 N
Hollywood Hǎoláiwū 好萊塢／好莱坞 PW
home jiājū 家居 N
home page shǒuyè 首頁／首页 N
homosexual; homosexuality tóngxìngliàn 同性戀／同性恋 N
honest lǎoshi 老實／老实; shízài 實在／实在 SV
Honolulu Huǒnúlǔlǔ 火奴魯魯／火奴鲁鲁 PW
hope/long for pànwàng 盼望 V
hopeful lèguān 樂觀／乐观 SV
horsemanship mǎshù 馬術／马术 N
hospital yīyuàn 醫院／医院 N
host zhǔchírén 主持人 N
hot water heater rèshuǐqì 熱水器／热水器 N
house: single-story house píngfáng 平房 N
housing zhùfáng 住房 N
husband lǎogōng 老公 N
hypocritical xūwěi 虛偽／虚伪 SV

I

idea: general idea dàgài 大概 N
ideal lǐxiǎng 理想 N/SV
identical to/very similar to *X* xiàng X yíyàng 像X一樣／像X一样 PH
idol ǒuxiàng 偶像 N
if . . . rúguǒ . . . de huà 如果……的話／如果……的话 C
if: as if ruò 若 A
illiteracy wénmáng 文盲 N
illness: serious illness bìngmó 病魔 N
illusion huànxiǎng 幻想 N/V
image túpiàn 圖片／图片; xíngxiàng 形象 N
impression yìnxiàng 印象 N
in addition cǐwài 此外 C
include fàng jìnqu 放進去／放进去 RV
include: be included; including zài nèi 在內 VO
increase zhǎng 長／长 V
independence dúlì 獨立／独立 N
independent dúlì 獨立／独立 SV
independently dúlì 獨立／独立 A
information xìnxī 信息 N
information technology xìnxī jìshù 信息技術／信息技术 N
inquire *(formally)* xúnwèn 詢問／询问 V
insincere xūwěi 虛偽／虚伪 SV
insist on jiānchí 堅持／坚持 V
instance: for instance bǐrú shuō 比如說／比如说 VP; lìrú 例如 C
instructor jiàoliàn 教練／教练 N
insurance bǎoxiǎn 保險／保险 N
insure; be insured bǎoxiǎn 保險／保险 V
intense jīliè 激烈; nóng 濃／浓 SV
interests àihào 愛好／爱好 N
intermediary zhōngjiè 中介 N
intern shíxí 實習／实习 N/V
Internet: go on (the Internet) shàng(wǎng) 上(網)／上(网) V
interrogation wèndá 問答／问答 N/V
interview cǎifǎng 採訪／采访 V; miànshì 面試／面试 VO/V
introduction jiǎnjiè 簡介／简介 N
introverted nèixiàng 內向／内向 SV
investigate diàochá 調查／调查 N/V
invite: respectfully invite jìng qǐng 敬請／敬请 V
invite applications for a job zhāopìn 招聘 N
involve shèjí 涉及 V
Islam Yīsīlánjiào 伊斯蘭教／伊斯兰教 N/PL

J

janitor bǎojié 保潔／保洁 N
Jesus Christ Jīdū 基督 N
jog: go jogging mànpǎo 慢跑 N/V
journal zázhì 雜誌／杂志 N
Journey to the West Xī Yóu Jì 西遊記／西游记 N
Judaism Yóutàijiào 猶太教／犹太教 N
judo róudào 柔道 N
jump over tiàoguò 跳過／跳过 RV

K

kick back ***(in soccer, etc.)*** tīhuíqu 踢回去 RV
kick into tī jìn 踢進／踢进 RV
kitchen ventilator chōuyóuyānjī 抽油煙機／抽油烟机 N
knight in shining armor; prince on a white horse báimǎ wángzǐ 白馬王子／白马王子
know: be known to all jìnrénjiēzhī 盡人皆知／尽人皆知 IE
know something/somebody well shúxī (*also pronounced* shóuxi) 熟悉 SV/V
knowledge zhīshi 知識／知识 N

L

labor: division of labor fēngōng 分工 N
landlord fángdōng 房東／房东 N
lane or alley hútòng 胡同 N
language: spoken/vernacular language kǒuyǔ 口語／口语 N
large pile yí dà duī 一大堆 N
large potful yí dà guō 一大鍋／一大锅 N
last: at last dàodǐ 到底 A
law fǎlǜ 法律 N
lay a foundation dǎ jīchǔ 打基礎／打基础 VO
lazy lǎnduò 懶惰／懒惰 SV
lease zūlìn 租賃／租赁 V
legend chuánshuō 傳說／传说 N
letter of recommendation tuījiànxìn 推薦信／推荐信 N
level píng 平 SV
library túshūguǎn 圖書館／图书馆 N
life (human) rénshēng 人生 N
life experiences rénshēng jiǎnlì 人生簡歷／人生简历 N
like: be like rú 如 V
limit: set a limit xiàn 限 V
link up with; get in touch with liánxì 聯繫／联系 V
liqueur lǐ 醴 N
list liè(shàngqu) 列(上去) RV
live: live in separate locations; live apart fēnjū liǎngdì 分居兩地／分居两地 IE
lively huópō 活潑／活泼 SV
lobby dàtáng 大堂 N
locality dāngdì 當地／当地 N
location: geographical location dìlǐ wèizhi 地理位置 N
London Lúndūn 倫敦／伦敦 PW
lonely; lonesome gūdú 孤獨／孤独 SV
long for kěwàng 渴望 V
long-standing yōujiǔ 悠久 SV
look after zhàogu 照顧／照顾 V
look forward to pànwàng 盼望 V
lots of ***(written style)*** zhūduō 諸多／诸多 ATTR
love: feelings about love; perspectives about love liàn'àiguān 戀愛觀／恋爱观 N
love each other xiāng'ài 相愛／相爱 V
lower: not lower than bù dī yú 不低於／不低于 VP

M

magazine zázhì 雜誌／杂志 N
mail yóujiàn 郵件／邮件 N
mail: sender of mail; From: ***(e-mail header)*** fājiànrén 發件人／发件人 N
mailing: group/mass/multiple mailing qúnfā 群發／群发 V
major part dàbùfen 大部分 N
make an itinerant living chuǎngdàng 闖蕩／闯荡 V
manage guǎnlǐ 管理 V
manage: cannot manage/attend to gùbushàng 顧不上／顾不上 RV
management guǎnlǐ 管理 N
manager: store manager màichǎng jīnglǐ 賣場經理／卖场经理; diànzhǎng 店長／店长 N
market; marketplace shìchǎng 市場／市场 N
marketing xiāoshòu 銷售／销售; yíngxiāo 營銷／营销 N
marriage hūnjià 婚嫁 N
martial arts wǔshù 武術／武术 N
Mass: go to (Catholic) Mass zuò mísa 做彌撒／做弥撒 VO
massage ànmó 按摩 N/V
massage therapy tuīná 推拿 N
match bǐsài 比賽／比赛 N
match: be able to match pèideshàng 配得上 RV
match: be well-matched in social and economic status ***(for marriage)*** méndānghùduì 門當戶對／门当户对 IE
matchmaker méiren 媒人 N
material wùzhì 物質／物质 N
matter wùzhì 物質／物质 N
mature chéngzhǎng 成長／成长 V
may kě 可 *(written style for* 可以 *kěyǐ)* AV
me; myself běnrén 本人 N
meaning: have meaning yǒuyìyì 有意義／有意义 V/VO
media méitǐ 媒體／媒体; chuánméi 傳媒／传媒 N
medical care yīliáo bǎojiàn 醫療保健／医疗保健 N
meditation míngxiǎng 冥想 N/V
meet/discover by chance zhuàngjiàn 撞見／撞见 V
membership (system) huìyuánzhì 會員制／会员制 N
memories huíyì 回憶／回忆 N
message: leave a message liúyán 留言 VO
messenger kuàidìyuán 快遞員／快递员 N
method fāngshì 方式 N
metropolis dū 都 BF
microwave oven wēibōlú 微波爐／微波炉 N
middleman jīngjìrén 經紀人／经纪人 N
miss xiǎng 想 V

model ǒuxiàng 偶像 N
modify xiūgǎi 修改 V
moment huìr 會兒／会儿 N
moreover cǐwài 此外 C
mosque qīngzhēnsì 清真寺 N
move: movement; motion; moves dòngzuò 動作／动作 N
movie theater diànyǐngyuàn 電影院／电影院 N
Muslim Mùsīlín 穆斯林 N/PL
mutton yángròu 羊肉 N
mutton kebab yángròuchuàn 羊肉串 N
mutually hùxiāng 互相 A

N

name qǔ míng 取名 VO
namely jí 即 A
narrate jiǎngshù 講述／讲述 V
natural resources zīyuán 資源／资源 N
naturally zìrán'érrán 自然而然 IE
negate fǒudìng 否定 V
negative side; negative fùmiàn 負面／负面 N
negligent cūxīndàyì 粗心大意 IE
netizens wǎngyǒu 網友／网友 N
new edition/version xīnbǎn 新版 N
new student xīnshēng 新生 N
news xīnwén 新聞／新闻; xìnxī 信息 N
news: cover; gather news cǎifǎng 採訪／采访 V
normally tōngcháng 通常 A
nose bízi 鼻子 N
nose: high-/long-nosed gāo bízi 高鼻子 N
novels: four great classical novels (of Chinese literature) sì dà míngzhù 四大名著 N
number: *(a number)* to be divided by chúyǐ 除以 VP

O

objective mùbiāo 目標／目标 N
obstinate gùzhi 固執／固执 SV
occasionally ǒu'ěr 偶爾／偶尔 A
occupation zhíyè 職業／职业 N
occur fāshēng 發生／发生 V
offensive player jìngōngqiúyuán 進攻球員／进攻球员 N
office worker wényuán 文員／文员 N
often jīngcháng 經常／经常 A
Olympic Games Àoyùnhuì 奥運會／奥运会 (*abbr. for* Àolínpǐkè Yùndònghuì 奥林匹克運動會／奥林匹克运动会) N
one another bǐcǐ 彼此 A
oneself běnrén 本人 N
online: be online zàixiàn 在線／在线 VO
open-minded kāilǎng 開朗／开朗 SV
optimistic kāilǎng 開朗／开朗; lèguān 樂觀／乐观 SV
ordinarily yìbān 一般 A
ordinary worker pǔgōng 普工 N
organize zǔzhī 組織／组织 V
orientation cháoxiàng 朝向 N
origin fāyuán 發源／发源 N
original yuánshǐ 原始 SV
original work yuánzhù 原著 N
originate fāyuán 發源／发源 V
other(s) qítā 其他 PR
outline dàgāng 大綱／大纲 N
overtime *(in sports)* jiāshí 加時／加时 N
own yōngyǒu 擁有／拥有 V

P

pack/ready one's baggage shōushi xíngli 收拾行李 VP
package bāoguǒ 包裹 N
palm leaves zòngyè 粽葉／粽叶 N
park gōngyuán 公園／公园 N
parking space/place tíngchēwèi 停車位／停车位 N
part: be loathe to part with shěbude 捨不得／舍不得 RV
partner bànlǚ 伴侶／伴侣 N
pass on zhuǎn 轉／转 V
paste/glue/stick to tiē 貼／贴 V
patriotic àiguó 愛國／爱国 SV
pattern shì 式 BF; xíngtài 形態／形态 N
peaceful píng'ān 平安 SV
peanut: shelled peanut huāshēngmǐ 花生米 N
penetrating jīngshēn 精深 VP
perfect wánměi; wánshàn 完美; 完善 SV
perform yǎn 演; biǎoyǎn 表演 V
perform in a traditional opera chàngxì 唱戲／唱戏 VO
performance biǎoyǎn 表演 N
performer yǎnyuán 演員／演员 N
periodical zázhì 雜誌／杂志 N
permit yǔnxǔ 允許／允许 V
person: base/mean person; person of low standards xiǎorén 小人 N
person: single person dānrén 單人／单人 N
personal gèrén 個人／个人 N/ATTR
personally qīnyǎn 親眼／亲眼 A
photo: take a photo together hé zhāng zhào 合張照／合张照 VP
photograph túpiàn 圖片／图片 N
photography shèyǐng 攝影／摄影 N
physical education/training tǐyù 體育／体育 N
picture túpiàn 圖片／图片 N
plan shèjì 設計／设计 N/V
play jù 劇／剧 N
play games wán yóuxì 玩遊戲／玩游戏 VP
player qiúyuán 球員／球员 N
pleasant gān 甘 SV
pleased mǎnyì 満意／满意 SV
plentiful fēngfù 豐富／丰富 SV

poet shīrén 詩人／诗人 N
point: key/focal point zhòngdiǎn 重點／重点 N
police station jǐngchájú 警察局 N
policy zhèngcè 政策 N
politics; political affairs zhèngzhì 政治 N
pompous: be pompous fúkuā 浮誇／浮夸 V
popular huǒ 火; rè 熱／热 SV
popular: explosively popular huǒbào 火爆 SV
portray chūyǎn 出演 VO
position dìwèi 地位 N
positive jījí 積極／积极; kěndìng 肯定 SV
positive side zhèngmiàn 正面 N
possess yōngyǒu 擁有／拥有 V
possible: Is it possible that . . . ? nándào 難道／难道 VP
post office yóujú 郵局／邮局 N
pour dào 倒 V
pour tea dàochá 倒茶 VO
powerful qiáng 強／强 SV
practical; pragmatic xiànshí 現實／现实 SV
practice shíxí 實習／实习 N/V
pray dǎogào 禱告／祷告 V
pregnant: be pregnant huáiyùn 懷孕／怀孕 VO
present to the public; come on the market tuīchū 推出 RV
president zǒngcái 總裁／总裁 N
press *(a keyboard)* diǎnjī 點擊／点击 V
Pride and Prejudice Àomàn yǔ piānjiàn 傲慢與偏見／傲慢与偏见 N
principle yuánzé 原則／原则 N
privilege quánlì 權利／权利 N
prize medal jiǎngpái 獎牌／奖牌 N
probably dàgài 大概 A
problem kùnnán 困難／困难 N
produce zhìzuò 製作／制作 V
profession zhíyè 職業／职业 N
professional zhíyè 職業／职业 ATTR
professionals; personnel in a specific field zhuānyè rénshì 專業人士／专业人士 N
profit: make a profit zhuàn 賺／赚 V
profound jīngshēn 精深 VP
program jiémù 節目／节目 N
project jìhuà 計劃／计划 N/V
promote tíshēng 提升 RV
pronounce fāyīn 發音／发音 V
pronunciation fāyīn 發音／发音 N
propagate chuánbō(kāi) 傳播(開)／传播(开) V
prudent jǐnshèn 謹慎／谨慎 SV
public parking gōnggòng tíngchēchǎng 公共停車場／公共停车场 N
publisher; publishing house; press chūbǎnshè 出版社 N
purchase gòumǎi 購買／购买; **purchase *(durable goods)*** gòuzhì 購置／购置 V
pursue zhuī 追 V
put up guà 掛／挂 V

Q

Qing Dynasty (1644–1911) Qīngcháo 清朝 N
qualify: be qualified for shèngrèn 勝任／胜任 V
quality: high/top quality yōuzhì 優質／优质 ATTR
quality of someone's character rénpǐn 人品 N
questionnaire wènjuàn 問卷／问卷 N

R

reach dǐdá 抵達／抵达 V
read *(usually aloud)* dú 讀／读; yuèdú 閱讀／阅读 V
real zhēnshí 真實／真实 SV
real estate fángdìchǎn 房地產／房地产 N
real estate agent fángchǎn jīngjìrén 房產經紀人／房产经纪人 N
reality show zhēnrén xiù 真人秀 N
reasonable hélǐ 合理 SV; yǒu dàolǐ 有道理 SV/VO
recall huíyì 回憶／回忆 V; xiǎngqǐ 想起 RV
reception jiēdài 接待 N
reception desk qiántái 前台 N
recipient *(of message, mail)* shōujiànrén 收件人 N
recommend tuījiàn 推薦／推荐 V
record: follow somebody with a camera to record an event gēn pāi 跟拍 V
recreation yúlè 娛樂／娱乐 N
red bean hóngdòu 紅豆／红豆 N
red date paste hóngzǎo 紅棗／红枣 N
reduce jiàngdī 降低 RV
reference book gōngjùshū 工具書／工具书 N
refined yǎzhì 雅緻／雅致 SV
reflexology zúliáo bǎojiàn 足療保健／足疗保健 N
refrigerator diànbīngxiāng 電冰箱／电冰箱 N
regard dàngchéng 當成／当成 VP
register *(at a hotel, etc.)* dēngjì 登記／登记 V
regress tuìbù 退步 V
regularly jīngcháng 經常／经常 A
rejoice kāixīn 開心／开心 V
relationships jiāo 交 N
release fābù 發布／发布 V
reliable kěkào 可靠 SV
religion zōngjiào 宗教 N
religion: believe/profess a religion xìnjiào 信教 VO
rely on kào 靠 V
remain (to be done) yǒudài 有待 V
remember xiǎngqǐ 想起 RV
rent zūlìn 租賃／租赁 V; zū 租 BF; ***(rent money)*** zūjīn 租金 N
reorganization chóngzǔ 重組／重组 N
reorganize chóngzǔ 重組／重组 V
reply dáfù 答覆／答复; huífù 回覆／回复 V

report bàodǎo 報導／报导 V
reporter jìzhě 記者／记者 N
request yāoqiú 要求 N/V
requirement tiáojiàn 條件／条件 N
resemble xiàng 像 V
residence zhùchù 住處／住处; zhùsuǒ 住所 N
residential area xiǎoqū 小區／小区 N
resources zīyuán 資源／资源 N
response huífù 回覆／回复 N
restaurant fànguǎn 飯館／饭馆 N
restrict xiàn 限 V
résumé jiǎnlì 簡歷／简历 N
revise xiūgǎi 修改 V
rice mǐ 米 N
rice ball mǐtuán 米糰／米团 N
rice dumpling zòngzi 粽子 N
rice dumpling: saltwater rice dumpling xiánshuǐzòng 鹹水粽／咸水粽 N
rich fēngfù 豐富／丰富; fùyǒu 富有 SV
right quánlì 權利／权利 N
ring quān 圈 N
rise shàngshēng 上升 V
river jiāng 江 N
roam guàng 逛 V
roam all over làngjì tiānyá 浪跡天涯／浪迹天涯 IE
roast kǎo 烤 V
role juésè 角色 N
Romance of the Three Kingdoms Sānguó Yǎnyì 三國演義／三国演义 N
rookie càiniǎo 菜鳥／菜鸟 N
roommate shìyǒu 室友 N
rotten làn 爛／烂 SV
row huá 划 V
row/paddle a boat huáchuán 划船 VO
run after zhuī 追 V
rush; dash (over to) chōngshàngqu 衝上去／冲上去 RV

S

sacrifice: offer sacrifices to ancestors jìzǔ 祭祖 VO
safe ānquán 安全 SV
safe and sound píng'ān 平安 SV
safety ānquán 安全 N
salary gōngzī 工資／工资; xīnshuǐ 薪水 N
salary: annual salary niánxīn 年薪 N
salary: monthly salary yuèxīn 月薪 N
sales xiāoshòu 銷售／销售 N
sales promotion cùxiāo 促銷／促销 N/V
saltwater rice dumpling xiánshuǐzòng 鹹水粽／咸水粽 N
sanitation: do sanitation work bǎojié 保潔／保洁 VO
satisfied mǎnyì 滿意／满意; mǎnzú 滿足／满足 SV
say: it is said that jùshuō 據說／据说 VP
scarf tóujīn 頭巾／头巾 N
scholar: visiting scholar fǎngwèn xuézhě 訪問學者／访问学者 N
school xuéxiào 學校／学校 N
school: enter school jìn xiào 進校／进校 VO
school: inside/within the school xiàonèi 校內／校内 PW/ATTR
school: this/our school běnxiào 本校 N
science and technology kējì 科技 N
score défēn 得分 VO
screen *(TV, computer, etc.)* píngmù 屏幕 N
scriptures jīngdiǎn 經典／经典 N
Seattle Xīyǎtú 西雅圖／西雅图 PW
sect ménpài 門派／门派 N
section zǔ 組／组 N
secure ānquán 安全 SV
security ānquán 安全 N
security: ensure public security bǎo'ān 保安 VO
security: sense of security ānquángǎn 安全感 N
security guard bǎo'ān 保安 N
see a doctor kànbìng 看病 VO
seek; search xún 尋／寻 V
seek: urgently seek jíqiú 急求 VP
seemingly ruò 若 A
select xuǎnzé 選擇／选择 V
self-confident zìxìn 自信 V
self-employment zìyóu zhíyè 自由職業／自由职业 N
sell shòu 售 V
sensation gǎnjué 感覺／感觉 N
separate fēn 分 V
series; set xìliè 系列 N
serious; solemn yánsù 嚴肅／严肃 SV
server fúwùyuán 服務員／服务员 N
service(s) fúwù 服務／服务 N
settle shuōdìng 說定／说定 V/RV
Shaolin form of boxing Shàolínquán 少林拳 N
Shaolin Temple, Henan Province, China Shàolínsì 少林寺 PW
shape xíngtài 形態／形态 N
share a room/lodging hézhù 合住 RV
shoot a movie pāi 拍 V
shoot arrows shèjiàn 射箭 VO
shop: go shopping gòuwù 購物／购物 VO
shopping: go shopping shàngjiē 上街 VO
shopping center gòuwù zhōngxīn 購物中心／购物中心 N
shortcoming quēdiǎn 缺點／缺点 N
show xiù 秀 N/PL
show a film shàngyìng 上映 V
shower; shower bath línyù 淋浴 N/V
shower stall línyùfáng 淋浴房 N
shrimp xiā 蝦／虾 N
sick leave bìngjià 病假 N

significant: have significance yǒuyìyì 有意義／有意义 V/VO
simple and honest hānhou 憨厚 SV
simultaneous: do V1 and V2 simultaneously biān V1 biān V2 邊V1邊V2／边V1边V2 C
sincere zhēnchéng 真誠／真诚 SV
sitcom qíngjǐng duǎnjù 情景短劇／情景短剧 N
situation zhuàngkuàng 狀況／状况 N
size: large size/scale dàxíng 大型 ATTR
skateboarding huábǎn 滑板 N; **go skateboarding** wán huábǎn 玩滑板 VP
ski huáxuě 滑雪 V
skill jìshù 技術／技术; jìnéng 技能 N
skin pífū 皮膚／皮肤 N
sleeping bag shuìdài 睡袋 N
slightly shāo 稍 A
so far qìjīn wéizhǐ 迄今為止／迄今为止 IE
so much so that shènzhì yú 甚至於／甚至于 C
soccer zúqiú 足球 N
soccer: play soccer tī zúqiú 踢足球 VO
social contact/interaction/life shèjiāo 社交 N
soft and gentle wēnróu 温柔 SV
softball lěiqiú 壘球／垒球 N
Sohu ***(one of the largest Chinese Internet companies)*** Sōuhú 搜狐 N
solar energy tàiyángnéng 太陽能／太阳能 N
solid; sound zhāshi 扎實／扎实 SV
solve a criminal case pò'àn 破案 VO
source fāyuán 發源／发源 N
sous-chef pèicài 配菜 N
space; open area kōngjiān 空間／空间 N
spare time; after hours yèyú 業餘／业余 N
speak incorrectly/unclearly shuōbuzhǔn 說不準／说不准 RV
special column ***(in a newspaper, etc.)*** zhuānlán 專欄／专栏 N
specialty zhuānyè 專業／专业 N
specific jùtǐ 具體／具体 SV
specify jù(tǐ)huà 具(體)化／具(体)化 V
spectator guānzhòng 觀眾／观众 N
speech: colloquial speech; spoken/vernacular language kǒuyǔ 口語／口语 N
spiral luóxuán 螺旋 N
spontaneously zìrán'érrán 自然而然 IE
sports tǐyù 體育／体育 N
spread kuòzhǎn 擴展／扩展; liúchuán 流傳／流传; chuánbō(kāi) 傳播(開)／传播(开) V
stabilize wěndìng 穩定／稳定 V
stable; steady wěndìng 穩定／稳定 SV
star ***(movie/pop)*** míngxīng 明星 N
stare at dīngzhe 盯著／盯着 V
state (of affairs) zhuàngtài 狀態／状态 N
state (of something) dìbù 地步 N
station tái 台 N
station: train station huǒchēzhàn 火車站／火车站 N
status dìwèi 地位; zhuàngtài 狀態／状态 N
stay; hang out dāi 呆 V
straightforward hānhou 憨厚 SV
street: go into the street shàngjiē 上街 VO
strength and beauty lì yǔ měi 力與美／力与美 N
stress: lay stress on zhùzhòng 注重 V
strike ***(here:*** **tackle*****)*** zhuàngjī 撞擊／撞击 V
string together chuànqǐlai 串起來／串起来 V/RV
stroll guàng 逛 V
strong nóng 濃／浓; qiáng 強／强 SV
stubborn gùzhi 固執／固执; juè 倔 SV
study: study hard so that you improve every day hǎohǎo xuéxí tiāntiān xiàngshàng 好好學習天天向上／好好学习天天向上 IE
study abroad liúxué 留學／留学 V
style shì 式 BF; xíngtài 形態／形态 N
subject zhǔtí 主題／主题 N
subject matter tícái 題材／题材 N
substance nèiróng 內容／内容 N
subway station dìtiězhàn 地鐵站／地铁站 N
successive liánxù 連續／连续 ATTR
such rúcǐ 如此 VP
such as lìrú 例如 C
summary dàgāng 大綱／大纲 N
supermarket chāoshì 超市 N
supervise guǎnlǐ 管理; zhǐdǎo 指導／指导 V
supervision zhǐdǎo 指導／指导 N
support zhīchí 支持 V
surf chōnglàng 衝浪／冲浪 VO
surfing chōnglàng 衝浪／冲浪 N
surroundings huánjìng 環境／环境 N
survey diàochá 調查／调查 N/V
suspense: hold someone in suspense ***(in storytelling)*** mài(ge) guānzi 賣（個）關子／卖（个）关子 VO
sweet gān 甘 SV
sweets tángguǒ 糖果 N
swim yóuyǒng 游泳 V
synopsis dàgāng 大綱／大纲; jiǎnjiè 簡介／简介 N
syntax yǔfǎ 語法／语法 N

T

table tennis pīngpāngqiú 乒乓球 N
take pictures pāi 拍 V
talent dárén 達人／达人 N/PL
talent: literary/artistic talent cáihuá 才華／才华 N
talent show xuǎnxiù jiémù 選秀節目／选秀节目 N
talk show tuōkǒu xiù 脱口秀 N/PL
target mùbiāo 目標／目标 N
task rènwu 任務／任务 N
taste wèi 味 N; pǐnwèi 品味 N, VO
tasteful yǎzhì 雅緻／雅致 SV

tasteless dàn 淡 SV
teach jiàoyù 教育 V
teaching jiàoxué 教學／教学 N
team duì 隊／队; tuánduì 團隊／团队 N
team member qiúyuán 球員／球员 N
technique jìnéng 技能; jìshù 技術／技术 N
tell about jiǎngshù 講述／讲述 V
temperament píqi 脾氣／脾气; xìnggé 性格 N
temple sìmiào 寺廟／寺庙 N
tenant zūhù 租戶／租户 N
tennis wǎngqiú 網球／网球 N
term; word cí 詞／词 N
terrace yángtái 陽台／阳台 N
territory tiānxià 天下 N
text: send a text message fā duǎnxìn 發短信／发短信 VP
Thanksgiving Day Gǎn'ēnjié 感恩節／感恩节 N
theatrical work jù 劇／剧 N
theme tícái 題材／题材; zhǔtí 主題／主题 N
then and only then fāng 方 A
thick nóng 濃／浓 SV
think over kǎolǜ 考慮／考虑 V
thirst for kěwàng 渴望 V
throw tóu 投 V
throw into tóu jìn 投進／投进 RV
thus rúcǐ 如此 VP
tie ***(in sports, chess, etc.)*** píngjú 平局 N
time: short time/period/term duǎnqī 短期 N
time limit qīxiàn 期限 N
time of use shǐyòngqī 使用期 N
time sent fāsòng shíjiān 發送時間／发送时间 N
title page shǒuyè 首頁／首页 N
toast kǎo 烤 V
toast: drink a toast gānbēi 乾杯／干杯 VO
together: get together jùhuì 聚會／聚会 N/V
together with (*used only in written Chinese*) yǔ 與／与 C
toilet (flush) chōushuǐmǎtǒng 抽水馬桶／抽水马桶 N
tongue twister ràokǒulìng 繞口令／绕口令 N
topic zhǔtí 主題／主题 N
toss tóu 投 V
touch pèng 碰 V
tough lìhai 厲害／厉害 SV
tourism lǚyóu 旅遊／旅游 N
tournant *(someone who does chores in a professional kitchen)* dǎhé 打荷 N
trademark páizi 牌子 N
tradition chuánshuō 傳說／传说; chuántǒng 傳統／传统 N
train péixùn 培訓／培训 V
train station huǒchēzhàn 火車站／火车站 N
trait tèdiǎn; tèzhēng 特點／特点; 特徵／特征 N
transact bànlǐ 辦理／办理 V
transfer zhuǎn 轉／转 V
transfer possession (to somebody) zhuǎnràng 轉讓／转让 V
transport zài 載／载 V
trouble dǎrǎo 打擾／打扰 V
trouble: sorry to trouble you bàoqiàn dǎrǎo 抱歉打擾／抱歉打扰 IE
true zhēnshí 真實／真实 SV
trustworthy kěkào 可靠 SV
truthful zhēnchéng 真誠／真诚 SV
tune into (TV) shōukàn 收看 V
turban tóujīn 頭巾／头巾 N
turkey huǒjī 火雞／火鸡 N
TV play or drama diànshìjù 電視劇／电视剧 N
TV series liánxùjù 連續劇／连续剧 N
type dǎzì 打字 VO
type lèi 類／类; lèixíng 類型／类型 N

U

Uighur *(ethnic group of Xinjiang Province)* Wéiwú'ěr 維吾爾／维吾尔 N
undergo guò 過／过 V
undergo a change yǒu biàn 有變／有变 VO
undergraduate course of studies běnkē 本科 N
undergraduate student běnkēshēng 本科生 N
underground dìxià 地下 ATTR
understand liǎojiě 了解 V
understand *(by reading or watching)* kàn míngbai 看明白 RV
understand thoroughly tōng 通 V
unite jiéhé 結合／结合 V
until now qìjīn wéizhǐ 迄今為止／迄今为止 IE
use shǐyòng 使用 V
used to: be accustomed/used to xíguàn 習慣／习惯 V
usually tōngcháng 通常; yìbān 一般 A

V

vacation: paid vacation dàixīn jiàqī 帶薪假期／带薪假期 N
vanity *(for sink)* xǐshǒutái 洗手台 N
video camera shèxiàngjī 攝像機／摄像机 N
view: number of "hits" or views diǎnjīliàng 點擊量／点击量 N
virus bìngdú 病毒 N
vivacious huópō 活潑／活泼 SV
volleyball páiqiú 排球 N

W

wages gōngzī 工資／工资; xīnshuǐ 薪水 N
wallpaper bìzhǐ 壁紙／壁纸 N
warm wēnnuǎn 溫暖／温暖 SV
warm oneself qǔnuǎn 取暖 VO

watch (TV) shōukàn 收看 V; **watch videos** kàn shìpín 看視頻／看视频 VO
water heater *(for kitchen sink)* xiǎochúbǎo 小廚寶／小厨宝 N
Water Margin Shuǐhǔ Zhuàn 水滸傳／水浒传 N
we; us; we all dàhuǒr 大夥兒／大伙儿 N
weak dàn 淡 SV
wealthy fùyǒu 富有 SV
Web page wǎngyè 網頁／网页 N
website wǎngzhàn 網站／网站 N
weight *(body)* tǐzhòng 體重／体重 N
welfare fúlì 福利 N
well-behaved guāi 乖 SV
whole family quánjiā 全家 N
wide-ranging bódà 博大 VP
wife: a good wife and a good mother xiánqīliángmǔ 賢妻良母／贤妻良母 IE
will jiāngyào 將要／将要 AV
willful rènxìng 任性 SV
win yíng 贏／赢 V
within yǐnèi 以內／以内 S
wonderful jīngcǎi 精彩 SV
word cí 詞／词; dāncí 單詞／单词 N
worker: ordinary worker pǔgōng 普工 N
workroom gōngzuòjiān 工作間／工作间 N
worldwide huánqiú 環球／环球 PREF
worship bài 拜 V
wrap bāo 包; bāoguǒ 包裹 V
wrestling shuāijiāo 摔跤 N
write *(books, etc.)* zhù 著 V

X

Xinjiang *(province in western China)* Xīnjiāng 新疆 PW

Y

year: that year; those years dāngnián 當年／当年 N
yoga yújiā *(loan word)* 瑜伽 N/PL; **do/perform yoga** zuò yújiā 做瑜伽 VO

Glossary of Measure Words

Following is a list of some common measure words, along with the nouns each of them is usually associated with. The nouns listed here are by no means exhaustive. They represent the ones you have encountered so far as well as some other common nouns. Note that a few measure words are themselves nouns and are not followed by other nouns; for example: *kè* 課／课, *suì* 歲／岁, *tiān* 天. We encourage you to add more measure words and nouns to this list as your Chinese advances.

bǎ 把 *(for things you can grasp in your hand)*
dāo 刀 *(knife)*
mǐ 米 *([a handful of] rice)*
qián 錢／钱 *([a fistful of] money)*
sǎn 傘／伞 *(umbrella)*
shuāzi 刷子 *(brush)*
shūzi 梳子 *(comb)*
yàoshi 鑰匙／钥匙 *(key)*
yǐzi 椅子 *(chair)*
bān 班 *(for crowds, scheduled transport vehicles)*
chē 車/车 *(bus [run])*
fēijī 飛機／飞机 *(airplane [flight])*
xuésheng 學生／学生 *([class of] students)*
bàn 半 *(half [of something])*
bàng 磅 *(pound)*
shuǐguǒ 水果 *(fruit)*
bāo 包 *(pack; package)*
táng(guǒ) 糖(果) *(candy)*
(xiāng)yān (香)煙／(香)烟 *(cigarettes)*
yáxiàn 牙線／牙线 *(floss)*
yīfu 衣服 *(clothing)*
bēi 杯 *(cup; glass)*
chá 茶 *(tea)*
kāfēi 咖啡 *(coffee)*
shuǐ 水 *(water)*
bèi 倍 *(times [as much])*
běn 本 *(for books, periodicals, files, etc.)*
shū 書／书 *(book)*
xiǎoshuō 小說／小说 *(novel)*
zázhì 雜誌／杂志 *(magazine)*
zìdiǎn 字典 *(dictionary)*
bǐ 筆／笔 *(lump sum)*
qián 錢／钱 *(money)*
biàn 遍 *(occasions; times; occurrences)*
bù 部 *(for film, large books, machines, etc.)*
diànyǐng 電影／电影 *(movie)*

cè 册 *(volume [of books])*
shū 書／书 *(book)*
céng 層／层 *(story [in buildings]; level)*
lóu 樓／楼 *(building)*
chǎng 場／场 *(for games, performances, etc.)*
diànyǐng 電影／电影 *(movie [showing])*
qiúsài 球賽／球赛 *(ball game)*
chǐ 尺 *(foot [length])*
chuàn 串 *(bunch)*
pútao 葡萄 *(grapes)*
yàoshi 鑰匙／钥匙 *(keys)*
cì 次 *(occasions; times; occurrences)*
kǎoshì 考試／考试 *(exam)*
lǚxíng 旅行 *(journey)*
cùn 寸 *(inch [length])*

dá 打 *(dozen)*
jīdàn 雞蛋／鸡蛋 *(eggs)*
dǎng (dàng) 檔／档 *(for programs and TV series)*
xì 戲／戏 *(TV series)*
dào 道 *(course [of food]; dish)*
cài 菜 *(food; dish)*
diǎn 點／点 *(clock time: hour on the clock)*
zhōng 鐘／钟 *(clock)*
dǐng 頂／顶 *(for hats, sedan chairs)*
màozi 帽子 *(hat)*
dòng 棟／栋 *(for houses)*
fángzi 房子 *(house)*
lóu 樓／楼 *(building)*
dù 度 *(angles; degrees; temperature)*
duàn 段 *(section; part)*
huà 話／话 *(remarks)*
duì 對／对 *([matching] pair)*
huāpíng 花瓶 *(vases)*
dùn 頓／顿 *(for meals, occurrences)*
fàn 飯／饭 *(meal)*
duǒ 朵 *(for flowers, clouds, etc.)*
huār 花兒／花儿 *(flower)*

fēn 分 *(clock time: minute)*
zhōng 鐘／钟 *(clock)*

fēn 分 *(unit of money: "cent")*
qián 錢／钱 *(money)*
fèn 份 *(for copies of newspapers)*
bào(zhǐ) 報(紙)／报(纸) *(newspaper)*
gōngzuò 工作 *(job)*
fēng 封 *(for letters)*
xìn 信 *(letter)*
fú 幅 *(for cloth, paintings)*
huàr 畫兒／画儿 *(painting)*
fù 副 *(for sets of things, facial expressions)*
shǒutào 手套 *([pair of] gloves)*
yǎnjìng 眼鏡／眼镜 *([pair of] eyeglasses)*
yào 藥／药 *([dose of] medicine)*

ge 個／个 *(non-specific measure word)*
bǐjìběn 筆記本／笔记本 *(notebook)*
dìfang 地方 *(place)*
jìniànpǐn 紀念品／纪念品 *(souvenir)*
lǐbài 禮拜／礼拜 *(week)*
qiú 球 *(ball)*
qǐyè 企業／企业 *(business establishment)*
rén 人 *(person)*
shǒujī 手機／手机 *(cell phone)*
wèntí 問題／问题 *(question; problem)*
xiǎoshí 小時／小时 *(hour)*
xīngqī 星期 *(week)*
zhōngtóu 鐘頭／钟头 *(hour)*
gēn 根 *(for long, slender objects)*
shéngzi 繩子／绳子 *(rope)*
(xiāng)yān (香)煙／(香)烟 *(cigarette)*
yáxiàn 牙線／牙线 *(floss)*

háng 行 *(line; row)*
Hànzì 漢字／汉字 *(Chinese characters)*
hào 號／号 *(days of the month)*
hào 號／号 *(numbered things or people)*
duìyuán 隊員／队员 *(team member)*
lóu 樓／楼 *(building)*
hé 盒 *(box; case; pack)*
huǒchái 火柴 *(matches)*
qiǎokèlì 巧克力 *(chocolate)*
yáxiàn 牙線／牙线 *(floss)*
hú 壺／壶 *(pot)*
chá 茶 *(tea)*
hù 戶／户 *(for families, households)*
rénjiā 人家 *(household)*
huí 回 *(occasions; times; occurrences)*

jí 集 *(for episodes in a TV series)*
jiā 家 *(for families, businesses)*
fànguǎnr 飯館兒／饭馆儿 *(restaurant)*
shāngdiàn 商店 *(shop; store)*
jià 架 *(for planes, radios)*
fēijī 飛機／飞机 *(airplane)*
jiān 間／间 *(for rooms)*
bàngōngshì 辦公室／办公室 *(office)*
fángjiān 房間／房间 *(room)*
wūzi 屋子 *(room)*
jiàn 件 *(for articles, items)*
chènshān 襯衫／衬衫 *(shirt)*
jiákè 夾克／夹克 *(jacket)*
máoyī 毛衣 *(sweater)*
shìqing 事情 *(affairs, matters)*
T-xùshān T-恤衫 *(T-shirt)*
wàitào 外套 *(overcoat)*
xíngli 行李 *(baggage, luggage)*
yīfu 衣服 *(clothing)*
jié 節／节 *(for class or game sections)*
kè 課／课 *(class session; segment; part; period [in a game])*
qiúsài 球賽／球赛 *(ball game period)*
jīn 斤 *(catty [Chinese unit of weight]; half kilogram)*
shuǐguǒ 水果 *(fruit)*
jù 句 *(sentence)*
huà 話／话 *(remarks)*
juǎn(r) 卷(兒)／卷(儿) *(for rolls, spools, reels)*
wèishēngzhǐ 衛生紙／卫生纸 *(toilet paper)*

kē 棵 *(for trees, cabbages)*
shù 樹／树 *(tree)*
kè 課／课 *(lesson [in a book])*
dì sān kè 第三課／第三课 *(Lesson Three)*
kè 刻 *(clock time: quarter-hour)*
zhōng 鐘／钟 *(clock)*
kǒu 口 *(for mouthfuls, people, wells)*
rén 人 *([number of] people [in a family])*
kuài 塊／块 *(for pieces, slices)*
(shǒu)biǎo (手)錶／(手)表 *(wristwatch)*
bīngkuàir 冰塊兒／冰块儿 *(ice cube)*
bù 布 *(cloth)*
dàngāo 蛋糕 *(cake)*
féizào 肥皂 *(soap)*
ròu 肉 *(meat)*
shǒujuàn 手絹／手绢 *(handkerchief)*
táng 糖 *(candy)*
kuài 塊／块 *(unit of money: "dollar")*
qián 錢／钱 *(money)*

lèi 類／类 *(type; category)*
dōngxi 東西／东西 *(stuff; thing)*
lǐ 里 *(Chinese mile)*
lù 路 *(road)*
lì 粒 *(for grainlike things)*
yào 藥／药 *(medicine [pills])*
liàng 輛／辆 *(for vehicles)*
gōng(gòng) (qì)chē 公(共汽)車／公(共汽)车 *(bus)*
kǎchē 卡車／卡车 *(truck)*
mótuōchē 摩托車／摩托车 *(motorcycle)*

qìchē 汽車／汽车 *(car, automobile)*
zìxíngchē 自行車／自行车 *(bicycle)*
liè 列 *(for [train] cars)*
huǒchē 火車／火车 *(train)*
lóu 樓／楼 *(story [in buildings])*
lù 路 *(bus route)*
chē 車／车 *(bus)*
luò 摞 *(for stacks of things)*
zhǐ 紙／纸 *(paper)*

máo 毛 *(unit of money: "dime")*
qián 錢／钱 *(money)*
mén 門／门 *(for courses of study)*
kè 課／课 *(course)*
mǐ 米 *(meter)*
miàn 面 *(for mirrors, flags)*
jìngzi 鏡子／镜子 *(mirror)*
miǎo 秒 *(clock time: second)*
zhōng 鐘／钟 *(clock)*

nián 年 *(year)*
niánjí 年級／年级 *(year in school)*

pái 排 *(for rows of things)*
zuòwèi 座位 *(seats)*
pán 盤／盘 *(for coils, dishes, etc.)*
qí 棋 *([game of] chess)*
shuǐguǒ 水果 *([plate of] fruit)*
pǐ 匹 *(for horses, mules, bolts of cloth)*
mǎ 馬／马 *(horse)*
piān 篇 *(for articles, chapters, etc.)*
wénzhāng 文章 *(article; essay)*
piàn 片 *(for slices of things)*
miànbāo 麵包／面包 *(bread)*
píng 瓶 *(bottle)*
hùfàsù 護髮素／护发素 *(hair conditioner)*
píjiǔ 啤酒 *(beer)*
xǐfàshuǐ 洗髮水／洗发水 *(shampoo)*

qī 期 *(for magazines and periodicals)*
zázhì 雜誌／杂志 *(magazine)*
quān 圈 *(lap around a track)*

shēn 身 *(for outfits, suits of clothing)*
yīfu 衣服 *(clothing)*
shǒu 首 *(for poems, songs)*
gē 歌 *(song)*
shī 詩／诗 *(poem)*
shù 束 *(for bunches of things)*
huār 花兒／花儿 *(flowers)*
shuāng 雙／双 *(a pair of)*
kuàizi 筷子 *(chopsticks)*
shǒu 手 *(hands)*
wàzi 襪子／袜子 *(socks)*
xiézi 鞋子 *(shoes)*
yǎnjīng 眼睛 *(eyes)*
suì 歲／岁 *(years of age)*
suǒ 所 *(for houses)*
gōngyù 公寓 *(apartment)*
xuéxiào 學校／学校 *(school)*
yīyuàn 醫院／医院 *(hospital)*

tái 台 *(for performances, engines, etc.)*
diànnǎo 電腦／电脑 *(computer)*
diànshì 電視／电视 *(television)*
zhàoxiàngjī 照相機／照相机 *(camera)*
táng 堂 *(class period)*
kè 課／课 *(class session)*
tàng 趟 *(for times [of trips])*
huǒchē 火車／火车 *(train trip)*
lù 路 *(trip)*
tào 套 *(set; series)*
gōngyù 公寓 *(apartment)*
shū 書／书 *(books)*
yīfu 衣服 *(clothes)*
tiān 天 *(day)*
tiáo 條／条 *(for long, narrow things)*
duǎnkù 短褲／短裤 *(shorts)*
hé 河 *(river)*
jiē 街 *(street)*
kùzi 褲子／裤子 *(pants; trousers)*
lóng 龍／龙 *(dragon)*
lù 路 *(road)*
máojīn 毛巾 *(towel)*
miànbāo 麵包／面包 *(bread)*
qúnzi 裙子 *(skirt)*
shé 蛇 *(snake)*
tǎnzi 毯子 *(blanket)*
yú 魚／鱼 *(fish)*
tóu 頭／头 *(for livestock)*
niú 牛 *(cow; ox)*
zhū 豬／猪 *(pig)*

wǎn 碗 *(bowl)*
fàn 飯／饭 *(rice)*
wèi 位 *(for people [polite form])*
kèren 客人 *(guest)*
lǎoshī 老師／老师 *(teacher)*

xiàng 項／项 *(for itemized things)*
xiē 些 *(small, indefinite amounts; some)*
dōngxi 東西／东西 *(stuff, things)*
rén 人 *(people)*
shìqing 事情 *(affairs, matters)*

yàng 樣／样 *(type; kind)*
dōngxi 東西／东西 *(stuff; thing)*
yè 夜 *(night)*

yìdiǎn(r) 一點(兒)／一点(儿) *(a little bit; small amount)*
qián 錢／钱 *(money)*
yuán 元 *(dollar)*

zhàn 站 *(stop [train, bus, etc.])*
zhāng 張／张 *(for flat things)*
chuáng 床 *(bed)*
dìtú 地圖／地图 *(map)*
huàr 畫兒／画儿 *(painting)*
míngxìnpiàn 明信片 *(postcard)*
piào 票 *(ticket)*
shūzhuō 書桌／书桌 *(desk)*
xìnyòngkǎ 信用卡 *(credit card)*
zhǐ 紙／纸 *(paper)*
zhuōzi 桌子 *(table)*
zhāng 章 *(chapter [in a book])*
dì sān zhāng 第三章 *(Chapter Three)*
zhī 支 *(for slender objects)*
máobǐ 毛筆／毛笔 *(writing brush)*
yágāo 牙膏 *(toothpaste)*
yáshuā 牙刷 *(toothbrush)*
zhī 隻／只 *(for animals, one of a pair of things)*
gǒu 狗 *(dog)*
jī 雞／鸡 *(chicken)*
lǎohǔ 老虎 *(tiger)*
lǎoshǔ 老鼠 *(mouse; rat)*
māo 貓／猫 *(cat)*
niǎo 鳥／鸟 *(bird)*
shǒu 手 *(hand)*
tùzi 兔子 *(rabbit)*
xié 鞋 *(shoe)*
yā 鴨／鸭 *(duck)*
yǎnjīng 眼睛 *(eye)*
zhū 豬／猪 *(pig)*
zhǒng 種／种 *(kind; type)*
dòngwù 動物／动物 *(animal)*
zhù 炷 stick *(for incense)*
xiāng 香 *(incense)*
zuò 座 *(for mountains, bridges, etc.)*
dàshà 大廈／大厦 *(high-rise building)*
qiáo 橋／桥 *(bridge)*
shān 山 *(mountain)*

Index

Credits

Illustrations:

Illustrations by Nora Guo unless otherwise noted.
Maps on p. 102 and inside back cover by Patti Isaccs/Parrot Graphics.

Photos:

Photos are taken from the video material for ***Encounters,*** unless otherwise noted.

Frontispiece courtesy of Hugo Krispyn, SWAMP, LLC.

p. 32 *(left to right)* © s_bukley/Shutterstock.com; © Bobby Yip/Reuters/Newscom; © Jaguar PS/Shutterstock.com; © Debby Wong/Shutterstock.com; © DFree/Shutterstock.com.
p. 37 *(left)* © Denis Makarenko/Shutterstock.com; *(right)* © AF archive/Alamy.
p. 53 *(top)* © PTSOlathe/iStock; *(middle)* © JStone/Shutterstock.com; *(bottom)* © szefei/Shutterstock.com.
p. 54 *(top)* © MichaelSvoboda/iStock; *(middle)* © mauro grigollo/iStock; *(bottom)* © Vladislav Nosick/Shutterstock.com.
p. 75 *(left to right)* © Debby Wong/Shutterstock.com; © Neale Cousland/Shutterstock.com; © Mitch Gunn/Shutterstock.com; © EdStock/iStock.
p. 79 *(top)* © Eye Ubiquitous/Newscom.
p. 81 *(background)* © SIHASAKPRACHUM/Shutterstock.com.
p. 82 *(left)* © Jim McIsaac/MCT/Newscom; *(right)* © Albert Pena/Cal Sport Media/Newscom.
p. 105 *(left)* © s_bukley/Shutterstock.com; *(right)* © Touchstone Pictures/ZUMA Press/Newscom.
p. 130 *(left photo)* © Professional photography/Shutterstock.com.
p. 162 *(left)* © karamysh/Shutterstock.com; *(right)* © Clive Postlethwaite/REX/Newscom.
p. 189 *(left)* © akg-images/Newscom; *(right)* Courtesy of Cynthia Y. Ning.
p. 213 © Charlesimage/Shutterstock.com.

Realia:

Realia photos on the following pages by Cynthia Y. Ning: pp. 16–20, 35–36.
Realia reproductions on the following pages by Nora Guo: pp. 52, 79 *(middle and bottom)*, 80–82 *(top)*, 101, 104.
Realia reproductions on the following pages by Wanda España/Wee Design Group: 53–54, 185, 214–216, 244.
pp. 101, 104: Courtesy of 58.com.
pp. 127–128, 130 *(text portions)*: Courtesy of baihe.com.
p. 187: Courtesy of Wiseway.com.
p. 237: Compiled by Alexander R. Pennock, Dartmouth class of 2001, under the supervision of Professor Hua-yuan Li Mowry and with generous support from the Byrne Foundation and the Dartmouth Presidential Scholars Program. Used with permission.

Outline of China's Geography

Borders:

- To the east: Sea of Japan, Yellow Sea, East China Sea, Taiwan Strait, and South China Sea.
- To the north, west, and south: North Korea, Russia, Mongolia, Kazakhstan, Khirghizstan (Kyrgyzstan), Tadjikstan (Tajikistan), Afghanistan, Pakistan, India, Nepal, Bhutan, Myanmar, Laos, and Vietnam.

Area: About 9.6 million square kilometers (3.7 million square miles). China is the third-largest country in the world, behind Russia and Canada. Its land mass is similar in size to the United States.

Topography: 1) the Northeast Plain, 2) the North Plain, and 3) the Southern Hills in eastern China; 4) Xinjiang-Mongolia in the west; and 5) the Tibetan Highlands of the southwest. Overall, the land is high in the west and descends to the coast in the east.

Major rivers:

- **Yangtze** (長江／长江), the third-longest in the world (after the Amazon and the Nile), which begins in Tibet, flows through central China, and enters the East China Sea near Shanghai.
- **Yellow River** (黄河), which begins in Qinghai and flows through north China, entering the Bohai Gulf of the Yellow Sea, through the Shandong Peninsula.
- **Heilongjiang** (黑龍江／黑龙江 Black Dragon River), which flows for the first three quarters of its length through northeast China and the last quarter through Russia, where it is known as the Amur.
- **Zhujiang** (珠江 Pearl River) of south China, which forms a fertile delta near Guangzhou, Macau, and Hong Kong.

Administrative divisions:

- **23 provinces** (*shěng* 省): Anhui, Fujian, Gansu, Guangdong, Guizhou, Hainan, Hebei, Heilongjiang, Henan, Hubei, Hunan, Jiangsu, Jiangxi, Jilin, Liaoning, Qinghai, Shaanxi, Shandong, Shanxi, Sichuan, Taiwan [currently governed by the Republic of China], Yunnan, Zhejiang.
- **5 autonomous regions** (*zìzhìqū* 自治區／自治区): Guangxi Zhuang, Inner Mongolia, Ningxia Hui, Tibet, Xinjiang Uighur.
- **4 autonomous municipalities** (*zhíxiáshì* 直轄市／直辖市): Beijing, Chongqing, Shanghai, Tianjin.
- **2 special administrative regions** (SARS, *tèbié xíngzhèngqū* 特別行政區／特别行政区): Hong Kong, Macau.

Agricultural divisions:

- One demarcation is made by the Qinling mountain range and the Huai River. To the north is the North China Plain—drier wheat and millet country; to the south are the wetter rice cultivation regions of the Yangtze River watershed.
- The other major division is east-west, based on the availability of arable lands. Western China is deserts and uplands; this is 57% of the land that is populated by only 6% of China's people (in 2002). Eastern China is arable lowlands; it constitutes 43% of the land but supports 94% of the population (in 2002).

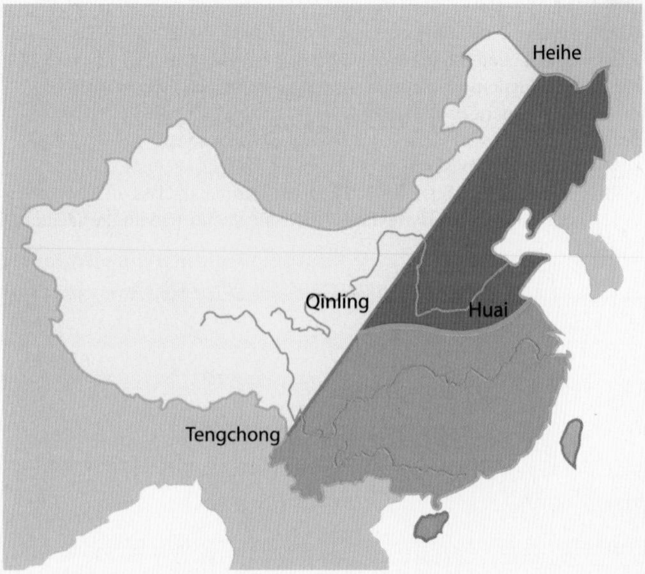